EIGHT TRAGEDIES OF SHAKESPEARE

A Marxist Study

VICTOR KIERNAN

VERSO

London • New York

First published by Verso 1996

Verso
UK: 6 Meard Street, London W1V 3HR
USA: 180 Varick Street, New York NY 10014–4606

Verso is the imprint of New Left Books

ISBN 1–85984–954–7
ISBN 1–85984–089–2 (pbk)

British Library Cataloguing in Publication Data
A catalogue record for the book is available from the British Library

Library of Congress Cataloging-in-Publication Data
A catalog record for this book is available from the Library of
Congress

Typeset by Keystroke, Jacaranda Lodge, Wolverhampton
Printed and bound in Great Britain by Biddles Ltd,
Guildford and King's Lynn

To
N.S.K.
Bear free and patient thoughts.
King Lear IV.vi.80

Contents

Foreword

In the first part of my attempt at a Marxist scrutiny of Shakespeare (*Shakespeare: Poet and Citizen*, 1993) I brought together, along with the Sonnets and other poems, the Comedies and the English Histories, two contrasting but converging series written mostly during the same years. In this second part it might have been desirable to combine the tragedies with the 'problem plays', belonging to the same period (and *Troilus and Cressida* itself a kind of tragedy). But as this would have required too much space, these and the later plays have been postponed, and the present survey is confined to the eight mature tragedies. It is divided between commentary on each play in turn, and discussion of questions arising in all or many of them. As L.C. Knights said, it is needful to take an all-round view of a drama as an experience in itself (19–20), but it is important as well to observe it as part of an unfolding sequence, whose leading preoccupations it shares.

Dates of plays are not always certain; I have followed what seems to be the most widely accepted order. But related ideas were fermenting together in Shakespeare's mind, and it is very possible that he, like Goethe, or composers like Beethoven or Wagner, was habitually revolving more than one project in his head at the same time. The bibliography supplied gives details only of works cited in the text, where brief references – author and page-number – are given in brackets. In view of the multiplying editions of the plays, and the unlikelihood of readers possessing complete sets of any one of them, references to plays are not always to the same edition, but should be easily traceable.

In pondering on Shakespeare a critic has hardly anything to go on except the outline of his life, what he wrote (or was published under his name), and the condition – social, political, ideological – of the England and Europe he lived in. My search has been for correspondences between one source and another; they have to be cautiously weighed together. Understanding of both writings and environment has greatly increased, but many difficulties still beset them; and what has come to be known about the texts in general may be a warning as much as an aid. Elizabethan and Jacobean theatrical texts had a fluid quality, and were modified from time to time by requirements of a particular production. Shakespeare's '*never existed as a stable entity*' (Patterson 4), and can be puzzling because they 'provide so many and such various possibilities' (Summers 97).

So do the outlooks, philosophies, convictions – political and other – of his readers and spectators. Shakespeare remains a highly controversial figure, and the problem of how to interpret him has never been more an apple of discord among critics than today. Hence readers of any study of him now want to know, it appears, not only what its writer has to say, but what his affiliations are, what flag he marches under. To meet this *Qui va là!* or challenge, I have begun with a sketch of some features in the evolution of serious thinking about Shakespeare, and made an effort to chart some influential currents of opinion today about him and his works; and to make my own point of view and its derivation as crystal-clear as humanly possible.

PART I

Programmatic

Programmatic

Medieval man was taught – how effectually we cannot tell – to abhor himself and the earth he dwelt on, and to wrap himself in meditations on other worlds to come. Renaissance man, or the élite known by that title to historians, was the product of a rebirth of knowledge and admiration of an ancient pagan civilization, Greek and Roman. He was very well pleased with himself and his surroundings, so well that his conception of art was a mirror that should reflect him and them in all their glowing colours. As the Renaissance spread out from Italy it overlapped, most strikingly in England, with that northern phenomenon, the Reformation. Two tides were meeting, setting up a vortex of cross-currents which were to form a significant part of the energy that went into Elizabethan literature and music. The Reformation was a turning back, like the Renaissance, but to medieval theology and austerity, though not to celibacy and monastic withdrawal from the world. It revived much that would have to be forgotten again later, like the doctrine of mankind's total depravity, but also did much to save Christian ethics from the very real threat of being forgotten.

Hamlet instructed his actors that the business of art was to hold a mirror up to nature: human nature, that is, and its social setting. Dr Johnson in turn found Shakespeare's greatest quality in his fidelity to truth and reality, his holding up 'a faithful mirrour of manners and of life' (3, 11). Clearly, however, this was a deceptively simple image. As Wordsworth was to realize, what we see is made up of both 'what the eye perceives,/And what it half creates' – the artist's eye to a special degree. A painter is expected to show us more in a face, or a landscape, than we have been able to decipher ourselves. Shakespeare observed the swirling life of London, and translated it into dramatic events. Hamlet wanted drama to be true to men's deeper feelings and interests, not to the minutiae of their external lives; the complex of what was meaningful in these lives and their relations with one another. The new times were making possible a fuller realization of all this than ever before; they were inaugurating what was to be an unending exploration of life in an ever-changing world. There had been peoples of old, it was known, who left memorials very different from those of the present; the question could begin to be raised of how one civilization came to be succeeded by another. Consciousness of time was stimulated by widening consciousness of space, thanks to the explorers and the finding of unknown lands and seas.

We must suppose Shakespeare to have been very exceptionally sensitive to other human beings and their heartbeats; most of us are, by comparison, usually obtuse, impermeable. Countless spectators and readers have found his characters 'life-like', as Johnson did; we can believe in the possibility of men and women like them, and are aware of kindred features in ourselves. Yet four centuries of vertiginous change stretch between them and us. On the other hand the underlying essentials of their social system and ours have altered far less than the means of transport we employ, or of communication; they are to be found in inequality of advantages, opportunity, education. Because of this, and still more as a result of their own long, slow evolution, the deeper structures of personality have been much slower still to change. There may be an indication of this in what we are told by psychologists, that our patterns of individual response and behaviour are permanently fixed by the time we have left infancy behind. This is not to say that 'human nature is always the same', a shibboleth dear to conservatives because it seems to prove that the comfortable position they occupy must always remain as it is. But each personality is a very complex bundle of elements not evolving integrally; and each community is capable not only of wider vision, higher aspiration, but also of precipitous relapses or disintegrations.

Writers have been allowed different places in society, and the pushings and proddings they have met with there have had a strong influence on their perceptions of life. To comprehend Shakespeare we must do our best to call back the England he lived in, the London he worked in. However, we must not try to imprison him there. Human consciousness, private or collective, roves backward and forward, and some of its wanderings may have more meaning than the common stuff of daily life. Elizabethans, especially the more literate, breathed the air of manifold epochs, from classical and biblical times to glimpses or fantasies of times still to dawn. Even the unlettered had their Golden Age fable, their land of Cockayne; countryfolk had their not altogether unreal legend of a 'Norman yoke' which had been fastened on them by invaders and was still resented (see Hill). It was in its way a genuine historical theory to explain a real historical situation. We too are products of our age, but not of it alone. We react against our age and its assumptions, as well as being indebted to it, much as we react to our parents and teachers.

Ideas can only take effect after men and women have been prepared by experience to open their minds. When civil war broke out in England in 1642 its causes, and the war-aims of Cavaliers and Roundheads, were too hazy (sometimes deliberately so) to excite the masses, particularly in the countryside where most of the population lived. There was, however, a huge outpouring, with populous London its centre, of reading and writing about matters of Church and State, and about relations between class and class. England was very considerably altered by the events of those two decades, if not very much outwardly for the ploughman or labourer. A great many people must have been left looking at their world with new eyes. Though defeated by Cromwell, the middle-class Leveller movement displayed a remarkably democratic and progressive outlook. Some of its pamphleteers took up the theme of the 'Norman yoke', and called for agrarian as well as constitutional reform. Seventeenth-century England ended as a country owned and ruled by aristocrats, but of a newer, semi-commercialized species, needing allies among the merchantry and financiers.

The conflicts of that era bequeathed to the next one an intelligentsia – a rarity in history –, professional writers with a reading public ready for new explorations. A vital culture is formed, however, out of many components, not all advancing in step like a well-drilled battalion; the age of Enlightenment in the British Isles was full, under its polished surface, of contradictory impulses, capable of pushing out in unexpected directions. In this it was aided by its diversity of four peoples and languages, English serving as lingua franca. Shakespeare was already an idol, as Fanny Burney heard George III humorously complain (*Diary*, 19 Dec. 1875); Johnson had readers who censured him for venturing to find any faults in the bard. At the same time economists and sociologists, as they would be called now, were unromantically setting themselves to lay bare the material roots of all civilization. Interest may have turned that way partly because the literary culture of the time (as of our time) was not of the most creative sort. Poetry was at a low ebb; poetic tragedy was lowest of all, and only kept alive to flatter well-dressed theatre-goers into thinking themselves highly cultivated. One of the best poets and critics, Thomas Gray (a historian too, like all good critics), remarked that none of the new tragedies ever made him shed tears, and only the least bad of them could keep him from laughing (letter to Dr Wharton, 26 Dec. 1754).

Academic minds of the time clung, as many still do, to a belief in the spontaneous generation of ideas and arts, free of any contamination from the rude world outside the college gates. But it was dawning on some minds that social institutions and culture cannot really be free-floating, but must grow out of our workaday activities. Knowledge of history, and of lands outside Europe, was growing under the stimulus of quickening change; capitalism was moving toward primacy in the West. A new world-view forms by degrees, and is in the air before anyone thinks of putting it into words. Coherent expression of this one seems to have been first attempted by two men about the same time, in the early 1750s: Turgot, French nobleman and administrator, and (though not in print before 1776) the Scottish professor Adam Smith. Others were quick to join, in both countries. France was drifting, though no one guessed it then, towards a profound transformation. Scotland was a poor country, lately shaken by its last feudal or clan outbreak, the Jacobite rebellion of 1745, and its educated classes were eager to see their country catch up with wealthy England. A distinctive 'Scottish Enlightenment' was in the making.

The theory that Smith, Adam Ferguson, John Millar, were developing rested on a division into four stages, identifiable by their prevailing 'modes of subsistence', or economic systems, each more productive than the one before it. Mankind had depended successively on hunting, animal-pasturing, agriculture and commerce; and there were regions still dependent on each of these, as most North American Indians were on hunting. Each basic activity generated its appropriate laws and customs, forms of property, institutions, manners and morals, and with them its culture. Smith, in his epoch-making *The Wealth of Nations* (1776), was very much concerned with the place of law and government in this scheme, and the kind of shifts that a new economy was ushering in. But his interests were wide and various, and his use of the general theory was 'all-pervasive': he could declare that 'in a certain view of things all the arts, the sciences, law and government, wisdom and even virtue itself tend all to this one thing, the providing meat, drink, raiment, and lodging for men' (cited by Meek 125; and see ch. 1 of this work generally).

It is not a formula to be applied woodenly or mechanically. No epoch begins with a *tabula rasa*. But obviously we have here a first version of the philosophy of history that Marx and Engels were to carry much further in the 1840s, with the stages rechristened 'modes of production', and a new one added, industrial (as distinct from mercantile) capitalism; and with 'base and superstructure' systematized, one tier over another, the arts at the summit. It is one of the many paradoxes in which the history of ideas abounds that what began as a leading thesis of the leading theoretician of early capitalism should in our time have been so anxiously hidden away and smothered by the high priests of the capitalist temple.

The march of ideas, the sharpening of men's recognition of the terms and conditions of their existence, has never been continuous for long; history interposes too many blockages, compels too many deviations. Between the onset of the French Revolution in 1789 and the final defeat of Napoleon in 1815 lay a quarter-century of European turmoil, a great divide during which many new truths were being learned, some older discoveries neglected. The Industrial Revolution, which began about 1770 in northern England and southern Scotland, was yet another vast complication. One result of this period of tremendous upheaval was the gushing forth of the magic fountain of Romantic poetry and with it came a far better critical understanding of literature. In England there was a rediscovery of Elizabethan drama, nearly forgotten except for Shakespeare. The Romantics shared with his era the experience of rapid change, of nations and classes struggling for power, of mass misery, foreign war, religious revival. On the other hand some of the most valuable eighteenth-century speculations about social evolution were being left in the lumber-room. Forces of reaction were mobilizing everywhere, with Tory Britain as their paymaster and religion a vociferous ally against all progressive thinking. Under these pressures, and still more through disillusion with the hopes of 1789, the elder Romantics in England – Wordsworth, Coleridge, Southey – decayed into Tories, and their poetry dried up. Among younger men, especially the exiles, Byron and Shelley, cut off from their own people, there can be seen an inclination to look for Promethean fire coming down from Olympus instead of emerging from history's subterranean depths.

Capitalism and bourgeois life-styles established their reign, and were soon having prodigious material successes (though everywhere they were, until the revolutionary year 1848 was safely passed, nervously hemmed in between older ruling classes and governments, and danger from below). The Victorian mentality, which did not die with Victoria, never ceased to be in many ways limited or adulterated by the survival of a very rich and powerful landed aristocracy, from whose younger sons the professional strata were largely recruited, including the legal, ecclesiastical and academic corporations, as well as the officer corps (see Harvie). Middle-class subservience to the gentry, and desire to join it, nurtured a cult of the genteel which has done a great deal to retard British progress, both intellectual and economic. None the less, the nineteenth century saw the decisive secularization of the English and European mind.

Marxian socialism, or communism (the names were for long interchangeable), was descended from early nineteenth-century German philosophy, chiefly Hegelian, by way of a critique of religion moving towards rational humanism, and desire for social and political change. When Marx (1818–83) became a refugee in London and his friend Engels a businessman in Manchester, Adam Smith's search for links between a community's economy and its culture could be renewed. Marx was a born sociologist, Engels a born historian, both versed in languages and literatures, both poets in youth, both Shakespearians. Together they could have done much more for cultural studies, beyond the broad outlines. Most of their free time was swallowed up in organizing the socialist movement, taking a share in the German revolution of 1848–49, analysing the mechanics of capitalism. Cultural problems were left to disciples to take up, not always judiciously, in later years. Still, interest in the history of ideas was spreading, and in England by the 1870s Sir Leslie Stephen, a man of letters and leading agnostic, could treat it as a 'commonplace' that at any time the 'prevalent conceptions of the day will somehow permeate its poetry', and that Shakespeare and Bacon were 'rooted in the same soil' (63).

Sigmund Freud (1856–1939), born in Habsburg Moravia, was another originator, like Marx, of transforming theories. He too was keenly interested in cultural and historical issues. He was not interested in overturning the capitalist system, but his work can be said to have done something obliquely to undermine its sustaining convictions by radically altering men's image of themselves. Marx looked outward for the evidence he needed, Freud inward.

Freud resembled Marx again in having forerunners as well as successors. Shakespeare wrote eloquently in his *Midsummer Night's Dream* (V.i.14–15) of the mysterious force of imagination (the word was already fairly old), which 'bodies forth/The forms of things unknown'. His tragic characters are often highly imaginative. They must be, if a great poet is to be able to speak through them; and this means also that they must be in a way mysterious, to themselves as well as to others – they must be surprised at times by what they are doing, as well as by what is happening to them. Nowhere were the Romantic poets closer to Shakespeare than in their absorbing interest in this faculty; and it brought them near to the concept of the unconscious mind, so seminal in later debate. Wordsworth made wonderful use of the word when he recalled in Book VI of *The Prelude* the visionary moment on his grand walking-tour when he learned that he had crossed the watershed of the Alps:

> Imagination – here the Power so called
> Through sad incompetence of human speech,
> That awful Power rose from the mind's abyss.

He came to be equally but painfully aware that our conscious feelings have their foundations 'fearfully low' in human nature – and, he might have added, in the societies men build. But whereas in his better days he could think of the hidden realm of mind as a treasure-house of inspiration and creative strength, Freudians have been more apt to consider it a breeding-place of noxious germs.

Literary criticism was being installed on a regular academic perch in an era when orthodox assumptions were heavily weighted towards conservatism: the National Poet had to toe its line, as Tennyson the Poet Laureate was doing so gracefully. History too, as a scholastic grind with examinations attached, was just establishing itself; from the first the two made little contact, though protests against the 'compartmentalizing' of knowledge began early. A competitive age and its sturdy individualism made for a focusing of Shakespeare studies on 'character', and an effort to blow up Shakespeare's *dramatis personae* into real-life beings, with regular life-stories. Bradley carried this as far as it reasonably could be, but did little to graft onto individual personality the social psychology derived from specific social relations.

Illogically enough, this obsession with the private self was coupled by most scholars with reverence for the Tudor doctrine of Order, of everyone having a fixed place in a strict social hierarchy. This had an odd parallel in similar Victorian notions, fed by suburban snobbery, of the duty of the 'lower orders' to know their place and respect their betters. History often repeats itself, Marx once said, but official ideologies are always more or less out of tune with social realities. Tudor order was backed by a mystical Great Chain of Being in which every sparrow was a link. Scholars have assumed that this was believed by everyone. There is no knowing how many Englishmen really took it seriously; in the absence of a regular police force, such abstractions, and religious exhortations, had to be relied on far more than now. But the Great Chain and Christian brotherhood were flagrantly at variance with the facts of Elizabethan life, where many were rising, many sinking, and multitudes were discontented. Monarchy stood at the pinnacle, and Shakespeare has been proclaimed a zealous loyalist. (In truth, his tributes to the throne are not very many, and must be weighed against his numerous condemnations of particular rulers.)

Strong forces of inertia discouraged fuller inquiries into cultural history. Throughout the nineteenth century Latin and Greek literature, plodded through in the most dry-as-dust fashion, continued to be the staple of upper-class English education. British academics concerned with German or Italian literature remained quite indifferent to any historical setting. The First World War shook things up somewhat; and in the field of drama, the study of environment was entertained at least to the extent of willingness to learn from those familiar with the theatre, and consider the pull of stage conditions and techniques on Elizabethan plot construction and dramatic method. A more far-reaching endeavour made some limited headway in Weimar Germany, more stormily shaken than Britain by the war. This was the 'sociology of knowledge', pioneered chiefly by Karl Mannheim, which emphasized the connections between all thought or culture and the social–economic structure they accompanied.

A second World War was needed to open, or reopen, windows to further progress in cultural studies. A young American came back from it, after finding time when off duty to read Aeschylus, full of a hope that 'Our nation would never return to the prewar insularity and cultural parochialism' (Kuhns 4). Unfortunately it did return to them very speedily, under the compulsions of the Cold War and its organizers' determination to outlaw progressive thinking. Since 1945 Britain and, more harmfully, the USA have had, most of the time, very right-wing governments; under their shadow, faith in Shakespeare's essential dislike of common people and of any changes for their benefit has seemed, in many quarters, unassailable.

Traditionalist thinking about Shakespeare and his England was presided over for years, in some ways very creditably, by E.M. Tillyard (1889–1962). His central conviction was that Shakespeare, being a great Englishman, must have been a great conservative. The only alternative to this view seemed to be the one adopted by Northrop Frye and others, who deemed it 'obvious' that 'Shakespeare had no opinions, no values, no philosophy, no principles . . . ' (*Perspective* 39). These negatives rescued the poet from the charge of being a willing lackey of authority, but at the cost of turning him into a kind of robot, or android, bereft of human sensation, indifferent to any human claims. Such a view suited the school known as the 'New Criticism', which treated literary works as 'self-sufficient objects apart from life' (Siegel 27).

Literary criticism has been professionalized since the days of Hazlitt and Coleridge, and this, Overton sees, has encouraged 'excessive specialisation, abstraction and forming of élites' (15) – cliques or factions. Such a situation is not altogether novel. Johnson commented on the fluctuations of opinion about authors like Shakespeare, from period to period, some judgments fading, others reviving. 'Thus the human mind is kept in motion without progress' (49), was his glum conclusion. E.J. Hobsbawm has pointed recently to the over-worked use by critics of French *avant-garde* jargon, disguising 'an essential scepticism' about any objective values (518): they are free, in other words, to rewrite Shakespeare as they please. He remarks also on how much can be achieved by dexterous use of the prefix 'post-', and specious phrase-making about post-modernism, post-structuralism, post-industrialism (287–8). The Greek prefix 'meta-' serves even better than the Latin 'post-'; we are always hearing of mysterious entities like meta-time, meta-space, meta-drama, or things metaphysical, even meta-representational. It is a great pity that Hamlet cannot be here to read some of this meta-criticism. Its business of course is to suggest great profundity, like that of the coffee-house politician who 'sees through all things with his half-closed eyes', or like Imogen's love, 'beyond beyond'. It is at least five times more sadly true now than when Thomas Carlyle wrote the words that we are living in 'an epoch when puffery and quackery have reached a height unequalled in the annals of mankind' (*Sartor Resartus*, Bk 1, ch. 2).

Half a century ago E.M. Forster amused an audience at Delhi by remarking that many critics seemed to be thinking of a Shakespeare 'subconsciously aware of the unconscious'. Since then Freud's name has become one to conjure with, and a great deal of conjuring has been done with it; we begin to feel, like Macbeth after first meeting the witches, that we are in a realm where 'nothing is but what is not'. If Bradley and other Victorians sometimes mistook fictional beings for flesh-and-blood men and women, Freudians carry this much further, by undertaking to reconstruct their inner, unspoken lives, unknown even to themselves. Since this enterprise depends almost entirely on guesswork, there is limitless scope for speculation.

Hamlet, of course, is a magnet. Ferguson diagnoses him as 'a man obsessed with a sense of sexual impotence' (303). Ophelia's family would have been relieved to know this. Listening to his self-communing while he watches Claudius at prayer, Erlich detects a desire for his uncle to be punished by God, a desire seeming 'to involve archaic castration imagery deriving from the unconscious' (33). Kavanagh informs us of 'Edmund's symbolic castration of Gloucester', his father, and talks of 'Lear's related tyranny and incestuousness' (156–7) – another note too casually harped on by Freudians.

'Literary criticism . . . is in crisis', Norman Rabkin (*Meaning* 1) felt obliged to admit in 1981; he was, however, not helping matters with his exposition of *Macbeth*. His hero is animated by 'unconscious hatred of a father'. True, he has no father; it may be agreed that he had one at some earlier date, but the fact is never alluded to by him or anyone else. He must be thinking of Duncan as his hated father (though he speaks of him only with the highest respect, even when alone), because the sleeping king's face reminds his wife of *her* father, so the murder is really an act of patricide (*Meaning* 107–8; *Macbeth* 126–7) – even though it has been planned in advance. Robert N. Watson follows a similar winding trail, and goes on to discuss social conflict in *Coriolanus* as stemming not from vulgar social–economic conditions but from 'the ambitious man's Oedipal conflict with his father-figures' (85–7, 143). Cavell feels that this play has less to yield to a political than to a psychoanalytical scrutiny. He classifies the hero and his mother as 'starvers, hungerers', because the play abounds in references to food, and is pervaded by the 'idea of cannibalization' ('*Coriolanus*' 248–50). As it begins with a dearth and food-riot, allusions to nutrition are not surprising. But Coriolanus and Volumnia are only metaphorically hungry, for power for themselves and their class. Some have been known to hunger and thirst after righteousness; but metaphors cannot be turned into physical actualities.

There have been some common-sense protests against such vagaries: by Franco Moretti for instance (35 ff.) and Harriet Hawkins attacking Freudianisms such as Coriolanus's alleged dread of castration (165). Drakakis warns against the tendency to 'vulgarize Freud' whenever psychological issues arise; he cites J.I.M. Stewart's treatment of Leontes' jealousy (9–10). A more general complaint must be lodged against the persistent neglect of social issues entailed by all this wandering in imaginary mazes. Westlund, for example, is interested in some of the plays because understanding them may 'help to repair our inner worlds' (9). These cannot be repaired, however, unless our social world is likewise being put in order. Coriolanus's essential link with his mother is not a 'latent sexual relationship' verging on 'an explicitly Oedipal attachment' (Watson 172), but the overweening aristocratic pride of family and class that they share. (Again, we know nothing of his father; indeed, the father–son relationship is conspicuously rare in the tragedies, and one of the few fathers is a ghost.)

To make sense of the psychoanalytical approach, we must first suppose that Shakespeare had no inkling of his own true meaning, that his unconscious self, or pen, was translating his psychic disturbances into symbolic action to be staged; and then that an audience's unconscious minds would translate his symbols back again into their own psychic disorders. This is both painful over-complication and lamentable impoverishment, a travesty of Shakespeare's plays worse than any perpetrated by their Restoration or eighteenth-century improvers. It is one facet of a many-sided retreat from reality into illusion, from a world of what often seem insoluble problems into a cave haunted by flickering shadows.

In Shakespeare's time, if not still earlier, women were beginning to claim a place in rivalry with men. A woman was on the throne for forty-five years. Some women who were not making history were writing it in the early seventeenth century (see Brant and Purkis). Women were active in religious movements; after the Restoration there were women playwrights. It is a good many years now since they began writing about Shakespeare, but only of late have they been debating his portrayals of women. Feminism may not yet have produced a work as striking as Caroline Spurgeon's study of Shakespeare's imagery (*Imagery*), now sixty years old, but feminist commentators may be asking more difficult questions. They must be listened to with special attention on relations between men and women, and on how far Shakespeare was able to throw off the prejudices of an earlier patriarchalism. Not at all, some would say. Linda Bamber begins by rejecting any thought of him as a supporter of feminist claims, and holds that in the tragedies 'the feminine Other is the object of intense suspicion'. This, she adds candidly, is no proof of what Shakespeare's own opinion was; and she tells us eloquently what she herself has owed to him (110–12, 43).

Women ought to be natural socialists, considering that in all societies founded on private ownership they have themselves been treated very much as a species of private property. A good many *have* become socialists. A good many, as students of culture, have also been drawn to modern psychoanalytic theory. Some have been guided by a religious outlook. Shakespeare has always had readers who have felt Christian ideas at work in the plays, and this has formed a distinct strand in recent commentaries. It is an encouraging sign of the times that what has been under discussion is genuine Christianity, very different from the bowdlerized version shared with the Tudor and Jacobean governments and harnessed to the cause of Order and Divine Right. A practical Christian can scarcely not be a socialist, in the widest meaning of the name at any rate; if he is reading Shakespeare he can scarcely avoid taking into account the many social issues raised in the plays.

Study of literary or cultural history could only emerge from its disoriented condition of recent years by a return to, and extension of, earlier ideas grounded in social reality. The end of the Cold War has made this easier. Marxist thinking had never been halted, particularly in Britain. It inspired Raymond Williams's *Marxism and Literature* (1977), though this was in part a corrective, a turning away from mechanical formulations standardized in the USSR. Williams began by looking back at eighteenth-century innovations, and the thought of history as not only in motion, but over long periods moving forward. Karl Marx, he went on, took up the concept of man making himself, and transformed it by maintaining that man did this 'through producing his own means of life'. This, Williams wrote, was 'the most important intellectual advance in all modern social thought' (13, 18–19).

For his own approach he coined the title 'cultural materialism'. This has been taken up, and given a wider or looser meaning, by a number of scholars, Shakespearians among them. A few of these may be regarded as – to paraphrase Boswell – 'fully impregnated with the Marxian aether'; others have distinctively different, often eclectic ways of thinking. Terence Hawkes, for one, has apparently become so advanced a thinker that Shakespeare has lost all meaning for him (see *Times Literary Supplement*, 7 April 1995, 16). All agree on the crucial importance of men's social–economic activity and relationships for any interpretation of cultural history.

Much emphasis is placed on technical progress in communication, with the advent of printing in the forefront; correctly enough, though it must not be forgotten that Elizabethan culture, or exchange of ideas, was still essentially oral, and that dramatists were writing for actors, far more than for publishers. A more general caveat to be entered is that printing, as well as all the later 'media', has oftener than not been under the control of conservatism, and must on balance have done more to promote inertia, or reaction, than innovation. What brings radical social change is not in any direct fashion the new machine – which grown-ups as well as children are apt to accept with surprisingly little surprise –, but the altered human relationships which it may help to bring about or accelerate. Hence Marxism has always rejected any simply or mainly technological explanation of history.

Two collections of essays appeared in 1985. John Drakakis introduced one of these by announcing its aim as to break down old stereotyped patterns of Shakespeare criticism, already undermined by historical and other inquiries, and thus aid in the poet's 'demystification' (23–4). A foreword to the other collection, edited by Dollimore and Sinfield, defined it as 'a combination of historical context, theoretical method, political commitment and textual analysis', in a spirit not of neutrality but of desire for the transformation of an unjust social order. Alan Sinfield made the apposite remark that if it is legitimate for Shakespeare to be called in by conservatives in support of their views, it should be just as proper for him to be quoted in favour of 'an oppositional politics' (132). This is enough to save today's Cultural

Materialism from any suspicion of having got no further than Adam Smith and his fellow-sociologists two centuries ago.

It may not be so easy to welcome a related trend known as 'New Historicism', spreading chiefly in an America where realistic thinking has for a long time been more severely frowned on than in Britain. Its spokesman Stephen Greenblatt prefaces his *Shakespearean Negotiations* with general propositions about culture growing out of social life, and the 'collective beliefs and experiences' that find their way into the arts; but these guidelines hardly seem to be followed out. He gives a long account of Catholic exorcisms and witch-findings, of antiquarian interest but only slenderly connected with *King Lear*. Hariot's well-known description of the early settlement of Virginia is likewise reported at length, but does not appear to throw much light on *The Tempest*. Such methods may call to mind Fluellen's contention that Henry V can be deemed another Alexander the Great because there is a river in Monmouth, where he was born, and a river in Macedon, 'and there is salmons in both'. What we have to look for are causal interconnections, not casual likenesses.

No such label as 'Cultural Materialism' can be very informative by itself. 'Historical materialism', as a title for Marxism, has the same limitations. A study of any form of culture, by a writer with eyes open for the influences of collective life, will be as much or little 'materialistic' as he is led to make it, and must be judged by the results. He may fix his eyes too exclusively on the ground, and forget to look up at the sky: his study then sinks into reductionism, or 'vulgar Marxism'. It is a necessary convenience of study to divide human experience into departments, such as the 'sociology of the arts and communication, as Cultural Materialism' might just as well be called, or the 'sociology of religion' that others have embarked on. What is vital is that the links among them all, and the fundamental basis of them all, the ways in which mankind earns its livelihood, are not left out.

Sprouting of art from productive toil can be very direct. Romanian shepherds invented dances simulating the movements of a shepherd with his crook. The *barcarole* or boatman's song, especially the Venetian gondolier's, can be felt to imitate the swaying rhythm of a boat gliding through still water. Motherhood inspired cradle-songs. Music has quite often had a functional role in the running of society. A woman's 'charm' began as a witch's spell, made more effective by being given the shape of a song ('carmen'). Soldiers have had marching songs to keep them going when they were ready to drop with weariness. In the Habsburg empire a special kind of 'recruiting music' was composed, to hypnotize young fellows into joining the army.

A modern orchestra, with its conductor and its intricate polyphony of instruments and harmonies, can be compared, not fancifully, to a regiment performing its complex parade-ground evolutions. These two evolved side by side, and in one celebrated case at least conductor and drill-master were the same man: Frederick the Great of Prussia might be seen drilling his soldiers in the daytime, directing his palace orchestra in the evening, perhaps in a composition of his own. Both these forms of organization were peculiar to modern Europe, with its unique social–political structures. Learning to imitate Europe, Japan has done so first with its army, secondly with its industrialization, and now, thirdly, with its orchestras playing Western instruments and music.

Monotonous repetition by painters of subjects like the Madonna and Child was not spontaneous, but was dictated by the Church, for centuries their chief employer. Nowadays artists of all sorts work on their own, but still under both pressures and stimulus from the collective existence of which they are part. This does not mean that we can overlook individual talent and imagination, which alone can lift the commonplace into true art. It means simply that the creative mind is moulded by the life round it, and in turn helps to remould this.

The present work is the second part of a scrutiny of Shakespeare's writings and outlook in the light of Marxist theory. Having been a Marxist all his working life, its author has learned enough at least to be conscious of how many problems and difficulties still beset the Marxist method, at least in the higher regions which it must seek to explore. It has always taken account of the range of general ideas adopted now by Cultural Materialism, but has endeavoured to go a good deal further, and to build a more coherent framework within which to analyse the history of societies and their cultures. Very much has been achieved; success can never be complete, if only because, for one thing, factual knowledge is always expanding; for another, because advance in one field may at any time compel renewed examination of others.

'There are many different kinds of Marxist approach to Shakespeare' (Overton 42). No two Marxist readers will have identical impressions of him, and this may be one of their best reasons for thinking and arguing about him. He is one of the grand test-pieces of civilization and its development. It is a special asset of Marxism, however, to have recognized from birth the interdependence of all human thought and action, the ways in which every-thing in human life influences everything else. Men mould and are moulded by the conditions they live under. It may be taken as a corroboration of this that some such insight was born, or struggling to be born, before Marx. Dr Johnson was quite close to it when he said that while in other writers a character is 'too often an individual', with Shakespeare 'it is commonly a species' (12). Johnson had in mind the detached, isolated individual as more or less a freak, as so many of those who crowd our contemporary novels are. Tragedy can only arise out of the collective feelings and experiences of mankind. Or as Michael Long puts it, tragic characters in Shakespeare are always 'seen in social situations'. 'Shakespeare's psychology is always social psychology' (3–4, 39).

Cultural history has an important contribution to make to our understanding of our past and our efforts to chart our future. Social progress without cultural progress can scarcely be possible, at least if it is to be of a kind worth having. Two adages may be cited from a study by one of the most gifted Marxist critics, Lukács, of modern realism. One is that in our age a writer (and therefore a critic) must be alive to the significance of socialism (or in the first place perhaps it should be said of social problems, like hunger). A writer may not accept socialism, but if he fails to take it into account seriously 'he closes his eyes to the future', and forfeits his creative faculty. The second maxim, subscribed to in their own ways by Ibsen and by Chekhov, is that a writer will be worth reading if he raises meaningful questions, whether he is able to supply convincing answers or not (Lukács, *Realism*, 60, 69).

PART II

Introductory

1

The Condition of England

Underlying the often crude excitements of the early seventeenth-century drama can be felt a deep layer of gloom or uneasiness about the health of a society where so many were excluded from the feast. Some day they might break in and demand their share. In 1603 the long-awaited dynastic crisis was successfully surmounted, but it sharpened anxieties, and new difficulties were soon coming in sight. Shakespeare's tragedies and 'problem plays' belong to a central point in the long-drawn transition from one era to another. Only some such critical turning-point of history could engender that rare phenomenon, Tragedy. A social order slowly decaying of inanition, like that of seventeenth-century Spain, and perhaps twentieth-century Britain, does not feel tragic; it breeds more Poloniuses than Hamlets. In Ireland an exhausted social–political culture was being knocked to pieces by English conquest, but the bards went on like sleep-walkers reciting sycophantic praises of their Irish or English lords (O'Riordan).

Tragedy as expression of a fundamental social mutation, and accompanying an outburst of national heart-searching, could flower uniquely in England because this country was undergoing an unprecedented transformation, ahead of all others, as it was to do again with the Industrial Revolution. From having been a random growth here and there in the economy, capitalism was turning into a whole social–economic system. What was happening was for very long hard to comprehend; men tried to explain it to themselves oftener in moral terms than in any language of economics. England was embarked upon 'a dangerous sea', like Othello sailing to Cyprus (II.i.46). An old order and its moral framework were crumbling, before anything was ready to replace them. The presence at this time of a supreme writer, not altogether a mere coincidence, ensured that the gathering forces of change would have a vast meaning in the history of poetry and human consciousness, as well as of men's ways of earning their daily bread.

Shakespeare's imagery of Time in labour with news or events reflects an era when every day might bring its novelty, great or small, and admonish people, or those with ears to hear, of how much they themselves were altering. A new face on coins, when few Englishmen of 1603 had lived under any other sovereign than Elizabeth, would be another reminder. Her quondam brother-in-law Philip II of Spain had died in 1598, ending an epoch of European history. James I had no inclination to keep the war going, and not many in England who had suffered under its burdens can have been sorry when peace came in 1605; but a war party, a bellicose tendency at least, persisted, with a glistening eye on colonies and treasure-ships. Suspicions of a Catholic menace could always be fomented; and James made room for them by cultivating Spanish friendship, as a conservative bulwark against radical currents in England. But the country was no longer bemused by patriotic drum-beating like Shakespeare's *Henry V*, and had more leisure to think about what was wrong with things at home, and the way it was being governed.

Bacon's *New Atlantis*, published in 1626, described a model state with a monarchy and – like all Utopias, as A.L. Morton said in his study of them (83) – a fixed, permanent constitution. Its author must surely have been too wise to suppose that England, beset with so many social shifts and discords, could expect a perpetual equilibrium. The propertied classes were feeling the need of a regime more responsive to their needs. These were not the same needs as those of common people, but broader support could be drawn in by religious propaganda. Puritanism appealed to an artisan and shop-keeping class, and the yeomanry or more thriving of the peasants. Together these might be called the aristocracy of labour; the lower masses had only deaf ears for the gospel of moral rearmament and hard work and thrift.

Among obstacles confronting James, finance stood first (Aylmer 52–5). Antiquated modes of taxation no longer brought in enough revenue; administrative expenses were inevitably swelling, partly because of inflation, and James was a lavish spender, after years of Scottish penury, which deterred Parliament from giving him more money to waste. Many of the gentry, equally overfond of spending, were being bought out by more businesslike landowners, or by wealthy townsmen. Lower down, since the Reformation days when Latimer launched his sermons at greedy rack-renting landlords, a very long-drawn process was reducing more and more of the peasantry with small farms into a race of labourers employed on bigger farms. Early in 1607 intensely cold weather was causing suffering to the poor, and to cattle; summer began with riotous protests in Warwickshire against enclosures of common lands by private interests; alarm was felt in Stratford. The poor have always been with us; 'poverty', in the sense of collective admission of its existence, only occurs when the poor show by some eruption like this that they realize how things are going against them. Some rough awareness of their condition had been shown by those in power, with the Poor Law of 1601.

In that year John Wheeler, secretary of the Merchant Adventurers, was impressed by the way all classes, and old and young, were continually chaffering, buying and selling, sniffing for profit (Southall, '*Troilus and Cressida*' 217–18). Those lacking money had to borrow. Laura C. Stevenson noted that whereas in the late Elizabethan years the grasping stage usurer had been dormant, in James's reign he was being reinstated by the playwrights (7). A harbinger of this revival was Marston's play *Jack Drum's Entertainment*, printed in 1601, where someone is warned against 'a yawning usurer . . . he'll devour your whole lordship . . . he is a quicksand . . . a gulf, as hungry as the jaws of a jail' (Act 1). A further factor making for social tension and disruption, side by side with the egotism of the new economy, was the frequent recurrence of plague. It struck the poor hardest, if only because they were less able to escape from the big towns. Dekker's pamphlet on the outbreak of 1603, which came so speedily to damp rejoicings over the smooth transfer of the crown, shows ghoulishly the traumas it could cause, its dehumanizing impact, its revelations of man's nature (*Wonderful Year* 178 ff.).

Modernity and its individualism were bringing liberation, enlargement; but by snapping or weakening old social ties they were leaving the individual in some ways impoverished, or unbalanced. Hence the clutching at newer, less personal ties, like aggressive nationalism, or salvationist religion. Class feeling was growing stronger. As usual it was most distinct at the top, most confused, except locally, at the bottom. There were intermediate strata, most important the newer 'Tudor aristocracy', with mixed feudal and bourgeois attributes. It stood at the apex of the more commercialized section of the gentry, an essential part of the capitalist advent. Differences between any propertied classes are always things of the surface by comparison with the fundamental gap between rich and poor.

Religion could do little to smooth this over. The Church of England, the only one with a legal existence, had emerged somewhat oddly from the hurlyburly of the Reformation with a State-controlled episcopal organization and a mainly Calvinist theology. From this disparity there resulted a greater potential of *fermentation*, or restlessness, than almost any other Church anywhere could claim. Wrangling divines were perpetually adding to the intricacies of the theological maze, until even the opinionated James confessed that he found predestination very hard to make sense of. His government was more and more anxious to curb theological controversy in the pulpits, as likely to have unsettling effects on ordinary men and women.

Semi-Pelagian ideas, free will carefully toned down, were being smuggled into Anglican teaching; they stemmed from one of Christianity's oldest heresies, of British origin. They were caught up in international controversy when the Dutch theologian Arminius (1560–1609), near the end of his life, put forward arguments in defence of free will, or a sufficient degree of it to open the door to the possibility – horrifying to the orthodox – of salvation for everybody, instead of only for the elect, those chosen by God long before their birth. In 1618 a conference of all Calvinist Churches, the Synod of Dort, met to pronounce on the issue. Tutored by their erudite king – who, like the House of Orange, had political as well as doctrinal considerations in mind –, the English representatives did their best for moderate views and agreement. But both camps were obstinate, and the canons finally adopted were firmly predestinarian. James endorsed them, as both Luther and St Augustine would have done, but in his later years he was drifting towards a not too clearly defined Arminian position. Under his successor this became a badge of the royalist, anti-Puritan wing of the Church of England. Within the higher social ranks it was accompanied by another widening division, between those who relied on ritual, or sacramentalism, and those with more faith in vigorous sermonizing, as the best spiritual diet for the nation. (On all this see Lake.)

With much abbreviation it may be tentatively said that free will has suited upper classes still feeling able to direct history; whereas a class aspiring to power will prefer to believe that the way it wants to go has already been chosen for it by an all-knowing Providence. For the majority with no prospect of rising in the scale, and much risk of sinking, these niceties could have little meaning compared with the burden of penury. A gloomy mood hanging over England must have owed much to material anxieties. Robert Burton understood this when he set himself to chart the malaise in his *Anatomy of Melancholy*, which appeared in 1621. He was a younger son of an old landed family, but first and foremost a scholar. His views – not his language – often sound so Shakespearian that an adventurous critic (A. Brownlee) has credited him lately with the authorship, not of all Shakespeare's works, but of all the best things in them. Burton defended amusements indulged in without excess, among them the theatre. Court life, on the other hand, he deemed a wretched existence. The English gentry he considered, in spite of his own descent, boorish philistines (II.106; cf. 157–8). He found some of the causes of depression in bad social relations, and could expatiate like Hamlet on patient merit unrewarded, and the insolence of office (II.218, 220, 225). He had plenty of sympathy, though no remedy, for the hardships of the poor, of mine-workers for instance (II.151, 186–8).

Burton dwelt with regret on the spread of religious doubts, and traced some of them to the arbitrary injustice of God's ways to men, as expounded by the divines. Puritanism discarded all the old comforting Catholic rituals, or sedatives, and left the human soul face to face with its destiny. There was something here not unlike the predicament of the tragic hero, hemmed in by perils seen or unseen. Poetic drama and religious faith may be regarded as parallel responses, one seeking to build order out of chaos with human materials, the other with supernatural aid. Drama's highest, tragic forms were half-religious in their gravity; men's worship in that age was very dramatic, and often poetical. Both had a close alliance with music, which helped to dignify them and to make music the second great Elizabethan art. Religious uncertainties and divisions had the advantage of giving a writer like Shakespeare a measure of freedom of mind and art very rare in his Europe. 'Atheism' was a charge often bandied about; Raymond Williams must be closer to the mark when he speaks of 'an anxious, serious, intermittently sceptical' frame of mind as one feature of Shakespeare's time (*Modern Tragedy* 223).

England was in an unstable condition: many ordinary people were discontented, while neither gentry nor burghers formed as yet a homogeneous class, and court and government were drifting apart from the nation. Only one country was ahead of England in modernizing, or some aspects of it at any rate: the United Provinces, or northern Netherlands, a federal republic with Holland the largest province. It too suffered from the instabilities of change, and was at times only narrowly to remain a republic. A well-developed bourgeoisie, with a political élite of 'Regents' or urban patricians – not unlike those who ruled London and the other big English towns, except in being more independent – confronted a small, compact nobility. This was under the leadership of the House of Orange, which had come to the front in the revolt against Philip II of Spain. It could make use of religious demagogy to sway the urban masses, swollen by refugees, embittered Calvinists from the southern Netherlands (Belgium), still under Spanish control. Germany and Italy were divided among a plethora of princes, but there were also city-states ruled by their wealthier citizens. Among these Venice, with territories in and outside Italy, counted as a European power, and part of Europe's defences against the Turks who were overrunning the Balkans. Poland by contrast was a semi-republican landowners' kingdom, not without an attraction perhaps for some English landowners. Everywhere else monarchy was in the saddle, busy with varying success in expanding its autocracy further, and fighting its neighbours for territory. Spain and the Ottoman or Turkish empire were the two examples of success often looked up to.

In 1609 Holland and Spain agreed on a twelve years' truce. There was to be further conflict between them, but from 1604 to 1618 most of western and middle Europe had one of its brief intervals of peace, amidst the perpetually recurring hostilities that did so much to mould its character and culture. Dutchmen were embarking on their conquests in the Indian Ocean, while England was completing its long-drawn conquest of Ireland and feeling its way across the Atlantic. Spain and Portugal, the original modern imperialists, were encountering their would-be successors. France was recovering from long civil wars. Germany was soon to fall into the chaos of Europe's Thirty Years War (1618–48), fought on German soil. Muscovy, or Russia, was learning to take a hand in European affairs, though between the death of Boris Godunov in 1605 and the election of the first Romanov tsar in 1613 there was dynastic and social turmoil. The Ottoman empire, like the Spanish, though still formidable, was passing its zenith. On a very general survey, the seventeenth century was a bad one for Europe.

Huizinga the Dutch historian sums up its situation at the outset by saying that after two centuries of a waning medieval civilization, in the sixteenth century a new start was being made, in many ways under adverse conditions (7). Only in parts of northern and north-western Europe was the new start to prosper for long. But the tragic spirit might be kindled by the clash between old forces decaying and the new emerging, a clash that sharpened poignantly the consciousness of both. In England, as in other countries in turn, nationalism was being forged, very much at first on the anvil of religion, as substitute for a national unity with little real existence. This pioneer country was to be tossed among currents never before met with, impossible for any steersman then – or any historian since – to chart very accurately. For a dramatist in Shakespeare's position there must have been more to excite imagination in an environment so fragmented, incoherent, than any later, well-ordered society could provide. There were windows half-open in every direction, boundless horizons whispering such messages as the 'thoughts beyond the reaches of our souls' that came to Hamlet on the dark battlements of Elsinore.

2

The Theatre

For Londoners the theatres were a collective Stock Exchange of ideas of all sorts, a running commentary on life. Inevitably they were held in doubtful esteem, all the more because so popular. They had been roughly attacked in 1579 by Stephen Gosson, a failed playwright who later entered the Church, in *The School of Abuse*; they needed the equally resolute defence given them in 1612 by Thomas Heywood in his *Apology for Actors*. In between Shakespeare had come and gone, and shed much glory on the stage. But authors had many problems to grapple with, 'agonized confusion' as Kernan says about their art and its purposes, and, most pressingly, how they were to pay their way (*Playwright* 17–19). Arts, like armies, have to march on their stomachs. Traditionally writers looked to private patrons, as they were still doing in the Celtic lands, men whose bounty did honour both to the donors and to the recipients. Self-respecting, or conceited, writers might feel it ignominious to publish their work and seek driblets of money from any willing to buy; this could keep such a poet as Donne away from the printing-office.

Massinger on the other hand was publishing his plays in the 1630s, with frequent acknowledgments to patrons who had supplemented his earnings. Few were so lucky. Princely patronage of the 'science' of poetry had fallen away, George Puttenham sighed in 1589, and aristocratic interest along with it; 'in this iron and militious age' rulers were engrossed in ambitions of conquest (20). James was anything but 'militious', and took himself seriously both as prose-writer and as poet, linguist and critic. He bestowed posts on several literary men, as did his queen and their promising elder son Henry. Plays were highly popular at court. Though only thirty-seven when he moved south, James was ready after years of harassment to relax and enjoy himself; he ruled carelessly rather than badly. His Danish consort Anne, eight years younger and fond of festivities, added sparkle, and sometimes tipsy jollity. Pleading for art and its claim to encouragement, W.B. Yeats once quoted Ben Jonson's flowery address to the court as a fountain watering England's choicest plants, a mirror for the land to guide itself by. Jonson was thinking of what it ought to be, rather than what it was. Still, its favours were not to be sneezed at.

It was nevertheless the theatre-going public that had to be looked to as chief patron; with the result that drama drew into its service some writers whose gifts were not really dramatic. Chapman was one, it has been suggested (Dixon 29). Only with drama as its carrier could poetry, above the topical ballad level, find a wide audience; and drama alone among the arts could be for the most part self-sustaining, kept going by the broad public support that large cities, of which Europe had very few, could afford. London's overgrowth and spreading slums were in many ways deplorable – James tried, vainly, to halt them –, but did help it to serve as a true metropolis. One of the theatre's functions might be called educational, or at least fashion-teaching. As in any era of change and social mobility, multitudes were having to adapt themselves to new ways, novel codes of behaviour, like actors impersonating new characters. Everyone was 'acting', those on the stage doing so the most skilfully.

It was acting, more than anything else, that many spectators were paying their money to see. Actors 'commanded the stage' (Thomson 78), while writing for the theatre was still in its infancy as a regular profession. Dekker talks of the impudent struttings of 'proud Tragedians' (*Belman* 268); authors may well have felt envious of their perfomers. This immature preference, shared by today's cinema-goers, was counterbalanced by willingness to listen to poetry. Blank verse could be a lingua franca of the theatrical realm, as a mode of speech not native to any class, but soaring above the daily level of all classes.

Neither higher nor lower spectators, it is true, could be reckoned ideal listeners. Playwrights were fond of carping at the more illiterate, perhaps in the hope of putting them on their best behaviour, perhaps to flatter their betters. Hamlet in his homily on acting distinguishes 'judicious' auditors from dull 'groundlings', the 'barren spectators' whom the clowns played to. Dekker (*Hornbook* 51) gives us another side of the story: the more genteel, he says, liked to affect a supercilious indifference, as though just casual droppers-in, and guffaw in the middle of a tragedy. If so, it may not be surprising that from 1599 to 1608 nearly all the plays put on at 'private' theatres were comedies, while the public playhouses were turning from history to tragedy.

On the whole it seems legitimate to think of Shakespeare's audience as a respectably intelligent one, with no doubt a fair sprinkling of young enthusiasts like Ralph the grocer's apprentice in Beaumont's *The Knight of the Burning Pestle* (*c.* 1608), fond of ranting in amateur theatricals. An advantage of poetic speech, lifting hearers above the dull earth, was that its speakers had no need to shut themselves up in a curtained box in order to make the indispensable separation between actor and spectator, and transport an audience into the magic realm where life's secrets are unfolded.

The finest specimen of the 'public' theatre, with projecting stage and galleries round an unroofed yard, was the Globe, built in 1599 on the south bank of the Thames as the headquarters of Shakespeare and his partners. New theatres of James's reign were of a pattern closer to the present day, rectangular in shape instead of round, and roofed all over, which made them more dependent on feeble artificial lighting. These 'hall', or 'private', theatres held smaller audiences, and charged higher prices. A corresponding demarcation between two kinds of dramatist, and of plays performed, courtly or popular, was not long in appearing. But in Shakespeare's day it was developing only slowly. In 1608 his company took over a private theatre in the Blackfriars, north of the river, and from then its year was divided between its two strongholds (Sturgess ch. 4). There is not often much sign of his being conscious of having to address two markedly different audiences; and his plays continued to form the staple repertoire of both stages, as well as of the company's performances at court.

In *A Midsummer Night's Dream* Duke Theseus rejects one proposed wedding entertainment as sounding too much like 'satire': its subject was the mourning of the Muses over 'learning, late deceased in beggary'. Such a jeremiad would find only too ready a hearing. An intellectual proletariat was appearing, of young men whose education left them unemployed and penniless. Attacks on society and its failings found their most convenient theatrical platform in the juvenile companies performing in private playhouses, whose popularity we hear of in *Hamlet*. Thomas Heywood condemned this recent vogue as a blot on the stage: writers sheltered behind their guileless young performers while 'inveighing against the state, the court, the law, the city, and their governments', and deriding men of position still living (61). In 1599 poems similarly objectionable, by several authors, had been ordered to be destroyed. The poets learned their lesson, but on the stage, with public favour, satire was more tenacious. Exposure of national ills, denunciation of abuses and those held responsible for them went on, and nowhere more – though without overt personal allusions – than in Shakespeare's 'problem plays' and some of his tragedies. Censorship of plays was growing more stringent under the early Stuarts than under Elizabeth; an admission of the growing importance of the theatre in a time of social and political hubbub (Heinemann, 'Political Drama' 168).

Now as earlier Shakespeare built on the past, as great artists in every field have always done, however far he was destined to travel beyond the literary traditions he inherited. Of his social or ethical outlook the same can be said. His fondness for everything belonging to traditional culture means, as Armstrong said, that he was adopting symbols 'from ancient, if not primaeval, folk-lore' (63; cf. 142). Some areas of the past that he looked back to were older than feudalism, as well as capitalism; though while he looked further back than most writers, he was also peering further into the future which he was so greatly to influence. His language fits this rootedness in the soil of the past, and through it in the feeling of the people. It is 'extraordinarily rich in the floating debris of popular literature' – scraps from the Bible, tags and proverbs and bits of song or ballad (Raleigh 74, 78). Here was his vital communion with his fellow-countrymen, a web of shared habits of mind and echoing words rather than any abstract ideas.

He continued to reshape readymade plots, with a turning aside every now and then to the *terra firma* of history. What was new in his world was exciting, but undigested, strange, hard to distil into coherent fictions. Life was growing more complex, mankind more unfamiliar, motives and actions less predictable. More sensitive than others to all this, Shakespeare faced a harder task in transmuting it into drama. A bewildering medley of old and new was waiting to be forged by poets into dramatic shapes. What must have come first with Shakespeare was some emotional thrill or turmoil, struggling for expression like the visions of a Delphic priestess. Myth or plot would be chosen to suit it; and it chose for itself, so to speak, a more transcendental aid, a gorgeous cloak of images. Concepts, sensations, memories, otherwise speechless, could be given wings by them. Hence the 'amazing and unique development' of his imagery, until it came to form almost 'a second world to that of the plot' (Clemen 1, 9, 89).

3

Shakespeare and Tragedy

Tragic drama must be in some sense an attempt at interpretation of the human condition and human destiny. It is one that, in a secular form of permanent value, has forced itself on men in a few times and places only. We have seldom had strength enough, it appears, to face what it has to tell us, or a poet equal to its demands. Shakespeare did not surrender to the tragic Muse without intermission; he must have been writing *Twelfth Night* on the heels of *Hamlet*, and his problem plays were interspersed with the tragedies and touched some of the same notes. Likewise his season of storm and stress had precursors in two early tragedies, *Titus Andronicus* and *Romeo and Juliet*, and two long narrative poems, both with tragical intent. There were prophetic hints also in some of the Sonnets. He may have had to find personal expression for his deepest feelings about life before he learned to give them effective dramatic form. England, for its part, may have had to imp its wings in dramatic fantasy before it could seek to lay foundations for a new future.

Dr Johnson, living in an eighteenth century which had almost lost the sense of the tragic, admired Shakespeare's comedies more than his tragedies (191), but thought his plays really neither one thing nor the other, but 'compositions of a distinct kind' (15). He was certainly not writing 'tragi-comedies', a label then coming into favour and signifying as a rule a medley, a throwing together of serious and lighter scenes, with little purpose but to avoid monotony. In Shakespeare we have instead, quite often, a dramatic fusion of the two, which is also a social interweaving, an interchange of feelings between higher and lower, when individuals are found in unaccustomed places: a Danish prince in a graveyard, a British king out on the moors, an Egyptian rustic in a palace. A passage like the porter's speech in *Macbeth* forces on us life's 'incongruities', reminds us of how grotesque much of it really is (Rossiter 282). We may be reminded of the young poet Rupert Brooke's cryptic remark about Webster: 'Good farce is a worthy training for a tragic writer' (84). Similarly Shakespeare's characters, though very seldom as artificially put together as those of some of his fellow-writers, can undergo alterations that take us aback.

Yet in this they may be close to 'real life', in 'complexity', 'inconsistency', even 'mystery' (R.M. Frye 121).

'Tragedy' was a term more impressive than precise. When we hear of 'the tragedians of the city' in *Hamlet*, we are hearing of *actors*, capable of performing all the miscellaneous species of play catalogued by Polonius (II.ii.363 ff.). Their being complimented with this honorific title shows at least that tragedy was recognized as the highest pinnacle of drama, even if to a good many spectators it may have meant not much more than blood-and-thunder, winding up with a pile of corpses. Every community needs outlets for its more lawless impulses, and England and London, with their manifold tensions, were finding them at every level down to bear-baiting and witch-hunting. Someone in 1654, talking of plebeian holiday moods, deemed it 'good policy to amaze those violent spirits with some tearing Tragoedy full of fights and skirmishes' (quoted in Wright 612). A writer of 1574 cited by Lily B. Campbell (7) may have come as near as anyone to a definition acceptable to more sophisticated readers of his time: tragic events spring from exorbitant ambition, greed, self-will, destructive to 'all estates'. He meant in short the sin known to the Greeks as *hubris*.

This has some considerable relevance to all Shakespeare's tragedies. They followed on from his English Histories, where political ambition was the dominant motive, and was taken for granted as such. Shakespearian tragedy is 'rooted in history', as Frye says (*Fools* 14). Verbal echoes from the Histories are many. In *Henry IV Part 2* rebels talk of their 'griefs', and are promised 'redress' (IV.i; IV.ii.59); Casca urges Cassius to be 'factious for redress' of Rome's 'griefs' (*JC* I.iii.118). No one but Falstaff would have thought of comparing the cold-blooded Lancaster to 'the hook-nosed fellow of Rome' who came, saw, and conquered (*2H.IV* IV.iii.37). While composing his first mature tragedy Shakespeare must have been struck by the likeness between murder and counter-murder in the Wars of the Roses and the proscription-lists of the Roman republic in its last convulsions.

Materially, by the time he was ready for a return to tragedy, he was doing quite well, and garnering property (cf. I. Brown 182). Such success would make the average writer a good friend of order, or things as they are, but in others might inspire the same sense of guilt as in Tolstoy. In 1603 Shakespeare and his eight partners or 'sharers' in the ownership of their theatre were promoted to the status of 'the King's Men', or company royal, with the title of 'Grooms of the King's Chamber', and scarlet cloaks. With his public too Shakespeare had the encouragement of knowing that he was liked and admired, even if not always understood; and this can go a long way towards reconciling an artist to his surroundings and their imperfections. One well-known tribute to his fame was the performance of *Hamlet* in 1607 aboard an East India Company ship off the African coast.

But we are compelled to think of a delicate equilibrium between the two sides that we know best of Shakespeare's nature, as thrifty investor and unequalled poet. Such extremes have very seldom met, though we can find a poetical banker in Samuel Rogers. We have to suppose a double personality, practical and imaginative. A too well-balanced, well-regulated Shakespeare would not have been our poet. Harmony in a personality, as in a community, easily settles into torpor. We know of a good many later artists who have combined discordant qualities and leanings, the outcome it may be of contradictory pressures – or parents – in early life. One so sensitive as Shakespeare to the vibrations of a society riddled with conflicting impulses could hardly be immune from their contrary influences. We may think of his dramas as fuelled by a continuing effort to overcome such disharmonies within himself – to control and direct them, rather than to erase them.

At one pole there was in him, as probably in all great artists, a 'classical' instinct for orderly form, for the whole as distinct from the parts, whether in works of art or in human communities. It shows in his love of well-kept gardens, his preference for restraint in stage-acting. At the other pole he believed also in the individual unfettered, or only governed by his own reason. He lauded the blessings of peace, and honoured the challenge of war. All his great characters are shaken inwardly by contending passions, as well as outwardly by hostile forces. They may reach, or fear they are nearing, the brink of madness. Some readers have guessed that Shakespeare himself must have been not far from the brink when he wrote *King Lear* and *Timon of Athens* (e.g. J.D. Wilson, *Shakespeare* 120). We know little about the effect on a mind of being frequently invaded and taken possession of by the daimonic powers of imagination.

In the Sonnets he was often gloomily introspective. Now he was entering on a period of life when he could, in those days, be reckoned an old man. In the tragedies he had opportunities to concentrate his feelings about it, and dispel them; this may have had a high therapeutic value. He was coming to terms with the departure of his own youth. In all kinds of ways, whatever the cathartic or purgative uses of tragedy for an audience, they must be felt first of all by the creator who frees himself of dark visitants by clothing them with visible shapes. Simultaneously he is in imagination purging society of its dark forces. Whatever is over-entangled with *self* in his sensations is immolated with the destruction of hero and villain, or hero-villain. By bringing himself closer to the afflictions of his fellows he discards illusions and pettinesses of his own, and confronts reality. Tragedy therefore shows the poet at his highest, as man as well as writer, and is only possible to great writers in great eras.

Musicians have often written cheerful music while themselves feeling wretched. Inspiration is drawn not from the surface levels of consciousness, but from accumulations deeper down, like the aquifers that store water underground, Shelley's 'inmost fountains of the brain'. Impressions that had been storing Shakespeare's mind were not all personal ones, but an intricate mixture of these with what he had seen and thought of the condition of England, and of humanity. All the tragedies are concerned with public as well as private happenings. Swinburne admired in *King Lear* not the 'divine indifference' he has sometimes been fancied to enjoy, but 'a sympathy with the mass of social misery' deeper than anything else in his works (174–5). The heights of poetry that he was able to soar to now would have been inaccessible if there had not been tumultuous energies in himself and in the life around him to hurry his thoughts onward. Each of the dramas makes its contribution to our conceptions of what genuine tragedy is; their most prominent common feature, apart from their poetry, is this interweaving of public and private themes. A Shakespearian tragedy is 'a vision of life', as L.C. Knights said, and what matters is 'our imaginative response to *the whole play*' (219; cf. Knight, *Imperial Theme* 79).

English tragedy had diverse roots; one was the old moralizing, semi-religious drama (see Hunter, 'Tradition of Tragedy'). A late example was Thomas Preston's *Lamentable Tragedie of Cambises, King of Persia* (*c*. 1569), lamentable indeed as a piece of writing, but with a clear political moral, announced by the Prologue. Kings must reign virtuously, and respect the laws, or heaven will punish them. There is no divine right for them to shelter behind. Shakespearian tragedy faces the same way. An indignation which must often have stirred in him, as he wrestled with the Gordian knots of human life, authorizes us to view these dramas from a standpoint which – in the most general meaning of the word – can be called revolutionary. A political revolution, such as was to follow before long in England, can be looked on as a narrower, more earthbound event, recording the outcome of collisions set in motion by outward conditions and people's imperfect awareness of them. For men and women as creatures who 'look before and after', the ideas aroused by world-shaking social change must be far vaster than the humdrum issues, the bones of contention, over which dispute rages in the marketplace.

Shakespeare's 'tragic period' must have started from something personal, some dislocation of his own life which could lay a magnified spell on him because it opened his eyes wider to the world round him and its martyrdom. Then the two levels of feeling would reinforce each other. It is too trivial to suppose, like T.S. Eliot, that he was merely trying, along with Dante (and with T.S. Eliot?), to 'metamorphose private failures and disappoint-ments' (49–50). Leavis showed more insight when he said that tragedy raises us above self-centred emotion to 'a kind of profound impersonality' (cited by Salingar, 82). This process of universalizing cannot be easy to put into words, involving as it does the whole molecular interconnection between individual and society. Coleridge's stock of philosophical terms may not give much help to his proposition that 'Shakespeare shaped his characters out of the nature within', but not 'out of his own nature as an individual person'; as a poet he 'had no *I*, but the *I* representative' (241). But the words may be taken to mean, rightly, that he was somehow digesting and transmuting what he could catch of the feelings and thoughts of others, together with his own, by virtue of a unique sensitiveness to the tremors in his social ether, and unique capacity to turn them into poetry.

There can be no finality in attempts to define his characters; as Hunter says, our judgments of personalities like Othello are 'capable of endless modification' ('Tradition of Tragedy' 131). In daily life too people have multiple and shifting impressions of one another, and often of themselves. And a dramatist with Shakespeare's breadth of response to human life could not be content to limit himself, in his greater works, to the doings of a few individuals, simply on their own account. Bradley quoted a dictum of Hegel's that tragedy since the Greeks had become primarily subjective, with collective concerns in the background at most (*Poetry* 76–7). The Shakespearian case that comes closest to fitting this view is *Othello*. Yet even here the concern is not simply with one woman's alleged sin, but with what appears to be a prevalent social malady.

Moreover the historical accompaniment, the conflict with Turkey, does not end with the wrecking of the Turkish fleet: it is 'a largely silent but eloquent presence throughout the play' (McAlindon 128). Timon, unlike Othello, is no more than a private citizen now, but he has been an important personage in Athens, and his fate has a bearing on everyone's life under its corrupt oligarchy. The speech in *Hamlet* about the king as a great wheel, to which all his subjects' fortunes are tied (III.iii.15 ff.), only expresses in archaic form the indivisibility of the two spheres, public and private. Shakespeare's protagonists are fully developed as individuals, but not cut off from the social whole; a complex one because Shakespeare, living on a borderline of history between pre-industrial and capitalist, could make use of promptings from both.

Coleridge lived through another great age of transformation and revolutionary upheaval; he was well placed to comprehend how drama must somehow embody social forces, historical currents. A tragic figure in Shakespeare is always endowed with admirable qualities, but is entrapped into undertaking actions that go against his grain, or else, by rash actions of his own, letting loose consequences he is unable to control. His passions are not his own solely, but well up from the social condition, or, more distinctly, out of the conditions men collectively forge for themselves at a given time. For a writer to experience life tragically, and find listeners, there must be in his society a poignant underlying sense of the times being morally and practically out of joint. There must be conflicts of feeling ready to force their way into consciousness by taking on the flesh and blood of poetical creations.

This should not be confused with allegory, a much more common-place mode of expression, which views things detachedly, from outside. Winstanley's treatment of *Othello* as an allegory of the ruinous Spanish conquest of Italy is ingenious, but no more, except as a reminder of Shakespeare's links with his west European background. Such artificial plot-construction would be quite out of key with the riches Shakespeare was drawing from currents flowing much deeper below the visible extent of life. His was an age of endings and beginnings, an old order changing and yielding place to new – but not tranquilly, painlessly, as Tennyson would have wished.

Britain is a deeply class-divided society, where one per cent of the inhabitants own more than half of the land, and where today the gap between affluence and poverty is wider than ever before since 1945. Here is a good reason for looking to earlier stages of its evolution, like Shakespeare's, for light on what it has become. His plays seem, however, to raise an immediate difficulty. Although we know his England to have been full of frictions and tensions, we do not often see these pictured in any literal way in what he wrote. They may stand out clearly enough in the way his characters talk of one another, or in collisions like the one compressed into the figures of Shylock and Antonio, or those between nobles and peasants in *Henry VI*, patricians and plebeians in *Coriolanus*. What is missing, in both Histories and Tragedies, is the middle class, the merchantry or bourgeoisie. Consequently we are shown no tragic clash between feudal aristocracy and the class destined to supplant it.

In fact, no such dramatic clash between them was ever to take place in English history, although some elements of it were present in the Civil Wars. The process of supplanting was to be extremely slow and piecemeal. Elsewhere too contests between these two classes have very seldom been fought out sword in hand. In the earlier stages, when lords were high and haughty and burghers impudent upstarts who wanted their loans repaid, feeling might be acrimonious enough. In course of time things softened into a milder warfare of manoeuvre, negotiation, skirmish, leading towards compromise; the hard-up gentleman ready to marry the wealthy citizeness, the businessman prepared to make it worth his while. Such social adjust-ments were proper matter for satirical comedy, like *The Merry Wives of Windsor*. But the envies and rancours lying behind them, along with the hostility of both sides to the hungry masses, could be sublimated into tragedy, a picture of a social whole under stress within the mind of a Macbeth, or between personalities like Othello and Iago, Lear or Goneril.

In ordinary conditions, rivalries dividing members of the same group are likely to be more in the forefront than the common interests which unite them. A grocer's worst opponent is the grocer in the next street. Barons and belted earls are rivals for local supremacy or court influence. It is a series of armed struggles between feudal factions that Shakespeare is concerned with in the English Histories. They culminate in the defeat of the more retrograde, recalcitrantly feudal party by the monarchy and its allies – including public opinion. Classes as well as nations and individuals are 'betrayed by what is false within'; the overthrow of the baronage had to be, as Shakespeare showed it, its own work, or the outcome of one of its members growing powerful enough to reduce the rest to submission. These plays – and Goethe's *Götz von Berlichingen* – may have been in Marx's mind when he said that 'the downfall of former classes such as the knighthood could offer subjects for magnificent tragic works of art'.

Public opinion counts in these plays, even when no bourgeoisie is visibly in the field. Shakespeare was increasingly aware that the Wars of the Roses came about not through forces arising within the dominant class in isolation, but in the configuration of an entire society, all of whose interests were in some way affected, so that the fate of the whole community was at stake. Shakespeare had to appear, and no doubt was, 'on this side idolatry', an admirer of the Tudor regime which completed the transformation of a medieval baronage into a semi-modern aristocracy. From other points of view he can be thought a surreptitious critic of it, or of the types of public men through whom it ruled, and whose qualities mattered more to the people under them. In his plays they show for the most part in a poor light. Ideally or in the abstract he may think an aristocratic monarchy a good thing, but usually the test-cases shown to us are less admirable.

A parallel might be drawn with the biblical story of George Peele's *David and Bethsabe*, produced in the late 1590s. David occupies a 'holy throne', but he finds very unholy means of indulging in a sinful amour; and when one of his sons rapes a half-sister and then turns her out of doors, David is displeased, but does nothing. He could scarcely be less deserving of the happy ending allotted to him. Or to take an analogy nearer home, Jane Austen may have felt comfortable with the thought of a cosy rural England presided over by benevolent squires and rectors, where the poor are taken good care of; but the well-fed personages in her novels are drawn realistically, and seldom fit into such an idyllic picture.

Shakespeare knew his audience, and the grievances always fermenting in many minds; he cannot have failed to guess what reactions he might be stirring up in them. If drama spoke for the many, the many might be capable of finding means of their own to express their grievances. England, not only London, was becoming literate, and was anything but inarticulate. All over the country, Adam Fox has shown lately, people were making known their dislike of individuals who misused wealth or power – squires, petty officials, dishonest traders, bullying parents – by producing lampoons, crude but telling satires in doggerel verse, and displaying copies wherever they could be seen. This was a feature of popular culture in other countries too, as far off as Russia and as late as the nineteenth century. In Shakespeare's time a grave view was taken of it as a subversive habit, in the highest quarters. A great many prosecutions took place in the court of Star Chamber itself.

Londoners had their own oligarchy to grumble about; any despot or bully on the stage might typify it for them. We may think of a bourgeoisie as an unseen presence, good or bad, in the plays. Aristocracy itself was being reshaped by the spreading commercialization of life, not always for the better. Few of its young sprigs could merit Ophelia's tribute to Hamlet as 'courtier, soldier, scholar' (III.i.153 ff.). This was an ideal derived from Renaissance Italy, a country untypical in not having passed through a period of strict feudalism and feudal monarchy; in the northern lands it was something of a misfit. A pamphleteer was expressing common opinion when he wrote that 'Pride, Riot, and Whoredom' were the young courtier's companions, and that the court was no place to look for virtuous women (Nashe 101, 133). Southall's study of sixteenth-century love poetry shows how heavily it was encrusted with imagery of wealth, treasure, jewellery, profit (*Literature*). Theatre and Puritanism really belonged to the same capitalist complex, Kernan notes (*Playwright* 89). Professional drama was very much a product of the new age, even if with one foot still lingering in an older world. The higgling of the market was going on all round it and its audiences. It cannot be a surprise to come upon stage characters showing traits of a mixed origin.

4

The Tragic Road

A sure instinct had led Shakespeare to history; it was his school or training-ground. He learned, more quickly than most later historians have done, that it must be made to reveal, as R.H. Tawney said, not only the externals of collective life but its 'hidden foundations', taken for granted until they begin to crack (8–9). By the time of *Henry IV* he was writing social as well as political history. His tragedies would explore the epoch of transition in a more searching, imaginative way than the Histories (Lukács, *Historical Novel* 155). This makes them at the same time the most realistic of all his plays, with the most 'real' characters and events. Unlike both the Comedies before them and the Romances after, they are firmly set in particular places, which may be far away in time and space but are so vividly conceived that each in turn becomes for the time being our universe. Variations of key are very wide. Groping into the future, he was taking his stories from a past more or less remote; what region he had got to, what soil he was standing on now, he can scarcely have known himself, until his play and its compass-points took shape round him. In its abrupt leaps too the sequence is remarkable, from civilization into the barbaric depths of *King Lear* and *Macbeth*, and back to classical antiquity; from urban bustle to blasted heath, and from Mediterranean sunlight to the forbidding skies of the north.

Poetic drama, with its heightened consciousness, investing everything spoken with a deeper significance, could not be at home with the here and now: the present, the actual, is too much clogged with the trivial and prosaic. Imagination it seems requires a pabulum already pre-digested, so to speak, by time – but not over-remote, not yet mummified. Shakespeare and his fellows could believe that they knew enough about Julius Caesar to show him as he was. About the common man of far-off ages they knew little or nothing: in these tragedies he is an Englishman, a villager or artisan licensed to talk plain prose. In French classical tragedy there could be no place for such plebeians, or for prose. In Shakespeare's theatre they provide a backcloth, sometimes a yardstick, for the heroic doings of their superiors; they supply also a sense of permanence, of the People as the enduring basis of social existence, always ill used yet always surviving.

In the Histories Shakespeare searched for a model of the man of action, successful without being too uncivilized, too much a Tamberlane. His search led to Henry V, but ended in disappointment. His efforts to lend variety to this hero by endowing him with a twofold nature, at ease whether in an East-cheap tavern or in a palace or on a battlefield, were awkwardly unconvincing, only saved from failure by the magnificent figure of Falstaff. There is no worthy business to be undertaken. Henry can only be packed off to conquer France, a mission which will do no good to his own country, far less to the French. Henry is what Granville-Barker called him, a dead end ('*Henry V* to *Hamlet*' 51 ff.). Shakespeare made haste to turn away from him in the first tragedies, where he could find heroes ready to face the most hazardous tasks for no advantage of their own. But Brutus and Hamlet perish with their duty only very imperfectly fulfilled. After Lear, whose quest leads him to a wild vision, there is a succession of men whose splendid abilities are squandered on selfish ambitions destined – not for Timon alone – to reveal themselves as delusions. Octavius is the only exception, the only winner, because in him private ambition and a sense of public responsibility form an amalgam. Perhaps this is how Shakespeare would have liked to portray his Henry VII, had he been free to treat Queen Elizabeth's grandfather as realistically.

Rome offered an appropriate starting-point. An odd image in *Love's Labour's Lost* compared Holofernes' visage in the masque, got up as an antique hero, to 'The face of an old Roman coin', worn and barely recognizable (V.ii.610). Old coins were being collected, memories of Rome taking on new life. All Europeans invested Rome with a peculiar grandeur and dignity, congenial to tragedy. Republican Rome was to remain for very long the model of civic virtue; veneration reached its climax with the French Revolution, but long before then 'Roman thoughts', like the one that roused Antony from Egyptian sloth, joined with the Bible to nerve Englishmen for their own revolution. Antonio in the *Merchant of Venice* was a pattern of 'The ancient Roman honour' (III.ii.296); Horatio at the side of his dying friend, and eager to follow him, is 'more an antique Roman than a Dane' (V.ii.320). In all the three Roman plays Rome is plunged into civil strife; they can all be regarded as tragedies of Rome itself.

Julius Caesar and *Hamlet*, the opening pair, might be called 'problem tragedies', because the hero in each case suffers from painful doubts and hesitations about what he ought to do. Something in Shakespeare's own life may have left him fascinated with the sensations of a man screwing up his courage or resolution to a perilous act; he may have thought of them as haunting Catholic fanatics, like the Guy Fawkes who followed close on these two plays. His own family had Catholic connections. It is conceivable that somewhere about that time he found himself on the fringes of a conspiracy among his high-born acquaintances; one or two of the Sonnets may lend colour to such a guess.

Brutus communes with himself on the likeness of an agitated mind to a country in a state of insurrection (II.i.63 ff.). Hamlet is troubled not by family duty alone, but by a sense of public responsibility, which he feels unequal to. Of the two, Brutus makes his decision and regains self-control much more quickly. He is after all a Roman, and has a party eager to follow him; Hamlet is solitary. Brutus's meditation on what to do with Caesar – 'there's the question' (II.i.13) – contrasts starkly with Hamlet's on what to do with himself – 'that is the question' (III.i.56). Hamlet has been thrown into an abruptly transformed situation, which we may take as crystallizing the more gradual pulsations of change that Shakespeare's contemporaries were all subjected to.

For Hamlet the shock turned all men and women into strangers, unknowable also to one another, even to themselves. He grew resentful of any intrusion into 'the heart of his mystery', his secret self, now acquiring an unfamiliar self-consciousness. Some such experience is shared by many of the heroic characters. A free openness, akin to the unclouded gaze of the 'clear gods' in *King Lear*, has been natural to them. It is one of Shakespeare's touchstones of true aristocracy, as well as the inheritance of a class moving, secure and confident, in a world which it belongs to, and which belongs to it. But this Eden is nearing its end; in the tragedies men learn the unwisdom of being over-frank and trustful.

In *Julius Caesar* and *Hamlet* hope and high endeavour can still confront the powers of darkness, and 'honour', wilting in the later Histories under Falstaff's derisive gaze, revives and is one of the keynotes. In Rome especially civic and personal honour flourish side by side. They stand now not for self-glorifying adventure, but for a rational, though élitist, conception of duty. With honour comes 'nobility', it too in a higher sense than before. It is not a mere badge of rank, as it usually was in the Histories, but betokens a moral quality. 'Think not, thou noble Roman – ' (V.i.110): in *Julius Caesar* this somewhat stilted form of address is habitual among men with true respect for each other. It is one of various legacies from this play to *Hamlet*. Here too noble attributes are at odds with an ignoble setting. Hamlet is addressed by the Ghost as 'thou noble youth' (I.v.38), very much in the style of Cassius summoning Brutus to action; the dying Laertes is reconciled with 'noble Hamlet', who has praised him as 'a very noble youth' (V.ii.308; V.i.191). The word suffers a relapse when Antony near his end consoles himself with the thought of having been the 'noblest' as well as 'greatest' prince on earth (*AC* IV.xv.55); it can mean no more here than splendidest, or most admired. Cleopatra remedies it with her last words to him: 'Noblest of men . . .' (IV.xv.59).

In spite of hesitations as to their right course, Brutus and Hamlet both accept a duty to act as soon as they are convinced of it, even though it is a duty to kill. For Macbeth there is no wavering between two alternatives that may each be right: he knows that what he resolves to do is nakedly a crime. With him there comes to its fullest a necessity to carry out a deed in order to prove his manhood, just as a soldier must show bravery in battle. In all three cases it is someone close to them whom they feel compelled to attack; each fatal act can be felt as a symbol or prophecy of national disruption. Brutus and Hamlet are readers, intellectuals; their successors are less and less given to thought, more under the sway of passion or instinct, like heroes of folk-lore. They behave like men 'possessed'. In a way Shakespeare is moving from the élite and its outlook towards the people with its elemental impulses. Distantly, if no more, this substitution of passion for reason may correspond to history nearing the waterfall, the whirlpool, swords breaking in on argument.

More evidently it goes with increasing closeness to Nature and the animal kingdom, especially in the murky depths of the middle plays. It is when the walls of conventional society totter that men feel their proximity to a realm not human, which may be welcoming or frightening. Closely akin to this awesome presence in the 'northern' tragedies is a mysteriousness in men's own behaviour, still more in their mentality. We catch sight of shadowy corridors, unopened doors, unexplained happenings. Heroes strive to uphold good things of the past, as Brutus does, or to pursue evil ambitions of the past, like Macbeth, when both have become anachronisms. Each drama 'shows a world at a further stage of decline' (Margolies 11).

In a diversity of States and epochs Shakespeare shows the processes of decay and approaching crisis at work. Everywhere his skies are darkening, something is going fundamentally wrong. The tragic climax is the funeral pyre of an old order doomed to perish in order to make room for a new and worthier one. It burns away in its conflagration thick clouds of human incomprehension, painfully yet healingly. In a few individual fates it seems to teach the historic lesson that nothing short of a cataclysm of some kind can jolt sluggish humanity out of its customary unthinking grooves. In this can be recognized the affinity between tragedy and revolution.

To ascribe to Shakespeare any 'fully-fledged political and religious philosophy' must, as Michael Hawkins says, be delusory; none the less the poet was familiar with the debates raging in his time (157–8). He must have had opinions, and it is in his tragedies that these can be expected to show most clearly. Dr Johnson was old-fashioned in wanting tragedy to administer 'poetic justice' all round. We know from Eckermann that Goethe did not write his works as vehicles for abstract ideas, as his philosophizing countrymen fancied (205–6; cf. 287). Shakespeare's spontaneous creativity was not fettered in any such way, and he had no programme to convert his audience to. He was content to let his men and women speak their contradictory minds, and to leave it to their words and actions to arouse *our* minds. He made conscious for us our own thoughts and those of our fellows;

our choice is our own. Yet a poet, as Wordsworth held, cannot but be a teacher; and Shakespeare's aim – how deliberate we cannot tell –, or at any rate the effect of his words, is to impress on us the duty of discovering as much as we can of the right conduct of life, public as well as private. He might have disagreed with a good deal of what Dr Johnson said about him; but not with his dictum that 'it is always a writer's duty to make the world better' (21).

5

The Others

Shakespeare towers above his contemporaries in literary quality, and above most of them in quantity of production as well. He began comparatively late, but was writing for a score of years. This longevity of his pen may have owed something to the sheltered placidity of his life (or the years we know about), by contrast with such stormy petrels as Kyd and Marlowe, Chapman and Jonson, or in Spain Cervantes, wounded in the great naval battle against the Turks, and five years in Moorish captivity – or Lope de Vega, serving in the army and sailing in the Armada. Much in Shakespeare is unique in its completeness; in a breadth of vision, an openness like that of his Globe to all the winds of heaven, a truly humane attitude to human life, which other Elizabethan playwrights achieved only at times. Similarly they touched poetic heights now and then, Shakespeare marvellously often; and in poetic drama the quality of the poetry must be the supreme test, on condition that it is dramatic as well.

He was, all the same, one of a flock, in which can be reckoned a greater number of truly creative writers than, for instance, among the English Romantics of about 1800. Notable artists have seldom been isolated figures, but have appeared in groups. Mid-sixteenth century France had its 'Pléiade' or constellation of poets, headed by Ronsard, who were giving their country's poetry its renaissance. They were among the first of many artistic fellowships banding together to revitalize their art. Early nineteenth-century England had its 'Lakers', France half a century later its Impressionist painters and Russia 'The Five' composers who set out to breathe new life into its music.

Elizabethan playwrights were not a 'movement'; they were all experi-mentalists, rivals, friendly or unfriendly, sometimes collaborators. Still, they faced many of the same problems, not only artistic but professional, as members of a new vocation, a precarious one as it has never ceased to be. They had to satisfy those who controlled the theatres, and if they could the publishers as well. All literary business was concentrated in London and its surroundings, and dramatists could scarcely avoid knowing one another. They worked for theatres with the same kind of construction and facilities, or for the 'private' ones added before long; this in itself imposed a family resemblance on their methods.

Few restricted themselves to tragedy alone, but they were often at their best there. Kyd (d. 1594) wrote the first real tragic drama; Marlowe (1564–93) came close on his heels, followed by Shakespeare, and by Chapman, active as a writer of plays until about 1610. He died, as many Elizabethan writers lived, in poverty. Still to come were Tourneur, born about 1575, Middleton in 1580, Webster about 1580 and at his best in his later twenties. Massinger was born in 1583, Ford about 1586. Shirley brought up the rear: *The Cardinal*, written about 1641, was one of his best attempts at tragedy. All these together form a veritable galaxy. There are passages in all of them that may remind us of Shakespeare. Many themes, situations, types of character were employed more or less by everyone. In Act I Scene 2 of Webster's *The White Devil*, the villain Flamineo's tale of his earlier life is that of an impoverished member of the gentry, corrupted by poverty; Shakespeare would have recognized him. Even in language there was a common stock of phraseology, such as not a few literatures have possessed. Walter Scott commented on this in his journal, after turning over one evening a bundle of Elizabethan plays.

Shakespeare earned an acknowledged supremacy in his lifetime, and continued to be performed until the Civil War; when the theatres reopened after 1660 he was the one most eagerly restored to the stage, as Charles II was to the throne. During the next century he got more and more of the limelight; Pope, Johnson, Warburton, edited him, critics quarrelled over him. Strolling players acted him in barns, with 'barn-storming' fire and fury. It needed the Romantics, another bevy of poets pining for success in the theatre, to recognize that Shakespeare had been one of a similar array. Charles Lamb opened the way with his annotated anthology in 1808 of striking passages from the old writers. This brought a number of them back into literary circulation, but Shakespeare's pre-eminence was never questioned, and instead rose still higher; and none of the others found their way, except very spasmodically, back to the stage.

Just as Shakespeare was not England's only important dramatist, his country was not the only one with a developing drama. The theatre was having a remarkable flowering, over wide areas of Europe from Norway to Hungary; the ideas it helped to spread were part of a grand modernization. Both Renaissance and Reformation – and Counter-Reformation –. were helping to awaken a consciousness, among town-dwellers and the literate, of life in a Europe leaving one epoch behind and entering another, like a bird moulting its feathers. Even in far-away Edinburgh in 1540 the approaching religious upheaval inspired a solitary but striking play, Sir David Lindsay's *The Three Estates*, a satirical morality-play on the maladies of the old Church. Three other countries share first place: England, France and Spain, or rather the leading Spanish *reino*, or kingdom, Castile. All three had many cultural features in common, but also wide differences: basically each was taking a distinct historical route.

Each was a conglomerate of regions and peoples, which its government was trying to bring under closer control, with the help of a dawning national spirit that the theatre, like the Church, could help to fan. England had its Celtic appendages; Spain, like England after 1603, was a combination of two countries, Castile and Aragon, both including provinces of alien speech. These latter were as a rule content with their local autonomies; but pressures of war-taxation could provoke the Catalan revolt of 1640, just as other irritations could provoke the rebellion of Scotland in 1638 and Ireland in 1641, and thereby precipitate the Civil War. Recurrent civil wars in France in the later sixteenth and earlier seventeenth centuries often had a partly regional basis.

Drama in western Europe was fertilized by complex interchanges and borrowings. Italy too had much to contribute, though its own early start was not sustained. It had no national unity, no nation-wide culture or even language, and its artistic genius was flowing chiefly into music and painting, arts by nature more cosmopolitan. The case of the Netherlands suggests interesting questions about the social bases of drama. What was needful, it would seem, was some sort of balance and interplay between an aristocratic outlook and that of a sturdy middle class, shading into an at least half-literate popular mass. On the cultural plane we may think of such a balanced tension as more readily achieved than on the political level, where Marx may have been too much in a hurry to suppose an equilibrium between old nobility and new bourgeoisie as the foundation on which absolute monarchy was being reared.

In the northern Netherlands, or 'United Provinces', the nobility was relegated to the background by the long struggle for independence from Spain. In the south, now Belgium, where revolt against Spain was crushed and Protestantism extinguished, there was a wealthy nobility and a vice-regal court, but the commercial and popular classes were enfeebled. Both sections of the divided country found their artistic outlet, like Italy, in painting (an art where England lagged far behind) and music. In western Germany too, the best developed part of the country, there was great political fragmentation. A medley of small principalities, some of them ecclesiastical, jostled with republican Free Cities; here again there was too wide a gap between the social strata on whose interaction the drama throve. There were local theatres, where English touring actors might be welcomed, but until much later there could be no rise of a national theatre.

In the three nurseries of drama, Walter Cohen observes, tragic and historical drama had a special affinity with the aristocratic mentality, that of a class undergoing many changes but still clinging to its social if not political ascendancy (108). Tragedy finds what we many call its centre of gravity in death; nobles were likeliest to feel death as something ever-near, because of their devotion to war, their sport of hunting, and the ritual of duelling, taking shape as the badge and seal of their code of honour.

By the time France had leisure from its civil broils to think much about tragedies on the stage, England was leaving them behind; Counter-Reformation and Catholic bigotry likewise arrived late here, when England was moving, if without knowing it, towards secularism. Paris did not acquire a professional public theatre until the early seventeenth century, and by 1630 its audience was more upper and middle class than popular. Its first great figure, Pierre Corneille, made his start in 1630 as a writer of comedies, but turned in 1637, with *Le Cid*, to the brief series of tragedies for which he was to be remembered. Tragedy may be in some senses an art of nobility, but few nobles have ever been able to write it for themselves. It demands a duality of vision, inward and outward, more likely to be found in writers from an intermediate class. Corneille was a provincial magistrate.

Plays like *Le Cid* had an ambivalent message, Cohen points out: an old feudal order was coming to an end, but its heirs could hope to survive by incorporation in a new centralizing state (112–13, 314). What was taking place in France, as in England earlier, was the curbing of an old undisciplined baronage by the monarchy, and its great minister Richelieu. This was a political reshuffle, leaving France's general structure and condition little altered. England was by now changing more fundamentally, and the depth of tragedy that its playwrights, Shakespeare most of all, were able to plumb was far greater, if less clearly charted. A French nobleman, Michel Hurault, writing in 1591 (and translated into English a year later), had analysed the historical trend as precisely as Karl Marx could have done. They would do well, he urged his fellows, to accept and support a strong monarchy, for if the common people were allowed to overthrow the king it would soon be all up with the nobility and its estates and privileges, whose natural protector was the king. A historical parallel in the twentieth century has been the willingness of capitalism, when under threat, to give up its cherished freedom and submit to the protection of dictators.

France, nation as well as State, was a largely artificial construct, a collection of territories and ethnic communities acquired and kept together by force. Its culture has been an instrument – less needed in England – in the welding together of these diversities, by dint of increasingly rigid bureaucratism, which the Revolution of 1789 only intensified. This culture has had some of the same flavour of artificiality, nowhere more evidently than in the subjection of French classical drama to the 'Three Unities' of time, place and subject; a doctrine about on a par with that of France's 'Natural Frontiers' or the law, invented in seventeenth-century France, which for two centuries obliged the gentlemen of Europe to wear top-heavy wigs.

Corneille's *Cinna* (1637), which had a great success, invites comparison with *Julius Caesar*, though with a leaning towards romantic love. It concerns a republican conspiracy against the emperor Augustus. Allusions to Brutus and Cassius are frequent, but the commoners of Rome are absent. Monarchy triumphs, but is magnanimously forgiving. Language is energetic, dignified, and inflexible, and almost destitute of imagery. It is rhetoric rather than poetry. In the theatre rhetoric is more effective than poetry, Heine was to say (221); a reminder of how extraordinary an achievement was that of Shakespeare and his fellow-playwrights – and their audience –, the more so when coupled with Heine's dictum that prose is inadequate for tragedy: 'the theatre is another world' from ordinary life (220–21).

Corneille's later plays were of failing inspiration. For him, by about 1660 with the consolidation of the monarchy under Louis XIV, history had come to an end, whereas for Shakespeare it was never more than beginning. He was replaced as a tragic dramatist by Racine – son of a provincial official, but a courtier by instinct –, whose first play was performed in 1664. His chief subject was the discreetly unpolitical one of love, in Greek or Roman settings. Napoleon greatly preferred Corneille, as the poet worthy to depict heroes like himself. He could have agreed with Goethe's spokesman Wilhelm Meister that Corneille chose men great by nature, Racine men of high rank, so that people of rank were sure to enjoy his pieces (vol. 1, 155). The great comedy-writer Molière, like Shakespeare an actor as well, spent his earlier years (1645–58) touring the provinces, chiefly in the south, and learning to write by imitating Italian comedy. After he and his company came to rest in Paris, when he was thirty-six, he wrote half of his best plays in prose.

In northern Castile, the old heartland of Spain, a challenge to the government from an urban, partly at least mercantile, quarter came with the Revolt of the Comuneros, or league of cities, in 1521. This was much earlier than any such challenge in England, but very premature; it was set off by fortuitous circumstances, and was quickly put an end to. No similar effort followed until the nineteenth century, and even then feebly. When the Comuneros rose the Spanish conquest of the New World had just begun. Profits of empire were more than outweighed by the cost of chronic fighting in Europe, where the Netherlands, most of Italy, and from 1580 Portugal belonged to the Spanish crown. In the long run, war with countries from England to Turkey had an exhausting effect on an economy too much limited to export of raw wool, with too little of the industrial development that Holland, England, northern France, were embarking on.

To this failure of development, hidden for too long by the excitements of war and religion, must be attributed some of the qualities of Spanish drama as a mirror of the national life. As H.A. Rennert showed long ago, the Spanish theatre grew up with remarkable similarities to England's; but in drama the differences were more apparent. Theatres were to be found in several provinces, particularly in Seville in the south. But the focal point was Madrid, arbitrarily fixed on as the capital in 1561 by Philip II. It was geographically central, but set in an inhospitable upland, and was much smaller than London, much less a home of trade or industry. There could be no clash of court and City values there, as so often in English plays. Seville handled the lucrative trade with America, and bred a class of rich merchants or financiers evolving more smoothly into gentlemen than their less parasitic London counterparts. Over much of Europe religious schism, if often productive of conflict, could have a stimulating effect; in Spain there was none, because social forces making for innovation were too weak, and the Inquisition, directed by the government, was too strong. Religious plays – *autos sacramentales* – continued to run their separate course throughout.

Philip II, that gloomy bigot, bestowed little encouragement on the theatre; courtiers gave more, and after his death in 1598 his successors. Actresses had a place on the Spanish as well as the French stage, and Philip IV honoured one of them with his special patronage and made her the mother of an ambitious commander in chief. A 'Golden Age' of Spanish music, painting, literature, drama, was in progress, though its material foundations were growing more and more inadequate. There was a harvest of genius and talent among the writers, playwrights and novelists in particular: Lope de Vega, from about 1580; Cervantes, from 1585; Calderón, from 1623. And the dramatic tradition shaped by Lope de Vega was of a 'highly nationalistic character' (G. Edwards viii).

These playwrights were not debarred from themes connected with public life, even if they could only display it in a somewhat subdued light. Spain had plenty of legal, but no constitutional life: the Cortes had never been more than a feeble substitute for a parliament, and was now moribund. There were plays dealing with national history. There were others about royal favourites, in the early seventeenth century when first the Duke of Lerma and then the Count-Duke of Olivares were taking over control from rulers frivolous or feeble (Cohen 213). They were drawn from the high nobility: in a sense feudalism was resuming its sway. Sometimes an unnamed king makes an entry, to set things to rights. In one of the Calderón plays translated by Edward Fitzgerald, *The Mayor of Zalamea*, it is Philip II himself who puts in a – not very impressive – appearance near the end.

An interesting point noted by Cohen is that when writers were not occupied with statesmen and grandees, they turned to peasant characters rather than bourgeois. A genre of 'peasant honor drama' flourished, where the farmer was endowed with a portion of the gentleman's respect for the code of honour, in place of the 'bourgeois tragedy' experimented with by some Elizabethans (301, 315). It was not the humble ploughman, however, who was being admitted to this distinction, but the *labrador*, the prosperous yeoman with labourers in his employment as in England. As Théophile Gautier in his travel-book on Spain was to say of the old drama, the *pundonor*, the point of honour, ruled everything (232 ff.). It controlled upper-class behaviour as rigidly as the Church directed belief.

So arbitrary a code of conduct, the *rigor mortis* of an obsolescent class, could only go with a type of drama of limited emotional range and depth. Lack of inner freedom was made up for by far more freedom of movement than French drama was allowed, and of transition from serious to comic: tragi-comedy might be called the norm. Variation of metres was another relief from monotony; an eight-syllable line, with rhyme or assonance, was the commonest. A flood of plays, hastily written even by Elizabethan standards, served to entertain audiences both aristocratic and popular, and may have done something to blur social differences, instead of crystallizing them as we may think of Elizabethan drama doing. Terms denoting social rank or status were many but muddled, and were used, as I.A.A. Thompson has pointed out, very imprecisely.

The 'comedy of intrigue', of *capa y espada* or cloak and sword, was the staple fare, one that a man of Lope de Vega's very chequered career was well fitted to set going. Spanish playwrights were admired abroad as well as at home for their ingenious plots and striking episodes, and were widely imitated. Corneille's *Le Cid* was an adaptation of a Spanish play. It was Tirso de Molina who set afloat in Europe the legend of Don Juan, or Giovanni. Molière took it up from him in 1665, in a play which is also a critique of the duel, and many others later. But whereas in drama at its best, incident only counts when it takes fire from real human passion, in too many of these Spanish plays, as in all melodrama, it took on an importance of its own. Tragedy failed to establish itself as the highest pinnacle, as it did in England.

Early on there were many tragic exercises in the Senecan style, as all over Renaissance Europe; and in the 1630s some plays of a darker than usual cast when the country's political and economic decline was beginning to force itself on the writers' attention. But too much of Castilian history in those years was external, remote; at home there was only a gradual running down. Enfeebled national energies were not rallying for a serious attempt to break away from the past, like the English Revolution. Religion tightened its hold still further, and monastic charity preserved a link between rich and poor that Protestant countries had lost. Fundamental divisions were blurred; revolution was as little possible as tragedy.

In each of its three chosen homes, the life-span of the great drama was brief, scarcely a half-century. This brevity, and the nearness of these countries, their many points of contact, suggest that drama was giving expression in fantasy to some ferment of change affecting western Europe as a whole. It was in England that the resulting transformation went deepest; and there poetic drama was before long followed to the grave by music, hitherto as rich in England as anywhere. Capitalist landowning laid its blight on music by destroying the old village community and the free peasantry, which everywhere else in Europe survived, however miserably, and preserved a reservoir of folk singing and dancing for composers to draw on.

Not only did Shakespeare's contemporaries fail to gain a footing on the modern stage, but the writers who rediscovered them equally failed to win entry there. Byron did not even try, though he went on writing tragedies; all the other Romantic poets tried and failed. So did Tennyson, in spite of the powerful aid of Henry Irving – and Browning, and Yeats and others in Ireland, and one or two dauntless spirits even since the last war, like Christopher Fry. It has not been very different in other countries. French Romantic poets tried their hand too, Italy had its Alfieri. In Spain Romanticism was too feeble – like bourgeois liberalism – to give birth to anything much better than the melodramas of the Duke of Rivas, one of which gave Verdi the story for *La Forza del Destino*. Apart from Pushkin with his *Boris Godunov*, inspired very directly by Shakespeare's Histories and helped to keep its place by Moussorgsky's operatic version, only Goethe and Schiller stand out from the ghostly throng. Goethe himself had to confess that he would have liked to write 'a round dozen' of tragedies like *Iphigenia* and *Tasso*, as a contribution towards the founding of a German national drama, if he had not been too much discouraged by their reception (Eckermann 99).

At least until the end of the nineteenth century genuine new poetry could still be written – and read – in English, even if it was shut out from the theatre. Since then it has seemed to be following poetic drama into the limbo of things we can only remember, not emulate. Whether the faculty of recognizing great poetry, of feeling a line of *Hamlet* in every fibre of mind and body, is today withering along with the creative impulse, is a question that cannot, unhappily, be evaded. Part of the blame must lie on actors who have tried to make Shakespeare more approachable by letting his blank verse sound as much as possible like prose. How many of them have known the difference?

PART III

The Plays

1

Julius Caesar (1598–99)

Turning from English to Roman history, Shakespeare was venturing onto remoter, though in some ways firmer, ground. He had taken his first steps there in his apprentice-tragedy *Titus Andronicus* and his long poem *Lucrece*. In *Julius Caesar* he rose far above these, in spite of what might be called a serious structural defect: the play has two halves, imperfectly joined. In a manner unique in the tragedies, unless some analogy can be found in *Timon*, two stories are told, one after the other, the last days of Caesar and the last days of the republic and its champions. In the second part most of the characters are newcomers, and memories of earlier events have dimmed. A survival of the earlier chronicle-play design has been suspected here; on the other hand the cutting off of the republicans from Rome dramatically emphasizes the completeness of their defeat in the capital. Other pitfalls might await a play about the death of a famous ruler, in the declining days of Elizabeth and the uncertainties of the succession. It belonged to 1599, the year of Essex's fiasco in Ireland and two years before his attempt at rebellion and his execution. It has been suspected that Shakespeare's text underwent some cuts, which might be abbreviations for the theatre, or the work of a nervous censor.

For us the chief crux concerns what Caesar and (a much later term) 'Caesarism' stood for in Shakespeare's mind. 'Great Julius' looms up as a towering presence, entitled by his victories within as well as outside the empire to be called 'the foremost man of all this world' (IV.iii.19–22). More than with almost any other character we are shown him through many different eyes, while he himself remains a great unknown: an opposite case to Hamlet, through whose eyes we see so many other people. Too often he has been invested with the same rights as an anointed king, or those of a necessary fulfiller of Roman destinies. Shakespeare spoke always with abhorrence of instigators of civil war, even if it can be admitted that his political philosophy included enough of the Hegelian 'What is, is right' to ensure a measure of respect for all winning causes. Before Philippi it is

Caesar's partisans who are allowed to hurl at the republicans the terrible charge of treason, sure to reverberate in the ears of any Elizabethan audience. In reality, in the republic's last flurry of faction-fighting Caesar had been the rebel general who attacked it, defeated Pompey and the conservative party at Pharsalia, and then Pompey's sons, and made himself dictator and now, in his last year, dictator for life. He had no shadow of a moral claim on any citizen's allegiance.

He has been extolled as embodying the grandeur of the Roman state (Traversi 40). He seems much rather to show us its weakness, fallen under the sway of an old, ailing man, behind whom, however, stand men of a new generation, determined to be his heirs. A senile dictator must have turned many spectators' thoughts to an aging queen closer at hand, still flattered by courtiers as 'Gloriana'. We hear nothing of any wholesome measures he may have used his authority to carry out. We only see him angling for a crown, to extend his sway even further and make it hereditary: he is still hoping for a son. For this prize he is willing – very unlike another of Shakespeare's Romans, Coriolanus – to smooth the arts of war with those of demagogy. Apologizing to 'their worships' the citizens for his fainting-fit (I.ii.271), he has a remarkable resemblance to the Bolingbroke of *Richard II*, doffing his bonnet to an oyster-wench.

Coleridge drew attention to an oddity in Brutus's soliloquy about killing Caesar: our stern republican seems only to be disturbed by the prospect of Caesar donning a crown, and to have looked on unmoved while his friend Caesar was dismantling the republic (313). Shakespeare has left out nearly the whole past, and this makes an undeniable awkwardness. He is drawing a marked contrast between the two republican chiefs, though not one of principles. By a later critic Brutus has been taxed with a monstrous 'violation' or 'perversion of love' in killing Caesar (McAlindon 87). It is true that he says he 'loved' Caesar, even while stabbing him; but this is intended to placate Antony, and Shakespeare makes very little of it. To Brutus the thought of murder is agonizing, but not that of murdering Caesar in particular.

He may well wonder how a royal title may alter Caesar's disposition, hitherto kept under restraint. Cassius has a very clear understanding of how power can inflate any puny human being. Caesar thinks himself 'more dangerous', 'more terrible', than Danger itself (II.ii.44 ff.). We are surely meant to see his arrogant boastfulness as stages in his corruption by power. There is quite enough in his bombast to warrant Cassius's picture of him as decaying, half-deranged, but also as something 'fearful', 'prodigious', a monster akin to the 'dreadful night' of the storm (I.iii.72 ff.). From having been a rationalist, as an educated Roman ought to be, he has of late grown 'superstitious', as if sinking into his dotage. But so long as others are willing to kowtow to him, he will be as great a menace as he proclaims himself.

There is deliberate iconoclasm in Shakespeare's handling of this traditional image of the Great Man.

Much of Rome's grandeur, in the eyes of Europeans of after-times, it owed to the republican annals, the ideal of civic freedom. In *Julius Caesar*, Swinburne wrote, Shakespeare made amends to republicans for often seeming to treat their faith with disrespect (159). It is thanks to the undaunted patriotism of Caesar's enemies that the drama is animating, not dispiriting. Their cult of honour, as an ideal of public service, is a vital part of the 'transvaluation of values' that we can associate Shakespeare with. It has its orchestration in a language not customary with Shakespeare, grand and simple like his theme, with little imagery, a formal regularity of beat and a frequency of end-stopped lines, as in Antony's finest speech: 'O mighty Caesar . . . ' (III.i.149 ff.). Monosyllables abound, especially when Cassius is the speaker.

Van Doren was one who thought the conspirators too statuesque (180–81). There is indeed something strained in their bearing at crucial moments. They as well as Caesar may speak of themselves in the third person, as if contemplating one of their heroic ancestors. They may strike attitudes, like actors anxious to perform their roles impressively. Behind all this lies the unreality of the worm-eaten republic they are risking their lives to prop up, when it is past rescue. But in other ways they are distinctly individualized, more so than most of the feudal barons or heavy dragoons of the Histories, hardly visible under helmet and shield. Casca even has a vein of sardonic humour. Shakespeare makes use of the quarrel scene – sometimes found fault with as lacking dramatic purpose – to display the two leaders as human beings subject to the stresses of a losing cause. He gives Brutus some less admirable traits, as a man of nerves and emotions, whose angry impatience with Portia has given a foretaste of this later outburst. Reconciliation quickly follows in both cases, but it is not Brutus who makes the first move. He confesses to 'a hasty spark' in his temper, Cassius to a 'rash humour' (IV.iii.111, 119). Brutus has more than a touch of self-righteousness, and is too complacent about his powers both as statesman and as man of action; but he has friends loyal to him to the end, and leaves an untarnished reputation.

It may be added that in painting these and some other portraits, Shakespeare is not always careful to hold the brush steady. There is a surprising moment when a conspirator proposes that Cicero should be invited to join them, on the ground that the elder statesman's 'silver hairs' and 'gravity' will throw a cloak over their own 'youths and wildness' (II.i.144 ff.). Brutus and Cassius at any rate can scarcely be thought of in these terms, and all their associates appear to be members of the Senate. They are resentful, like some Englishmen in the next reign, of a prospect of being reduced to what the tribune Flavius at the outset calls 'servile fearfulness' (I.i.79). He and his colleague are 'put to silence' for interfering with Caesar's triumphal procession (I.ii.286–7): the phrase has a more sinister ring than Plutarch's remark about their being deprived of their offices.

Nominally these tribunes are representatives of the people, whom in fact they look down on with contempt. They belong to an élite trusting to its ability to recover its rights, and bring Rome back to the true path, by itself. There is no debate about needful changes or reforms, or alliance with the people; all that is required is swift action by a few patriots of unshakeable courage. Much of their ineffectiveness was to be repeated over and over again in later days, in constitutional and nationalist movements from Ireland to Poland, by high-class leaders chagrined by the deafness of common people to their high-flown talk.

Among these 'noble Romans' fear is the worst reproach, as honour is the prime virtue. 'Cowards die many times'; fear makes 'coward lips' (II.ii.32; I.ii.122). It is not peril that they, Brutus above all, have to steel themselves against, but the nature of the act they are called on to perform: until it is done, life is for Brutus a 'hideous dream' (II.i.65). They are forced into it by the 'hard condition' of the times (I.ii.174). Such men have no need of a vow to bind them to their cause; any thought of it would be a confession of mistrust. Brutus's speech on this – 'No, not an oath' – may be counted one of the grandest of all declarations of political faith, as well as of the anguish of free men subjected to the yoke of 'high-sighted tyranny' (II.i.114 ff.). It has a Protestant as well as a Roman flavour; as Gellner says, the Reformation brought a dislike of private rituals and oath-takings (109–10). Brutus has a good deal of the Puritan gentleman in him, and the coming rebellion in England was to be known as the 'Puritan revolution'.

Cassius has often had less justice done to him than any other character in Shakespeare (e.g. Muir, *Sequence* 46; Leggatt 142; Evans 61), on the strength of Antony's epithet 'envious', and of a perverse assumption that Shakespeare deemed Brutus a good man led into a bad act by a bad man. This travesty has been bolstered by a crass misreading of the lines 'Well, Brutus, thou art noble' (I.ii.309 ff.), as meaning that Cassius is, and knows himself to be, *not* noble. They mean simply that Brutus is a true patriot, but his good relations with Caesar make it hard for him to recognize a duty to overthrow the dictatorship. Brutus makes it clear in their first colloquy (I.ii) that he has already been thinking on much the same lines as Cassius, whose appeal only hastens his decision; though hitherto his delay in reaching it, and his silence, have been responsible for a coolness between them, painful to his friend.

A conclusive reason for rejecting any notion of Cassius as an envious or ambitious schemer is Brutus's respect and love for him, whose depth is only fully shown later in the play, after the dispute and on the battlefield. The best evidence of Cassius's remarkable talents is Caesar's rich, though reluctant, tribute to him, and his admission that Cassius is the only man he might fear (I.ii.198 ff.). He must have tried, and failed, to win Cassius over to his side. This account of him, contrasting with the same speaker's words about Antony's fondness for revelry, is one of an ascetic, even closer than Brutus to the Puritan type of public man. He is not without some jealousy of Caesar as a rival for Brutus's esteem. He feels more personally than Brutus the humiliation of having to live under the shadow of a man whom he feels no need to look up to; he despises other men who are willing to crouch and submit, and he shows insight in arguing that Caesar's apparent great-ness is only a measure of his subjects' servility. There is a touch in him of the aristocrat's resentment at being fettered, but it is a usurper's arbitrary will he dislikes having to submit to, not a legitimate authority. He never reveals any self-interest, or resentment at having to play second fiddle to Brutus, by whom he is so often overruled. He is a man of emotion and imagination as well as practical shrewdness. It is he, after the murder, who starts the thought of its being acted over again, in times to come, on the stage (III.i.111 ff.). Brutus takes it up; to these Romans with their strong sense of history, and self-dramatizing bent, it is a congenial fancy.

Friendship was to Shakespeare one of the choicest blessings of life, and *Julius Caesar* was the play where he made most of it: it is very much a study of loyalties, human as well as political, and of the two supporting each other. Cassius despite his realism can cherish his idealized picture of Rome all the more because he sees the old Roman spirit embodied in Brutus. His friend's bitter regret when he supposes that Cassius's attachment to him has waned (IV.ii.18 ff.). is a testimony of what such a bond could mean to Shakespeare; and their final leave-taking before the battle is one of the poet's great Roman utterances. If the play, with all its tragic accents and sparseness of speech, has so much of inner warmth, much of the reason lies here. On the enemy side, in the camp of the triumvirs, there is no friendship, only the knife-edge competition of a bleak new age.

The play finds room for love as well, between one man and woman, and affection and respect at least between another pair; here too there is an escape from the chilly England of the late Histories. Both women want to know, like Hotspur's lady in *Henry IV*, but with better response, what is in their husbands' minds. Calphurnia does not hesitate to give Caesar good advice (II.ii). Portia's high ideal of marriage as a partnership of equals, sharing all secrets with each other (II.i.180 ff.), is a true manifesto on behalf of womanhood. Portia of Venice had expressed the same thought. But Brutus's consort, born into the republican élite, is as warmly attached to its ideals as any of the men. She can only persuade Brutus to confide in her by a display of resolution which deceives both him and herself. Before long she is to realize that she may have a man's mind, but only a woman's strength (II.iv.8), and her end is solitary despair and suicide.

The fatal weakness of these ardent republicans is their inability to make common cause with the people: partly their own fault, partly that of the citizenry, politically degenerate because too long excluded from any real share in civic life. With unconscious egotism the conspirators take for granted that because Republic and Liberty will be good for them, they must be good for ordinary folk as well. It is a matter of course that the new government will be set up by *them* (III.i.178–9), without any consulting with tinkers or tailors. Among some of them class prejudice or snobbery is as strong as we see it later in *Coriolanus*. Casca derides a group of young women in the crowd applauding Caesar, who he says would have cheered just as loudly if he had stabbed their mothers (I.ii.272 ff.). To him 'the common herd' (I.ii.265) – a phrase which has stuck – is a mere sweaty rabble, even when it applauds Caesar's affected reluctance to be crowned.

His companions do not talk in this strain, but they listen without dissent; and it is true that the commoners have been behaving in a foolishly volatile fashion. Sufficient warning has been given to the plotters of how little they can rely on them for even tacit support. We are seeing the politics, long familiar in Rome and growing familiar in Shakespeare's England, of the grandiose public spectacle, the *tamasha* as Englishmen learned to call it in India, and the readiness of the populace to flock to any colourful display. In the opening scene the crowd is in a boisterous holiday mood, rather than under the sway of any serious feeling. Their 'basest metal' may be moved, the tribunes fancy, when they are reminded of their hero-worship not long ago of Pompey, Caesar's dead foe (I.i.65); but this weathercock shift of mood is brief.

Brutus can still think of them as worthy Romans at bottom, only needing to have the facts laid before them. But he makes no attempt to rouse them to a higher political consciousness: that would require a serious programme, which he has no inkling of. His message after the assassination is that all is now over, and they can go quietly home. The 'freedom and liberty' he promises (III.i.111) have a glowing reality for him, none for them. It is a fine irony for this devoted republican to be saluted with a cry of 'Let him be Caesar!' Brutus's place is at once taken by Antony, an adventurer ready for any demagogy, and we have the opening scene over again: a crowd easily diverted from one allegiance to another, though now in the opposite direction.

In each case the speaker plays on 'patriotism', in the jingoistic style of the English Histories where conquest in France seems a good enough answer to everything, even with Cade's rebel followers. Pompey is extolled by the tribunes as an enlarger of the Roman dominions; Antony makes the same claim for Caesar as an empire-builder, whose plunderings swelled the public treasury, and backs it with the solid testimony of Caesar's will, bequeathing to every citizen a sum of money out of the spoils of his wars. What Brutus could offer was pallid compared with this. Otherwise the funeral oration is a tissue of thin sophistries and emotional tricks, none of it making any political sense. It plays on Tudor stock-responses to the words 'treason' and 'traitors'. But it touches, for almost the only time in the play, on the curse of poverty. 'When that the poor have cried, Caesar hath wept' (III.ii.92). Highly improbable as this may be, it helps to transform the hearers into a bloodthirsty mob, revelling in the sensation of being free to lynch a literary man and sack aristocratic mansions.

Demagogic arts, chiefly as practised by upper-class politicians, were a subject in which Shakespeare had shown keen interest in the Histories, especially in his studies of Richard Crookback and Bolingbroke on his way to becoming Henry IV. It was a modern craft growing out of the contests of later feudalism, and further cultivated by the Tudors, most carefully by Elizabeth. Antony is not to be bought over by the other party: his attachment to Caesar has been genuine. Caesar's death has roused him from a life of hedonism, and revealed him as a man of bold, independent action, as happens again in *Antony and Cleopatra*. But the moment his speech has done its work, from heart-broken mourner he turns into a ruthless calculator, and he and Octavius will soon be arranging to cheat the people out of part of Caesar's bequest. He demands an equal share of the empire with his old leader's adopted son, young Octavius, along with their partner Lepidus, who can be pushed out of the way when he has served his turn (IV.i.18 ff.).

For the present the three triumvirs sit amicably together and plan to crush opposition by wholesale murder; in the proscription-list they are drawing up are a nephew of Antony and a brother of Lepidus. Shakespeare is under-lining a contrast between their gangster mentality and Brutus's lesson to his friends: 'Let us be sacrificers, but not butchers' – Caesar alone must fall (II.i.166). There is nothing in the Histories like this blood-chilling scene (IV.i), and no dramatic requirement for it here; it is introduced as if on purpose to blacken a villainous trio beyond redemption. Most of political Rome seems to be against them; they scent 'millions of mischief' behind the smiles that surround them, and can only counter it by terrorism. They, like their foes, have no programme of renovation to win men's allegiance. Shakespeare reminds us of their list of names, in one of the few linkages between the two parts of the play, when news reaches the republican camp of scores of senators being put to death, among them the great orator and writer Cicero (IV.iii.171 ff.).

Between repression and lack of popular support the republican party has been paralysed in Italy, and left to make its last stand far away in the east. There Brutus and Cassius have to raise money for their high-minded struggle by high-handed levies of money from peasants who have no interest in it, a sordid need which comes close to dividing them. They alone are left of the old guard. There are new faces, strangers to us, most of them officers or retainers loyal to them rather than to a cause. One is Pindarus, a Parthian war-captive and faithful bondsman of Cassius (V.iii.47 ff.). Brutus is now addressed as 'my lord', by Messala at the council of war as well as by underlings. The common soldiers appear to be serving only for pay. We hear of no republican zeal among them, and their commanders do not harangue them before the battle. During it Cassius complains of 'villains' running away, and has to kill one 'coward' and snatch the standard from him; while Brutus's men, having got a temporary advantage, fall to plundering (V.iii.1 ff.).

Life has gone out of the old republic, whose people no longer believe in it. This gives the drama its underlying pathos, though because the citizens have dropped out of sight the last Act does not sufficiently display it. There is no political discussion among the republicans. Brutus and Cassius have no regrets for what they have done, and no reflections on the hard lessons that their expulsion from Rome should have taught. What concerns them now is their inner life and faith. The faithless plebeians are shut out of memory by Brutus's consoling thought: 'I found no man but he was true to me' (V.v.35). This Roman nobleman feels the same revulsion as an Egyptian queen was to feel not much later at the thought of being taken to Rome in fetters and paraded before a jeering populace (V.i.110–11).

Under so many strains he is experiencing again the nocturnal torments of the time before the murder; he has hallucinations of Caesar's ghost, come to haunt and distract his slayers. Cassius has been forced into a half-belief in omens of defeat (V.i.76 ff.). A spreading credulity, misting the lucid classical mirror, seems to reveal a weakening of the old Roman confidence. We are not obliged to suppose that Shakespeare shared it, and the contrary interpretations of Calphurnia's dream (III.ii), each as plausible as the other, suggests a note of scepticism. But first for Caesar, and now for his opponents, it seems as if their approaching end is something unescapable, the last in a chain of preordained events. The tide in the affairs of men is running against the republicans. Philippi closes in gathering darkness, with torchlight signal and setting sun, Cassius's death and Rome's fall. Brutus hails his dead friend as 'The last of all the Romans' (V.vii.99), even though the final engagement is still to be fought.

The play is not the tragedy of Julius Caesar, or of the republic, both of them long past their prime; its poignancy is concentrated in the group of idealists in whom the old Roman virtues still live on, with Brutus as their foremost representative. His intentions are frustrated, partly by his own temperamental faults and his miscalculations, but far more by the blind alley of history in which he is caught. He is living in a dream, even if a noble one, and sacrificing himself to the behests of a dead past. Here the significance of tragedy as a clash between old convictions, good or bad, and new realities is very clear. 'Honour' has come back to life, but only to doom its devotees to failure and ruin; and Brutus, the most honourable of them all, has been less effective as a leader than a realist like Cassius might have been. Cassius himself, however, has no greater understanding of the inevitability of change, and his realism only extends to questions of tactics.

G. Wilson Knight sees Caesar's imperial entry into Rome as announcing a return of order and harmony, which is wrecked by Brutus and restored by Brutus's death (*Imperial Theme* 61–2). There is very little in the play to indicate that this was how Shakespeare felt about the events he set himself to narrate; and Caesar's death, however it might come about, could not be long delayed, and would infallibly unleash further civil wars. On the other hand, while Shakespeare could admire republicans he could see that there was no longer a place for them in the Roman polity. Empire loot had suffocated whatever of democracy there had been, and degraded political life to faction-fighting. At Philippi the worse men triumph, the better perish; the most that can be said for the winners is that they confess to having destroyed, in Brutus, a finer man than themselves. Their motives are purely self-seeking, and they already show signs of falling out among themselves; but they have a 'mission', to terminate a bankrupt regime and open the way to a new one. Ultimately order will be established on the basis of unlimited – and unstable – monarchy, as the sole kind of government that Rome is now fit for.

An old order, with many achievements, but reduced now to an anachronism, has been overthrown by a new one, whose virtues are still to appear, but which has in its favour a kind of historical necessity. Shakespeare does not deny this necessity, but his heart is in the coffin with Brutus. It is the republicans whom he watches at Philippi, in their last hours; the victors only come forward after the fight. 'I shall have glory by this losing day', Brutus declares, more than his enemies by their 'vile conquest' (V.v.36–8). Memories of what Rome has stood for in its better days, the example it has set, will survive and inspire generations to come. The tragic impression left on us is very strong, but it is not one of un-relieved defeat and negation. All is not lost; baffled hopes and ideals will reappear in other, less ill-omened days.

Shakespeare's guide to classical history was Plutarch, whose bias was towards republicanism. Medieval man looked up to Augustus as organizer of the empire in which Christ was soon to be born; Dante lodged Brutus and Cassius in his Inferno, with Judas. Humanists of the Renaissance city-states magnified them instead; Shakespeare followed their lead, but less uncritically, stripping away pretence and illusion from both 'the mightiest Julius' and the mighty republic he subverted. Hobbes the philosopher of absolute monarchy was to complain that too much classical education was fostering a spirit of insubordination, by teaching young men to admire 'liberty' and decry 'tyranny' (Curtis 25, 27). English political life was showing some likenesses to that of the earlier Rome. In 1601 Parliament won its first momentous success against the government, in the heated controversy over grants of monopolies. Englishmen were learning to band together in newer forms of association, in a line of development towards the modern party; Shakespeare was showing them a group of men brought together by regular principles and goals, very unlike the feudal factions now left behind.

Opposition to monarchy in Europe might come from the 'towering individual', the feudal malcontent; or from movements more in harmony with a spreading bourgeois influence (Heinemann, *Puritanism* 173–4). In the Wars of Religion in France and elsewhere, following the Reformation, these two kinds of discontent might be jumbled together; and while some Catholics did not shrink from advocating regicide, some Calvinists were ready to justify rebellion, if the call was given not by common folk but by men holding responsible positions. Plutarch reminds us, though Shakespeare does not, that Brutus and Cassius both held senior magistracies, as praetors.

In the Histories Shakespeare had started with orthodox warnings against civil broils, but had gone on to recognize the opposite drawbacks of arbitrary rule. Power corrupts, as Brutus is thinking when he reflects on Caesar's growing dominance and how it may 'change his nature' (II.i.13). Tyranny if not checked in good time will go on 'Till each man drop by lottery' (II.i.119): here is the converse of the maxim, familiar to Shakespeare, that a ruler has to sustain his authority by eliminating the too prominent individuals whom, as the wise Prospero says, he must 'trash for overtopping' (*Tempest* I.ii.81). Here are the two horns of the dilemma of government as seen by the poet. Nevertheless, wherever we find monarchy in the tragedies, it is in a parlous condition. So no doubt, in all cases but one, are the republican governments whose acquaintance we make in his company.

2

Hamlet (1600–01)

In the opening scene of *Hamlet* Horatio recalls the portents that heralded Caesar's death; in the last scene he wants to emulate Roman example by committing suicide. Something of the pattern of *Julius Caesar*, with its hero condemned to a repugnant task of murder, is repeated in this next tragedy; a good deal also of its mood and its use of keywords like 'honour' and 'noble'. But the honour reborn in Rome was a collective ideal, binding men together; Hamlet is left to act alone, and we see it sinking back into 'the bubble reputation' chased by the reckless adventurer Fortinbras, as before him by Hotspur. A shadow from Brutus's defeat lies heavily over Hamlet's – or Shakespeare's – mind, and makes this an inward- instead of outward-looking drama.

It seems to be agreed that Shakespeare, following a practice that to us seems freakish, took as his basis an earlier version of the Hamlet story, 'almost certainly by Kyd', author of *The Spanish Tragedy*, most celebrated of revenge-plays (Boas, *Elizabeth* 3; cf. Maxwell 209). How obtrusive and how intractable this borrowed framework proved, J.M. Robertson was among the first to demonstrate, though he considered Kyd 'a natural play-maker', if no great poet (129; cf. Bradshaw 123–4). But the story of fratricide, ghost, revenge, was far older than any writer of Shakespeare's time, and looks like a deliberately archaic choice, as does the winning of Norwegian territory by Hamlet's father in single combat.

'Our text', Empsom confessed, is 'a weirdly baffling thing', only account-able for by the audience being expected to know the story's outlines already (97). Some of its more sensational episodes may seem incongruous, though a play so introspective might well need something of the sort as relief. Shakespeare's uncontrollable ability to bring new life into characters he was interested in, even if these are a minority of his *dramatis personae*, might bring on the stage figures to whom the plot offered no proper elbow-room. Nashe had lately written scathingly of the Danes as barbarians (93–6, 121), but this play, of 1600–01, when James VI and his Danish wife were likely to be translated before long to London, depicts a breathingly modern, sophisticated society, where the primitive elements of the tale, led by the

Ghost, can hardly feel at home. Incongruities of detail are easy to find. In the first scene Marcellus, a regular officer of the castle guard, has to enquire why Denmark is resounding with preparations for war. Claudius asks about the subject of the play he is to see, when the dumb-show has just informed him – the subject of Robson's intriguing essay on the *Mousetrap* (*Dumb-Show*; cf. Bethell 151 ff.). Ophelia's drowning makes a pretty idyll, but if there were spectators, why was she not rescued? Why does Hamlet, back in Denmark, at once notify his wicked uncle, who he knows has just tried to have him killed, and rejoin the court circle as if nothing had happened? It is puzzling to try to work out, as Bradley does (*Tragedy*, App. B), where Hamlet has been living lately, and his connections with the fellow-students who reappear in his life. A plethora of characters and episodes may leave us with 'a sense of bewilderment' (Danby, *Nature* 146).

All these, however, are trifles that Shakespeare does not care about, and does not want us to. A misty, irregular backcloth of events goes well enough with the hero's preoccupations, which hinder him from looking at things round him coolly. His mind is obsessed with conscience, duty, will, anger, not with practical business. We must take the play as we have it, and be guided by its poetical accents or signposts, while keeping in mind the existence of vistas unexplored, uncertainties unexplained. These stretch away into unknown distances, as they do in the lives of all of us, lives whose indistinct contours Shakespeare was perhaps consciously setting himself to reproduce.

Hamlet talks far more than any other character in Shakespeare (Lee 367). All the play is built up round him, whereas in *Julius Caesar* we have two rival camps, in *Othello* two great opposite personalities, in *King Lear* a main plot and a sub-plot. If some of the figures seem at times blurred, part of the reason is that we are seeing them chiefly through the eyes of an emotionally disturbed Hamlet. Shakespeare himself was in a way doing the same. In this play, the first of his incomparably great dramas, he may be thought of as writing not simply a tragedy, but a play *about* tragedy and its inner nature. He throws his hero into a laceratingly 'tragic' predicament, and Hamlet tries hard to seize his cue: he is anxious to work himself into the emotions and carriage of a true tragedian. Yet he succeeds only by fits and starts. Something seems wrong with him – or with 'tragedy' itself as hitherto conceived. In exploring the obstacles, Shakespeare is finding his way towards new conceptions of his own, while we, like Hamlet, listen to stirrings of 'thoughts beyond the reaches of our souls' (I.iv.56).

It may not be too bold a guess that Shakespeare felt, or often felt, more like Hamlet than any other creation of his. Hamlet's soliloquies have a marked resemblance to some of the best sonnets. Hamlet resents being spied on by Rosencrantz and Guildenstern; Sonnet 121 complains of 'spies', worse men than himself, reporting the poet's 'frailties' and traducing him.

Hamlet's story is one of indecision; the poet may have been suffering from an attack of this commonest of human moods, and thereby been able to make the human race his audience as no other play has ever done. Frequently Hamlet seems to be speaking for all of us, rather than for himself. Or it may be that he is always peering into himself and finding all of us there. All the same he 'comes to life' as a human being seen at close quarters, more than any other tragic protagonist of Shakespeare's.

We may be surprised by his age, thirty, as the gravedigger reminds us near the end (V.i.150 ff.), though his mother has just remarried. At first sight he has a more youthful aspect, with his sable costume and Byronic gloom. But a young man like Romeo could only be chosen for a youthful tragedy. Hamlet *must* be older, if he is to speak for an author now approaching forty. And yet he has just been spending his time at a foreign university, while quite lately – whether or not at the same time – the 'warlike state' of Denmark (I.ii.9) has been at war with England, and he might have been expected to be busy with his sword instead of his pen. But what Shakespeare may be aiming at is to make us see him as a man who has remained young – too young, too full of trust in life –, until he is abruptly shocked into maturity by devastating experiences. What is ordinarily a long-drawn process, for Hamlet is sudden and traumatic.

Eager life, and world-weariness, compete in him. He has a streak of Richard II's hesitancy, as well as his love of words and of discursive talk. Yet he has a realistic understanding that words without action are nothing. Crisis, demanding activity, liberates him by releasing his instinctive self from the pale cast of thought. Still, he is a born intellectual, one of the first in modern literature. Men like him belong oftenest to times when the air is full of a confused onrush of new thinking, as yet only half making sense. They are not the ones who know how to make profitable use of ideas, but people who are seized and as it were made use of by ideas seeking entry into the world. Hamlet looks young because, for another thing, he has been living in a bookish atmosphere of student cleverness. 'You might have rhymed', Horatio comments when he improvises some mock-heroic lines, after the *Mousetrap* (III.ii.287 ff.). But events are opening his mind to the meaning of a throng of impressions that life must have been gradually infecting him with; he sees everything, quite suddenly, in a new and sombre light.

He was to become in later days a mirror for frustrated nations or classes, as well as Romantic poets, to see themselves in. A poem written in 1844 by Freiligrath bore the title *Deutschland ist Hamlet*. In the later nineteenth century he was similarly a national poet for Russians, in the early twentieth century for Indians. In Hamlet's own day – or Shakespeare's – his next of kin were the best educated of the English middle classes, conscious of their potential worth but also of their present cramped footing. Even near the play's end, the foppish manners and chatter of an Osric can rouse Hamlet to brilliantly sardonic talk. But the bungling, costly fulfilment of his mission, even in its most limited sense, owes nothing to his intellectual gifts.

Hamlet is a person made for friendship, another theme carried over from *Julius Caesar*; but he cannot say like Brutus that no friend of his ever deserted him. Rather, it is one of his misfortunes to feel driven to retaliate against two of them by engineering their deaths, an apparent vindictiveness only palliated by the feeling we can attribute to him of breach of friendship being a heinous sin. His true friend Horatio is somewhat inscrutable, seeming at times to be in the cast only because Hamlet cannot be always soliloquizing; there must be a confidant for him to talk to. Shakespearian characters may take shape only during the process of writing, so that to look back on their first appearance may be puzzling. Horatio is a Dane, but can manage to sound more like a foreigner. He has to learn from Hamlet, who is 'native here', that heavy drinking is a Danish national vice (I.iv.14).

He has left Wittenberg to see the royal funeral and wedding, and in Scene 1 he is in the castle, on a friendly footing with the sentinels; but it is two months before he presents himself to his old friend and lately fellow-student the prince. When others prove hollow, Hamlet pays a warm tribute to Horatio as the single person he can still have faith in, and tells us that they have been companions ever since he came to years of discretion (III.ii.56 ff.; cf. III.i.57–8). Horatio has remained poor, a proof perhaps of disinterestedness; what Hamlet admires most in him is his stoic ability to bear good fortune and bad equally, and his 'judgment', firm against any gusts of passion; these are qualities that Hamlet can envy. Yet he never turns to Horatio for aid or advice; his taciturn friend has to be kept in the background.

Hamlet can hail the actors too with charming amiability, as if greeting old friends. It is agreeable to suppose that Shakespeare himself conversed with the juniors and employees of his company in the same affable style. At any rate, in Hamlet he is showing us a patron such as any artist or scholar would be happy to have; a man of high degree, with the bearing proper to one who respects talent and its possessors – unlike Polonius, who looks down on both: he must have derived some of his traits from court grandees known to the poet.

That Shakespeare was bringing his own profession so prominently into this drama is one encouragement to us to think of it as having more than usually intimate meanings for him. His reflections on the player's epic speech, and the question 'What's Hecuba to him?' may suggest some misgivings about the genuineness of his art. If an actor can work himself into so much pretended emotion, so perhaps can a poet. An author composing a play whose chief focus is on self-doubt must surely have been perturbed by doubts about himself and his place in the annals, as well as his hero's. Later on he holds in his hand the skull of the old court jester Yorick, once a brilliant wit and entertainer, now a forgotten thing in a nameless grave. Hamlet's view of the theatre is not that of a man about town wanting to be amused and tickled, but of an earnest, thoughtful, reforming class, seeing it as the business of the stage to instruct and improve as well as beguile. In line with this is his Miltonic conviction that man has been endowed with 'godlike reason' not to let it rust, but to put it to good purpose (IV.iv.35–9). And we are free to associate Shakespeare, whatever taste for indecencies can be charged to him, with Hamlet's praise of a good though not popular play he remembers which had 'no sallets in the lines', nothing salacious, but was content with 'an honest method, as wholesome as sweet' (II.ii.451–2).

Gertrude married again within a month of her first husband's death, Hamlet tells us twice in his first soliloquy (I.ii.145 ff.). He was already shaken and disgusted before the Ghost's revelation and the terrible duty imposed on him. We are encountering Shakespeare's only fully evolved ghost – 'the best in all drama' as Robson called him (*Prologue* 67) – and with him treading hazardous ground, as Hamlet does when he follows him across the battlements. Catholics still believed in ghosts, Protestants in principle did not: for them this apparition might well be diabolical, a possibility briefly in Hamlet's own mind. The Ghost's best credentials may be looked for in his noble bearing and lofty language, surely beyond the reach of any counterfeit. On the other hand, in the bizarre close of his visit he seems to shrivel incomprehensibly into something, as Dover Wilson says, 'like an underground demon' (*Hamlet* 83; cf. on ghosts Thomas, *Religion* 703–5; P. Edwards 39; Alexander 33). Did Shakespeare half-imagine a second, lower entity, parodying the old king? At any rate the Ghost is no illusion; unlike those of Caesar and Banquo, it is seen by others besides the hero. The truth of his story, which Hamlet probably never doubted, is confirmed when we hear Claudius's confession. A third question remains, about the morality of what he demands from his son – revenge. He claims it as a matter of conscience; it is to be noted that he never tempts his son with thoughts of the throne.

Hamlet's first reactions show him becoming at once a prey to a secretiveness and mistrust that force him further into isolation. He refuses to tell his companions what he has learned, and swears them elaborately to silence; the idea of feigning madness comes to him at the same moment. He knows, of course, as the audience would, that his life will be in jeopardy if his uncle discovers that his guilt has come to light. He is by nature, as Claudius admits, 'Most generous, and free from all contriving' (IV.vii.135), the last man to be fit for conspiracy and ambush; he cannot 'look fresh and merrily', as Brutus tells his friends to look, while plotting a deed of blood, and one that will be judged so harshly. Pretended madness gives him, as many have seen, relief from his feelings (e.g. Lucas 54), an escape from tor-turing suspense, and from the 'prison' that his Denmark has turned into (II.ii.234).

All this is half hysteria, and must at times have been close to the border-line of real insanity. But it is also the kind of derangement believed in primitive times to contain an inspired wisdom. To Hamlet, as a year or two later more visibly to Lear, it brings an enlargement, not a narrowing, of moral vision. Awareness comes to him of things he has known unthinkingly, or heard of, or can now guess at. Sins of individuals open his eyes to deep faults in the society he has hitherto taken for granted. To his generalizing mind everything round him suddenly appears false. All sorts of acquaintances, not an uncle only, may be smiling, and yet be villains – as Octavius felt in Rome after Caesar's death. He can denounce them under cover of his 'antic disposition' (I.v.172), as we may guess Yorick the jester was wont to do.

Gertrude has been called 'one of Shakespeare's more careless productions' (Danby, *Nature* 156). It might be too much to suspect him of leaving an unfinished portrait on purpose, as an admission of the impossibility for men of seeing women clearly. More matter-of-factly we can blame a ready-made story difficult to straighten out. Hamlet being thirty, his mother's role as *femme fatale* can scarcely be convincing (even if Cleopatra's age cannot be much less); her time of life is impressed on us by the player-king and queen having been married for thirty years. She is necessary to the plot, but in what we see of her is curiously inert. She is devoted to her son, as Claudius knows (IV.vii): her love for him is part of the general affection he has been enveloped in until abruptly he finds himself alone. Yet she is quite unaware, until very rudely awakened, that her marriage can have given him any ground for resentment.

We are left in what Coleridge called 'an unpleasant perplexity' about her (153). Much debate has gone on as to whether she was committing adultery with Claudius before her first husband's death, and whether she had any hand in his death. Dover Wilson has no doubt on the first count (*Hamlet* 292–4; also P. Edwards 42–3, 107 n. 46). Yet it seems safest to be dubious of both indictments, especially the second. Conceivably Shakespeare may have wanted to avoid any distinct charge of complicity in view of the murder of King James's father and the prompt remarriage of his mother Mary Queen of Scots. In the play that Hamlet gets the actors to perform there is nothing to warrant suspicion of unfaithfulness by the queen, or anything worse than shallowness of feeling. At the point where it is broken off, Hamlet is saying that the villain, having committed his crime, will go on to win the widow's love (III.ii.269–70). Gertrude seems too colourless a woman to be connected with anything as positive as murder; and as a devoted mother she must know how deeply Hamlet is devoted to his father.

In the closet scene, the only one where we see the two alone together, when Gertrude exclaims at Hamlet's 'rash and bloody deed' in killing Polonius (III.iv.28), Hamlet, beside himself, retorts by accusing her of the same sin. She is uncomprehending, and the accusation is not repeated. Nor is the charge of adultery pressed. Unchastity among wives must have been widespread in Shakespeare's England, if only because of the frequency with which girls were forcibly married to rich but decrepit old men. It was a stock Elizabethan joke, and to be said to have had an unchaste mother was a stock insult, from which today's colloquial use of 'bastard' must be descended. Laertes will prove himself a bastard, and so bring shame on his mother, if he does not punish his father's killer. But Hamlet has been pushed beyond any such merely personal feeling, to revulsion against sex altogether. All the rest of his reproaches are concerned with Gertrude's disgusting sensuality in wanting another sleeping-partner at her matronly age. It is the thought of this behaviour that torments him; in his eyes, as in Church law of the time, she is also committing incest, though no one else cares about it. We are hearing from Hamlet an outpouring of the horror of physical lust, animal passion, which began in *Venus and Adonis* and was to continue with Iago, Lear and Timon, as one of the loudest notes in the whole of the tragedies.

Gertrude can neither see nor hear the Ghost when he breaks in on them, or rather on Hamlet's fevered imagination; Hamlet's distraught looks at this point startle even the usually phlegmatic queen into a wild flurry of images. She is more than ever convinced of his madness, in spite of his solemn assurances, except that his indignation at her hasty remarriage does make her see it to have been wrong. Even the most easy-going of women could not be impervious to such language from a dear son. The sense of guilt she admits to later on (IV.v.17 ff.) may seem to convict her of worse things (Flatter 25–6), but it can be explained on other grounds. She must have come to believe that her union with Claudius has been the cause of her son's madness, and therefore of Polonius's death and the train of mischiefs this has brought on; among them Ophelia's madness, the calamity which is weighing on Gertrude when she speaks of her 'sick soul'. She like Claudius is undergoing punishment before death overtakes her. Questioned by him after her meeting with Hamlet she can assure him without intentional deceit that her son is mad – as she has promised Hamlet to do, and that he killed Polonius in a fit of frenzy. Hamlet's parting words to her, about the masterly plots he is working up against his enemies (III.iv.203 ff.), have made no impression on her.

We are left in the dark as to whether his rebuke has had a lasting effect, and altered her relations with Claudius. Shakespeare may simply not have found time to answer this, or have lost interest in it. When Claudius is in danger from Laertes and his rioters she tries to shield him, at some risk. This must prove that she does not think of him as a murderer, but does not prove that she is still sleeping with him in defiance of her son's injunction.

It is over Hamlet and Ophelia that the play's ambiguities cluster so thickly that even Shakespeare cannot have failed to notice them, and must knowingly have left us in doubt. Much devious speculation about motives and feelings is possible, if not very helpful. One missing datum is the time when Hamlet was pressing his suit. 'Of late', she says (I.iii.99–100), but *how* lately? She is talking after the ominous marriage, but before the Ghost's denunciation. Ophelia has a quality of naïve simplicity; still, she is an emancipated young woman, who has grown up at court, not in a nunnery, and is not overly shocked by Hamlet's loose words during the play-scene. She is well educated, and can make a very well-turned reply to her brother's homily (I.iii.45 ff.). In her meeting with Hamlet, where they are under observation, her language takes on a bookish or stilted tone, with phrases like 'I have longéd long to redeliver' (III.i.93), a mode that drops away when she goes out of her mind and reverts to a homely vernacular. (Again, *how* long?)

She has been 'most free and bounteous' in allowing Hamlet to approach her with his gifts and his 'holy vows' (I.iii.93, 114), without telling her father and brother what is going on. They have been left, as Polonius says, to hear of it from others, from servants very likely. They both – very properly, most of the audience will have agreed – deem it their duty to lay an embargo on the affair, on the rational ground explained by Laertes with some tact, by Polonius with blunt crudity: Hamlet as a royal prince and heir presumptive to the throne cannot be free to marry as he chooses, and any connection with him must be perilous to a young woman. Lord Clarendon, when chief minister of Charles II, was so deeply shocked by his daughter's secret marriage to the king's brother that he considered her guilty of *lèse majesté*, and wanted her to be executed. Desdemona would have rejected a parental ban; Ophelia submits, and consents to break with Hamlet. She can put the blame on a falling off of affection on his part, not hers.

Bradley noticed the absence from the soliloquies of any mention of Ophelia, and found it hard to measure Hamlet's feeling for her (*Tragedy* 153, 157). It is Hamlet's misfortune to be in love when plunged into his sea of troubles, which he cannot disclose to the woman he loves; and hers to be in love with a man in the clutches of a dark fate, which she can do nothing to relieve, and cannot even understand. His pretence of madness comes most naturally to him while he is with her, because then he is incapable of behaving rationally. Like his mother, she is sure that he really has gone out of his mind. It is another of the play's many ironies that his pretence of insanity helps to bring insanity on her. The impression of most readers, that his attachment to her is blighted by his mother's conduct, must be correct. Her marriage, he tells Gertrude, 'takes off the rose From . . . an innocent love'; it discredits the good faith of all women. 'I loved you not', he tells Ophelia (III.i.119): it seems to him now that he can never have been foolish enough to fall in love.

Ophelia assures her father that Hamlet's wooing has been 'in honourable fashion' (I.iii.110 ff.). Polonius brushes this aside. He has seen more of life than she has – and more of Hamlet than we have --, and we need not doubt his sincerity when he tells Hamlet that he loves his daughter 'passing well' (II.ii.375–6). But we may have to wonder, or Hamlet in his gloomy mood may be forced to ask himself, whether the affair was as innocent in intention on his side as on hers. Speaight is one sceptic (16–17). Hamlet has at any rate been making ardent love to a girl without, so far as we know, saying anything of marriage. One strand in the moral turmoil that paralyses him may be a recognition that he has been acting thoughtlessly, selfishly, and drifting close to the edge of something worse; that he and his mother are tarred with the same brush, and he has little right to condemn others. His mother, he knows from the Ghost, was corrupted partly by 'traitorous gifts' from Claudius (I.v.43): does this throw a shadow over the gifts that Hamlet has been making to Ophelia, and that he now disclaims (III.i.95–6)? Polonius changes his mind, as Margolies notes (52: II.i.108 ff.); but is he more right now, or less?

Here once more are reminders of some of the Sonnets, and the view they give of sex relations as they were in the London known to Shakespeare. Hamlet tells Ophelia he is no more than 'indifferent honest', or honourable, and talks of how 'honesty' can be perverted by 'the power of beauty'; Sonnet 142 is about Shakespeare being tempted into self-delusion and sin by his mistress's charms, and how he has 'sealed false bonds of love'. The climax of Hamlet's tirade – 'thou shalt not escape calumny', except by taking refuge in a nunnery – evokes the sonnet-atmosphere of intrigue, unfaithfulness, jealousy, slander (e.g. 64, 107). In the next tragedy Desdemona suffers the 'calumny' that Hamlet foretells for Ophelia. If we begin to feel afraid that he has actually seduced her, his 'be thou as chaste as ice' may be taken as dispelling any such notion. A critic determined to make the worst of things might, indeed, take them to mean that whether he has done this or not is of no account, since no one will believe her virtuous in either case.

Polonius likes 'a jig or a tale of bawdry' (II.ii.488), and may have been a gay dog in his time, as he fears his son is now. He and Laertes do not say that it would be wicked of Hamlet to trifle with Ophelia's affections, but only that it would be foolish of her to let him. His self-suspicions must extend to this part of his life, as to all the rest. He may be regretting that he was not more open about his love. To the new king and queen he could not of course bring himself to apply for sanction, as he might have meant to do in his father's lifetime. Gertrude seems to have known or guessed that he would like to marry Ophelia, and she saw no objection. She says so twice, before and after the girl's death (III.i.38 ff., V.i.246–8), which makes her touching words less likely to have been afterthoughts of Shakespeare, or inspirations of the moment such as he did not always bother to reconcile with earlier passages. In any case her good will can be of no service to Hamlet after his killing of Ophelia's father makes marriage with her an impossibility; he is either too stoical to say anything about this, or no longer cares.

Politically this is a drama that points away from monarchism, though not towards any alternative, just as *Julius Caesar* pointed away from republicanism – as hitherto known. Only in this negative sense can it be said that *Hamlet* is 'republican in sentiment', as a historian of political theory writes (Morris 101). There are fulsome laudations of monarchy, in conventional Tudor–Stuart terms; but it is a regicide usurper who expatiates on the divinity that doth hedge a king, and a pair of self-interested sycophants who revere the crown as the supreme institution with which all national well-being is bound up (IV.v.124–6; III.iii.7 ff.). Hamlet's opinion is just the opposite: 'The King is a thing . . . of nothing' (IV.ii.28–30). And when he talks of a royal corpse eaten by worms and then journeying through a beggar's guts (V.iii.19 ff.), the same disparagement shows. There can be little sanctity left in royalty when a royal family tears itself apart as his is doing.

Claudius it must be allowed comes to the throne just before Denmark is threatened with invasion, and rides out the storm ably and coolly. He has a copious flow of well-sounding words, advertises his own reasonableness, and would impress an audience very favourably if it did not learn before long what he really is. When the populace turns against him he falls back, like Richard II, on his right to divine succour, from which he quickly goes on to a fresh murder plot, as if judging this a more useful safeguard. He is growing more brutal and unscrupulous as his fears mount, like Macbeth. He bewails the swamp he has fallen into, the rumours and 'muddied' public opinion that are spreading unrest (IV.v.75 ff.). For him too death will be a kind of release.

Not only monarchy itself, stripped of its mask, but its ordinary procedures, or those of its employees, are taking on an unwholesome complexion. Hamlet talks of a court favourite being allowed to suck up wealth, until it suits his master to squeeze the wealth out of him, as if out of a sponge (IV.ii.15 ff.). Polonius takes pride in his talent for ferreting out secrets, in a scene where he instructs his private agent Reynaldo to follow Laertes to Paris and spy on him (II.i). It has been objected to as irrelevant, but we must welcome it as a side-glance at the way secret services were being built up in England and elsewhere. Polonius must have been helpful in securing the election for Claudius, who rewards him with high praise and talk of public regard for him (I.ii.47–9). But the minister's artificial mode of speech, when on his mettle, cannot conceal his senility, carried almost to caricature in his consultation with king and queen (II.ii). This is part of what stamps the government as out of date, fit to be discarded.

Hamlet may decry kingship, but there are hints of sour grapes in his attitude to it, resentment at being passed over for the succession, and in favour of such a man as his uncle. Gertrude and others may have thought him too young and inexperienced, and disinclined to responsibility. From classroom bench to throne would certainly be a high jump. Claudius assures us that the councillors have fully approved of his marriage also (I.ii.14–16). He has no children to follow him: he addresses his nephew as 'the most immediate to our throne' (I.ii.109), and Rosencrantz cannot be alone in assuming that Hamlet will be the next ruler (III.ii.309–10). If so, he has only to wait. His explanation of his gloom – 'I lack advancement' –, and his words to Ophelia about unsatisfied ambition (III.ii.308, III.i.122), are not to be taken literally. But he is speaking soberly, alone with Horatio, when he makes it one of his grievances that his uncle 'Popp'd in between the election and my hopes' (V.ii.65). We are free to guess that this added fuel to his indignation against his mother as well. Little as he might care about the throne for its own sake, his being denied it would be another wound to his self-confidence and capacity for action. There was, moreover, his oppressive sense of an obligation to find remedies for a time out of joint, a positive task over and above the negative one of ridding Denmark of a usurper.

In his impromptu verses after the court play he calls his father a Jove, dethroned by a peacock; again when trying to rouse his mother's conscience he compares his father to Jove, and other gods, a man and king vastly superior to his brother. But there is no sign of Hamlet and his father having ever been very close. They were very different personalities, offspring of discordant eras. One is a warrior, of the age of chivalry, whom we hear of fighting Poles, Norwegians, Englishmen, but doing little else. It is in martial guise that he returns to earth, in full panoply of arms. The other is a young man of modern and speculative turn of mind. We are surely meant to suppose that Hamlet's sharpening vision could not leave his image of his father unaffected.

Apart from the disgrace that has befallen 'the royal bed of Denmark' (I.v.82), the Ghost has no thought but of revenge pure and simple. He shows no more interest than his overwrought son in the foreign menace to Denmark, though this arises directly out of an action of his own. He is equally oblivious of the social ills that are taking hold of his son's mind. Moreover he is undergoing grievous punishment for misdeeds when alive, and confesses to 'foul crimes' (I.v.12, 25, 117). All this adds to the doubts which must be felt about his right to impose his will on his son; and

Hamlet's mind, even if he never speaks of this, must be painfully divided over where his real duty lies. Shakespeare's next tragedy king, Lear, was another doughty fighter in bygone days, but one who came to see that he had 'taken too little thought' for the sufferings of his people (III.iv.32–3).

In Denmark as in Rome, though not in ancient Britain, we see the common people in revolt, not, however, against their own afflictions but on behalf of others, their superiors. In Rome it is to protest against the murder of Caesar, in Denmark that of Polonius; in both cases they show good feeling but less sense. Having pondered the Roman record, Shakespeare could scarcely want Hamlet to put the same misguided trust in the people as Brutus had done. Claudius testifies to a public affection for Hamlet which makes any open action against him impracticable – a good deal is heard in this play of the weight of public opinion –, but it never occurs to the prince to enlist popular support as Laertes does.

The mob at whose head Laertes breaks into the castle is one more of the play's conundrums. He seems not to have stirred it up himself: he is reported, Claudius learns, to have been lying low and listening to 'buzzers', or rumour-mongers, who talk to him about his father's death and do not hesitate to blame the king (IV.v.90 ff.). This may sound as if agitators are looking for a pretext in Polonius's death and hasty burial, and are making use of Laertes as their figurehead. We see the rioters only for a moment: bidden to wait outside the king's chamber, they withdraw, and disappear. They seem to be inflamed by sympathy for a bereaved family, but politically are light-headed. They have been shouting for Laertes to be made king (IV.v.106–8), as their Roman kinsmen wanted Brutus to step into Caesar's shoes; their love for Hamlet is forgotten. Claudius may well grumble at 'the distracted multitude' and its unreasoning excitability (IV.iii.4–5). A long-winded announcement of its approach, by a horrified courtier, is too lengthy and rhetorical to sound dramatic; it must be taken as one of Shakespeare's authorial 'asides'. It depicts a scene of the wildest anarchy – 'Antiquity forgot, custom not known', as if the whole fabric of an old world were tottering (IV.v.103–4).

The masses once unchained, it would appear, can be expected to sweep away everything in their flood. There seems no connection between this and the death of a good old fellow like Polonius. It is an alarming glimpse of the lower depths erupting, a sort of parallel to the terrors of Purgatory that the Ghost is condemned to. An insurrectionary crowd was delicate work for any Elizabethan playwright to handle. Shakespeare's description of a wild, momentary outburst is an alarm-bell to the respectable of all grades in the audience, but less likely to frighten the censor because it is unpolitical. Socially it is all the more threatening. Laertes is now a man of property, as well as a good son, and cannot feel comfortable with his dangerous allies. He is easily steered by Claudius away from his design of public exposure and punishment of whoever may be responsible for his father's death, to a plan of covert, cowardly revenge which will do nothing to right his father's name and fame.

Old Hamlet's talk of his married life, his exemplary faithfulness to his wife, holds up a standard of conduct which Gertrude has woefully demeaned. Marriage as well as monarchy is shown in its opposite aspects, ideal and debased, and in its social setting, which helps to lift the story above melodrama. Young Hamlet's disillusion is with society, not with individuals alone. He turns more passionately to the task of opening his mother's eyes to her moral shame than to that of retribution against his uncle; his bent, or 'mission', is that of a reformer. His alienation from Ophelia is the visible, romantic expression of a single-handed idealist's inevitable failure.

As for social evils arising from oppression of class by class, or man's inhumanity to man, it must be an equal blow for him to realize that these things have flourished whether his admired father or his detested uncle has been on the throne. It seems that 'whatsoever king may reign', the poor will be the ill-used poor. He never puts this into words; but neither does he ever speak to us or to himself of the painful link in his mind between Gertrude and Ophelia. Dowden was critical of an over-schematic reduction, by the German theorist H.A. Werner, of the man Hamlet into a symbol of social crisis; but he did not question Shakespeare's recognition of the individual's involvement in the social and moral conditions surrounding him, and saw that Hamlet's predicament lay in his being 'called upon to assert moral order' in a demoralized world (127–30). Similarly Boas – another of the elder critics with more perspicacity on some matters than most of their successors – saw how Hamlet's 'inward disease' was fed by 'the rank poison' circulating in the body politic (*Shakspere* [sic] 387). 'Hamlet's discontent is not merely private', wrote the Marxist scholar Arnold Kettle, citing as an analogy Donne's 'First Anniversarie' poem of 1611 about a broken, incoherent society, lying 'all in peeces' ('From *Hamlet* to *Lear*', in Kettle, ed., 150–51, 160–61).

Francisco is 'sick at heart' when we meet him briefly at the outset; Marcellus has a misgiving of 'something rotten' in Denmark (I.i.9, I.iv.90). Hamlet is seized, possessed, by the same unease, and goes through the play chewing on it, as Brutus would say. In his first soliloquy he makes use of Shakespeare's favourite image of the unweeded garden, abandoned to 'Things rank and gross in nature' (I.ii.135–7). Caroline Spurgeon shows how the play's imagery reeks of infection and corruption (*Imagery* 316, 332), and how pervasive is 'the idea of a tumour, a hidden corruption, needing the surgeon's knife' ('Iterative Imagery' 256). 'Denmark is diseased', writes Rossiter: 'we are never allowed to forget that' (182). The gravedigger shows us some of the work of venereal disease (V.i.166–8). All this must mean that the life of the community has somehow suffered a blight. What this is, we are never explicitly told, but we are given an array of pointers to how human beings are living and treating one another.

Shakespeare had to have characters to speak for him, as well as for themselves, and Hamlet may have been better adapted to this double duty than any other. No dramatist could be a perfect ventriloquist, and Dr Johnson was only one of many critics who have seen that Hamlet's table of the ills that flesh is heir to includes some that a prince is unlikely to have been exposed to. Still, he has been a student as well, and students have traditionally been drawn to radical ideas. None of his classroom friends have much money; his one true intimate, Horatio, is definitely poor. Hamlet must have come in contact with men of middling rank in government service, as well as the nobility. As an intellectual he stands in some degree outside the classes; he chats with a gravedigger, must often have been approached by humble petitioners. In daily life a semi-feudal society, as Shakespeare's still was, segregated high and low less sharply than full-blown capitalist life was to do.

Above all, it belongs to the profession of tragic hero to be in some sort a spokesman of humanity at large. Even Macbeth, crushed by the load of life and failure, is so. W.H. Clemen draws attention to the distinctive quality of Hamlet's images, mostly concrete, simple, familiar, and revealing very wide-ranging interests or knowledge (107). He communes with himself in verse, often with others in prose, of which this play contains an abundance. He is a thinker, but not a cloistered one, and his firmest interest is in mankind. Shakespeare confronts him with the ordinary lives of his fellow-beings, instead of leaving him statuesquely pedestalled like the patricians of Rome. Experience has prepared him in advance for some at least of the discoveries now breaking over him, the realization of how much the human condition stands in need of mending.

Denmark's social framework is Shakespeare's customary binary society, of high and low with little between apart from impecunious young gentlemen. There is nothing to be seen of a bourgeoisie, the class destined to inherit the earth. Hamlet's talk, however, is leavened, like so much other dialogue in Shakespeare, with much legal–commercial phraseology. 'Quietus' is a quittance or discharge of some liability (III.i.75): he is thinking of life as a bondage. As he stands pondering whether to stab the king he asks himself how his dead father is faring – 'how his audit stands' (V.iii.82). Gazing at the skulls, he fantasizes about three of them as remains of professional men, each with the worst proclivities of his business. A 'politician' is 'one that would circumvent God'; a courtier is a smooth-tongued flatterer; worst of the trio is a lawyer, 'a great buyer of land', who provokes Hamlet to a burst of legal jargon about the 'tricks' needed to amass wealth (V.i.83 ff.). In all this his standpoint, or Shakespeare's, is that of a man of education and independent means, free of the trammels of any particular walk of life, but conversant with the ways and the mentality of many, especially at the professional end of the social spectrum. It was towards some such situation that Shakespeare was working his own way; he reached it in his few years of retirement at Stratford, before his discharge from the 'vile world' of Sonnet 71 (or *Macbeth* III.i.108), and the panorama of social evils in Sonnet 66.

At the bottom of the social pile is the labourer condemned to 'grunt and sweat' under his burden (III.i.77), words that seem themselves to sweat with physical exhaustion. When Hamlet, soon after his brooding on suicide, accuses himself to Ophelia, more seriously than Malcolm denouncing himself, of so many vicious qualities, he is in the process of growing aware of hardship and exploitation in the life around him, hitherto disregarded. But as social critic he, unlike Lear not much later, is preoccupied chiefly with the vices or foibles of the higher ranks. His strictures begin with a criminal ruler, a minister in his dotage, fawning courtiers. Claudius and Polonius themselves, who ought to know whereof they speak, are cited by Shakespeare as witnesses. Claudius in his self-reproaches deplores 'the corrupted currents of this world', where the highly placed sinner dodges censure, and ill-gotten gains can bribe justice (III.iii.57 ff.). When Hamlet maintains that there is only one honest man nowadays in ten thousand, Polonius can but assent (II.ii.178 ff.). And when later on Polonius remarks that a pious exterior is often a mask for guilt, the royal conscience shrinks as if from a stroke of the lash (III.i.50).

Hamlet seems to know a good deal about fashionable ladies, with their cosmetics and camouflages, always abominations to Shakespeare; his tirade to Ophelia about them (III.i.140–41) is one of the play's attacks on aristocratic frivolity. Polonius wants women to be virtuous, if chiefly for prudential reasons, but his standard of conduct for young gentlemen is less strict. It is part of the purpose of his instructions to Reynaldo (II.i) to let us know what this standard is. Youth must have its fling: it has a natural taste for gambling, along with 'drinking, fencing, swearing, quarrelling, drabbing'. Reynaldo, who may suffer from middle-class prejudices, is taken aback by this last item; but the whole curriculum has a convincingly Elizabethan tone.

Like this scene, Osric has often been regarded as superfluous (eg. Raleigh 147), but he would not be brought in at the tragic crisis without good reason. He adds a touch of sour amusement to Shakespeare's picture of the decadence of an old order, and Hamlet's disgust with it and its pretentious silliness. Like Thurio in *Two Gentlemen of Verona*, he is 'spacious in the possession of dirt', and stands for a whole class or genus: Hamlet knows others like him, whom 'the drossy age dotes on' (V.ii.87, 166). Unlike Thurio, but like many foppish Cavaliers in the Civil Wars, Osric may not be a poltroon; but bravery, if he has it, will be his sole saving grace.

Face to face with his mother, Hamlet unexpectedly repeats the thought, familiar in the English Histories, of peace generating plenty, and plenty bringing degeneracy (III.iv.154–5). Virtue can claim no right to speak 'in the fatness of these pursy times'. Clearly the meaning cannot be that everyone in Denmark, or England, is well-off, overfed, pampered. It is the same meaning as the Archbishop's in *Henry IV Part 2*: the *rich* are too prosperous and self-satisfied to pay any heed to moral restraints (IV.i; Kiernan 60–61). Hence an indifference to right or wrong, which the ruling class of Denmark has shown by allowing Claudius and Gertrude to behave as they have done.

In such times – a frequent regret of Shakespeare's – men, even the greatest, are quickly forgotten once they are gone, as Hamlet's father has been. This forgetfulness is one source of his revulsion from mankind. His words about it are followed by the lament of the player-king, falling sick and gloomily clear-sighted about the brevity of love or gratitude. 'The great man down, you mark his favourite flies . . . ' (III.ii.192 ff.). Shakespeare's sensitiveness to human relations was too acute not to be touched. Hamlet drops his 'madness' at once to welcome his 'excellent good friends' and fellow-students Rosencrantz and Guildenstern; but it is not long before he is forcing from them the confession that they have been sent for by the king, to watch him (II.ii.227, 280 ff.).

Laertes' mob, a stylized prophecy of a revolt of the masses, is followed closely by the graveyard scene, a crucial stage of Hamlet's dark enlightenment, where impressions that have been struggling into consciousness grow distinct. Foremost among them is the gulf between higher and lower ranks. Contemplating the gravedigger, dully careless of the bones he is turning over, Hamlet reflects that 'The hand of little employment hath the daintier sense' (V.i.88–9). Only the leisured can cultivate delicacy of feeling. What is pitiable is the insensitivity of the poor to their own degrading lot. Yet the sexton plumes himself on superiority to his assistant in his grasp of the law (I ff.), and quibbles and puns like the shoemaker in *Julius Caesar* (I.i) – or like Shakespeare in his comedies. This taste for word-play leads Hamlet to his comment on how, in this refined age, 'the toe of the peasant' almost treads on 'the heel of the courtier'; which may sound like a levelling up of social inequality. It has been taken as a prince's supercilious disdain of the workman's attempt at wit (Patterson 103); it is better to find in Hamlet's words a sense of the emptiness of court culture, which any ignoramus can pick up, and the folly of the poor in wanting to ape it. All the doings of the world he belongs to are now for him no more than play-acting, as meaningless as the fine feelings of their betters to men of common clay.

Fuming at his own inactivity, Hamlet had cursed himself for 'a rogue and peasant slave' (II.ii.502). 'Peasant' and 'slave' could both be terms of abuse for any inferior, a reminder of how English ploughmen were being degraded into a dispirited race of hired labourers. But the gravedigger is no mere clown: he is a serious, saturnine, even menacing presence. He and his mate take comfort in the thought that toilers like themselves are the only true aristocracy (V.i.24–6). Such ideas were fermenting in the brains of many hard-driven toilers in Shakespeare's Europe. Class resentment is turned grotesquely into a grievance about Ophelia being buried in holy ground, as a suicide has no right to be, only because she is a lady, and it is a shame that 'great folk' should have more licence to 'drown or hang themselves' than ordinary people.

When Hamlet is awaiting the Ghost, and talking on and on to quieten his nerves, he wanders from a diatribe against drink, or against his hard-drinking uncle, to the weaknesses that individuals may be sullied with from birth, however praiseworthy otherwise (I.iv.14 ff.); as if, maybe, alive to some such failing in himself, a fault of indecisiveness. He has meant so much to so many because he expressed for them the curse of inability to act, in a world that has lost its meaning, or simply grown too complicated. All such moods in Shakespearian drama must be intensifications of feelings shared in some measure by many or most men and women.

In the traditional view, Hamlet had a clear duty laid on him, and was to blame for his failure to carry it out. Goethe's Wilhelm Meister, in a discussion of the play, takes Shakespeare's theme to be 'the effects of a great action laid upon a soul unfit for the performance of it' (Bk IV, ch. 13). No soul could really be equal to Hamlet's task, a far larger and more complex one than Wilhelm perceived. Coleridge's portrait of an inward-turned Hamlet and his natural 'aversion to action' (150) makes one suspect that he was examining himself more than his prince. Dover Wilson is emphatic as to Hamlet being a failure, and 'through weakness of character' (*Hamlet* 268). Robertson explains his long delays better as due to disgust with his mother making him feel that no effort was worth making (161–2). Disgust with everything round him as well, we must add; nothing less could make a young man of so ardent a temper feel that life had suddenly grown 'Weary, stale, flat and unprofitable' (I.ii.133).

Pyrrhus, son of the dead champion Achilles, would be more quickly identified in an Elizabethan theatre than today (Scragg 117). He is both a model for Hamlet and a warning against brutal revengefulness (Kernan, *Playwright* 97). In the Trojan War speech he halts for an instant before killing old king Priam in revenge, 'like a neutral to his will and matter' (II.ii.491–3). Hamlet pauses for much longer, in much the same half-hypnotized state, until he can only explain it to himself as the will of fate. As a result the last two and a half Acts form 'a series of detached episodes' (Wilson, *Hamlet* 203; cf. Bolt 17), giving life itself the random, fortuitous look that it usually has for us. There are practical obstacles in Hamlet's way, which we must take account of though Shakespeare leaves this to us, and Hamlet never reaches the point of considering a plan.

He has all the strength and means needed, he tells himself (IV.iv.45); but this is to urge himself on. To kill Claudius would be easy enough, as we see; but to be the prelude to any meaningful advance it would have to be carried out in the light of day. A muffled assassination may be enough to satisfy Laertes, but cannot be enough for Hamlet; it would have no better effect on the the public mind than his killing of Polonius. Any attempt at a public exposure of Claudius would be nullified by his being thought a madman. The fear he expresses with his dying breath, of leaving behind him a stained reputation, must have been with him all the time.

More important for latter-day critics has been the question of whether blood-revenge *can* be a duty (e.g. P. Edwards 60; Alexander 10). Hamlet assumes that it is, but his inaction belies him; his instincts rise up against it. We may find here Shakespeare's clearest recognition of the difference between a conscious and unconscious mind. Conventional morality, backed by religion, was against any private revenging, any taking of the law into an aggrieved man's hands. A ghost's demand for revenge, and a son's pledge to satisfy it, could on this view only be satanic, as McGee's summing up of the issue makes clear (41–2, 102). To Hamlet himself it could hardly seem a righteous way to set things right, once he had cooled down from the first flush of anger at the Ghost's revelation. Antony's bloodthirsty prophecy of Caesar's spirit 'ranging for revenge', with the goddess of vengeance 'come hot from hell' (III.i.255 ff.), belonged to another world than Hamlet's. What justice required was a regular impeachment and trial of the usurper, but Hamlet is tied to the primitive code under which only a son's sword could wreak sufficient retribution. More practically, he has no evidence to produce except the word of a ghost; and Claudius is not, like Macbeth, a notorious oppressor of his country. It would, moreover, hardly be possible to denounce him without incriminating the queen as well.

Hamlet's *Mousetrap* is part of his delayings. Its purpose is not to make Claudius give himself away publicly – and it has no such effect on the court, or his wife – but to lay to rest his nephew's dubitations, unreal as these may be, about the truth of the Ghost's story. There could be no thought of forgiveness for the criminal; but Hamlet is stranded between two eras, two conceptions of right conduct. We can think of him as suffering the same pangs as the men on whom for centuries the code of honour of their class imposed an obligation to fight duels, with the brand of cowardice to be incurred if they refused, of murder if they fought and killed. To Brutus murder even of a tyrant was 'a dreadful thing', wearing a 'monstrous visage' (II.i.63, 83). It must have looked more forbidding still to one like Hamlet, suddenly waylaid by a resurrected past and its imperatives, which men of the new age were trying to shake off.

In Hamlet's mouth his ruminations on the duty so abruptly thrust on him sound only self-regarding. We may none the less be meant to guess at other trains of thought, such as the risk that killing his uncle might well, like the death of Caesar, let loose anarchy. The 'conscience' that makes cowards of us (III.i.83) must have its earlier meaning of 'consciousness', or thought and awareness as opposed to instinctive, unreflecting action. This self-reproach of cowardice torments him, even though we have seen him prove his daring by following the Ghost over the battlements, by himself, in spite of his companions' anxious warnings. He knows that to men in general of the higher classes his hesitations would be simply lack of courage, which invents so many excuses.

Beyond this is the changing shape of his mission, as it seems to broaden from mere revenge into something more portentous, a sweeping national regeneration. If the time is out of joint, as he feels from very early in the play (I.v.189), if Denmark is sick, getting rid of Claudius will not restore health (cf. Mehl 36, 47; Smirnov 86 ff.). What the mass of its people are suffering is the social injustice which compels the poor to pay for the pleasures and follies of the rich. In Shakespeare's time, as he very likely knew, Osric's peasants were being reduced to serfdom. Hamlet might well feel it a 'cursed spite' of destiny to make him responsible for finding a remedy. Critics of a different sort from those who blame him for neglecting his revenge have also underestimated the obstacles in his way. A Soviet enthusiast may have imagined a Hamlet boldly slaying Claudius, seizing power, carrying out a political purge, initiating agrarian reforms. No such programme could possibly be practicable. In the end what Hamlet accomplishes is nothing more than the primitive task of revenge which had been too meagre, as well as too repulsive, to inspire him to action.

Hegel accounted for consciousness undergoing disintegration by seeing in it a reflection of a social order decomposing. In the stale atmosphere of Denmark, Hamlet's isolation shows us in miniature this crumbling of an old order, with nothing ready as yet to take its place. It is really the air of England that Hamlet is breathing, and Shakespeare himself, as Boas said, must have felt at times like him, stifled and repelled by the decadence and discord all round him (*Shakspere* 388). Once Hamlet begins to recognize this for what it is, he becomes a kind of censor of morals, but it is only with words that he can play the part of a 'scourge' of iniquity. The 'inky cloak' in which we see him first (I.ii.77), among the gaudy courtiers, is an emblem not of grief alone, but of something akin to a religious conversion. This was a phenomenon common in Shakespeare's day with its spreading Puritan influence. Gloom, self-doubt, self-disgust, were its hallmarks, and all these sensations were fed by the condition of social life, with its many dislocations. It is for Hamlet now to 'wipe away all trivial fond records' of his former days (I.v.99), those of love among them, and the vanities of high life whose 'glass of fashion' and 'mould of form' he himself, Ophelia says, has been (III.i.156). As an earnest scholar lately in a small provincial town

– Luther's town –, he may have been asking himself what such caperings were worth. Exaggerated self-reproaches, such as he pours out to Ophelia, were another compulsive habit of the convert.

Hamlet's dualistic sense of a human race half-angel, half-beast (II.ii.286 ff.), is not all pessimism, but it is not likely to give him the strength he needs. If mankind has grown honest, in the cynical joke between him and Rosencrantz, doomsday must be near (II.ii.240–42). Revolutionary energy requires faith in man, not the scepticism that was engulfing him. A morbid fear of sharing in a general human corruption – 'We are arrant knaves all; believe none of us' (III.i.128–9) – is the other side of his poignant sympathy with the human lot. When links with others lose their meaning, it becomes hard for him to act, because there are only shadows to be acted on, and the earth itself is turning into 'a foul and pestilent congregation of vapours' (II.ii.311). When excited he can kill human beings without compunction; they have no real existence. He is a mystery to us because he has become a mystery to himself, as all human beings are when they are rash enough to think about it. He is only now being compelled to realize how greatly his deepest beliefs have been altering. His uncertainties open the way to a moral vacuum where 'There is nothing either good or bad but thinking makes it so' (II.ii.239–40).

His only ostensible duty is one which he has at first embraced with alacrity, but which becomes as he ponders it useless and inhuman. With an easy chance to kill his uncle, he cannot overcome his repugnance to a treacherous blow; unable to admit this to himself, he concocts an excuse that allows him to sound splendidly ferocious. Its being no more than a pretext is clear if only from the fact, which he must know at least as well as Claudius, that a criminal cannot wipe away his guilt without making restitution of what he has got by it. Johnson, Tillyard (App. B.), and many others, going back, Tillyard observes, as far as William Richardson in 1784, have seen through the pretence. Sydney Bolt's conviction, in agreement with Coleridge instead of with Johnson, that in this scene (III.iii) Hamlet shows true 'calculated ruthlessness' (15) is persuasively argued; but it is irreconcilable with the impression Hamlet gives throughout of a man unable to perform such acts except in a fit of passion. He is in such a fit very shortly after, when he kills Polonius by mistake for Claudius – a Claudius still fresh from prayer. The notion of killing an enemy's soul as well as body was taken up by some other playwrights; it would make thrilling melodrama, but would repel more serious auditors, those whom Shakespeare was most concerned with. An ideal prince turning murderer would be an unbearable thought, Summers writes; and it is not any flaw in Hamlet that makes him tragic, but an 'evil and intolerable situation' (53, 58–9).

But Hamlet's self-rebukings show that he (like his uncle) is not always wrestling with his conscience. He drifts into the spells of apathy, of 'almost blunted purpose', which the Ghost – or his fevered mind – reproves (III.iv.110), and which his mother observes alternating with bouts of frantic excitement (V.i.251 ff.). There is an oblique reflection on his instability in Claudius's words to Laertes on the sad impermanence of love (IV.vii.110 ff.). It is one of the play's many fine strokes of irony that Claudius should be urging Laertes not to be slack in his revenge on Hamlet, who has been so slack in his revenge on Claudius.

Hamlet's opponents, unlike him, are men of prompt action. 'Am I a coward?' he vainly asks himself – 'Who . . . plucks off my beard?' His uncle tells Laertes not to suppose him 'so flat and dull' as to let his 'beard be shook with danger' (II.ii.582 ff.; IV.vii.30 ff.). Hamlet's temperament goes with a self-dramatizing inclination, which his solitude encourages. Called on to avenge his father, he thinks himself summoned to act as 'minister' to out-raged heaven (III.iv.176). The deaths of Rosencrantz and Guildenstern he dismisses as the reward of their own rash folly in coming between the angry swords of 'mighty opposites' – himself and Claudius (V.ii.60–62). A morbid consequence of this romanticizing is that Hamlet can let himself be put to the blush by the heroics of war, however unmeaning.

Shakespeare had been coming to feel an aversion from war, with its cruelties and stupidities; but the values enshrined in its nobler aspects always remained very real for him, and his heroes, whatever else they might be, had to be brave. When Hamlet's world is fractured and splintered, he can seek refuge in contemplation of war as a time-honoured occupation, the one in which his father had shone, socially approved and evading criticism by its very irrationality. All the other tragic heroes have had long familiarity with battle; Fortinbras can only say of Hamlet that if he had been brought to the test he would have been likely to do well. Had this happened already, he would scarcely be so willing to suspect himself of timidity.

He is irrationally thrilled by the spectacle of Fortinbras's motley army marching off to raid Poland (IV.iv.32 ff.), and stirred to thoughts which, as Bradshaw says, defy any logical scrutiny (6 ff.; cf. Scragg 125 ff., 135). They are indeed hopelessly confused. No cool thinking can help Hamlet, an intellectual thrown back among the clamours of wilder times. He talks of man's endowment of 'capability and godlike reason', when the fighting in prospect is utterly senseless on both sides. He calls it 'divine ambition' in Fortinbras to be prepared to risk his life and those of thousands of others, merely for 'a fantasy and trick of fame'. 'Rightly to be great', a combatant must have a great cause – as Hamlet has; but it is Fortinbras, strong in the arm as his name implies rather than in the head, who is finding 'quarrel in a straw', putting his honour at stake when his whole expedition to Poland is no better than self-display and vainglory. This is Hotspur over again, ready to 'cavil on the ninth part of a hair'. Hamlet's killing of Polonius must have left him disoriented, over-dependent on stray impulses from outside.

Fortinbras and his fantasies stand at the opposite pole of Europe's thinking from its religion, so elusively prominent in the play. What we hear of an afterlife can at times sound perfunctory, lifeless as it does to Frye (*Shakespeare* 87), and may well have done to Shakespeare. Reliance on a ghost to set his story moving makes it unavoidable, and he can at least make some poetic capital out of it. We are to feel that a Providence is presiding over events, another reader holds (Kitto, 157). If so, it is a more than usually inscrutable one, moving in a mysterious way to litter the stage with corpses. Is the Ghost one of its instruments? Hamlet is at first doubtful whether it is 'a spirit of health or goblin damned', but is quickly convinced of the truth of its statement, which justifies his already strong animus against his uncle (I.v.9 ff.). Theology Shakespeare has to dodge, skating round such questions as why his father is allowed absences from purgatory on business so un-Christian – for it is revenge he comes to call for, not justice. As R.C. Levin points out, he cannot be placed in any orthodox category (18–20). He is an upholder of old pagan custom, much more than a Christian penitent; a figment of folk-tale imagination, endowed by Shakespeare with a vitality not his own.

Religious turns of speech are oddly mixed up with other matter. 'Flights of angels' are summoned to bear away the hero's soul; no other favourite of Shakespeare departs under such escort, but a military salute adds a more audible send-off. In his reproaches to his mother Hamlet can sound a good deal like a Puritan chaplain; her sin has turned 'sweet religion' into 'a rhapsody of words' (III.iv.47–8). Shakespeare very likely felt that a good many well-known Englishmen were doing this. His uncle hopes that rain from 'the sweet heavens' may wash the blood off his hand (III.iii.45–6); but when he prays he is already resolved to get rid of Hamlet, presumably by having him killed. Yet he is well-taught enough to know that he must throw himself on divine mercy; no gifts to the Church, such as that good Catholic Henry V set store by, occur to his mind. Like Hamlet we may expect Ophelia not to forget her morning prayers, but religion is no help to her when her ordeal comes on her, or when a 'churlish priest' refuses Christian rites at her burial (V.i.207). Dislike of clerical bigotry stands out here.

This peculiar religious atmosphere goes with the haze hanging over the play, the fog of history and an unknown future, very unlike the Mediterranean clarity of the Roman plays. Hamlet himself can be thought of as, probably like many Elizabethans, a mixture of Christian and pagan or sceptic. His visitings of religious compunction seem like fugitive recollections of a creed he has outgrown. His Providence may watch over the fall of a sparrow (V.ii.192–3), not seemingly over that of a king. In the Histories death was an 'eternal night', swallowing up good men and bad; in the tragedies Hamlet and his uncle are nearly alone in their forebodings of a life to come. Hamlet has the Ghost as evidence of survival, but he can only picture the beyond as a nightmare, worse than extinction: there is no paradise anywhere. He talks of being held back from suicide by fear of 'something after death', but it is really fear of confessing himself a weakling by not killing Claudius instead of himself. It is one more of the play's contrasting parallels of situation or language that Laertes breaking into the castle, reckless of the next world as of this, can 'dare damnation' to revenge his father, while Hamlet entangles himself in fine-spun cogitations (IV.v.133–6). But Laertes' goal is revenge alone, whereas Hamlet's is something far more complex.

Not born for action, Hamlet when he does act does so on impulse, thoughtlessly, and he rationalizes this into an idea of our 'indiscretions' sometimes serving us better than any 'deep plots' (V.ii.8–9): fate, or Providence will turn them to account. When by error he kills Polonius he takes a step that leads tortuously to his own death. From now on he is a changed and not always better man. Only bloody thoughts can serve him, he concludes from the fiery Fortinbras's example. How far Rosencrantz and Guildenstern deserve the doom he sends them to may be arguable, though it is in any case, as McAlindon says (10), unnecessary. Polonius's death and Hamlet's wild behaviour might well portend danger to the king, and make it the 'holy and religious' duty (III.iii.8) of good subjects like this pair to enter into whatever their royal master's protection might require. For Hamlet, their being chosen to accompany him to England is enough to condemn them, as 'adders fanged' (III.iv.204); his retaliation is as revengeful as what his father wants him to do.

Out on the waves, Hamlet was quick to seize opportunities he thought – then or subsequently – Providence was holding out to him. As its instrument he could feel irresistible, though it was an impersonal power to which he never thought of praying. On his safe return he could assure Horatio that he had learned, and was a stronger man than before. It is another facet of the play's enigmatic cast that readers have so often been divided about this. Bradley found some trust in Providence in the Hamlet of this final stage, but more of a fatalistic waiting for things to happen (*Tragedy* 143–5). Harry Levin sees 'a new man who . . . has attained his full stature' (*Hamlet*, 94); Charlton finds only a paralysis of the will, abandonment of any attempt to steer his own course (103; cf. Dowden, 158; Boas, *Shakspere* 403; Bolt, 79–80). Even now, the truth seems to be, Hamlet cannot bring himself to be the first to strike. He knows that his uncle has tried to have him killed, but others do not know it. He can only wait for Claudius to give himself away publicly by a fresh attempt on his life. 'The readiness is all', he tells Horatio (V.ii.223): readiness to seize opportunity when it comes. It does come, in the fencing-match when the dying Laertes confesses the plot he and Claudius have been guilty of. If we are bent on finding Providence at work, we can detect it in the poisoned rapier changing hands.

'My fate cries out', Hamlet had exclaimed as he followed the Ghost to their meeting-place. It was natural to him, we may guess, to think of a 'fate' rather than of any more intelligible power. Left with the others, Horatio asked 'To what issue will this come?' and gave himself the commonplace answer: 'Heaven will direct it' (I.iv.81 ff.). When Hamlet assures him that 'heaven was ordinant' in the sending of Rosencrantz and Guildenstern to their deaths – as if wanting to put the responsibility off his own shoulders –, Horatio acquiesces uncritically (III.iv.207 ff.). His attitude of acceptance is rudely disturbed by the final catastrophe, where the will of heaven, if there was any at work, seems indecipherable. He can only sum up the record as a tragedy of errors, a medley of 'purposes mistook/Fall'n on the inventors' heads' (V.ii.385–6). If there is a lesson, it seems to be that evil committed by man or woman multiplies incalculably in the rank soil of the human, or social, condition. Others will catch the infection, as Laertes does most fatally; Hamlet himself is not immune. Crime brings inexorable retribution, but through a web of tortuous and costly accident. Hamlet is able in the end to give the villain his deserts, with the whole court watching, better than any planning of his own could have brought it about; a symbolic blow at all the rottenness of an old Denmark.

When the play was written, the fable of an enlightened prince rebuilding his country on ideal lines could still be taken seriously, and in daydreams of the commonalty it was to have a long life. Shakespeare could feel its attraction, but as a realist he could see its unreality, and relegate it to the Romances of his last plays. The 'Hamlet mood' of hesitation would beset for centuries a European reformism chronically held back by fear of change making things worse. Hamlet is too deeply estranged from his country to be able even to think of how to change it. Yet his last thoughts are for it and its future, in which the true story of his own life and death will have a part to play.

But with no alternative in sight he can only give his vote for Fortinbras, returning 'with conquest' from Poland (V.ii.351), as next ruler; a choice we can only see as making Denmark's future highly problematic, and chiefly made up of irresponsible foreign quarrels. Hamlet has been enthralled, perhaps Shakespeare too in some moods, by the glamour of a man so entirely opposite to himself. He is turning away from the kind of political life represented by Claudius and Polonius, or the defunct politician of his graveyard fantasy, to the martial virtues, frank courage and freedom from sordid greed. Another tragedy, *Timon of Athens*, was to end with a soldier installed in power, this time specifically as a reformer. Countless Europeans in times to come were to put their faith in similar paladins, and find their hopes turning to ashes.

As for Hamlet, he has performed all that it was in him to achieve of what he heard his fate cry out to him, on the dark ramparts, to do. He is entitled in his turn to bequeath an unwelcome duty to Horatio. His friend must renounce for a while the 'felicity' of death, in order to see that justice is done to his memory. Hamlet himself has made this renunciation, by going on living when life ceased to hold anything for him, except a remorseless task. Life must have a purpose, however sombre, and whatever a man has tried to do to better it ought not to be forgotten. The prince of Denmark has earned his rest. His countrymen have earned and deserved much less; and monarchical rule in Denmark, which can only be rescued from itself by the killing of the man on the throne, has reached an impasse.

3

Othello (1603–04)

In more than one way *Othello* follows on from *Hamlet*. Both plays have a very 'contemporary' flavour, compared with later tragedies. Both begin with loud preparations for war, which quickly die down, leaving the main conflict to emerge within a family. But whereas what happens within the Danish royal family affects the fortunes of a kingdom, in *Othello* there is an approach to a type of drama which came to be known as 'domestic tragedy'. It is very untypical of Shakespeare, with his absorption in grand public issues, but he was helping to initiate a vogue; it has been pointed out that *Othello* had much influence on the later Jacobean and Caroline mode, turning away to themes of private life (Hibbard, '*Othello*' 40). Shakespeare is on his guard, however, against any too sharp or steep a withdrawal. In Cyprus Othello is invested with plenary power, and when he and his bride come ashore out of the storm Cassio greets them in terms like those of a royal couple's welcome. Othello's profession is the 'royal' one of war, and Shakespeare bestows on him a magnificence of bearing which often extends to his language. He is a stranger to Venice, a great unknown. All this raises him high above the commonplace level of a jealous husband. He is a figure portentous enough to embody or personify the social whole, or serve as mirror for the social whole to see itself in; he emerges from and sinks back into the brooding mist of fate or capricious fortune that Shakespeare throws over his scene.

Like its predecessor, this play bristles with difficulties of interpretation. As to its plot, the simplest explanation is the one reached by Ned B. Allen, after a review of discrepancies between the first two and the three later Acts: 'Shakespeare wrote the two parts of *Othello* at different times', and joined them together not very carefully (17; cf. Council 14). Sanders (16) thinks there may have been no more than a revision. In either case not all the awkwardnesses are disposed of. Iago is hard up, he tells Roderigo at the outset; yet Roderigo's purse has been open to him for some time, and is not the only one that he has tapped (I.iii.365). No reason is given for the abrupt recall of Othello from Cyprus, and the disgraced Cassio being put in his place. And why should Desdemona be happy at this news? Hardest of all are the problems of the time-scheme, the fact especially that the charge of long-continued unfaithfulness against the heroine cannot be reconciled with probability, or even possibility. A hundred years ago an over-earnest American, Welker Given, argued that the high-minded poet had planned this confusion, with the subtlest skill, so as to make it impossible for Othello, as well as Cassio, ever to sleep with Desdemona: race and colour had to prohibit their love from consummation, and preserve its heavenly purity.

Othello lets himself be duped by Iago with ridiculous ease, and in one long scene passes from unalterable love to raging hatred; he goes on to plan his wife's murder without any serious attempt to question her, without questioning her alleged paramour at all. No inner discords hold him back from action, as they do Hamlet; the deed follows automatically on the thought, because this springs from other sources than tangible evidence; Iago has only to set them flowing. If we can sympathize with Othello it must be that we are all likely to have an uneasy sense of how the warmest attachments may be at the mercy of accident or error. Shakespeare's unique gift of portraying vital relationships between human beings was joined to an equal sensitiveness to the pathos of ties ruptured – as they seemed about to be in the quarrel scene of *Julius Caesar*, and as they were irretrievably in the scene of Hamlet with Ophelia.

As a whole this play, like *Julius Caesar*, is in verse, with only 541 lines of prose out of 3324, far fewer than in *Hamlet* (Smeaton 373). This by itself helps to keep it well above the plane of humdrum daily life; and some of Othello's speeches are pitched at a poetic altitude that has seemed to some readers to border on the excessive. Boas points out, on the other hand, that some of the most impressive scenes are either in prose or in verse with little embellishment (*Shakspere* 431). And this dual style is appropriate to Othello's dual place in the world: he is a towering alien figure, a legendary hero, and also a soldier of fortune in a modern European army. He stands at 'the disastrous meeting point' of two worlds (Charlton 123).

Othello can claim royal descent (I.ii.21–2). Shakespeare does not make much of this; there are no kings in Venice, and he has long been telling us, through royal as well as other lips – an exiled duke's in Arden, Henry V's on the eve of battle, Hamlet's in the graveyard –, that a king is no more than a man. What counts is the individual's endowments, and Othello's are doubtless remarkable. He alone of the tragic heroes has risen by unaided merit; when he imagines himself steeped in poverty 'to the very lips' (IV.ii.49) he is remembering what it was like. But a tragic hero must impress us as being in some fashion a representative, or reflection, or a current of history that is somehow altering the landscape of an era, and of the mind. Each tragedy grows out of the social turmoil of Shakespeare's time, but each is translated from the narrowly local into a different, timelessly exotic guise. Othello may be seen, from his far-off origins and wanderings, as one of those Noble Savages who haunted writers of the Age of Discoveries like Montaigne and his reader Shakespeare, and for two centuries to come. He has remained uncorrupted, free of the artificialities of 'civilized' life that Hamlet detested. He bolsters his self-respect, Rossiter has some ground for thinking, with 'a habit of self-approving self-dramatization' (200, 202). But as a successful member of a profession growing in size and importance in Europe, who has risen by merit from nothingness to the rank of General, he is an early beneficiary of the career open to talents, the principle enshrined in years to come by the French Revolution and Napoleon.

Eligibility for public employment has been for many years of immense importance to rising classes in Europe and native aspirants in colonial regions like British India. In Europe constant warfare was making the new regular armies a ladder of promotion for individuals combining energy with luck, and a man reaching the top in spite of manifest disadvantages like Othello's was a standard-bearer of progress, as well as one of the very many foreign mercenaries to be found in all the armies. He and his fellow-soldiers give great importance to what Iago calls 'good name' (III.iii.156), and others 'reputation' (eg.II.iii.175). Shakespeare had used this word as early as *Richard II*, in a feudal context, but now he was making it one of his shibboleths. He was moving amid a generation of newcomers, competitors, self-made men, for whom it was essential to stand well in the eyes of employers.

With it went the ideal of honesty, or reliability. 'The key word of *Othello* is "honest"', Empsom wrote: it and 'honesty' occur 52 times, something with no parallel in any other play (cited by Lerner 106–7). Shakespeare was now thinking more in the idiom of the middle classes, for which 'honesty' was to be the cardinal virtue, whereas among the noble Romans of *Julius Caesar* it had been honour. In the two social orders, older and newer, these two values occupied the same relative position. Brutus was 'armed so strong in honesty' as to fear no threats (IV.iii.67). 'Are you honest?' Hamlet asked Ophelia (III.i.103). Othello in his last extremity couples the two terms: 'why should honour outlive honesty?' (V.ii.245).

In him we see the old heroic values going out into a world of common men to justify themselves by their deeds. His work is in the truest sense his vocation; he has been all his life, like the Clifford of the Wars of the Roses, 'truly dedicate to war', enthralled by its 'royal banner', its 'pride, pomp, and circumstance' (III.iii.354–5), with a romantic ardour ready to be extended to the bride whom it wins for him. At the same time he is in his way, or the way of the old military orders of chivalry, a puritan who finds positive virtue in hardship and asceticism, and has learned to make 'the flinty and steel couch of war' his soft 'bed of down' (I.iii.227–8). Many soldiers of later empires were likewise to pass their lives on remote frontiers, making a fetish of their removal from the fleshpots and vices of the city. Othello has a hero's 'free and open nature' (I.iii.405), but it can only keep him safe in his proper sphere. Marriage, into an aristocracy, lands him among traps and deceits which will be his downfall. When he imperiously halts the brawl in Cyprus (II.iii), it is the last moment of his career as man of action. From now he becomes the only one of the heroes who is acted upon instead of acting (Sanders 20).

Iago is another professional soldier, whom his homeland Venice will ruin with temptations of a different sort. Some day he will be discovered by some critic or film director to have been a secret agent of the Turks; in the meantime his significance lies in his being Othello's counterweight, or mirror opposite. Between them these two do more than half of all the talking, and it has been noticed that Iago has more lines than Othello, in verse as well as in prose. He too has risen by merit, though not as high as he feels he deserves, in spite of being no older than twenty-eight. To make up for this he has got into the habit of resorting to less reputable methods of adding to his income. They have not made him a contented man. For one thing, as a married man he has long been, as Othello will soon be, a prey to jealousy and mistrust, and, as McElroy says (165), is well qualified to lure Othello into the same pitfall.

Shakespeare had written a great deal about romantic love, nearly always with a hint of scepticism; of late his faith in it had been drifting into the doldrums, as we can see from his talk in *Twelfth Night* of 'women's waxen minds', and Cressida's display of one. After its breakdown in *Hamlet* he shows it now for a while triumphant, even though loaded with handicaps. His romantic unions had sometimes brought together men and women from unequal social backgrounds; now, it would seem, a young woman must look outside civilized Venice, outside Europe, for a man unusual enough, or close enough to Nature, to share her feelings.

In the comedies Shakespeare shrank from letting us be privy to his young people's love-making, and was apt to fall back on the conjuring-trick of love at first sight. This would hardly do with a pair like Desdemona and Othello, and he furnishes an explanation with Othello's tales of danger and daring, which find their way to Desdemona's heart. Rosalind in *As You Like It* fell in love from watching Orlando in his hazardous wrestling-match with the champion. Romantic love has been the antidote, in times like Shakespeare's, to sordid money-grubbing and egotism; its spell has been the stronger because it promises to make up for all other ties lost or weakened. Venice has been an uncongenial home to Desdemona; she can vow, in the spirit of Shakespeare's most hyperbolical sonnets, that even if Othello turns her adrift, a beggar, his unkindness will never taint her love (IV.ii.156 ff.). Othello's long, lonely, homeless years have left him predestined, if he ever loves, to love with something like a mystical fervour. If their union is ever fractured, Chaos will have come again (III.iii.91–2), life will be meaningless. This is indeed what is fated to happen, and here again we may find a representation of a whole era of European feeling, a mirage revealing itself like so many others as a tapestry of contradictions.

In the flush of love and success Othello can hail his ill-starred match as the copingstone of a grand career. Marriage to a much-admired Venetian beauty, with the sanction of the Doge and his council, means for him full acceptance into the life of a State which he has served and looked up to from afar. In Venice, like England aristocratic though also highly commercial, he has been a stranger, as Shakespeare once was in London; now he can boast himself worthy of 'as proud a fortune' as the one he has reached (I.ii.23–4). Shakespeare is reaffirming his belief in merit and in the equality of 'true minds'; but the play is also an acknowledgment that a happy outcome is not to be expected within the close walls of things as they are. Venice as well as Denmark is a prison. An unequal society must first be broken down, as it is in the Romances where men and women alike are exposed to the adventures that Othello has undergone.

What might be thought a serious obstacle, religion, stage convention allowed Shakespeare to turn a blind eye to. Neither Brabantio nor anyone else raises the question of Othello's creed, past or present. Perhaps he brought an army chaplain with him to perform his wedding ceremony. We may assume that he shows a befitting respect for his employers' official tenets, as well as a proper loathing of Mohammedans. For himself he seems content with the same ill-defined 'natural' religion that serves so many of Shakespeare's people. Race is a more tangible matter, and a recurrent theme of Shakespeare's. Racial prejudice has always shown most virulently where sex relations are concerned. Portia of Venice was disgusted by the thought of wedlock with a swarthy Moroccan (of unspecified faith again). It does no credit to the empress in *Titus Andronicus* to have a Moor for her lover, nor to Antony to have an Egyptian mistress.

None of Othello's associates except Iago find fault with his marriage, but Iago and Roderigo have a receptive listener in Brabantio when they harp on Othello's colour. He insults his unwanted son-in-law with talk of 'the sooty bosom Of such a thing' (I.ii.70–71); from this his mind jumps quickly to social anarchy, with 'Bond-slaves and pagans' in the saddle. His daughter, he tells the Doge, has always shunned the 'wealthy curled darlings' of her own people; he attributes this to a very retiring nature, which only black magic can have warped into love for Othello. We can guess rather that aversion to cosseted young fops, and fear of some day being bestowed on one of them, has made her shut herself up. Aristocracy is sinking into decadence, as in Denmark with its Osrics; Desdemona (unless Shakespeare's idea of her changed a good deal from what it was when he began the play) is not afflicted as her father supposes with shrinking over-modesty; she has been daydreaming of real men, real action, and of a manly hero who will one day discover her.

When he comes she welcomes him with impetuous warmth. Her elopement gives their union, as Iago says, a 'violent commencement', a reminder of the Friar's misgivings in *Romeo and Juliet* about 'violent delights' and the violent ends that may await them. She herself must be feeling a pang of uneasiness when to win the Doge's sympathy she pleads the 'downright violence and storm of fortunes' that has befallen her (I.iii.245). But a heroine must expect ordeals, and face them bravely. We know from Othello that it was she who put the thought of love into his head, and drew him on: she was 'half the wooer', Brabantio comments bitterly, even more indignant with her than with Othello (I.iii.174). She comes near the close of Shakespeare's long series of attempts to conjure up ideal women combining traditional with newer qualities, courtly accomplishments tempered with the seriousness of a later time, or Renaissance culture blended with northern Protestant morality. In Cyprus we see a well-educated, emancipated young lady, gifted with a 'high and plenteous wit and invention' for Othello to admire (IV.i.179–82). 'My wife is fair, feeds well, loves company,/Is free of speech': he has no objection, being a husband equally liberal-minded, for all his Moorish blood, with no desire to play the jailer. She can even join in badinage of the free and easy sort Iago is given to; such vivacity is enough to stir Iago's malign suspicions (II.i.96 ff.).

Clearly Brabantio would not have consented to the marriage, if asked. Desdemona can be assumed to have known this when she gave him the slip instead. Shakespeare makes her a test, so to speak, of how far the audacity of love ought to be carried, an opposite case to that of the bashful and biddable Ophelia. He does not censure her, but he makes it hard for us not to do so, or to reflect that a claim for complete independence may or must mean a considerable degree of egotism. Shakespeare was a father himself, after all. Brabantio is abandoned with no more of a farewell than Shylock when his daughter vanishes; and he is forced to learn what has happened in the most humiliating fashion. He has no other child, and is left to die of a broken heart, while we watch his daughter in Cyprus undisturbedly gay, meeting her relative Lodovico with no sign of embarrassment and asking no news of her father. We are told of his death by his brother, contemplating Desdemona's lifeless body and expressing relief that Brabantio has been spared at least this: it would have been enough to make him turn his face away from heaven (V.ii.204 ff.) Romantic love may be a fine thing, it seems, but in an unromantic world it is all too likely to prove destructive as well as self-destructive.

Othello has been a stranger since childhood to family life and its obligations. We cannot but ask whether his off-handed treatment of Brabantio is not marred by something of the tragic sin of hubris, over-weening presumption. Brabantio is a powerful member of the Venetian oligarchy; he is 'an old man', who seems to have treated Othello like a son. With no sense of having made him an ill return, Othello declares that 'he loved me; oft invited me', and allowed him free access to Desdemona (I.iii). When the guest turned from story-teller into lover he was throwing dust into the trustful father's eyes. Warned after the clandestine wedding that Brabantio is searching for him, Othello dismisses his anger as mere 'spite' (I.ii.17). Frye agrees, calling Brabantio a 'spiteful old pantaloon' (*Fools* 102; cf. Long 41).

Othello relies on his services and (more remarkable) his 'perfect soul' to carry him through (I.ii.31). What really saves him from official displeasure is the impending Turkish attack, which makes him indispensable. All the aggrieved parent gets is the cold comfort of a string of commonplaces from the Doge, on a par with Gertrude's sermon to Hamlet on why he should not mourn over-long for his father. He takes refuge in a stoic dignity, and parts with Othello with a warning – 'She has deceived her father, and may thee' (I.iii.289.) From now on the shadow of a prophecy of doom hangs over the marriage. Iago has heard the words, and when he is stirring Othello's jealousy he brings them up, with powerful effect (III.iii.208). There can be no breaking away of the new from the bonds of the old with-out harshness and embitterment; no smooth transition from one era of social habit to another. In the interim the opposing claims are irreconcilable. All judgments of conduct are in flux. Othello is both right and wrong in virtually abducting his bride; we are meant to appreciate Brabantio's state of mind as well as Desdemona's.

It could not escape Iago's cynical eye – and Shakespeare's audience is unlikely to have overlooked it altogether – that Brabantio is a rich man, and Desdemona his only child and natural heir, who may yet have a chance of inheriting, to Othello's profit. Their commander, he tells Cassio sardon-ically, has 'boarded a land carack' – captured an heiress like a privateer capturing a ship –, and 'If it prove lawful prize' (if the courts confirm his ownership) 'he's made for ever' (I.ii.50–51). We may give the lovers the benefit of any doubt by guessing that they made no approach to Brabantio because they wanted it to be clear that they had no thought of getting his money. But what others would be likely to think is not something for us to disregard. In the end it is Brabantio's brother who inherits Othello's property (V.ii.361–3). Not many modern readers have found fault with this heroine, but Harry Levin recalls that Thomas Rymer did so in 1678, when patriarchal authority was more in esteem (*Revolution* 156).

A more tentative speculation may be that Othello felt able to ignore Brabantio because the married life he was looking forward to was meant to rise above ordinary passion – such as Roderigo told Brabantio the 'lascivious Moor' was already indulging in (I.i.127) – and to be of a more refined, spiritual kind. In his Tragic years nothing marked Shakespeare's outlook more strikingly than the distrust, often even disgust, of physical sexuality that he shared with the Puritan preachers. Certainly Othello intends his marriage to be a fully real one, not a disguised celibacy. He is nevertheless an aging man with a much younger wife, and may be making a virtue of necessity when he talks of his love as inspired by something higher than mere desire, whose 'young affects' are in him 'defunct' (I.iii.264–5). He may half-consciously be expecting his partner's thoughts on wedlock to be as ideal and restrained as his own. It has occurred to some readers that he may be disconcerted by finding himself mistaken (Cavell, *Disowning Knowledge* 136; cf. Smith 40–41).

Venice in the seventeenth century could be regarded by many as a model republic, and Shakespeare may partly have shared this view; but he clearly thought of it as having, in common with his London, a more disreputable side. To this Iago belongs; he is 'native here, and to the manner born'. He and the licentious Roderigo are shoots of a latter-day generation, whereas the worthier Venetians we see are of an older stock. We may be reminded all the same of the corrupt Senate of Timon's Athens when Brabantio shouts at Iago 'Thou art a villain', and Iago retorts 'You are – a senator' (I.i.99).

Iago is one of those 'smiling pickthanks' denounced in *Henry IV*, by whom 'the ear of greatness' is often abused; he breathes the air of a jostling, self-seeking existence, where the weaker go to the wall. He has no mind, he tells Roderigo, to go on serving a master for mere subsistence, like an ass, and then be turned off when worn out, as happens to simpletons (I.i.41 ff.). He must have seen many dutiful servitors, and soldiers, treated like this; so had Shakespeare, with his poor old faithful Adam in *As You Like It*, or his prediction of Lepidus being dropped from the triumvirate like an 'empty ass' in *Julius Caesar*. Massinger's plays abound in army officers who have done their work honourably, only to be left hungry when no longer needed.

Cassio's image of billows and lurking rocks as 'Traitors ensteeped to clog the guiltless keel' (II.i.69–70) has an ominous suggestion of good men or women slandered, as the 'divine Desdemona' he is speaking of will soon be. An atmosphere of pervasive suspiciousness was one that a man like Iago, whose tendencies it had fostered, would know how to profit by. In the Comedies every married man was supposed, not altogether in jest, to wear a pair of horns; now the joke takes on a grimmer flavour. To Othello, the outsider, 'A horned man's a monster and a beast' (IV.i.62). Iago must believe a good deal of what he says when he tells Othello that the highest standard of conduct known to Venetian women 'Is not to leave't undone, but keep't unknown' (III.iii.202–4), and that 'millions now alive' are cheated by their wives; even though, thinking aloud as he often does, he reflects that 'many worthy and chaste dames' are maligned, and their husbands, 'credulous fools' like Othello, are deceived another way (IV.i.46 ff.).

Some of Iago's information on such topics may have come from his own wife Emilia, who becomes Desdemona's attendant and is devoted to her. Her mistress is naïvely shocked by her bantering talk of how willing she and other wives would be to cuckold their husbands, for a big enough reward – which she adds (with a laugh) might benefit their men as well as themselves (IV.iii.63 ff.). Behind this lay the habits of a society where husbands, even of the highest station, often did prosper by tactful winking at their wives' peccadilloes. Emilia goes on in a more serious key, rising as she talks from prose into verse, and into an outburst against husbands that may be called one of the revolutionary declarations of English literature. She is one of Shakespeare's heterogeneous feminists, very open-eyed about men and how they tyrannize over women. We are hearing an assertion of women's equality, a parallel to Shylock's language about the Jew's right to be treated as a human being. It is men's fault if their wives play them false; they neglect them, chain them up, beat them, give way to 'peevish jealousies'. They must learn that 'Their wives have sense like them', the same 'Desires for sport, and frailty', and if ill used will know how to retaliate in kind. Many a married man in Shakespeare's audience must have felt and looked uneasy.

Nearly all the action or movement of the play is set going or kept going by Iago. Critics have been taking more interest in this strange being, a hardened sinner yet with some of the same title to our admiration as Richard III. Neither Coleridge's 'motiveless malignity' nor a later writer's 'spirit of evil, pure and undivided' (Speaight 88) can be adequate for him. If Othello is a poet, Iago is a vigorous though warped thinker, with a pungent, incisive mode of speech whether in verse or prose. He has earned the respect, though he is incapable of valuing it, of Othello and Cassio, and, according to himself (I.i.8–10), of several influential dignitaries in Venice. He speaks of his 'trade of war' (I.ii.1 ff.): it is not for him a glorious vocation, as it is for Othello. But his talent and energy must have made him an efficient officer, one who might have risen high. Instead he trips himself up, through over-haste and by giving way to gnawing hatreds which he tries to hide under his pose as a sternly objective calculator.

He is a denizen of a moral no-man's-land between two epochs. Values of an older time have been fading, new ones are still embryonic; to a malcontent who can never feel that he is receiving his due, anything like altruism is folly. He has a grievance against all his fellow-men, and feels justified in any reprisals he can take against them. He is the most highly evolved specimen of a genus not rare in Shakespeare, men like Macbeth's murderer itching to 'spite the world' which has treated him ill (III.i.110).

Some traumatic experience in the life of this young soldier may have curdled his nature and left him brooding on his grievances. He is a man of education as well as ability, middle class by his profession. Unscrupulous, cut-throat competition has become his governing instinct.

He possesses in short the vices of an acquisitive class, without any of its better qualities except intelligence and determination, unless we count his strong streak of the puritanical. In him, a man exiled from human kindness, it has taken a morbidly twisted form. When he talks of women and sex, as he is fond of doing, he uses pulpit phrases quite spontaneously. He pretends to know that Desdemona has been unfaithful, but he is sincerely convinced that she *will* be unfaithful before long. In Iago's philosophy our own bodies and their cravings are the unweeded garden of Shakespeare's favourite image, to which reason and will must be the gardeners. Like Claudius he talks of wickedness knowing how to cloak itself, but he talks as if revelling in his own expertness. Yet his pious turns of phrase do not always sound merely flippant, though they do not point towards heaven. He hates Othello as he does 'hell-pains'. No mischief can be too hard for his wits, aided by 'all the tribe of hell' (I.i.153, I.iii.344).

Iago is an intellectual, if a warped one, proud of his unclouded vision of everything human. He takes life seriously, and has a turn for preaching. Good and bad are to him no more than matters of opinion; he can sound like the Ranters and Antinomians of the Commonwealth, free by divine grace to indulge in anything they liked. On the other hand he has learned to keep a wary watch on himself, as well as on others. He is scornful of drunkards, as well as philanderers. Self-mastery elevates him above his mindless fellows, ruled by 'carnal stings' and 'unbitted lusts'. If we are not on our guard, 'the blood and baseness of our natures' will drag us to 'most preposterous conclusions' (I.iii.319 ff.). This is orthodox Christian language about human depravity, a Christian dogma. For him, we may guess, every night spent with a woman is a kind of black sacrament. He is very close again to Puritan rigour when he declares that we must learn self-control so that our lives may be 'manured with industry' instead of 'sterile with idleness' (I.iii.317–18). Iago stands in the tragic succession of alienated man beginning with Hamlet and culminating in the imprecations of Lear and Timon on mankind and all its vileness.

There has been endless debate over Iago's 'motives'. Coleridge's 'motive-hunting' may be the best summary, Bradley held, adding that Iago is 'moved by forces which he does not understand' (*Tragedy* 226). We can understand them as products of historical change and social tension, working on the sick places of one personality; even if all our actions are ultimately in-explicable, governed by accumulation of forgotten experiences and buried thoughts. As Bradley also said, Iago gives us a confusing medley of reasons for what he is doing (*Tragedy* 222 ff.). An estranged malcontent, a chronic grumbler, will keep thinking of grievances, some more real than others. But Saintsbury too was right in saying that any of those alleged by Iago may be real, and that his complaint of being passed over for promotion in favour of Cassio *must* be real (202).

He dwells on it no doubt in order to impress Roderigo with his zeal in the cause of helping him to seduce Desdemona, but Shakespeare would not devote thirty lines of an opening scene to what could be said adequately for this purpose in three lines, if it were not a matter of weight. Iago had counted on promotion 'by old gradation', or length of service, and instead it has been decided, he maintains, by private influence: Othello has bestowed the lieutenancy on his personal friend, Cassio. Iago's discontent was shared by unnumbered officers and other professional men in England. When Othello turns against Desdemona, Emilia is quick to suspect that 'Some cogging, cozening slave, to get some office', has been slandering her (IV.ii.129 ff.).

Lunacharsky thought of Iago as a gambler, unable by temperament to collect his winnings and leave the table in time (38, cf. Evans 131). He cannot bring himself to stop, and has to go on at all hazards until he can feel he has revenged himself on Othello, not only for appointing Cassio, but because he more than half believes that both Othello and Cassio have been making free with his wife. We know that his jealousy is genuine, because Emilia complains of it, and has evidently been plagued by it. All husbands, she says, are liable to such suspicions, even without any cause: they are 'jealous for they are jealous' (III.iv.159 ff.). She asserts too that some rascal must have sown suspicions of her and Othello in Iago's mind (IV.ii.145–7).

It would not be a hard task, considering his low estimate of all women. Early on he is given an opportunity to expound it; in a light tone, for Desdemona listens tolerantly, but he has nothing to gain by such talk, and is simply giving vent to his feelings. He takes an anti-romantic view of women, with a rancour sharpened by his relations with Emilia; he is provoked by her long tongue, she by his domineering ways. They have lived a camp life together; the same setting that must help to make Othello so ready to distrust Cassio, who, though always respectful to his commander's high-born lady, has a loose woman at his beck and call. (Alcibiades in *Timon* has two.) Emilia must be a young woman, and may well be an attractive one, and her husband looks on Cassio as a man 'framed to make women false' (I.iii.380). Further to inflame him, 'it is being thought abroad', not by himself alone, that he is a cuckold (I.iii.393).

Smarting under this, he is all the more resentful of being cuckolded by a coloured man, an African. The idea torments him like 'a poisonous mineral' in his body (II.i.306); he seems to hug it with masochistic tenacity. Pretending to help Roderigo to win Desdemona, he secretly longs to get her for himself: 'not out of absolute lust', he hastens to assure himself and us, in one of his most revealing soliloquies, but partly to get his own back on Othello (II.i.300 ff.); a much lesser breach of the prudent self-discipline that with him takes the place of morality. 'Iago hates Othello because he is a Moor', it has been said (Matthews 131): still more, we may surmise, because he resents being under the orders of a Moor. He has been called 'a masterly social portrait' of the poor white, the resentful inferior (Long 56). He has risen in the world, it is true, but emotional disturbances in early life are not easily overcome. It is a necessity with him to have a secret life of his own, where he talks to himself and revels in his own cleverness, his superiority to all the dullards round him, and cannot keep from weaving schemes in order to assure himself of it.

Not content with talking cleverly to himself, Iago cannot always check his desire to impress others. Like Hamlet he comes to grief through excess of a theoretical bent (Muir and O'Loughlin 175). It cannot profit him to lecture Roderigo on the foolishness of love, when his hold on the poor dupe depends on his remaining desperately in love. He is indiscreetly frank in telling Cassio that 'Reputation is an idle and most false imposition' (II.iii.268–9), like Falstaff deriding honour. He is a thinker who must prove his theories in action. 'I'll set down the pegs that make this music', he says of Othello's and Desdemona's love (II.i.192), which in his scheme of things has no right to exist. He must give his talents full range – 'To plume up my will' (I.iii.375). His designs, deep-laid or hastily improvised, do not always look as impressive as he thinks them; and the further he goes, the more entangled his web-spinning, until he is no longer free to draw back. By inducing Othello to strangle Desdemona instead of quietly poisoning her, he ensures an official investigation and the downfall of Othello, now his useful patron – and very likely his own fall.

Roderigo is in most ways a familiar Elizabethan wastrel, a young man about town with all the makings of a 'gull', or dupe, and with notions of morality that bear out Iago's estimate of Venetian manners. Iago has a true bourgeois sense of the value of time, and would 'profane' his talents if he threw it away on such a 'snipe', except for 'sport and profit' (I.iii.366–8). Money, he impresses on his love-lorn friend, is the key to success. Eight times in the speech where he advises him on tactics he reiterates the necessity of having money in his purse (I.iii.339 ff.). We are left in no doubt that Venice is a very mercenary place, where the almighty ducat reigns. Iago takes over the cash and professes to be buying jewels to bribe Desdemona with on Roderigo's behalf. Romeo tried to win his Rosalind with 'saint-seducing gold', and Claudius won Gertrude with 'traitorous' gifts. At last Roderigo will want to know what has become of all his resources, and threaten to give the game away, and Iago will see that it is time for him to be got rid of.

But there is a different side to Roderigo; he is a study of love from a special angle, as abnormal in its way as Iago's. A would-be seducer of a married woman is a great rarity with Shakespeare; so is a man madly infatuated with a woman not interested in him, for in his plays amorous passion is nearly always mutual. Iago pays an unexpected tribute to the power of love (it may really be more of an 'aside' to us from Shakespeare) when he tells Roderigo that even 'base men being in love have then a nobility in their natures', lifting them above their ordinary plane (II.i.217–18). Roderigo has no interest in Desdemona as a human being, he is simply infatuated with a beautiful woman; but for this he will talk of drowning himself, and follow her to Cyprus in a storm, at the risk of a watery grave – disguised presumably in the false beard recommended by Iago (I.iii.346) –, and bankrupt himself, and do his best to commit murder, with the consoling thought that "Tis but a man gone' (V.i.10). No common philanderer would do all this. But it is another symptom of the crisis into which love and sex are drifting.

We have two statements from Iago about Cassio as a soldier: that he has learned much 'bookish theoric', but has never 'set a squadron in the field' (I.i.22 ff.), and that he is 'a soldier fit to stand by Caesar' (II.iii.105). The first is the likelier to be true, if we allow for Iago's prejudice against a learned 'arithmetician' as compared with a seasoned fighting-man like himself. Cassio, we may conclude, is a better-educated officer, of a new breed. His gentlemanly manners, which Iago ridicules but probably envies, likewise mark him as coming of a better family. There is a gulf of class between them as well as rank, though Cassio never presumes on either. He is besides a foreigner, a Florentine.

'Good Michael', as Othello addresses him (Iago has only a single name), has earned his commander's friendship, and Desdemona's, by accompanying him on his 'wooing' visits to her. We need not think that he was performing this service in the hope of being made Othello's lieutenant; but the two things did happen close together. Iago must again be expressing his rancour at Cassio's more well-bred manners when he speaks of 'a daily beauty in his life', by contrast with which he himself appears 'ugly' (V.i.19–20): he is clearly thinking of manners, not morals. Cassio is a serious-minded officer, and repents bitterly of the drunken scuffle that Iago lures him into. 'To be a sensible man . . . and presently a beast!' He has lost, with his reputation, 'the immortal part' of himself (II.iii.242 ff.). But he has no qualms about toying with the courtesan Bianca, and feels only amusement when she falls in love with him and puts on jealous airs. He is on his way back from supper with her when he is set on by Roderigo. 'This is the fruit of whoring', comments Iago primly, and not ungenuinely (V.i.116). His wife does not tax him with any such strayings, as he does her.

Desdemona begs to be allowed to accompany her husband to the wars;

like the two Portias and other good wives, she wants to have a full share in her partner's life (I.iii.244 ff.). Yet they remain strangers, in a way that outward disparities only emphasize. We cannot think of them having a frank discussion and dispelling their misunderstandings. She can find no way to the enraged Othello's mind, as she did to his heart. When trouble comes she is too humbly submissive, while he is too ready to play the master. 'We can call these delicate creatures ours . . . ' (II.iii.271). Iago is only half right when he assures Roderigo that their marriage cannot last because it is one between 'an erring [wandering] barbarian and a supersubtle Venetian' (I.iii.343); she is too simple rather than too subtle. In the natural course of things their relations must have cooled; he would age and die, she would remarry. Instead, thanks to the extraneous factor of Iago, there was to be catastrophe.

He and Othello were both fated to be sufferers from jealousy, ready to distrust those closest to them. Iago has been in 'sweet England' (II.iii.75), and perhaps listened to preachers there. He believes he has seen Desdemona, greeted by Cassio, 'paddle with the palm of his hand' (II.i.240–41), as Hamlet thought of his uncle 'paddling' in his mother's flesh. Under his prompting Othello can soon feel 'a young and sweating devil' in his wife's soft hand. (III.iv.308). As McElroy sees, it is his own disease of jealousy that enables Iago to infect Othello with its germs (105; cf. Hawkes 109–10). Othello thinks him, as Caesar thought Cassius, a man versed in the windings of civilized life, with 'a learned spirit of human dealing' (III.iii.261–2), which he himself, an outsider, lacks.

Bad men and women in the tragedies pave their downward road with crimes; good ones, beginning with Brutus, do so with their illusions and errors of judgment. Desdemona, it must be admitted, gives Iago some ground for his conviction of Othello being 'so enfetter'd to her love' (II.iii.312) that she can get him to do anything, even what he ought not to do. Cassio in his drunken folly has committed a grave offence against both civil and military law; he has wounded Montano, Othello's predecessor in the governorship, and Othello has very properly cashiered him. Desdemona is already pleading for his reinstatement, in the name of private friendship, before he comes to beg her advocacy, and Othello is promising to reinstate him when things have quietened down (III.iii.75–6). He ought not to have done this; he had pledged his word to the government, when asking leave to take Desdemona with him, that he would never allow love to distract him from his duty. She ought not to have said to Cassio, in the pride of her influence with the general and in the friendly generosity of her heart, 'I give thee warrant of thy place' (III.iii.20).

Desdemona and Othello are a union of opposites; so are Othello and Venice. To him Desdemona *is* Venice, the idealized city whose service has come to be his anchor. But there is an ambivalence in such attachment, which undermines it. Venice is a magnificent exterior which may cover inward corruption. He has admired Desdemona as a lady 'of so gentle a condition', of so aristocratic a breeding. 'Ay, too gentle', Iago replies (IV.i.181–3): high breeding may not mean high morals. The extreme celerity with which Othello's trust in her evaporates is proof of how little confidence he has at bottom been able to feel in their love. Iago's slander is persuasive because to Othello it must sound plausible, even, to his inmost self, not unexpected. 'Why did I marry?' he exclaims almost as soon as he understands what honest Iago is saying. His counsellor is only saying aloud what has been whispering in the depth of his consciousness. George Eliot describes a similar process in chapter 20 of *Middlemarch*: the stab of 'hearing in hard distinct syllables', from a bystander, the 'confused murmurs' we have tried to suppress as sickly. Harry Levin (*Revolution* 161) finds a lack of tragic inevitability in Othello's ruin; but with his nature and his situation, it is as inevitable as any hero's.

Othello thinks he is learning about his wife, what Brabantio really did have to learn about his daughter, that outward behaviour may be no gauge of inner feeling. He is deceived by what Iago tells him, but not as to the bitter truth lurking in his mind, that sooner or later he will lose Desdemona's love, even if not her faithfulness. He is being put in a humiliating position akin to that of a London burgher whose wife is admired by young gallants from court circles. His marriage had marvellously set the seal on his career; its blighting makes it impossible for him to think of continuing in it. 'Othello's occupation's gone' (III.iii.357). Brabantio had accused him of witchcraft; he now has some kindred feeling about Desdemona, as a witch who should not be suffered to live. He kneels to take a 'sacred vow' to punish her, and honest Iago follows suit (III.iii.460–62). About to kill her, Othello three times invokes the 'cause' of his deed. In his mind, it would seem, she has not only betrayed him, but has broken the moral code on which society is founded: it is his duty to society as well as to himself to kill her – much as it was Hamlet's duty to kill his uncle. Nowhere more clearly than now, we feel the distance that separates Shakespearian from simply 'domestic' tragedy.

Othello lives to learn his error; Lodovico speaks for all when he expresses more pity than anger for a man so 'rash and most unfortunate' (V.ii.280). There is time for a brief reconciliation between him and Cassio, whom he has tried to have assassinated. For a moment Othello is lost in helpless bewilderment; it is the finding of a sword that restores his manhood, and allows him to quit the world with Roman dignity. His final boast of having killed a Turk, on Turkish soil, for an insult to Venice reveals the same extreme nature that led him to love and then kill his wife.

Iago's last act is to kill his own wife, an act of vindictive haste by which the man of cool reason gives himself away. His last words are a dour acceptance of defeat. All his schemings and philosophizings have come to nothing, except that he has involved Othello in his own ruin. We leave him to crown what must have been an irksome existence with a painfully protracted death. It fits his nihilistic outlook that in the end this man of many words, alone among the prominent figures of Shakespearian tragedy, has nothing to say, no recourse but to shut himself up, like an Indian at the stake, in a stoic silence which will soon turn into the silence of the grave. To the rest he is a 'damned' soul, a monster or devil, 'More fell than anguish, hunger, or the sea' (V.ii.362).

More charitably he may be thought of as a scapegoat, laden with the sins of many. Granville-Barker found this drama repulsive, because 'a tragedy without meaning' (cited in Gardner, 349). But it is a wise reminder that 'In tragedy the private, the public and the universal are one' (Heilman, *Lear* 31). The other tragedies move towards crisis and collapse in national life, opening the way to wholesome change. Here it seems otherwise: the Venetian State is unshaken. Morally, however, it has been shown to suffer from a creeping malady of which no end can be foreseen. Iago, destroying others and finally himself, is its symptom, or a harbinger of the evils of an age of ruthless egotism now taking shape and destined to stretch far into Europe's future. Venice has been able to enlist in its service a great captain from far away, but unable to keep him, because of the corrosive poisons of its own life. And this man, 'the nature whom passion could not shake' (IV.ii.276–7), has been the death of a woman in whom the charm and virtue of Venice seemed embodied. Thunderstruck by what he has done, Othello wonders why 'a huge eclipse' has not blotted everything out (V.ii.99–101). At the back of Shakespeare's mind may be stirring a memory of the Crucifixion. Venice has undergone at any rate a profound, perhaps a purgative and life-renewing, shock.

4

King Lear (1605–06)

Into Othello's mind, as death drew near, came the thought of a 'huge eclipse'; early in *King Lear* Gloucester talks of the 'late eclipses' which had in fact darkened England in 1605. There are other likenesses between the two plays, in spite of the vast interval of time and space between their happenings. Iago and Edmund are fellow-rationalists who overreach themselves. Desdemona and Cordelia are two daughters who banish their fathers from their lives. Even in the remoteness of ancient Britain, Old and New confront each other, in some of their endlessly varied masks, which stand out even more sharply here than in Venice or Denmark. A salient contrast is between older and newer attitudes to age. 'You yourselves are old', cries Lear, appealing to the heavens. Goneril's favourite term for age is 'dotage' (II.iv.187; Heilman, *Lear* 141).

In the opening scene, where the old autocrat sets his daughters to vie with one another in fulsome compliments to him, we may guess at some scar left on the poet's mind from having to compete with others for a capricious patron's bounty. It may be permissible also to imagine him, now middle-aged and prosperous, feeling qualms of self-reproach at joining the ranks of the comfortably off, amid multitudes of famishing men, women and children. Such sensations might lead him, for self-relief and to make the best amends in a writer's power, to give expression through his art to what the poor could not or were not allowed to express for themselves. It would be a grand undertaking to teach a mad king to rebuke all supposedly sane kings and grandees for their neglect of the hungry.

Among these was King James, before whom the play was performed in December 1605, even if his resemblance to King Lear in other respects was less remarkable than one critic has held (Mangan 103–4). His elder son Henry was now, as heir apparent, duke of Cornwall; the younger, Charles, still a boy, had until that year borne the Scottish royal title of duke of Albany – once a region of Scotland, whose name now vaguely covered all Scotland. Thus the two magnates of Shakespeare's play represent (very indistinct though its geography is) the two extremities of Lear's kingdom of

Britain, whose two realms were now governed by James. An earlier duke of Albany had trodden the stage in *Gorboduc*, the first Elizabethan blank-verse tragedy, by Thomas Sackville and Thomas Norton. That ambitious lord, the 'foe of all our liberties' (lines 1621, 1637), took advantage of a civil war in Britain between two brothers, whose father had rashly partitioned the country between them. If James knew of *Gorboduc* he must have been pleased now to see an Albany so much improved.

Shakespeare's play was probably written late in 1605, between *Othello* and *Macbeth*. In print it was twice-born, in a Quarto edition published in 1608, and in the First Folio. These two texts differ appreciably, and there are complex problems about the relation between them. Most editors have dovetailed what they approve of from the two, whereas in reality there may never have been a single definitive text (Warren 176–7; cf. Jackson 177). Many have conjectured that Shakespeare made a revision of his play. If so it may have been for the purpose of removing things that might sound tactless in a court performance. Shakespeare, or his Edmund, had derided astrology; James's queen was a firm believer in it, as well as a half-believer in Catholicism, and was consulting astrologers in 1604.

It is one token of the stresses inseparable from the patriarchal family that folk-tales about someone like Lear have been ubiquitous across Europe. Turgenev emulated them in his *King Lear of the Steppes*. In England there was for long a practice of parents at a certain age handing over their farm or other property to their son or sons, but retaining a legal right to living quarters and provisions. For his plot Shakespeare had several sources to draw on, among them a hobbling play acted in the 1590s and printed in 1605, just in time for him to make use of it. In outline the story, though he made important alterations, would be familiar to a good part of his audience. As often, he took up and developed the parts of it that interested him, and left the rest more or less as it was. He was infusing a new consciousness bred by his own age into a time-honoured saga; to modern readers the distinct planes on which events unfold may appear discordant. Hoeniger speaks of a 'curious interplay of realistic and unrealistic, at times even fantastic, episodes' (13). There is almost a kind of surrealism at work, as Shakespeare blends drama with inspired social commentary, or descends from poetic flights to the cold earth. Physical sensation and experience have a prominent place: food, hunger, cold, fatigue, pain. Prose opens the play, and alternates with verse, 903 lines of one to 2395 of the latter (Smeaton 413).

This greatest poem of our greatest writer is set in a land of poverty, oppression, misrule, the grinding defects of a whole social machine. Disintegration has gone very far now; through the cracked walls we see not simply contending individuals or factions but the crushed mass of humanity, by whose enslavement these walls were reared. It is because the subject is now so vast that the drama cannot be neatly realistic. In ordinary life human beings often find it impossible to make sense of other people's behaviour, or even their own; in *King Lear* this opacity is thickened. Outside and all round the speck of earth, on which we see a group of castaways, a demented rush of events is taking place, events with little meaning except some mysterious affinity with the inner turmoil of mortal souls.

It was Lamb's feeling that the old king's physical presence on the scene wanes as time goes on, because the drama is at bottom not centred on any individual, but on the social order and the destinies of mankind. Failure to comprehend this led Wilson Knight to judge the whole tragedy 'purpose-less, unreasonable' (*Wheel* 188–9). It is Shakespeare's most 'Gothic' tragedy, because the closest in feeling to the masses, the experiences of the poor, and some of their modes of thought and speech. They are not – not yet – in revolt; what is breaking in on the minds of at least a few among their masters is the fundamental wrongness of the social fabric, whose axioms or truisms are turning out to be lies.

We may be closer in touch here with Shakespeare's own deepest feelings than anywhere else. His Britain is all bleakness, grimness, barbarity, as of a boundless desert. There is scarcely a bush for miles round Gloucester's castle (II.iv.297–8). But in spite of this phantasmagoria the play, like any other great production of art, is rooted in the same corner of human history as its creator. It forms part, as Cohen points out, of a tradition of English popular radicalism continuing from medieval times (356). Such drama cannot be reduced to allegory, as it was very absurdly by the religious reader Creighton, who saw in it a portrayal of the English Reformation, with Lear as Conscience blended with superstition, Goneril as the papacy, Regan as the Anglican clergy. There must all the same be a significance beneath the surface, as inseparable from the story as mind from body. Bradley is conscious of an indistinctness in nearly all the characters, and refers to Sonnets where Shakespeare shows himself not unable to move at a symbolical or Platonizing altitude; though his comparison with the *Faerie Queen* is much less convincing (*Tragedy* 263–5; cf. Muir, *Sequence* 140).

From what we get to know of Lear, he may have been a good-hearted monarch, scarcely an intelligent or hard-working one; hunting was probably his chief avocation, as it is after he quits the throne (and as it was King James's after he quitted Scotland). He has been a warrior, and can look back on days when he and his good sword 'would have made them skip' (V.ii.277–8). Fantasies of horrific revenge come to him when he has fallen out with his daughters; one thing he has to learn is to renounce them, as the ghosts of Caesar and old Hamlet could not, but as Prospero does. In abdicating, at the age of eighty, he is not doing amiss, being obviously unfit to go on ruling. To tax him with dereliction of duty (Moretti 51) is unfair. By giving shares to each daughter he is partitioning the country, but no one objects to this: as we see again in *Cymbeline*, ancient Britain is not properly a nation. Principalities in the Germany of Shakespeare's time were frequently divided among heirs. Lear's purpose, he says, is to avert future strife, a worthy aim enough (Council 140), though unlikely, as we soon have reason for thinking, to be successful. The abdication has been decided on hastily, 'upon the gad' (I.ii.26–7); there has been no consultation with Lear's most reliable friends. He wants to enjoy life like a carefree landowner, but still live in royal state. We can believe Regan when she says that he has always 'slenderly known himself' (I.i.291; cf. Goldberg 16); the phrase recurs (I.iv.252), and it enshrines one of Shakespeare's chief teachings – that men must shake off false imaginings and face things as they are.

It has been noticed by some readers that the few who remain faithful to Lear seem to do him more harm than good. Cordelia, it may be added, sets the example. The Fool may have some unpleasant memories of an irascible master, and it is easy to surmise that his true attachment was to Cordelia, in whose absence he pines (I.iv.74–5). Kent is too blunt to be capable of tact. Shakespeare has to make these characters behave in ways that help to push Lear into madness, because no milder medicine can jolt him into a new consciousness. The Fool goes on taunting him in a manner that would be heartless if it were not needful for the play's unfolding (cf. Danby, *Nature* 104). When Lear's thoughts turn contritely to his youngest daughter, he breaks in with an idiot riddle about an oyster; it is after one of his sour witticisms that the old king exclaims 'O, let me not be mad!' (I.v.25 ff.; I.v.45–6).

Edgar's behaviour parallels the Fool's. It is his abrupt apparition as Mad Tom that topples Lear into insanity, and the more frantically he overacts his part, the further Lear's mind is whirled away into similar ravings. Edgar treats his father in much the same way. Guiding the blind old man towards Dover he mutters to himself 'I cannot daub it further . . . and yet I must'. He must, in order to rouse Gloucester from his despair by trifling with it (IV.vi.33–4, 51–3). 'I'm almost mad myself' were Gloucester's last words to his mad king (III.iv.166). He comes very close to lunacy when he is made to believe that he has fallen over the Dover cliff and been saved by a miracle. But it is a derangement like Lear's, detaching him from his old worldly self and floating him into a mood that no sane thinking could have brought about. He can only go on living by hugging the illusion that heaven has preserved him, in spite of 'men's impossibilities' (IV.vi.74–5).

Hamlet's father was sent to purgatory to have his sins 'burnt and purged away'. Lear and Gloucester have to undergo a more real purgation here on earth. The mirror that the fallen Richard II looked into takes a subtler form in the lessons that make all the world a mirror for Lear to see himself in. He has to learn that his present sufferings are related to his past conduct, his neglect to befriend those weaker than himself, as those stronger are now neglecting him. It is part of the retribution that his elder daughters share his own worse qualities. He may have been a kindly man, in indulgent moods, but he has been arrogant and arbitrary as well. Regan's consort the duke of Cornwall may be of 'fiery' temper (II.iv.88), but not more than the Lear who bursts out, at Goneril's first remonstrance, 'Degenerate bastard!' (I.iv.254). Later on his mode of speaking grows plainer and simpler (F.P. Wilson 115).

Restoration is beginning when in the storm he feels sorry for the Fool (III.ii.71–2), and before entering a wretched shelter prays, not for himself, but for the earth's 'Poor naked wretches', whom he has taken too little thought for (III.iv.28 ff.). It is, as Bradley said and many have felt, a sublime moment (*Tragedy* 287). A writer in *The Adventurer* on 15 December 1753 declared that the words of this speech, 'Take physic, pomp . . . ', deserved to be inscribed 'in characters of gold in the closet of every monarch upon earth'. Lear has been forced to realize, on this wild night, that he is only 'A poor, weak, and despised old man', not a god; a lesson forced on several of Shakespeare's rulers before him, but never before with this intensity. His mind is giving way, but a new vision is dawning on his former blindness. He recalls later how the tempest delivered him from the falsities instilled into his mind by flatterers; and it is a little after this that he begs Cordelia to 'forget and forgive' (IV.vii.83–4).

His paradox has been that while madness might give him relief from private troubles, it set him free to think about his past, and ponder what he has seen in bygone days, unnoticingly, of human life and *its* troubles. What to others is madness, to himself is sanity; his world is turned upside down. His sharpest insights come, like revelations, while he is still out of his mind, or his mind has been taken possession of by a collective consciousness. The lustful beadle whips the whore; wealth protects injustice – 'Robes and furred gowns hide all' (IV.vi.149 ff.). He wakens from his purgatory freed from the flashes of vindictive revengefulness that have haunted him (IV.vi.183–6). Even self-pity can make him say 'I should e'en die with pity to see another thus' (IV.vii.53–4); a measure of his transformation.

Shakespeare has been holding up his mirror to the royal absolutism that was on the march in his Europe, more sophisticated but no less irresponsible than Lear's rule has been. Monarchy itself, not a single old monarch, is under scrutiny, anachronistic yet eager to react savagely when defied. In all this is pictured the tormented process of historical change, the whirlpool at the conflux of two eras, and the impossibility of any smooth, easy progression from one to another. Lear's last act as king, a fitting close to his reign, has been to banish the loyal earl of Kent. The social hierarchy he has presided over has not been without some good characters, but these are now scattered, confused, slow to combine. Each goes his own groping way, obeying instincts of fidelity, however unwise. Kent and Gloucester are men of the old school of nobility, one with more of its energy, now unavailing, the other of its weaknesses. In terms of the amount of speaking allotted to him, Kent comes third in the play (Bentley 54). Honest conservative as he is, fervently devoted to the king he has served, he has no awareness of anything having been amiss under Lear's rule, and no notion of any need for change. All he wants is to go on living in the past, or bring the dead past back to life.

Unshakeable loyalty makes Kent disguise himself and take a lowly post in Lear's service, where zeal does not make him very helpful. He has a great deal to say about cunning servants who fawn on and corrupt their employers, and a rooted dislike of Goneril's steward or factotum, Oswald. This man may be the self-seeking plebeian that Kent calls him, but the earl is giving way to the arrogance of his class when he abuses him as a 'lily-liver'd, action-taking whoreson' (II.ii.14 ff.) – a cowardly fellow who would rather protect himself by law than by the sword. Oswald is destined in fact to die in a fight with Edgar. At Gloucester's castle Kent cannot help venting his discontents on this man, and then brazenly insults Regan and her duke of Cornwall, and is, it must be said, lucky to be punished only by being put in the stocks. On Lear's arrival he hastens to denounce them (II.iv.4 ff.), as if on purpose to precipitate a quarrel; and it is the sight of his servant in the stocks that destroys Lear's attempt at self-control (II.iv.101 ff.; cf. Boas, *Shakspere* 447). In Cordelia's camp at Dover he tells her mysteriously he must still hide his identity, in order to achieve his aim. This is to restore Lear to the throne of what he assures him is his 'own kingdom' (IV.vii.8 ff., 76). What good this could do either to Lear or to Britain, Kent cannot have asked himself.

Schücking finds fault with the 'breakneck pace' of the story at some points: Gloucester's giving instant credence to the lurid tale told him by a son who has been a stranger for nine years, against his legitimate son and heir, seems to him unbelievable (191). So it would be, in any quiet times; but, somewhat as with Othello's immediate succumbing to Iago, we are watching an insecure individual in an unhealthy society. Gloucester's soliloquy, a short while before, about signs and portents heralding, not now the death of a great man, but a rupture of all human ties (I.i.206 ff.), fixes our attention on an atmosphere of mistrust and estrangement (cf. Dollimore 197). Not only monarchy, but the social framework itself is in decay, and any accusations against anyone can be believed.

Gloucester is the reverse of the rugged Kent, but likewise with his portion of the better and worse traits of their generation. He is an amiable, foolish, credulous old fellow, with frivolous notions of morality. Lear is the king he has lived his life under, and he will risk life and fortune to save him. Yet he can clamour for his son Edgar's arrest and execution (II.i.56 ff.), when his own turn is coming to be accused of treason and 'tied to th' stake' (III.vii.53). Blindness opens his moral eyes, as the storm opens Lear's.

Giving his purse to the disguised Edgar, who is to guide him to Dover, he reflects that the rich should all share with the poor, 'and each man have enough' (IV.i.63 ff.).

'Edgar is the most complex of all Shakespearean parts' (Isaacs 104–5). It is central, together with Lear's madness, to all that is non-naturalistic in the story as Shakespeare tells it. In a historical light he can be seen as one of those well-meaning members of every decaying class who, as Nemesis draws near, feel the sins of their fathers visited on their heads. He echoes and strengthens Lear's probing of the social conscience. He is duped as easily as his father by Edmund, who looks down on him as 'noble', un-suspicious, full of the 'foolish honesty' (I.ii.182 ff.) derided by Iago; a frequent heirloom of aristocracy, trustful because deeming itself secure. A false sense of security is 'mortals' chiefest enemy', we are told in *Macbeth* (III.v.32–3). Brutus, Hamlet, Othello, Timon, are all of this race, too slow to put themselves on guard. Edgar's taking the disguise of 'Mad Tom', a half-naked beggar (*King Lear* is a play where men disguise themselves, as women did in the Comedies) may be sensible enough, with the country-side full of pursuers. But it may have a symbolic as well as practical meaning. Gloucester's heir is not likely to have been brought up on very straitlaced lines. He is Lear's godson, and is said to have consorted with the old king's 'riotous knights': Regan seems genuinely to think this a sufficient cause of his supposed plot against his father (II.i.94–5). We may at least feel that he too has a conscience now stirring, something to reproach himself for in the life he has hitherto lived. He too has a purgatory to undergo.

He invents a history of himself as a former debauched servitor, a hanger-on of corrupt nobility, brought down to misery by his own vicious self-indulgence (III.iv.84 ff.). No doubt this is far too highly seasoned, like Hamlet's confession to Ophelia, and Malcolm's to Macduff; but the broader significance of all three self-accusations is a general confession on behalf of a selfish, sinful ruling class and its creatures. Mad Tom's crazy moralizings are close to Lear's; they are saturated with the same horror of sex, and hold the same piercing realization of what poverty means to the poor – to the vagrant 'whipped from tithing to tithing, and stocked, punished and imprisoned' (III.iv.133–4). It is this spectacle of humanity stripped of all social 'lendings' that fascinates Lear. 'Thou art the thing itself' (III.iv.106).

Edgar passes from one character to another. He turns into 'a most poor man', who has learned pity 'by the art of known and feeling sorrows' (IV.vi.219–20), just as Lear and Gloucester are learning. Confronting the self-important Oswald, he mimics the dialect of an uncouth peasant. He is impelled, it would seem, to think himself into the skins of as many as he can of the suffering, heavy-laden with the burden of those above them. Why he goes on with his mystification when his father has realized him to be innocent, and has surely undergone enough, has always been a question.

Cavell imputes a streak of cruelty to Edgar (*Disowning Knowledge*, 54–5). But we should recall rather the indistinctness, or morality-play aspect, of many of these characters, with faces of men walking in a dream. Hamlet was overwhelmed by the magnitude of social evil: now it has swelled and broken its bounds still further, until individuals are helplessly adrift in it.

Sole member of his trade in the tragedies, the Fool seems to belong naturally to one where the clock – or one of the clocks – is turned back to antediluvian beginnings. He has been looked at through many sentimental spectacles, whereas to Goneril he seemed 'more knave than fool'; and his master addresses him, though sympathetically, as 'Poor fool and knave' (I.iv.316; II.ii.68). If he stays by Lear when others desert, it may not be unfair to observe that there is not much else he can do. Lear's manner with him suggests a more or less juvenile person, which need not imply that he is a young innocent. He is not unfamiliar with the whip that Lear more than once threatens (I.iv.111, 181 ff.). One of his rhyming jingles is a warning that these are times calling for caution, distrust, secrecy, thrift (I.iv.119 ff.) – everything that Lear has lacked. He is not a wit, a Touchstone, affecting courtier-like manners. His humour is part of the play's descent into lower social levels; it clothes a rough common sense. His talk, 'abrupt and bewildered' (Danby, *Nature* 103), sounds like that of a rustic, with mouth full of folk-sayings and ballad-snatches, a Sancho Panza protestingly trailing after his lord. Lear's choice of such a homespun court-companion prepares us to see him, in adversity, able to come so close to the feelings of his poorer subjects.

From this voice of the people we hear things that swell the chorus of indignation at social evils and upper-class vice and folly. He ought to have a 'monopoly' of folly, he complains, by virtue of his office, but 'lords and great men', and ladies too, keep infringing it (I.iv.153 ff.). Granting of monopoly patents to court favourites was a recurrent grievance of the public in Shakespeare's time. Fool and king are one and the same, he makes us see (Willeford 217). A madman, he says, is 'a yeoman that hath a gentleman to his son', a young sprig wanting to rise above his class (III.vi.12–14). His 'prophecy' at the end of Act III Scene ii, with its grotesque conclusion, is a jumble of bitter allusions to familiar targets: prosing priests, usury, prostitution. Pollard doubted its authenticity (14), but it is really the same prophecy that Shakespeare is making all through the play; 'the realm of Albion' is sinking into 'great confusion'. When there is no more need of the Fool's vinegar, he disappears, leaving in his place the image of a suffering people. He and his master are returning to nothingness. Lear seems obsessed with the thought of *nothing*. 'Nothing will come of nothing', he angrily warns Cordelia in the first scene; he answers the Fool's riddle with 'nothing can be made out of nothing' (I.iv.131–4).

It must be as patron saint of family reconciliation that Cordelia has won such nearly unanimous applause. But it is reconciliation with her father alone; she has made no attempt to come to an understanding with her sisters on his behalf. According to Danby, 'To understand Cordelia is to understand the whole play' (*Nature* 114), a dictum that could scarcely be more misleading. Siegel looks up to her as a Shakespearian Christ-figure (34). M.D.H. Parker commends Bethell for having been the first to notice how many phrases link her with Christ, and considers her, despite some failings, 'the most nearly perfect woman' in all literature (141–2). Bransom on the other hand is not the first to observe that Shakespeare does not endow her with much remarkable language (29), and R.M. Frye (234) points out that she is only given about 100 lines, out of a total of close to 3300, and has an active part in only four scenes. To Bayley she seems out of place, 'not made for tragedy' (38). There must be reason to guess that she did not fully capture Shakespeare's imagination; and the cause of this may be that she is a well-meaning woman caught between two eras, belonging in part to them both, and suffering from this, dramatically, more than her sisters do. We first see her as partaking, with the 'problem play' heroines, of a certain angularity, a virtuousness which can only preserve its purity, in a tainted soil, at the expense of some more ingratiating qualities. She is very much a puritan, almost a Quaker in her adherence to absolute truthfulness and refusal to compromise, when called upon to emulate her sisters – who have, we guess, memorized their lines in advance – by assuring her father of her love and devotion.

This has seemed to some readers over-rigid, a kind of self-love (e.g. Sewell 62–3). After all, for an aged parent to ask his children for warmer expressions of regard than they really feel is not unlike the need of a beggar, which Lear pleads later on, for some small luxury to sweeten his existence (II.iv.260 ff.). But Lear is a ruler as well as a father, even if about to abdicate; and he is continuing to set a pernicious example by publicly demanding another dose of the poison of flattery. Someone has to make a declaration against this court fraud, which, as Lear comes to realize, has done him and all monarchs so much harm, by inspiring a sense of omnipotence and encouraging irresponsibility. Cordelia refuses to join in the dishonest game; again we see a woman making something like a revolutionary stand, with an inevitably high price to be paid by her and by Britain.

We next see Cordelia, now queen of France, leading a French army of invasion into her native land (her royal consort tactfully absenting himself). She is enmeshed now in an older code, on a par with that of the fighting dynasts in the Wars of the Roses – or of Hamlet's father. She is planning a counter-revolution, in league with conservative adherents in Britain; servants of both Albany and Cornwall are spies in French pay (III.i.22–5). Schemes are afoot early, as we seem to learn when Kent sits in the stocks reading a secret letter by moonlight (II.ii.160 ff.). Edmund purloins and gives to Cornwall a missive received by his father, revealing his complicity (III.v.11 ff.). Cornwall and Regan have therefore good ground for arresting Gloucester as a traitor. Their prisoner had wanted his son Edgar killed out of hand; Cornwall has scruples about taking his life without a trial, though he sees no harm in inflicting a worse penalty on him.

Cordelia is bringing a foreign army to uphold her dear father's 'right' (IV.iv.27–8); in other words to restore Lear to the throne. But he has no right to a throne he has given away. His safety is assured when he is brought into the French camp at Dover, and he could have been taken to complete security in France. Cordelia is careful to disclaim any motive of 'ambition'; but she has found her father 'mad as the vexed sea' (IV.iv.2): if he is put on the throne she and her foreign husband will be the real power. All this Shakespeare has to pass over; his fable and its inner meaning, however, are slipping far apart. In the feudal or aristocratic view, only exalted individuals count; the essence of tragedy is its concern with humanity, as Shakespeare saw most clearly of all in this play. Danby falls into the older conception when he declares that 'Cordelia's invasion of Britain is simply right' (*Nature* 133). Goldberg is more faithful to the spirit of the play as a whole when he blames her for ignoring the horrors she is letting loose (142). It can be no more than a charitable guess if we suppose her conscience to be pricking her for her obduracy in the first scene, and what it has led to; but what she is doing now is worse.

Shakespeare could not expect his audience to welcome a French victory, any more than in *King John* when a French army had to be brought into England, with however good a pretext. The French threat helps Lear's opponents to close their ranks, at Goneril's call for postponement of 'domestic and particular broils' (V.i.29–31). Shakespeare drops hints, but does not make much use of them, that we should view Cordelia as a liberator, like Malcolm with his English army in Scotland. It is only with reluctance that the worthy Albany takes the field against the invaders. Some others, alienated by the way the country has been governed, may be joining them. Edmund fears that the soldiers, who are conscripts, may be won over by sympathy with the old king (V.i.22 ff., V.iii.46 ff.), which implies that Lear personally had not been unpopular. Cordelia, too well intentioned, is the cause of his death, as earlier of his being left at the mercy of her sisters. She shares his fate, becoming with him a part of tragedy's necessary offering. 'Upon such sacrifices, my Cordelia,/The gods themselves throw incense', are the last words of his that she hears (V.iii.20–21). It is tempting to think that when he begs for her pardon he is expressing a symbolic contrition to his people as well, to all those he has wronged or allowed to suffer wrong.

Goneril and Regan have always had a place among Shakespeare's most repulsive creations. They unite power-hunger with cruelty, to which

Goneril adds depravity as a wife and as a murderess. They too belong to a historical borderland between two eras, but in this case it is the worse features of an older time that they inherit, while their newer qualities are of the most overbearing sort. Shakespeare cannot have meant us, nevertheless, to fail to see the necessity of change, or a move forward into a new age. As long ago as 1844 a Dr A. Brigham ventured – like Morgann as counsel for Falstaff – to urge that Goneril and Regan were entitled to a measure of indulgence: they showed no wish to ill-treat their father, he argued, until provoked by the 'outrageous' conduct of his retinue of knights (Furness et al. 413 ff.).

More recently others have recognized some justice in their protests. Heilman finds them, in terms of everyday logic, 'almost unanswerable' (*Lear* 7). Frye allows them 'a certain hard common sense' (*Fools* 108). Kettle agrees that the sisters were shrewd enough in their censure of the knights as roystering backwoodsmen, but too inflexible, 'morally impervious' ('From *Hamlet* to *Lear*' 164–5). Tudor statecraft had early taken steps to disband the old feudal retinues, as a menace to law and order; this saved money for great families, though on the other hand Elizabeth's progresses through the country, with a long train of courtiers and hangers-on, could be ruinous to those who had to house them. By the time Shakespeare's play was written we may suspect some reference in it to growing criticism of court extravagance and disorderliness. There are signs of *King Lear* being considered in some quarters 'dangerously political' (Heinemann, 'Political Drama', 193–4).

Goneril and Regan have anticipated trouble with their father from the start. At the end of the first scene they agree to keep in touch against possible explosions of his rash temper, which he has just displayed by his treatment of Cordelia and Kent. He and his knights make their first stay with Goneril, and she soon has to complain of his continual grumblings, and his latest conduct in striking her gentleman for rebuking his jester. 'His knights grow riotous' (I.iii.1 ff.): not surprisingly, with their master setting such an example. Even the well-disposed Albany's hospitality is cooling. In the next scene the humourless Goneril is indignant at being insulted by the Fool the moment she enters her own hall. She breaks in on his and her father's prose in glacial verse (I.iv.201 ff.). Few such abrupt modulations can have so arresting an effect on the ear; the constricted rhythm of the opening line leads into a long, tortuous sentence, civil so far as her nature allows it to be, but with menace glittering through its ice.

Lear's assertion that his followers are 'men of choice and rarest parts' (I.iv.264) must be taken as ludicrous. We have indeed seen them before, in a frolicsome vein, in the Sir Toby and Sir Andrew of *Twelfth Night*, vainly reprimanded for their nocturnal jollity by Olivia and her steward. Lear's own behaviour is as undignified as can be, whether he is bawling for dinner, laughing over a clown's scurrility, or pettishly running in again after launching his terrific malediction against Goneril (I.iv.91–2, 276 ff.). He winds up his tirades with a threat to resume power, and the same thought comes into his mind in the next scene (I.iv.310–11; I.v.39). With a hundred armed men he would have means to seize control of any castle, as a start. Both sisters express willingness to have their father with them, on condition that he brings no armed force with him (II.iv.298–9). There is no reason to disbelieve them; if there is already 'division between the dukes' (III.iii. 8–9), custody of the old king would be an asset to either side.

Whatever the sisters' native asperity, it is the plot against them of Lear's adherents, with foreign backing, that brings out their tigerish qualities. Regan plucks hair from the pinioned Gloucester's beard, and stabs the servant who is resisting her husband. This might be reckoned a wifely duty; and as soon as she becomes a widow, she is entitled to fall in love with Edmund, whereas Goneril has to instigate Edmund to murder her husband, in order to clear the way for her (IV.vi.259). Women are claiming the right to do all the things that men do. Quite early Goneril is finding fault with Albany for his 'milky gentleness', as Lady Macbeth does with her husband, and she is soon impatient of the timid shuffler she supposes him to be. 'A fool usurps my bed' (I.iv.342; IV.ii.28). There can be no doubt that Shakespeare regards her as a terrible creature, an evil offspring of the times. Albany's sombre prediction of humanity preying on itself 'like monsters of the deep' is coming true (IV.ii.49 ff.).

One such monster is Edmund, a critic of the old dispensation all the more trenchant because he belongs to it himself, at least left-handedly. He is another Iago, less morbid and more rational in his motives. He has not much to thank his father for, and much reason to envy his half-brother. Like Faulconbridge in *King John* he can make a virtue of his 'base' blood, as carrying with it a new vitality lacking to the 'whole tribe of fops' or effete legitimate heirs (I.ii.14). Exulting in his independence, he appeals to Nature, which to him means the law of the jungle; cleverness and energy are what he relies on in place of an inherited silver spoon. He too is one of the line of Shakespearian characters who take their stand on natural as against artificial rights. Why should an elder brother inherit everything, simply for being a trifle older? Such a custom belongs to what he calls, in the letter he forges in Edgar's name, men's 'idle and fond bondage', only submitted to because they lack spirit (I.ii.47 ff.).

It might be of interest to speculate about what policies this young adventurer would have set himself to carry out, if he had come to power as he hoped by marriage into the royal family. Incongruously he throws his life away by accepting Edgar's challenge to ordeal by battle; Edgar's name and rank being unknown, he was not bound to fight him, as Goneril tells him too late (V.iii.151 ff.). Puffed up by his new rank as an earl, he was giving way to the lure of that discredited deity Honour. It is another irony that the two unsentimental sisters both fall in love with Edmund, and pay the forfeit with their lives. To be modern-minded may be good, it seems, but to do it by halves is perilous. Many contradictions of such a time of history as Shakespeare's stand out in dramatic guise. Characters like these were as Danby says 'projections of the psychology of Shakespeare's time' (*Nature* 59). They were comprehensible to him because he was in part a New Man himself.

Edmund's existence is proof of something wrong in the life of the family, so closely entwined in these tragedies with that of the nation. Shakespeare has not escaped a feminist charge of being the grand 'patriarchal Bard', restoring parental dominance through Lear's reconciliation with Cordelia (McLuskie 106) – which to most eyes must appear to signify the opposite. To Shakespeare the family which he found in being, at diverse social levels, was far from sacrosanct; his plays might rather be called one never-ending critique of it. In *Othello* this had been concerned primarily with relations of love and marriage; in *King Lear* we see instead a loveless marriage, and relations equally deformed among three sisters and between two half-brothers. Much more in the foreground are relationships between parent and child: a conflict of generations, between old fathers still hectoring and children impatient of worn-out claims.

Lear must have had a much younger wife, to be at eighty the father of three young daughters; this exaggerated gap emphasizes the widening gulf which it typifies between two social epochs. Royal and patriarchal authority have run riot together. Lear storms at the faithful Kent instead of listening to his reproof, and – as McFarland says (97) – answers Goneril's with thunderbolts, instead of being turned by it to self-scrutiny. Autocracy in both its forms has helped to bring about a moral collapse. Family disruption is the central emblem of a disintegrating world, a breakdown of even the closest human ties, so complete that normal relations no longer seem possible. And underlying all this is society's neglect to strive towards a reasonable relationship between the two great classes of rich and poor.

Thanks to the warping of family life, by the faults of both generations, the play, and Lear's mind most of all, is saturated with disgust for sex altogether. This is accompanied by running imagery which has much to do with the sense of smell. It is part of the disharmony between instinct and reason that marks an age of changing values. Lear goes out into a storm that he hopes will 'crack nature's moulds', and 'all germens spill at once/That make ungrateful man' (III.ii.8–9). Sexual passion stands for 'the sulphurous pit, burning, scalding, stench, consumption', in place of the 'good sport' that Gloucester remembered from his carefree days. Yet after all, animals breed, and men and women are only a species of animals: all that has made them seem different is vanishing with the collapse of their false civilization. 'Off, you lendings' (III.iv.108): Lear's cry means a stripping off not of clothes merely, but of everything artificial that has overlaid human life. He and Edgar are pilgrims finding their way back to Nature, a different one from Edmund's. Animal images and allusions abound. Lear, denouncing Goneril, thinks of 'the sea-monster', that most terrifying of things (I.iv.262), the same that Albany thinks of as creation's ultimate horror. But the Lear of Act I has spoken of his royal self as a 'dragon' (I.i.121).

We are seeing the crisis of an old order that has come to depend more and more on deceit and make-believe. Supple adaptability has been the pathway to success. 'An thou canst not smile as the wind sits, thou'lt catch cold shortly' (I.iv.101–2). At court, packs and sects of great ones ebb and flow, Lear has known without comprehending, and cunning politicians pretend as much wisdom as if they were God's spies (I.iv.101–2). It is the abuse of *power* that strikes him most forcibly now as harmful; not long since he felt satisfaction at being told by Kent that *authority* was stamped on his face (I.iv.28–30). He has come to realize how little thought he has given to the poor; but his thinking now is not so much about what can be done for them, as what ought to cease being done *against* them. Power corrupts; the best the governor can do may be to leave the governed alone. Power looks imposing only because it is kowtowed to. A beggar fleeing from a dog's bark is 'the great image of authority', Lear discovers (IV.vi.153 ff.). And authority is itself too guilty to have a right to punish anyone. As to blue blood – 'The Prince of Darkness is a gentleman', according to Mad Tom (III.iv.143), as good we may suppose as any other. There is another contrast between this preoccupation with government and the rough folk-shrewdness that makes the Fool see *property* as the apple of discord. 'Fathers that bear bags shall see their children kind' (II.iv.48–9); no more money-bags, no more good-will, as Timon of Athens was to learn.

Shakespeare must have heard daily gossip about depravity in high places of his own Britain, and forebodings of worse things, such as Gloucester saw written in his eclipses and portents. Edmund alarms his brother with talk in the same strain, of 'death, dearth, dissolution of ancient amities; divisions in states . . . ' All these fears, and 'maledictions against the king and nobles' (I.ii.148 ff.), must have been audible to Shakespeare, sensitive as he was to the stirrings of life around him. They were destined to go on swelling until they merged into the noise of an English revolution.

Lear's last thought before his mind gives way is that the rich ought to expose themselves to what the poor feel, and 'shake the superflux', their surplus wealth, to them (III.iv.33–6). On the stage we see very little of the hungry poor, nothing of riotous crowds; Shakespeare works on our imagination instead, keeping the poor an invisible but compelling presence. Most of what he says is not about overworked toilers like the farm labourers, but about the outcasts, jobless vagrants, cripples, of whom there was a multitude for Edgar to conceal himself among. These were the images of destitution most visible to the better-off, and could well serve to represent the hardships of poverty at large.

Some of Edgar's 'mad' speeches have been objected to as unnecessary, but their purpose is to exhibit the depths of degradation into which human beings can be forced by hunger and friendlessness. Lear's mad speeches pass into a denunciation of corruption and injustice that makes Hamlet's catalogue sound academic. Hamlet contemplated a skull and philosophized in traditional style on death as the great leveller; Lear, encountering the disfigured Edgar, contemplates with a greater revulsion a living man crushed down to the level of a beast. 'Is man no more than this?' (III.iv.103). When an unfortunate nobleman laments that the gods treat men as boys do flies, we are surely meant to think that this is also the way the rich and powerful treat the poor and weak.

In one extraordinary scene, which only Shakespeare's near-omnipotent art could have ventured on, he gathers on his stage a mad king, a Fool, a young aristocrat playing mad beggar, his father driven to feel 'almost mad'. Insanity in an individual opens hidden caverns of a mind; derangement as pictured in this drama shows tragedy weaving together the fates of mankind. It liberates thoughts otherwise barred from expression, things buried in the collective mind of an era. It amounts to a revolt against reason, of the narrow dehumanizing sort devoted only to self-interest. It is surely made clear that the order trumpeted by Tudor mouthpieces is only 'orderly' for the well off, for whose benefit it exists, while life for the poor is chronic disorder. The rich must repent, not for the good of their souls in another world, but because failure to repent makes them unworthy to live and may bring on a social cataclysm. While the upper classes fall into moral decay, it is left to humbler folk to preserve human decency. Gloucester's servants are horrified by his blinding; one of them loses his life in trying to prevent it. Regan, who stabs him to death, is indignant at this mutiny – 'A peasant stand up thus?' (III.vii.79). Shakespeare leaves us to hope that some day the masses will stand up, for themselves.

As Danson remarks, Shakespeare was in some ways 'a profoundly conservative writer', yet with some very radical views (8). In the advent of any new social order its more aggressive and repulsive elements can be expected to thrust themselves forward in advance of the better. We see a milder side of the old paternalism when the countryman who has been a lifelong tenant of Gloucester, and of his father before him, comes to the blind man's aid. Gloucester has not been an exemplary family man, but he cannot have been a grasping landlord. Old men in this play are foolish rather than, like the more ambitious of the young, wicked; but their time is done. 'The great world', Gloucester sighs, listening to Lear's ravings, 'Shall so wear out to naught' (IV.vi.135–6). A ruling class going downhill is always convinced that its own end must spell the end of the world.

It is one aspect of the play that it records 'a stage in the emergence of the modern European consciousness' (Knights 84). Amid the turmoil of a confused, many-sided shift, men would try to orient themselves by the light of 'Nature' and its long-revered law. But Nature's oracles were too discordant. Edmund has a rational scepticism about astrology, and equally little regard for any moral restraints. 'The younger rises when the old doth fall' is his maxim (III.iii.24) – and the quicker the better. Goneril and Regan have much of the same cold-blooded rationality. One of its social consequences would be to deny to labourers a right to anything more than bare subsistence for as long as they were needed. When Lear declares that even 'basest beggars' must have some little indulgence to hug, he is recognizing for the first time what a king may have in common with the most forlorn of his people.

Goneril and Regan come from the old order, like a good many of those who were, in history, to subvert it; but they have imbibed much of a newer spirit, calculating and utilitarian; they have a not too remote kinship with emerging capitalism and its standard-bearers, who in turn had affinities with Puritanism. Lear's retainers with their 'Epicurism and lust' seem to Goneril to be turning her residence into something more like 'a tavern or a brothel' (I.iv.244–5). It is Nature's revenge on her and Regan that they fall wildly in love. At least they are subscribing to the same doctrine as Edmund, of talent mattering more than birth, when they offer their royal hands to a bastard. Oswald is a humbler member of the same camp, with an irreverent contempt for fallen majesty, who is killed by Edgar while trying to earn a reward by seizing Gloucester. Edgar, like Kent, thinks him 'a serviceable villain': to them he is an upstart. On his side he abuses Edgar, in his rustic masquerade, as an impudent 'peasant', 'dunghill', 'slave' (IV.vi.244 ff.).

Of the religious or philosophical ideas astir in Shakespeare's day, *King Lear* offers a good compendium. Religious and secularist outlooks were in competition, as they would be for long years to come. 'What is the cause of thunder?' Lear gravely asks his fellow-'philosopher' Mad Tom. Much of the play's floating tide of questions can be traced to Montaigne's essays, favourite reading with Shakespeare (Salingar, ch. 7). Heaven's smiles or frowns are recognizable reflections of forces contending on earth. Doubts and disagreements centre, as they are likely to do at every crossroad of history, on problems of fate and free will, fundamental also to the theological controversies of the age.

Edgar's mode of thinking, hammered out by danger and hardship, must seem the one closest to Shakespeare's own mind; and in terms of Danby's distinction between Stoic and Christian patience (*Fortune's Hill* 108 ff.), it seems distinctly closer to the former. It turns on acceptance of calamities, as trials of our strength or as unescapable consequences of our misdeeds. We turn them to good purpose by learning sympathy with our fellow-creatures;

this harmonizes with the will of heaven, a figurative title for human impulses that in the present state of mankind cannot be free-standing. Men must endure life and death, because they are men. Edgar bids his sightless father, who can do nothing better, to 'pray that the right may thrive', while he himself goes to fight (V.ii.2); neither prayer nor courage avails. There is a peculiarly haunting note in his simple words, after the scene at Dover cliff: 'Bear free and patient thoughts' (IV.vi.80). Patience, constancy, are sovereign virtues with Shakespeare, as sources both of inner strength and of the individual's ability to play his part among his fellow-men. Lear himself, who has gone through life impatiently, recommends patience to the blind Gloucester (IV.vi.177).

To explain anything incomprehensible, men fall back on the stars. Kent is a conventionally religious man, one of those who 'fear judgment'; at the close he feels that doomsday has indeed come (I.iv.17; V.iii.263). But for him only the stars, strong though insentient powers which 'govern our conditions', can have been responsible for the difference between Cordelia and her sisters (IV.iii.33–6). To a decaying class fate is likely to seem hostile, and Gloucester has an acute sense of the malignity of unknown forces. Phenomena like eclipses may be rationalized, but as the storm over Rome moved Casca to say, there is no dodging their effects, or what they portend. Emancipated from fatalism by birth and temper, Edmund dismisses as 'an admirable evasion of whoremaster man' any pretence that we are 'villains on necessity, fools by heavenly compulsion' (I.ii.124–5). Here is a highroad leading towards true science.

Of recognizably Christian consciousness there is little sign, except in ethical terms. Cordelia and Edgar each protect and forgive their fathers. But Providence keeps well out of sight, as it does throughout the tragedies. The bad come to grief, but they destroy most of the good with them. Albany is the one who shows most faith in the triumph of justice. Where human strength to enforce it is lacking, heaven must be called in, but what is asked of it is justice here and now, not in the beyond. 'This shows you are above, you justicers', Albany exclaims at the news of Cornwall's death (IV.ii.78–9). He has a Puritan conviction of mankind being so vile as to be incorrigible without heavenly grace; but likewise a Puritan readiness to draw his sword in furtherance of heaven's will. As Frye says, however, not much happens in 'this dark, meaningless, horrible world' to warrant Albany's faith (*Shakespeare* 111–13). And as Muir says, his cry 'The gods defend her!' is at once followed by Lear's entry, bearing Cordelia's dead body (*Sequence* 137).

Royalties like Richard II had been wont to summon celestial help as something they were entitled to *ex officio*. Lear can only appeal to the heavens for sympathy with an ill-used old man; neither we nor Lear think of this as other than a poetic outburst. Religion and Shakespearian tragedy are in fact incompatible. Lear while still king might pay his respects to

Apollo, or the sun; his later deities were the vast dim shadows of his own faded power. They shared its vindictive qualities; they must have stirred up the storm in order to 'Find out their enemies' (III.ii.49–51). Now they too, like mortal men, are relapsing into nothingness. In their place have come the twin ideals of patience and penitence. Yet his sufferings are not his own punishment alone; in something not unlike a Christian sense they are an atonement for the sins of all those who have wielded power and used it selfishly.

The story labours towards an incoherent battle, followed by the stirring duel between the brothers. Edmund, mortally wounded, is touched at last by remorse; for one reason, because of the astonishing feeling of having been *loved* by other human beings, even the terrible sisters. 'Yet Edmund was beloved' (V.iii.238) – a sensation unknown to Iago, or to Richard III solitary at Bosworth. A brief moment is left for the brothers to 'exchange charity' (V.iii.165), and for a vain effort by Edmund to undo his latest crime.

Contrary to his sources, and his later would-be improvers, Shakespeare decided that as part of the tragic climax Cordelia must die. So must Lear. It would be too incongruous for him, after the spectacle of human misery he has been shown, and can do nothing to remedy, to live a contented old-age pensioner's life with his daughter. He dies of exhaustion, consoled by an illusion of Cordelia being still alive. There is in his death a tragic reconciliation with life, perhaps a hopeful augury for his people's future. But now that he is 'sane' once more, the revelations brought him by madness have faded. Of those close to him he has been reconciled with Cordelia alone. His sympathizers he denounces as 'murderers, traitors all', responsible for her death. This alienation is part of the tragedy he, like Macbeth, has brought on himself, if in a very different way. Gloucester has gone before him, when Edgar – belatedly, as he confesses – revealed himself before the duel, and his father's heart, torn between 'joy and grief/Burst smilingly' (V.iii.195–8). Kent is dying, worn out (cf. McAlindon 178). He wants to die, and follow his master, who has forgotten all about him. Suicide is denied, however, to the good, as Gloucester had been made to learn at Dover, and is left to Goneril: only in Rome can it be admirable. All those belonging to Britain's past are being dismissed, with the exception of two of those who have broken away from it, Edgar and Albany.

It remains for the country's future and its guidance to be faced; a harder problem than in other tragedies because not merely a political solution is required, but a new social structure. Lear's purgatory, of which Edgar is the one who has seen most, is a warning example to those who are to follow him. Albany's first, and very inept, proposal is to restore 'absolute power' to Lear, whose mind he knows has gone, for the remainder of his life; on Lear's death he offers it to Kent, who refuses, and Edgar. (V.iii.296 ff.). In

Bradley's opinion Albany shows weakness in not wanting to share responsibility himself (*Tragedy* 297–8); but this misses the direction of Shakespeare's thinking. Power is too fearful a burden; only one like Edgar, who has been plunged into the lowest depths and been reborn there, can be fit, or least unfit, to shoulder it. He is a young man exiled from the old world, unconnected with the old ruling family, but ennobled by hardships, his own and others'. In a way he can be thought of as a champion of the people, a people ready to shake off its servitude. His words of acceptance are modest, indistinct, enigmatic. These speakers are peering into an unknown future.

Some lessons at any rate stand out clearly enough from the play. One is the claim of the poor to what used to be called 'natural rights', and nowadays are known as 'human rights'. Annabel Patterson has pointed out that Lear only recognized them in his mad fits, and forgot them when restored to sanity (116). He had little time left him then; Shakespeare, moreover, may well have judged it prudent to keep Lear's vision of the abyss to the privileged sphere of inspired madness. We can keep it alive for ourselves by thinking of Lear and Cordelia themselves – Cordelia in captivity at least – as images of suffering humanity.

A more political lesson is the duty of those close to a ruler to speak the truth, and of the ruler to listen to it. 'To plainness honour's bound when majesty falls to folly', Kent tells Lear bluntly (I.i.147–8). 'Truth's a dog must to kennel', the Fool grumbles when threatened by his royal master with the whip (I.iv.111–12). Before long his master is ready to agree. 'To say *Ay* and *No* to everything I said!' is his reproach now to the supple courtiers he looks back on (IV.vi.98–9), among whom we may number court preachers with their servile adulation. And this insight into the crooked ways of a court is *not* forgotten when he recovers his wits; his talk about them to Cordelia reveals an unexpected realism, even a sardonic humour (V.iii.11 ff.).

If not the whole of the closing Act bears on the main theme (Evans 178), the reason is that individual destinies and their secrets have expanded so prodigiously as to involve with them all humanity; mankind itself becomes the tragic Hero. Few probably have reached the play's end feeling, like Hoeniger (19), 'exhilarated, uplifted, by a transforming vision of life'. We have listened to 'a most profound commentary on the passing of the old order' (Kernan, *King Lear* 27); if we are left with hope for the future, it may seem little more than a forlorn hope. We have indeed been shown much of human virtue and strength, as well as wickedness. Still more momentous, we have seen human beings capable of learning and changing. 'Men are as the time is', says Edmund to the officer he is bribing to kill Lear and Cordelia for him (V.iii.26 ff.) – one of Shakespeare's many hired murderers: this is a ruthless age, we must be ruthless too if we want to get on. Edmund is expounding historical determinism; but we have come to know in his

Britain a few individuals who can defy the force of social gravity. Lear himself, another reader has said, is 'the greatest of Shakespeare's dramatic affirmations of the human capacity to grow, to learn' (Snyder 170). And this, the play leaves us to feel, is the quality mankind needs above all if it is to survive and move onward.

5

Macbeth (1606)

Macbeth is the second of two usurpers of a throne in the tragedies, both of them murderers; a better man than Claudius, and less happy therefore with his stolen sovereignty. Claudius could fortify himself with wine and good cheer; Macbeth never does this. Unlike his forerunner he is the central and dominant figure of his drama, which, unlike *Hamlet*, is brief, swift, intense, tragedy unrelieved. It seldom descends to prose; the mood is one of sustained tension and excitement. Imagery is more varied and striking than in any other play, with more complexity of interweaving, and images clustering in groups, concerned with themes such as children, or clothes (Spurgeon 324; cf. Brooks 238, 245). Recurrent talk of sleep, wholesome or haunted, may suggest that Shakespeare was conscious of approaching exhaustion, and pining for rest. He may at some point have given up acting, the heaviest part of his burden. Ironies abound, as they do in *Hamlet*, and seem to show all apparent good in life turning into illusion. Duncan has just admitted his hitherto 'absolute trust' in Cawdor (I.iv.13–14), now revealed as a traitor, when another whom he has complete trust in enters, Macbeth.

There may have been some fortuitous reasons for the brief duration of this play, besides its chosen method of placing the focus on one or two figures, with little secondary development. All the earlier part has a truncated appearance, with sections required by the story missing. Shortage of time for writing might account for this; so might a need to avoid giving offence to the court, for whose benefit a subject from Scottish history must have been undertaken. Macbeth is close to the succession; its rules are not fixed; fresh from his victories over the country's enemies, he may well feel that he has a better claim than Duncan's fledgeling sons. But he never says so, even to his wife or to himself. To handle the murder of a Scottish king, only a year or two after the Gunpowder Plot, would call for care. Moreover *King Lear*, with its harping on the defects of government, may have failed to give unmixed satisfaction. Players would always be sensitive to court reactions, reaching them through one channel or another. When Shakespeare's draft was discussed with his colleagues, it may have been decided to remove some passages, and perhaps pad the witch-scenes by way of ballast, witchcraft being one of the topics on which the royal pen had been employed. J.M. Robertson's contention that a number of hands had a share in the text cannot, as Empsom said (155), be ignored.

In sharp contrast with *King Lear*, this play has very little to say overtly about social injustice. If the poor suffered under good king Duncan, it was not from any ill-doing of his, though his government may well have failed, as governments usually did, to check ill-doing by others. This is implied in the porter's allusion to 'a farmer who hanged himself on the expectation of plenty' (II.iii.4–5) – who had been hoarding grain, as many did, in hope of a scarcity which would drive prices up. Scotland is profoundly shaken by events, but these are of a political nature, feudal revolt and foreign invasion and regicide. We seem to be faced with a reversion to the earlier, simpler keynote of the English Histories, unbridled pursuit of power. Resemblances to *Richard III* are many. But in the Histories, before *Henry IV* at least, or some of the later scenes of *Richard III*, it had been action viewed for the most part from outside; now we are being shown how it can feel to embark on such gambles, and the searing effect of crime on the human spirit. Again, in the Histories there were always two factions, stemming from a dynastic feud; now the nobility is not divided in any such way, though it lacks courage to combine effectively against a tyrant.

Feudal broils did go on longer in Scotland than in England, mixed up in the later stages with other developments, such as the Reformation. James VI and I was the son of a murdered father and exiled mother. Shakespeare was aware that Scotland was largely Celtic, and that from the Highlands and Western Isles 'kerns and gallowglasses', or irregular mercenaries, were ready for hiring by malcontents like the rebel Macdonwald (I.iii.112 ff.). Under all the surface instability, however, we can feel a pervasive, undefined malady in the body politic. A recurrent imagery of 'purging' suggests a Shakespeare obsessed with the thought of a society contaminated in some fashion and requiring to be somehow cleansed. Caithness hails Malcolm as 'the medicine of the sickly weal': inspired by him they must be ready to shed their blood in their country's 'purge' (V.ii.27–8). Macbeth is at the same time wishing that the doctor called in to treat the queen could 'cast/The water of my land, find her disease,/And purge it': a moment later he asks 'what purgative drug' could rid him of the invading English (V.iii.50 ff.). His own misrule, not the invasion, is what Scotland is suffering from now; but it is only the culmination of an older, more deep-seated ailment, of which his crime of murder, like Cawdor's treason, was a sudden eruption. This ailment must have ramifying connections with the social evils brought to light in *King Lear*. If Duncan's pious queen 'Died every day she lived', and was oftener on her knees in prayer than on her feet (IV.iii.109–11), it cannot have been for any faults of her own; she was praying for a sinful Scotland.

In this remote environment there is no urban life, no burgher class beginning to come forward as in the Histories; all we see is gloomy fortress or blasted heath. But Shakespeare's epochs tend to run into one another, and his Scotland is not without a degree of polish which gives it more likeness to Denmark than to ancient Britain. 'And the rich East to boot' (IV.iii.37) – Macduff's words about those fabled riches is far more Elizabethan than medieval. Most of Scotland by Shakespeare's time shared a common language and much historical experience with England. He probably visualized Macbeth as not much more behind the times than the Scots nobles of his own day, some of them now to be seen in the streets of London. Macbeth knows what it is to shiver over 'a dismal treatise' (V.v.11–13), on demonology or theology we may suppose; his witches are denizens of the Europe of 1600, near the height of the witch-hunting craze, rather than of any earlier era. Cawdor is a 'gentleman' who dies confessing and repenting like a good Tudor conspirator, and with the same aristocratic sang-froid (I.iv.3 ff.). A wounded officer reports the fighting at the outset in surprisingly literary style, and Ross speaks of Macbeth's share in it as worthy of 'Bellona's bridegroom' (I.ii.7 ff., 55).

Feudal greed for power like Macbeth's cannot be translated directly into bourgeois greed for wealth. Morally or psychologically, however, they occupy similar ground, and here as very often in Shakespeare we must remember the new atmosphere in his England of remorseless competition, unchecked acquisitiveness, shifting now from the political into the economic, but helping him to breathe reality into bygone conflicts. It helped him also to hear the inward reverberations of an action like the murder of Duncan. Hence the play's emphasis on 'obscurer regions' of human psychology, on 'secret forces' holding men and women in their grasp (Bradley, *Tragedy* 338). Yet these remain inseparable, as always in Shakespeare, from the *res publica*, the marring of a nation by the neuroses of private ambition, and of a hero by those of the nation.

A scattering of topical allusions would make it easier for spectators to relate what they heard to what was happening around them. Cawdor secretly in league with foreign foes would call up a familiar bogy, thanks to years of Catholic plotting and Spanish menace. We hear of an 'equivocator', or Jesuit, who 'Committed treason for God's sake' (II.iii.8 ff.) – or really believed he was doing so, as the poet may have been willing to think. Sidney Lee catalogued items that could be counted on, like this one, to tickle James's ears (394–5). James had been pestered with plotters in Scotland, and must have found it agreeable to look back on dark hours left behind. Macbeth's words about 'humane statute' having 'purged' the country since lawless days of old could be taken as a compliment to James, who really had made Scotland a somewhat less disorderly place, as he continued to do, with greater success, from London. He was soon pressing on a reluctant Parliament his plan for a full integration of his two realms into a single nation, and the play can be viewed as lending some encouragement to it. In *Henry V* Shakespeare had pointed towards a union of the British Isles, led by England, and now he was showing England in a 'civilizing' role, its army entering Scotland with no aggressive intent but as a rescuer.

Shakespeare could not think, or at least could not talk, of any other government in Britain than monarchy. But *Macbeth* is the only major tragedy where monarchy is shown, first in Scotland, then in England, functioning both practically and legitimately, or *de facto* and *de jure*. In several preceding plays he had seemed to reveal a deep-seated distrust of any autocratic power, as a mode of government too dependent on individual qualities. James, on the other hand, had enjoyed only limited power at Edinburgh, but had made up for this by developing theories, expounded in 1598 in his book on monarchy, which went a good way towards the doctrine of Continental absolutism. This was to be more and more a part of royalist thinking as time went on and civil war approached.

Shakespeare may appear to be falling in with this lofty assessment of monarchy; or to be trumping it by setting rulers an impossibly high standard of conduct. He bestows a stained-glass kind of virtue on that 'most sainted king', Duncan, a counterpart of 'the most pious Edward', 'the holy king' reigning in England and devoting himself to the service of his people in distress (III.vi.27, 30). Edward has a 'most miraculous' gift of healing, and a 'heavenly gift of prophecy' (IV.iii.141 ff.). All later kings, the Stuarts in England among them, inherited the ability to cure the 'King's evil'; and prophetic power too could be ascribed by admirers to James, as by Shakespeare to his witches. On the other side is Macbeth's reign of terror; between his 'fiend-like queen' and Duncan's consort the contrast is even more glaring. We are left to consider which colour autocracy is likely to wear, especially when it functions in isolation. Macbeth has no adviser except his wife, who is critical of him for shutting himself up alone with his anxieties (III.ii.8–9). What he oddly calls a 'council' (III.i.22) is only a banquet for the notables. Duncan left no Polonius behind him.

Fulsome protestations of devotion and loyalty, like those lavished on Lear by his elder daughters, are heaped on Duncan too. Lady Macbeth welcomes him with assurances that all his subjects are his 'servants', and all they own is entirely at his disposal (I.vi.25–8). Doubtless she hopes they will all have the same sentiments when they are her husband's subjects. Stuart doctrines of passive obedience were to give such protestations a more literal and absolutist meaning than they could have in 1606; but Shakespeare is hinting that those round a ruler who 'protest too much' are unlikely to be the most sincere. Regicide has of course to be condemned *fortissimo*. But the note of divine right, of the king as heaven's lieutenant, comes out very clearly in

Macduff's outcry about 'Most sacrilegious murder' having violated 'The Lord's anointed temple' (II.iii.67–8). Sincere though he is, there is something strained and artificial in his language here, as well as in Macbeth's. Shakespeare cannot really have his heart in this rhetoric; his aim, as it had taken shape in the later Histories, was not to deify monarchy but to make it a useful and law-abiding part of government and public service. And in reality the Duncan whom he read of in Holinshed was a quite unsatisfactory ruler, Macbeth for many years a much better one.

Duncan's transfiguration is followed by Malcolm's long list of 'king-becoming graces': temperance, mercy, lowliness, etc. (IV.iii.91 ff.). Again we may wonder whether Shakespeare was spreading rosy illusions about royalty, or laughing at it in his sleeve. The long-drawn scene where these matters are argued out between Malcolm, pretending at first to be a hardened reprobate, and the honest Macduff, whom he is trying to sound, does little to forward the action, and seems tiresome to readers who fail to see that Shakespeare is venturing into a field of vital concern to him, but only to be approached circuitously. The parley comes from Holinshed and from old tradition (Muir, *Sequence* 153–4), but Shakespeare was making it very much his own.

Malcolm has to be introduced to us as a young prince of a new strain, one who would have been at home in folk-lore, the wishful thinking of the people. He has undergone peril and exile, like the Edgar on whom power is conferred at the end of *King Lear*. This is the only royalty admissible by Shakespeare now: responsibility entrusted to bearers who have been sobered by suffering and by rubbing elbows with ordinary fellow-mortals. Malcolm displays very little of Hamlet's spasmodic ardour to revenge a murdered father; and he is not returning to Scotland to claim any unmeaning 'rights' of his own, as Cordelia came to Britain to do on behalf of her father. He is Scotland's servant, not master, 'my poor country's to command' (IV.iii.131–2). A fantasy prince of this kind could not be given much flesh and blood; he represents a dumb aspiration towards a recovered innocence, a fresh start for humanity. There is heavy stress on his virginal chastity, as a symbol of all this, after his overdone pose of being an omnivorous devourer of women. Monarchy is being sanitized, or puritanized.

James liked to speak of himself and his brother-kings, figuratively, as 'gods'; intentionally or not, there is a sardonic comment on this when Malcolm refers to the bloodthirsty Macbeth as 'an angry god' (IV.iii.17). Caithness and the other nobles resolve to join Malcolm, not at all in the name of any sacred hereditary right, but in the hope that he will restore Scotland to health. Macduff explicitly denies any such right to a claimant as perverted as Malcolm has made himself out to be (IV.iii.101–3). From this must follow the question of a people's right to throw off the rule of a man as vicious as Macbeth. He is a usurper, but the argument would seem to hold good even against the most legitimate monarch; the dividing-line is at any rate faint. Shakespeare is not free to follow it to its logical conclusion; but he is in effect challenging James's doctrine that the worst conceivable ruler, once anointed and sceptred, must be submitted to unmurmuringly. To strengthen the rebel case Macbeth is taxed with every species of guilt, including – as against Malcolm's stainless purity – lawless lust, of which there is no evidence, and which seems foreign to his nature.

Attributes befitting a king are not confined to men of royal birth. Macbeth fears Banquo because of his 'royalty of nature' and kindred attributes (III.i.40). Banquo of course is to have the honour of being King James's ancestor; and in the course of the play it is increasingly taken for granted that the crown must become hereditary, instead of semi-elective as it was in old Scotland or Denmark. Macbeth is accused, though not by Malcolm, of withholding from the latter 'the due of birth' (III.vi.24–5); and at the end Malcolm is the unchallenged successor, as his father had designated him. Shakespeare is interested, moreover, in the desire of ambitious men not only to win power but to hand it on to their heirs, to found a dynasty, and thus pre-empt a sort of immortality. Banquo and Macbeth both feel this strongly, though it seems to drop out of Macbeth's mind as his wife drops out of his life, even if the thought of Banquo's heirs being the winners still gnaws at him (IV.i.102 ff.). Merchants of Shakespeare's time had an equal longing not only to become rich but to become gentlemen, even noblemen, and found families to perpetuate their name.

The crown that tempted Macbeth stood for unchecked power; it would give them, in his wife's ecstatic – or hissing – words, 'solely sovereign sway and masterdom' (I.v.69). In both these two a hyperactive imagination – with which the Celtic peoples, as represented by Glendower in *Henry IV*, were already being associated – could paint the delights of kingship in ravishing colours, as well as conjure up horrible hallucinations. It was Macbeth, not his wife, who first conceived the idea of seizing power. In the moral code of his historical time it would have been more surprising of him not to think of it. Hence his immediate thrilling at the witches' prophecy, though this brings up with it the horrid thought of murder. He would have gone no further if his wife had not pushed him. She taxes him with having not only proposed it to her, but even sworn to carry it out. His wanting now to draw back is enough to turn her into a virago and accuse him of cowardice (I.vii.35 ff.), in spite of the bravery he has just shown in two hard-fought battles.

We can scarcely admire a man who commits a crime simply to satisfy his wife (Rossiter 216–17). But when a mind is so evenly and painfully divided as Macbeth's, any push from outside may tip the balance. As Bradley said, Macbeth is persuaded to act as a sort of 'appalling duty', necessary to prove his manliness afresh (*Tragedy* 358). In an opposite way from that of *Hamlet*,

Shakespeare gives us a remarkable study of the psychology of fear and courage, and shows how unstable a compound each can be. Macbeth cannot simply tell his wife that honour and obligation forbid the deed, because he knows that to her this will only appear, as his own shrinkings do to Hamlet, contemptible, 'three parts coward'. To his wife he must at all costs be a flawless hero, knowing instinctively that what she loves in him is her own fanciful image of a man of limitless, inflexible daring. Since *Julius Caesar* the task of killing has grown harder and heavier. With Macbeth it is for the first time a crime, pure and simple, against both a trusting kinsman and a nation.

To kill as unhesitatingly as an Iago a man must be completely callous, and Lady Macbeth deplores the excess of kindliness she knows to be part of her husband's disposition (I.v.15–16). This has been called in question (Schücking 181), but unconvincingly. Stewart observes that 'There are in a sense two Macbeths', and that some degree of such dissociation may be universal (90). There is a curious reminder of his better side in some words, when he is planning Banquo's death, about 'the tender eye of pitiful day' (III.ii.47). He can only feel murderous at night. We see it again in his frustrated longing – like Tarquin's in *Lucrece* (lines 141 ff.) – for the respect, loyalty, friendships, that ought to be the consolations of old age. He cannot relegate a crime to a corner of his mind, like that healthy, well-balanced assassin Claudius. The 'Amen' that he is unable to utter after the murder will stick in his throat for ever. He never thinks of trying to expiate his guilt by prayer. Its effects must sink deeper and deeper into him, morally ruinous because he has sinned against his own better nature. Before long both he and his partner are suffering from 'terrible dreams', and from realization that they have only 'scotched the snake', and must complete their work by killing Banquo (III.ii.4 ff.). Crime begins to fascinate him. He shows unexpected mastery of a new skill when he instigates his puppets to murder Banquo. After seeing Banquo's ghost he tries to convince himself that his hysteria was only due to his being still 'young in deed', a failing of which 'hard use' will cure him (III.iv.141–4).

It does, in a way, but only by alienating him from mankind. The more he struggles to make himself safe, the more enemies he stirs up, and the more impossible his longed-for security comes to be. The opprobrious name of tyrant, first used against him in Act III scene vi, is heard more and more frequently. To make room for Malcolm he has to be kept off the stage for a long time in the second half of the play, but meanwhile he is felt as a monstrous presence, a ruler running amuck. Some can guess how guilt and inner turmoil are paralysing him, how he must feel his kingship hanging loose 'like a giant's robe upon a dwarfish thief' (V.ii.20–22; cf. Spurgeon 327). His followers are deserting him, and a tyrant abandoned can be challenged and grappled with. From this point we can look back at the grand fanfare of Macbeth's first introduction, in the glow of his martial triumph. Since then he has striven to make himself greater still, but has shrunk instead of expanding.

Macbeth and his wife have been lovers, as well as fellow-plotters, and their tragedy is in part one of love. They are the first couple since Brutus and Portia capable of debating affairs together with mutual trust, and the only pair in the tragedies capable of joint action. Lady Macbeth cannot be more than in her thirties, since her husband believes she can still give him the heirs he craves for, 'men-children only' (I.vii.72 ff.). She must be an attractive woman, with an amiable side which is hidden from us, or he would not bestow on her more endearments than any other married man in Shakespeare gives his wife. She is his 'dearest love', his 'dearest partner of greatness' (I.v.10–11, 58), his 'dear wife' (III.ii.36), and even – a pet-name also used by Othello (III.iv.45), and by Antony to Cleopatra (IV.iv.2) – his 'dearest chuck' (III.ii.45). We never see her free enough from weightier thoughts to return his affection. She is devoted to her image of him, and what he may come to be, rather than to him as a human being, and recoils from him as soon as he recoils from their grim plan. 'Such I account thy love' (I.vii.39) – something as feeble as his resolve. She meets him after his desperate battles without a single word of them, her mind fixed solely on the further ordeals she wants to plunge him into. He must choose between giving way, or forfeiting his only close attachment in life, as well as his chance of the throne.

Nietzsche may have been thinking of her when he said that a woman always conspires against the higher soul of her lover. She stands, as all women before yesterday have in a sense stood, outside the man-made conventions which have moulded society and its patterns of good and ill. Some of her first words show her prepared to carry out the murder herself, and only awaiting Macbeth's assent; it is one of her redeeming touches that in the end she cannot bring herself to kill Duncan, because in his sleep he reminds her of her father (I.v.51; II.ii.12–13). Even for her own limited part in the business she has to embolden herself with wine (II.ii.1–2). Before Macbeth's return we have seen her screwing up her courage with a hysterical invocation to the spirits of evil to take possession of and 'unsex' her. Goneril would have had no need of such a frantic outburst to smother 'compunctious visitings of nature', or of her talk of dashing her child's brains out rather than break a wicked oath (I.v.39 ff.; I.vii.54 ff.).

She must have shared responsibility for other deaths than Duncan's. She hints at the same fate for Banquo and his son Fleance, before learning that Macbeth has already planned it (III.ii.16 ff.). Evans (194) asks why she has not been informed of the plan. Here is one of the blanks that in this play more than others we feel we may claim some licence to fill in. The answer surely is that now Macbeth is king he must assert his leading role. But when he has to face Banquo's ghost he collapses, while she remains firm. Neither, however, can hold out long without the other's support. At the outset she believed to be easy a path he knew to be full of perils. Unnerved by the spectacle of his weakness, she in turn succumbs to her overwrought nerves. Left solitary, he can only plunge into mindless violence. There must be wormwood for him in the thought that he has let this woman, with her supposed 'undaunted mettle' (I.vii.73), lure him like another witch to his doom. His words on being told of her death are among the most poignant ever written, but they are quite impersonal; that she was once his darling has long been forgotten.

Darkness broods heavily over Macbeth's Scotland. In the dagger speech he thinks instinctively of night as evil, full of 'wicked dreams' (II.i.50; cf. III.ii.52–3). Untroubled sleep eludes the exhausted. After his crime 'Macbeth shall sleep no more'; one of the play's many internal echoes is his wife's attempt to comfort him after the banquet-scene: 'You lack the season of all natures, sleep' (III.iv.141). Gloom is moral as well as physical. Malcolm and his brother are foolish to flee after their father's death, but they are already mistrustful, as Malcolm shows himself later with Macduff (II.iii.140–41). Macduff's little boy is not too young to know that there are more 'liars and swearers' in the world than honest men (IV.iii.55–7, 75–6). Children's voices are among Shakespeare's choric devices for displaying the world as it is. As Knight says, everywhere are rumours, uncertainties, actions unexplained (*Wheel* 158–9).

A death like Duncan's must bring others in its train. This begins at once, with the two grooms in Duncan's chamber, whom Lady Macbeth has drugged into slumber. Macbeth feels no compunction at all about killing them: they are underlings, insignificant – a reminder of the feudal morass out of which Shakespearian tragedy has to find its way. Other ordinary folk have scant place in the story, but when we see them at odd moments they preserve the better qualities of human nature, as they do in *King Lear* and *Timon*. One of these few voices of the people is the old man of seventy whom the thane of Ross talks with in neighbourly style (though both of them in verse) about the portents attending Duncan's death (II.iv). He ends with a pious wish for bad men to reform and enemies to become friends. A sympathetic messenger who comes to warn Lady Macduff calls himself 'a homely man', and is nervous and hurried, though well-meaning (IV.ii.64 ff.): he too speaks in verse, not of the homeliest sort. In Act III Scene i the episode of Macbeth inciting two men to murder Banquo is drawn out longer than dramatic need requires; Shakespeare seems to be telling us that many in his England suffer from wrongs, at the hands of great men, such as these two complain of, and to imply that society must be insecure while oppression is allowed to breed such thirst for revenge.

Scotland is falling under a reign of terror, something only sketched in *Richard III*, or, with the proscriptions, in *Julius Caesar*, but now depicted with grim realism. England in the Histories had often suffered by having too weak a government; now a country is suffering from excess of power, arbitrary and irresponsible. After the fiasco of the feast Macbeth's guilt must be plain to all, as the talk between two noblemen in Act III Scene iv confirms; from now on fear and suspicion stalk the land (IV.ii.17 ff.; IV.iii.164 ff.). Macbeth has spies in all the great households, a precaution not unknown to Elizabeth's government, and other agents trying to get rid of Malcolm for him. There were not a few models on the Continent for Shakespeare's imagination to draw on; among the most lurid was the Spanish persecution of rebels and heretics in the Netherlands, which had driven multitudes of refugees to England and brought English troops to assist the revolt. In Macbeth's Scotland bloodthirsty despotism was setting its people afloat, as Ross says to Lady Macduff, 'upon a wild and violent sea'. Among the worst sufferers is the tyrant himself, clear-sighted enough, unlike many autocrats, to understand how deeply he is hated, pursued by 'curses, not loud but deep' (V.iii.28–9).

Macbeth's own class, the nobility, is more exposed than any other to the repression. Its members are only lightly sketched, though G.R. Elliott distinguishes 'the time-serving Ross' and 'the cleverly satirical Lennox' (174). Macbeth begins by courting them, but no support gathers round him. Banquo is a somewhat ambiguous figure, whom we do not see distinctly, just as men under such a regime can no longer see one another clearly. Macbeth has a very high opinion of him, and makes tentative advances to him after the first meeting with the witches, and just before the murder of Duncan (I.iii.153 ff.; II.i.22 ff.) Banquo is 'not without ambition', and on hearing the witches' promises to Macbeth at once asks what *he* is to get (I.iii.54 ff.). It may be either because he has vowed to see Duncan's death cleared up, or because he wants to open the way for his heirs to reign, as foretold, in Scotland, that the new ruler is uneasy about him. On his side he is secretly dubious about Macbeth's conduct but seems to be nursing his own hopes more than thinking of the country.

Macduff is a more forthright character, not unlike Lear's earl of Kent. He alone is certain of Macbeth's responsibility from the start, and defies him by not attending his coronation; but he then over-hastily takes refuge in England, leaving his family and household to be butchered. Part of the misery of Lady Macduff's ending is that she dies resentful of what she thinks his desertion of her (IV.ii.6 ff.). This massacre, before our eyes, like Banquo's death earlier, is needed to lend vivid reality to our general impression of a country under the harrow. It is worth notice that the ruffian who stabs the defiant little boy exclaims 'What, you egg! Young fry of treachery!' – the same thought that Brutus had of Caesar as 'a serpent's egg', venomous if allowed to hatch. Good men and bad may be swayed by the same arguments.

It is another sign of social disruption that the family, the microcosm of society, is being torn apart, as in varying ways it was in *Lear*. A weighty aspect of Macbeth's crime, and one he is very conscious of, is that Duncan is his kinsman. Duncan's sons, and then Fleance, can be accused of parricide (III.vi.6–7), as Edgar was of plotting it. Macduff and his wife are never seen together, and in the embitterment of her last hour she tells her boy that she can buy twenty new husbands at any market (IV.ii.60). Love as we see it in Macbeth and his wife has recovered from its ineffectiveness in preceding tragedies, but only to become a force of destruction. The revulsion from sex so marked in *King Lear* finds a devious entry into this play when Malcolm accuses himself, as well as the tyrant, of 'boundless intemperance'; and then when Macduff reluctantly assures him that Scotland has 'willing dames enough' to satisfy the greediest libertine (IV.iii.73–7), Malcolm retracts his self-blame, proclaiming his complete chastity, as if only a youth 'unknown to woman' could be fit for the sacred task of liberating his country.

'Nature', 'natural', 'unnatural', are ubiquitous terms, again as in *Lear*. Nature's realm is the ambience of human life, and may share in it or mirror its convulsions. A storm accompanies Duncan's death, as it did Caesar's, with strange 'lamentings' and 'prophesying' (II.iii.57 ff.). These are auguries of coming woe for Scotland, not simply lamentations over a king's death; they link heaven, throne, people, in a single macrocosm. Religion is really, as often in Shakespeare, 'natural religion', even if, more than in most of the plays, embroidered with pious phrases. Some of these must have been offerings to King James, a deep theologian as well as statesman. They do not always sound merely conventional. There is true feeling in Banquo's 'In the great hand of God I stand', or in the doctor's 'God, God, forgive us all' (II.iii.130; V.i.74).

For Lady Macbeth only a child's eye 'fears a painted devil' (II.ii.54–5), though 'fate and metaphysical aid', as announced by the witches, can help to inspirit her (I.v.28). Macbeth cares little for heaven or hell, but his life is blighted by thoughts of what he has done; at bottom, by his violation of the ties that should unite human beings. He may feel at moments that he has 'given to the common enemy of man' his 'eternal jewel', or soul, but what really galls him is that he has sacrificed so much only to make 'the seed of Banquo kings' (III.i.63 ff.). Unnerved and frantic, he can quail at the idea of a secret power bringing murder to light by magical means, like the flight of birds (III.iv.123 ff.). Really, however, Providence, if at work at all, can work only through human means. Macduff wonders in vain how heaven could look on unmoved at his family's butchery (IV.iii.223–4). 'Heaven' is becoming more and more evidently a name for man's collective will towards social good. Duncan is in his grave, not in paradise; his reward is not bliss, but sleep.

Near the end we hear of 'the Powers above' setting their 'instruments' on, using men to good purposes. Young Siward perishes in the battle as 'God's soldier' (IV.iii.238–9; V.i.16). There are countervailing 'instruments of darkness', which Banquo, like Hamlet, fears are at work to trap men's souls (I.iii.123 ff.). 'Fiend' is a recurrent word, used by Macduff of Macbeth, and by Macbeth of the witches (IV.iii.233; V.viii.19), and deepening an impression of diabolical forces at work. On the whole, however, this is the tragedy with least of recognizable religion, most of superstition. In Shakespeare's England interest in magic of all kinds, from astrology down, was very strong, quite as strong we may guess as in Church doctrine: a hallmark of an age of social break-up like our own, when individuals cast on their own moral resources must grope through a murky universe in search of aid and comfort. Orthodox belief comes nearest, and shows most grotesquely, in the ramblings of a tipsy gatekeeper playing St Peter.

Few denizens of Shakespeare's world have divided critics more than the witches. Dowden thought them 'terrible and sublime' (246), McElroy dismisses them as 'filthy old hags' (212; cf. Rossiter 222). Poetically the witch scenes are poor, compared, for instance, with the opening scene of Jonson's *Masque of Queens*; proof either that Shakespeare did not write them, or that he cobbled them carelessly, though they are as indispensable to his plot as the Ghost in *Hamlet*. They have mysterious powers, chiefly for evil; but we are sometimes made to feel that their evil-doing is more petty and silly than frightful. One sister is nursing a spiteful grudge against a sailor whose wife has refused her a few chestnuts (I.iii.4 ff.); this has the flavour of village gossip, old wives' tales. Taken together they may be said to incarnate all egotistic, anti-social, blighting instincts, seductions rife in any environment but taking on different shapes. Their promptings only add force to the cravings of ambition already astir in Macbeth. At times they may, as F.L. Lucas suggests, symbolize hidden thoughts (77), among them 'the cursed thoughts' that Banquo prays for relief from (II.i.7–9).

There are intense moments in this drama where time seems to be warped or dislocated, sucked into a vortex. Glowing hopes and 'horrible imaginings' kindled by the witches throw Macbeth into a sort of trance (I.iii.137 ff.). He is 'rapt', Banquo twice says. His message throws Lady Macbeth into a similar intoxicating state of consciousness, transported 'beyond this ignorant present' and feeling 'the future in the instant' (I.v.55–7) – but a future in which her own wretched death, soon to be followed by her husband's, has no place. Little as Shakespeare may have cared about his witches, his always absorbing interest in questions of time, the future, fate and human will, to which beliefs in witchcraft and stars were primitive answers, was powerfully stirred.

But whereas he had been teaching himself to study past and present rationally, and learn from them some part of what the collective future might hold, Macbeth – concerned only with his own and his descendants' fortunes – is morbidly obsessed with his search for a magical short cut to foreknowledge. Banquo's mind runs, less obsessively, on the same lines. If Macbeth's accession to the throne is written in the book of fate, he may feel no need to blame himself for hastening it. But the inscrutable force at first his ally is to turn before long into a menacing foe, embodied in the strength of the human resistance that his rule will provoke. He must wrestle with this single-handed; he does not ask the witches for help, only for knowledge, not seeing that such reassurances as they may offer can be no more than delusions. Only the revelation of a future belonging to Banquo's heirs, not his own, is true.

Stung by this thought he is ready to challenge Fate to mortal combat, like a knight in the lists (III.i.70–71). Thinking of Macduff he resolves to destroy him, and thereby 'take a bond of Fate', extort from it a guarantee of safety (IV.i.83–4). Planning Banquo's death he rises to a pitch of defiance far beyond any other tragic hero's, a threat not against society, or humanity merely, but the whole universe: 'let the frame of things disjoint, both the worlds suffer' (III.ii.16): he will turn everything upside-down, a consummation Lear or Timon could only wish or pray for. In the witches' cavern he demands their secrets, at whatever cost, in tempest or earthquake, to all the germs of life, 'Even till destruction sicken' (IV.i.50 ff.). The extremity of his isolation is showing itself on a titanic scale. Whatever likenesses there may be between him and Milton's Satan (M.D.H. Parker 163), they break down here; Satan always had a loyal following. From another viewpoint Macbeth may seem instead a Faust-figure, a solitary forerunner of mankind's headlong rush towards limitless power and limitless crime and peril. He has been called 'a sacrificial victim' as well as a criminal (Mariestras 79–80).

Scotland is rescued by the English invasion, a virtuously disinterested one very unlike the many that were to follow it in Scottish history. With it comes Malcolm, as a pledge of Scotland's future; the commander, Siward earl of Northumbria, is his uncle. Macbeth feels that he could have beaten them if they were not being joined by so many Scots (V.v.5–6). Helpless unaided, Scotland is ready to join in its own liberation. Some of Macbeth's soldiers are joining the enemy; many are only 'wretched kerns, whose arms are hired' (V.vii.17–18). He is irrevocably alone in a land he has outraged. Desperation, indifference, as well as the moving forest of Birnam, induce him to give battle outside the impregnable castle where he could have waited for its besiegers to starve. Like the shadowy encounter in *King Lear*, this one gives place to a duel between mortal foes. Macbeth has lost everything except his courage; sword in hand he, like Othello, can still face anything. He has the same horror as Brutus or Cleopatra of being captured and 'baited with the rabble's curse', but he cannot 'play the Roman fool' and commit suicide (V.viii): a Roman death required its proper setting in tradition.

It has been said that we find ourselves looking for reasons to be not too hard on Macbeth (Sanders and Jacobson 57); but also that this drama fails to reach the highest tragic level, because his death does not leave us with a sense of unutterable loss (Van Doren 252). Yet he and his wife are the only grand personages of the play, the only ones who really captured Shakespeare's imagination, and therefore cannot fail to capture ours. Macbeth first comes before us as a national hero, winning 'golden opinions' which he is loth to sacrifice (I.vii.32–5). We know him also as a fond husband, with a disposition open to friendship. Close to death, he can feel a flicker of remorse at the sight of Macduff (V.viii.5–6). In his painful days of power it redeems him, from seeming to us an utterly lost soul, that he is anguished by knowing he has bartered the gold of men's esteem for the tinsel of sovereignty.

His opponents are less impressive than those faced by any of Shakespeare's other heroes (McElroy 215–16): he is his own worst enemy. We see in him a sinner undergoing penalties he has brought on himself, and recognize in him something of ourselves. Evil-doing, we are made to feel, is self-eroding; all wrongs men commit against one another will rise up in judgment against them. The play is a study of crime and punishment, raised to a far higher level than that of conventional morality. Action purely egotistic must alienate the doer from his fellows, and thereby render the gain valueless. Numerous touches point to the limits, imposed by men's mutual dependence, to the individual's ability to profit by self-aggrandizement at the expense of others.

Lear and other monarchs have had to learn that they were no more than men; but now Shakespeare is saying also that, while a craving to dictate to others diminishes the individual instead of enlarging him, achievement of simple manhood, as a human being worthy of a place among human beings, is not a descent but an elevation. Men can only be great as having a share in human greatness. Macbeth sees the truth when he says

> I dare do all that may become a man;
> Who dares do more is none –,

and his wife is wrong when she tells him that by performing the deed she is thrusting on him he will make himself 'so much more the man' (I.vii.46–51). Macbeth offers his murderers no fee, only the revenge due to any manly spirit; and their reply is 'We are men' (III.i.91). 'Are you a man?' his wife asks him impatiently when he quails before an imaginary ghost. 'What! quite unmanned in folly!' The ghost vanishes, and he can answer 'I am a man again' (III.iv.58, 73). We must stand up to tyranny 'like good men', Macduff says to Malcolm; and at the end of the scene, when all have shown their resolve, Malcolm can exclaim: 'This tune goes manly' (IV.iii.3, 235).

Such dwelling on *manhood*, the plain essence of humanity, belongs to a historical progression stretching far into the future. 'Ein Mensch zu sein' is the philosopher-king's teaching in Mozart's *Magic Flute*: to be truly a *man* – or rather a human being – is a high enough aim. Lady Macbeth is only too eager to claim more than her portion of manliness, to the exclusion of the feminine side of humanity. Yet she too can be reckoned a tragic and 'representative' character, as an example of womanhood excluded from a full share in the corporate life and intent on breaking into it, without knowing how. It is an essential thread of what makes this play a tragedy that it involves the wilful ruin of what ought to have remained a splendid alliance between a remarkable man and woman.

Macbeth makes an apt symbol of times when men feel mysterious forces at work, at bottom social forces not yet clearly recognized for what they are, which turn individuals almost irresistibly against their fellows. He felt it somehow dishonourable to shrink from a challenge to reach the summit, whatever the hazards. In Lukács' words, the play is an illustration of how 'great historical collisions could be translated into human terms and imbued with dramatic life' (*Historical Novel* 137). In a time like Shakespeare's a society may be ripe for change, but only individuals ruthlessly prepared to defy old rules of conduct can lead the way towards a shattering of the old order, and an opening towards a new one. Macbeth oversteps all bounds; the old virtues are degraded, or run wild: courage becomes readiness for murder, monarchy degenerates into despotism, religion into magic. An era is breaking up; new energies, still unharnessed and chaotic, are arising out of it.

In a different fashion from Hamlet, Macbeth was caught in the maelstrom of changing times, the clash of archaic ideas and their compulsions, and newer ones more inviting but less compelling. It led him to a nihilistic rejection of life, as a cosmic failure, without meaning. Hamlet came close to this sensation now and then. But nihilism cannot in itself be tragic. It is Macbeth, not Shakespeare, who tells us that life is a walking shadow, signifying nothing (Bradley, *Tragedy* 359). We forgive him for the sake of his confession, a warning to all his fellow-men, of what his insensate pursuit of power has brought him to. Giving himself up to ambition, he has sunk from superman to something lower than manhood.

Feudalism was giving way to capitalism, even if neither of these terms had yet been invented. There are things in this drama, as in the other tragedies, that make it look like a new picture painted over an old one. For the first time society's most dynamic class was giving itself up body and soul to the struggle for wealth, with many painful searchings of conscience and seeking of 'metaphysical aid' or warrant. To none more truly than the Puritan bourgeoisie could it be said

> What thou wouldst highly,
> That wouldst thou holily;

no class could have more need to steel itself, like Lady Macbeth, against self-reproach. None could be more bitterly aware of an incessant need to go on and on in its course, never free to enjoy the fruits of its triumphs. No era could have a better right than its descendant, the twentieth century, after all the wars and reigns of terror it has lived through, to borrow Macbeth's words: 'I have supped full of horrors . . .'

6

Timon of Athens (1606–08)

If the unrestricted competition, the struggle of each against all, that was taking hold of Shakespeare's England may be seen through a glass darkly in earlier plays of his, in *Timon of Athens* it comes openly, raucously, into the foreground. Here the new social system is firmly established: it is in control of the State, able to dictate its own laws and mould social conduct. A story to crystallize this new mode of life could not be easy to find, and the one Shakespeare hit on gave him a poor drama, though a good enough platform for social criticism. Not all the text we have can be from his pen, though agreement is hard to reach about what is authentic and what is not. If critical opinion of late has favoured a view of the Folio text as derived from 'a not-quite-finished manuscript of Shakespeare', probably dating from 1607 (Soellner 186, 201), it has surely been too easy-going. Many have thought it, with its frequent unmetrical lines and crudities, and its prose in particular, a rough draft only (e.g. Muir, *Sequence* 187–8). If so, it tells us something of Shakespeare's working methods, and indicates that composition did not always come easily to him. One suggestion has been that a good deal had to be cut out because the Essex rising of 1601 made the staging of any kind of revolt indiscreet (Jorgesen 279–80). But Alcibiades' *coup d'état* is shown in full and given the author's blessing. Essex has probably been blamed for too many things.

A different guess might be a wholesale shift of time and place, for political reasons, such as Massinger made when he transferred his *Believe As You List* from modern Portugal to ancient Rome. Another conceivable interpretation would be that Shakespeare was seized by an impulse to return to narrative poetry, this time in the lately fashionable vein of satire, as a means of working off his feelings about contemporary abuses. Oscar J. Campbell finds in *Timon* some of the same 'satirical devices' made use of in several plays by Jonson (183). But if this was the case Shakespeare found his material swelling too much, and could not help drifting back to drama, with a poet's sketch in the opening scene of an intended work on the fall of someone resembling Timon – perhaps Shakespeare's own plan, turned into a kind of dumb-show introduction.

Soellner finds the play 'deliberately anchored in a pessimistic intellectual tradition' (12); Hazlitt, who may be said to belong to this tradition himself, and had a good share of Timon's misanthropy, declared the play to be 'written with as intense a feeling' as any work of Shakespeare (47). In this light it is tempting to see Timon as the successor of Lear, as Bradley did (*Tragedy*, 246–7; cf. Farnham 7). Both men have succumbed to the sweet poison of flattery; both come to grief through too liberal giving, one bestowing his kingdom, the other his fortune, on undeservers. Timon may have been given some furious tirades for which there was no room in *King Lear*, but with none of the wild grandeur of the Lear story to justify them. Lear is driven out into the wilderness; Timon turns his back on the city and walks out into a desert conveniently close by, to discharge his storms of invective. Shakespeare's disgust with mankind, which strains *King Lear* to the limits of dramatic form, here overflows them altogether; it is a play virtually without a plot. Timon has far too little warrant for his indiscriminate excommunication of mankind, and – lacking inspired madness – even less opportunity than Lear to have acquired the detailed familiarity with human depravity which he suddenly displays. It is clearly the author himself who is finding vent for feelings of his own, inflamed by awareness of similar indignation among many others. There is no lack of evidence elsewhere that Shakespeare sometimes suffered from such inflamed moods, at the opposite pole from his keen relish at other times of life among his fellow-men. It was a fundamental of his nature to be compounded from opposites and contraries.

Lear's ordeals finally emancipate him from self-absorption; Timon's do not. His only way out will be the escape from life that Gloucester learned to renounce. He undergoes no 'genuinely tragic remoulding' (Maxwell, cited by Lerner, 271; cf. Hunter, *Studies* 254). Probably Timon was too well known a character for even Shakespeare to be able to alter much. Dekker was writing in 1609 of 'Timonists' who 'truly loath this polluted and mangy-fisted world' (*Hornbook* 18; cf. 75). Timon was seen, that is, as typifying the alienation of man from man that people were growing uneasily conscious of, not as a bringer of new ideas for curing the malady. In the play he may condemn men's heartlessness towards one another, but it is always their treatment of *him* that infuriates him. *King Lear* is concentrated on the miseries of the poor, *Timon of Athens* on the callousness of the rich; not much, however, or not manifestly, towards the poor. Here the levelling tendency apparent in the two previous plays becomes a morbid one, downward instead of upward. Men are equal in being equally worthless; when Timon wants all 'degrees, observances', ranks, swept away (IV.i.18–20) it is not for the sake of enfranchisement, but to set mankind free to destroy itself. Lear's frantic denunciations of the human race are palliated by his age, whereas Timon seems to be in the prime of life.

We can suppose Shakespeare to have abandoned work on the play, leaving it perhaps to be cobbled up by a 'prentice hand, when he realized that it was not flowering into a true drama. A hero without distinct personality, raging at a set of ingrates who are only names to us, could not be lifted from the ground by even a whirlwind of poetry. There is something in Timon of Hamlet, unpacking his heart with words, but unlike Hamlet he has no specific mission to urge him on, and no impulse to do anything more than talk. His world is too degenerate to be worth saving; his jeremiads are on a par with those of the pulpit against a human nature incurably defective. They miss the crucial fact that what is wrong is not, at bottom, human nature, but the institutions it has locked itself into. Shakespeare does end by pointing this out, in however rough and ready a manner, not through Timon, but through Alcibiades.

Tragedy cannot for Shakespeare be confined within any circle of personal life, eventful though this may be: it must cast huge shadows of collective concern. A hero's fate and that of his fellow-men must in some fashion be bound up together. In *Timon* this vital factor is for a long time missing. True, the protagonist has been at some time in the past a true hero, a pillar and protector of the city, both with his purse and with his sword, against foreign attack. But we learn this belatedly; through the first two Acts he shows merely as a rich man indulging his foolish whims. It would almost seem as if Shakespeare suddenly perceived this, and brought in Timon's services of bygone years as an afterthought. They are what entitles him, he believes, to call on the Senate for an immense subsidy when he goes bankrupt (II.ii.193 ff.), and to charge the government as well as his friends with ingratitude.

Romantic love had become for Shakespeare a very questionable ideal; he turns now to another fashionable Elizabethan cult, romantic friendship, and finds it even more fallacious. It meant much to him, but only, in his maturity, when cemented by shared principles and sense of duty. In *Julius Caesar* it is the threatened breakdown of a noble friendship that affects us most painfully of all. In Athens things are too one-sided. Appealed to by an associate, in jail for debt, Timon declares that he is not one to desert 'My friend when he most needs me', but little guesses how his friends will behave when he needs *them*. In Shakespeare's calendar ingratitude was always a sin, 'more strong than traitors' arms' against Caesar (*JC* III.ii.186). Timon's misfortune is foretold in *Hamlet* – 'who not needs, shall never lack a friend' (III.ii.188); he is as deeply outraged by his abandonment as Coriolanus, deserted on political grounds.

Timon is alone in the world, without kith or kin, so that his friends mean everything to him. He is a nobleman, often addressed as 'Lord Timon'; a great landowner, living in a pipe-dream nourished by his riches and his ardently generous nature. 'We are born to do benefits', he proclaims, finding a 'precious comfort' in the thought of friends, 'like brothers, commanding one another's fortunes!' (I.ii.94 ff.). His healthy social instinct, formerly dedicated to the commonweal, is now frittered away in useless waste. His philosophy of mutual aid is a kind of collectivism, but of an élitist kind, limited to a clique of men rich enough to exchange valuable gifts. It is, though Timon does not rationalize it so, a method of mutual insurance, such as the poor have always been compelled to practise among themselves. There is no thought of aid to those really in want. It is with savage irony that the disillusioned Timon, in his grace before meat, begs the gods to 'Lend to each man enough, that one need not lend to another': lending and borrowing must always breed rancour. He includes 'the common tag of the people' among those 'suitable for destruction' (III.vi.72 ff.). It was an obtuse critic, of a century ago, who hailed the play as a demonstration that socialism, community of goods, cannot work (Smeaton 434).

There is something in Timon's self-deception, all the same, of Shakespeare's haunting nostalgia for a lost Golden Age, free of private property with its dividing and corroding taint – that property which on a modest scale he himself felt obliged to devote so much of his life to putting together. In this play he is setting against the acrid self-interest of the new age an opposite conception (however much it leaves out) of how life ought to be lived. Timon has never expected to be reduced to poverty: he thinks his wealth inexhaustible, and in any case counts on always having faithful friends to buoy him up. Still, he has a laudable indifference to possessions, except as a means of making others happy; and he accepts voluntary penury rather than return to riches bereft of the sanction of any ties of brotherhood.

Yet the ideal glow he basks in at first is no more than a feeble glow-worm light. As Soellner notices (54), he is an isolated figure even in his palmy days. He has no genuine friend, no confidant to turn to; a strong contrast with Brutus's many loyal friends, and one that reveals Timon's lack of judgment. Costly gifts are no substitute for a communion of beliefs, political allegiances, high purposes. Rome too was an oligarchy, but its best minds dwelt on a vastly higher level than is to be found in Athens. Hugging the dear friends whom he has never tested, Timon is one of Shakespeare's Don Quixotes, a fantasist of the past. There survives in his daydreams at least a negative truth, that 'civilized' life, perennially athirst for gain, corrupts human beings and makes any advance to truly civilized life impossible. Constructive social thinking would for long be out of sight; Shakespeare can only dodge insoluble riddles by going out into the wilderness with Timon in an unavailing protest against the reign of Mammon.

Timon has been called a memorial to the old spirit of open-handed feudal bounty (Siegel 17); but Machiavelli had long since warned readers of *The Prince* against throwing away their money and taking the highroad to despised poverty. Spendthrift habits, of the Rake's Progress sort, were beggaring a wide swathe of the English landed classes. Another factor here must have been simple inability to count. Numeracy was spreading much more slowly than literacy, and ignorance of the use of Arabic numerals and decimals, of even the most straightforward arithmetic, was still common in England (Thomas, 'Numeracy'). Doubtless the Merchant of Venice could count well enough, but he had been wont to lend money without interest; Timon outdoes him by refusing to accept money lent to Ventidius when the latter's son, now well off, wants to return it (I.ii.1 ff.). There is an ostentation verging on vulgar display in his lavish gifts. He can only keep it up now with borrowed money; all his vast estate is gone, as he is at last forced to learn from his steward. Antonio found no one to lend him money when *he* was in dire straits; and Timon's creditors and critics think of his extravagance as Shylock did of Antonio's. It cannot be supposed that Shakespeare, himself a hard-working man careful of his funds, admired Timon's folly. Some lines in *Troilus and Cressida* show what kind of giving he approved: Troilus is generous, 'Yet gives he not till judgment guide his bounty' (IV.v.102).

Timon's denunciations of mankind are still more excessive than Lear's, yet no one is to blame for leading him astray but himself. He has been flattered, or buttered up, no doubt, but so are all rich men; and he is one of the plutocrats who have been enjoying life in the Athens whose wickedness he now excoriates. No sooner is he angry with his false friends than he is ready to curse everyone wholesale, including women, who have done him no injury that we know of, and commoners. 'Timon will to the woods' (IV.ii.35 ff.), but not in the resigned spirit of *As You Like It*, or the hopeful spirit of the Romances. His maledictions may be magnificent, but there is something in them of the Byronic, or the spoiled child. He does not call on his fellow-men to improve, but to vanish from the earth. He runs some risk at times of sounding like a thunderous echo of the crusty cynic Apemantus. He cannot speak for mankind against its oppressors; all its better qualities he is blind to. He urges Alcibiades to massacre every soul in the city. There is nothing of Lear's devouring remorse, first for his foolishness and then for his wrong-doing or neglect. We can only feel good-will for Timon by reflecting that he is really condemning not the individuals he thinks have wronged him, but the accumulated cankers and corruptions of society. It is Shakespeare, in however unbalanced a mood of *saeva indignatio*, who is speaking to us.

He can indeed find fault, through Apemantus, with his hero's 'unmanly melancholy' (IV.iii. 203–4), a phrase recalling the prominence of 'manly' and 'manliness' in *Macbeth*. Yet Timon can in his way impress us as a tragical figure, because an embodiment of the better, if wasted, qualities of a passing age, horrified by the new age into which he is shaken from his dream; and those qualities have earned him the staunch fidelity of a humble few. It is not merely personal mortification, but the shattering of a faith, that transforms him overnight into a half-crazed misanthropist. Some such loss of cherished illusions is part of the experience of every tragic hero, and therefore also of ours as spectators. Timon could be rich again if he chose, but there can be no way back to Athens for him, any more than for Lear to a throne he has learned to despise. For him only death remains, and he looks forward to it in splendid poetry (IV.iii.372–3; V.ii.213 ff.). He will have a grave washed daily by the tide: he must leave behind not only earth's vile inhabitants, but the infected soil that breeds them.

Shakespeare might be in principle an admirer of republicanism, but his Athens is a very unattractive republic. He must have had in mind his own London, very much a little republic as far as its domestic affairs went, and governed by an oligarchy of the rich. In this play alone Shakespeare shows us a bourgeoisie in power, and his senators have an evident resemblance to the aldermen familiar to us from the works of other playwrights. These London dignitaries were never on cordial terms with the theatres, and Shakespeare's choice of plot allowed him to retaliate against them by proxy.

Timon and his milieu epitomize a time when propertied classes are in a shifting condition, individuals rising or falling, novel sources of wealth being found; when opportunity and insecurity reign jointly, and profit or bare survival can both depend on credit. Little distinction is made between friends whom Timon has enriched and businessmen he has borrowed from to keep up his wasteful style of living. He has inhaled enough of the commercial air of the times to feel that his 'honour' is injured by his failure to pay his debts (II.ii.41) – a notion that Falstaff would have laughed heartily at. It is a sign of how much his outlook has altered that when he discovers gold it does not occur to him to use it for clearing off his debts.

The senators who refused to rescue him from bankruptcy are 'old fellows', he complains, their blood cold and 'caked' (II.ii.211 ff.). Athens is a home of the new or nascent capitalism, but the only mode of enrichment singled out is the most opprobrious, one that any writer could attack and be sure of having the public on his side, – usury. But money-lending in the modern sense of credit, or provision of capital for useful enterprise, was becoming an indispensable part of the economy, which the playwrights were apt to overlook. A senator who has lent money to Timon, and wants it back, may not be a monster, but a rational man of affairs, who sees that Timon's 'raging waste' must soon ruin him. 'My reliances on his fracted dates', he tells his assistant, 'have smit my credit', and though he holds Timon in esteem he has no wish to follow him downhill (II.i.4, 20 ff.). Timon is soon beset by duns, employees of other 'usurers'. There can be no lending of money nowadays 'upon bare friendship, without security' (III.i.39–40); even the gods would find it hard to borrow from men (III.vi.73–4). There is no room for pity in business affairs, 'For policy sits above conscience' (III.ii.87–8). A banker today would say, or think, just the same.

Hitherto Timon has found nothing objectionable in the ways by which money circulates among the prosperous; and of course as a landlord he has found it quite natural that others should dig the soil while he collects rents from them to be spent on feasting and junketing. This is something he never feels any need to think about. Still, Shakespeare can invite us to sympathize with him in spite of his egregious folly. He brings in a group of 'strangers' to express this feeling and protest against all cut-throat money-making (III.ii.64 ff.). 'Religion groans at it.' At bottom the issue presented is between two classes, two eras, and their philosophies.

Timon had many forerunners in inveighing against the encroaching power of money. Erasmus, who spent a good deal of time in England, had elevated Plutus, god of wealth, to primacy on Olympus, as the deity at whose nod 'All public and private affairs are decided' (103). In earlier plays of Shakespeare pecuniary values creep in through many channels, among them the Bastard's tirade on 'Commodity', or profit, in *King John*. Now their blight is intensified into Timon's ferocious denunciation of Gold, the real villain of the play. Kenneth Muir counts two hundred allusions to it, and points out that Shakespeare's play followed close on Jonson's plays about avarice, as the motive force of an acquisitive society (*Singularity* 66, 68). Its contagion can no longer be closed up, shut off, in any single personality like Shylock; it is an impersonal, omnipresent social force. Timon's worthy servant longs for his master's false friends to be compelled to swallow molten gold, a penalty traditionally inflicted on the greedy in hell (III.i.49).

All time-honoured social principles are being subverted by the unfettered pursuit of riches; this play is a manifesto against what is happening. Timon himself has been a casualty, long before his fall; it is his exorbitant fortune that has turned his wits. He has been trying to bribe people, with lavish gifts, into being his bosom friends, and been rewarded with nothing better than flattery – always, like ingratitude, one of Shakespeare's targets. It seems from what his honest steward says that his house has often been the scene of noisy, 'riotous' revelry (II.ii.154 ff.), which must have detracted from the respect earned by his public services. Such feudal profligacy recalls the revelry of Lear's knights, which so disgusted Goneril. 'O, the fierce wretchedness that glory brings us!' the steward is left to lament: this is where 'pomp' and 'state' lead to (IV.ii.31 ff.). Great wealth, like overmuch power, is dangerous both to the possessor and to those whom it enables him to enslave. Timon comes to see this very clearly, of everyone except himself. More than once he thinks of gold, like Erasmus, as the 'god' of this new age (IV.iii.380; V.i.48–9). Even when he is about to make ready his grave and epitaph, he turns back to apostrophize gold – that 'ever young, fresh, loved, and delicate wooer', and destroyer – the 'sweet king-killer', the 'divorce' between father and son, that magnet that can join together things impossibly incongruous (IV.iii.375 ff.).

Timon may seem emotionally involved, to an unnatural degree, with his male friends, though not with any one of them in particular, and to be indifferent to women until, as soon as he is soured, he feels a maniacal loathing for them. There are no reputable women in the play; it might have seemed indecent to bring any onto the stage that is to be drenched by Timon's torrents of abuse. There could be no partner for such a man; he must be alone, like Lear, to pour out his vituperations. These are not so much of government or institutions, as of individual vice, especially sexual. But public and private depravity go together, whether we are to conclude that government corrupts or is corrupted by those it rules.

In the passages from *Timon* quoted with most relish by Marx, the black magic of gold, and the sexual debasement it can cause, stand out together. In a society ruled by gold there can be little room for love. At best it can be looked back on by a mercenary old father as no worse than a fit of youthful silliness: the man for his daughter must have money (I.i.112 ff.). Gold can join couples, and it can drive them apart: it is the 'bright defiler of Hymen's purest bed' (IV.iii.376–7). For the first and only time in Shakespeare we see and hear of women only at their tawdry worst. The only speaking parts, both small, are those of a pair of trollops kept and openly paraded by Alcibiades. 'We'll do anything for gold', one of them assures Timon (IV.iii.150), speaking, we must suppose, for her sisters in general. They provoke another outburst from Timon, and bode ill for their protector's future as reformer of Athens; but by the time he appears under the walls they have disappeared.

In Timon's fevered imagination, at least, sexual vice overflows all bounds of class, age, rank; lust is the great leveller. In a not very Shakespearian colloquy, but with some resemblance to the brothel-scenes in *Measure for Measure* and *Pericles*, a 'Fool' apparently attached to some such establishment is asked the meaning of 'whoremaster': he replies that the term may denote any male from thirteen to eighty, lords, lawyers, philosophers, and, most of all, knights (II.ii.104 ff.). Disgust with everything sexual is carried to an extreme. Intercourse is seldom alluded to without mention of disease as well. Timon can welcome immorality as helping to hasten the extinction of the human race. He bestows gold on Alcibiades' women, adjuring them to further this good work (IV.iii.134 ff.).

Of any interest in social reform he shows only an occasional flicker. There are touches of the puritanical, as when he censures wine and gluttony as likely to cloud or 'grease' men's minds; he goes on to talk disparagingly of 'the subtle blood o' the grape' (IV.iii.193–4, 422 ff.). We have heard things like this in *Hamlet* and *Othello*. In one long speech he sounds as if suddenly transformed into a revolutionary agitator, calling on debtors to cut

147

their creditors' throats, servants to steal, all law and order to be thrown to the winds (IV.i.1 ff.) – as they were by Laertes' anarchical mob. Lear wanted authority dissolved, Timon wants class war to take its place, but, apparently, without any plan or leadership.

Timon winds up by extending his curse to 'the whole race of mankind', of most of which he can scarcely know much. Earth, the all-mother, 'sick of man's unkindness', should no longer breed 'ingrateful man', but only venomous creatures like adders, or savage beasts (IV.iii.176, ff.). Human beings will outdo the devil himself, Timon's man Servilius remarks. Apemantus seems to hint at recent English history as confirming his belief that a great man's neighbour at table is 'the readiest to kill him; 't has been proved' (I. ii.42 ff.). No remedy is to be looked for from the educated, who have a full share in the iniquities of the mass. Timon sees 'boundless theft' practised by the liberal professions. Lawyers in particular indulge in 'uncheck'd theft' (IV.iii.420 ff.). They are also oppressive. 'Religious canons, civil laws, are cruel': what can we expect war to be? (IV.iii.60–61). Many in Shakespeare's audience would have said Amen to this; lawyers were second only to usurers in the Englishman's list of social plagues. Alcibiades the soldier speaks apprehensively of 'the law, which is past depth' to those who rashly plunge into it (III.v.12–13). As for the medical faculty, its 'antidotes are poison' (III.iv.424–6). In all this, as in Lear's curses on mankind, the fundamental Christian doctrine of total depravity, rendered still more strident by Puritanism, must be borne in mind. Without it such maledictions would have sounded hysterical, as they do to us today. All men and women were corrupted, according to the Churches, by the sin of Adam; *society* is corrupt, Shakespeare is saying, because of the unbridled greed and egotism which have come to be the breath of its life.

The play opens with a poet and painter waiting, along with skilled crafts-men, for a chance to sell Timon their wares. Shakespeare must have recalled his early days of dancing attendance on a rich patron and offering homage; a memory that, as Armstrong said, must have disgusted him (155). Since then he had shaken off this degradation by taking the public, with all its shortcomings, for his chief patron. Both poet and painter deplore Timon's reckless spending. But artists must live, and these two are as acquisitive as any other toadies when, getting word of his discovery of gold, they hurry out from Athens hoping to lay their hands on some of it. He overhears them talking, and quickly sends them packing; though it is to his credit that he recognizes in poetry a species of 'alchemy', able to turn base materials into gold (V.i.1 ff., 111). And whatever shifts artists may be reduced to in a soulless society, the poet's intended composition, approved by the painter, amounted to a warning against Timon's blindness, unlikely to have wrung many thanks from him. Artists are finding the new climate unpropitious, we may conclude.

Apemantus is a dull creature on most days of the week, with nothing to do in Athens except snarl at the gay world he sees in Timon's mansion, where his admission speaks well for its owner's tolerance. He has somehow got himself an education, which has left him an intellectual without occupation. Embitterment like his was no small ingredient in the cauldron of English social feeling. He has turned satirist, and occasionally shows wit. He has good warrant, after watching Timon's banquet, to ask 'what need these feasts, pomps, and vain-glories?' – and to sneer at elaborate upper-class etiquette as turning men into creatures more like 'baboon and monkey' (I.i.239 ff.). After Timon's fall Apemantus is seen in a better light, and is capable of some true eloquence. He claims a contentedness with poverty superior to never-satisfied grandeur; Timon retorts that he was born poor, and would have been a debauchee if he could (IV.iii.239 ff.). In their altercation in the wilderness Apemantus sensibly points out that Timon knows no mean, no moderation, but has always been at one of two opposite extremes. (IV.iii.300 ff.). But their talk falls off into an undignified exchange of abuse, sinking from poetry into prose.

Timon illuminates class-society in a few words when he says that life is brief, but sweet

> to such as may the passive drudges of it
> Freely command.
>
> (IV.iii.253–5)

His catalogue of human ills includes, like Hamlet's, the 'pangs of love', but not poverty (V.i.195 ff.). The lives he adds joy to are those of his fellow-aristocrats; we hear of no donations to the poor, no benefactions such as both lords and opulent merchants often preened themselves on. If he had sought companions among humbler folk, as Hamlet did, his disillusionment would have been less crushing. Here as in ancient Britain, simple virtue has taken refuge among the poor. Everyone makes promises nowadays, says the painter, but fulfilment lags very far behind, except among 'the plainer and simpler kind of people' (V.i.22–5). Timon has no ear for such talk. In one of Shakespeare's most terrible utterances he recommends his steward to give no charity to beggars,

> But let the famish'd flesh slide from the bone.
>
> (IV.iii.521)

There were famines in Shakespeare's Europe, one of the worst in Ireland, as there are today in our world. Through Timon's ravings Shakespeare is telling us that this is how the rich do, too often, treat the poor. Through Lear he has told us something of how they *ought* to treat the poor. Misfortune has turned the two men's minds in contrary directions.

In *King Lear* we meet good men of both high rank and low. Timon has faithful adherents only among the lower ranks, as if Shakespeare had lost hope of all grandees. To his servants Timon has doubtless been an indulgent master, in the old style of the great household, and their devotion to him is unbroken. Cast adrift, their 'hearts wear Timon's livery' still (IV.ii.18). Even the servants of the ruined man's creditors, sent to dun him, feel how basely his old associates are behaving (III.iv.22 ff.). Having vainly done his best to dissuade Timon from his fatal liberality, the steward gives his humbler fellows a share of his savings, and goes out to Timon's cave to offer the rest to him, together with his free service. For once Timon feels his now 'dangerous nature' almost subdued, and admits to the 'perpetual-sober gods' that there is one good man left alive. His steward, he knows, could have done better for himself by deserting and betraying him: many get employment with new masters 'Upon their first lord's neck' (IV.iii.485 ff.) – another piece of social realism.

By way of parody (and a reminiscence perhaps of his burlesque brigands in *Two Gentlemen of Verona*), Shakespeare brings into his procession of visitors to Timon's new abode a group of 'banditti' (IV.iii.392 ff.). They try to pass themselves off as soldiers, in distress as many always were, but Timon sees what they are, or it may be is implying that there is not much difference between the two occupations. They call their trade a 'mystery' – mastery, craft; a joke, like Falstaff's 'vocation' of highway robbery, that Shakespeare never tired of. When Timon assures them that all men are thieves, he comes close to saying 'Property is theft'. He urges them to go to Athens and break into shops: they take this as differently meant, and are moved to thoughts of giving up their anti-social life. Here, still more evidently, Shakespeare is teaching back-handedly.

Religion, like all else, is in a bad way. Gold can 'knit and break religions' (IV.iii.34); priests are among those who ignore 'the general weal' in their chase after private gain. A servant speaks of 'those that, under hot ardent zeal, would set whole realms on fire' (III.iii.31), fanatics bent on stirring up broils. Amid this hubbub morality is abandoned to the lowly and unassuming. 'Man was wished to love his enemies', the good steward reminds us (IV.iii.459). There is frequent invoking of 'the gods'. Timon calls on them to confound mankind. They are 'righteous', the steward believes (IV.ii.4); he does not ask why they have made so unrighteous a world. As in *King Lear*, such epithets tell us what virtues human beings feel their rulers most lack.

Nature partakes far more now of human malignity than of heavenly innocence. Apemantus's warning to Timon of how little 'these moss'd trees/That have outlived the eagle' will care about his wishes contains some of the play's superbest poetry (IV.iii.221 ff.). Timon himself makes no attempt to idealize Nature. All living things prey on one another; here again allusions to the political jungle are thinly disguised. For good measure Timon goes on to accuse even sun and moon, earth and sea, of thievery (IV.iii.326 ff., 429 ff.).

We expect a Shakespearian tragedy to work towards events crucial to the public weal or woe. It is never the hero who is commissioned in the end to launch a reconstruction, as new kings could be in the Histories with their simpler requirements. Hamlet and Lear can catch sight of the needs of a new age, but they must leave it to others to provide for them. Timon is so hopelessly overwhelmed by the evils surrounding him that he cannot even dream of reformation; the only cure for mankind is to be wiped out. Change cannot be inaugurated by any legitimate means, or by insurrection, but only by a *coup d'état*. Its leader Alcibiades is an admirer of Timon, which supplies a degree of continuity. With his army on the march, the Senate begs Timon to come back to Athens, assume full power, and save the city, as he saved it once before from foreign attack. He repels its deputies harshly, but twice in the colloquy rises into a mood of tragic serenity. His thoughts are on his coming death, his sea-washed tomb. 'Lips, let sour words go by, and language end' (V.i.183 ff.): we can fancy we are hearing Shakespeare, in his mood of this play, bidding farewell to poetry, like Prospero, reconciled to life, later on.

Unlike all the other heroes, Timon disappears unseen, careless of how he will be remembered, and leaving no more of a message than the necessity of root and branch change. Salvation from a mutinous army chief is a very new departure in Shakespeare's political thinking, though Fortinbras and Albany are in their own ways forerunners, and Antony and, more distinctly, Octavius successors. Shakespeare is far from wishing to romanticize war, as he had sometimes done before. Timon talks with aversion of 'contumelious, beastly, mad-brain'd war' (V.i.171); a far cry from Othello's glorification of it. There is in Alcibiades' closing speech a return to something like the notion, so frequently met with in Shakespeare, that peace breeds maladies which only war can cure (V.iv.80–82); but the gist is now rather that each must be kept in its proper place. As to army service, Shakespeare is making explicit what he must always have been conscious of more or less: the sacrifices of war fall on the soldier, the benefits go to his sleek employers (III.v.108 ff.), a ruling class as Timon has called them of 'large-handed robbers', who 'pill [pillage] by law' (IV.i.11–12).

Plutarch's portrait of Alcibiades was a mixture of praise and blame; he was not much admired in England (Soellner 51–2). Like his disgruntled men he deems himself ill-rewarded, but the issue over which he takes up the cudgels is a comrade's condemnation by the Senate for killing a man in a fight. It is the only occasion when Shakespeare debates the ethics of duelling seriously; his old problem of Honour comes up afresh. In Alcibiades' view the culprit showed a noble disposition by fighting, because his 'reputation' (so much heard of in that military play *Othello*) had been 'touch'd to death', or traduced. A senator states judiciously the case against duelling: it is 'valour misbegot', or mere revengefulness, and for a man to risk his life without need is folly. It emerges, moreover, that though a bold soldier this man was often drunken and riotous. How many good soldiers are not, Shakespeare – always severe on drunkenness – may be asking? What will an army be, Alcibiades asks, if courage is to be stifled, or why keep an army at all if it is right to swallow injuries (III.v.18 ff.)?

Once again we are witnessing a clash between the outlooks of two eras, two dominant classes. Alcibiades wants law to be its old feudal self, flexible and pliable, taking account of individual claims to favour; the Senate answers him, as it answered Timon's appeal for financial aid, in a spirit of cold, formal legalism. Justice has no room for pity; mercy only encourages law-breaking (as it did in *Romeo and Juliet*): 'We are for the law; he dies.' No person is entitled by his services to ask for law to be set aside. 'My wounds ache at you', the general protests. He is banished for his persistence, and breaks out in fury, telling his masters to banish their own 'dotage', and the practice of usury 'That makes the Senate ugly'. He is left resolving to stir up the soldiers against their employers, who have been enriching themselves by money-lending while he has been out fighting, like his men, for miserly pay (III.v.95 ff.).

Alcibiades marching on Athens has a resemblance to Coriolanus marching on Rome; but his intention as it takes shape is a far better one. It is truly revolutionary, the overturning of a selfish government of the rich. The trumpets sounding his 'terrible approach' (V.iv.1–2) reverberate like Bolingbroke's 'brazen trumpet' outside Richard II's crumbling castle. England, like Athens, must have harboured some hankerings for an armed saviour; if Essex had come back from Ireland a triumphant conqueror, as Shakespeare had predicted in *Henry V*, he might have had better fortune. Alcibiades' philippic against the senators and their abuse of power, now grown intolerable, is a powerful expression of patience worn out (V.iv.3 ff.). New spokesmen of the Senate assure him that his enemies have died of 'shame'. It is not very clear what is the dividing line between sheep and goats; but those now in the lead offer dignified submission, and appeal to Alcibiades' feeling for his 'Athenian cradle'. He responds in statesmanlike tones: only a few of the most guilty will be punished, the army will be kept in order, Athens can make a new beginning. Forgiveness, so often spoken of in the tragedies, has a place here too; he proclaims a 'more noble meaning' than revenge (V.iv.40 ff.), very much as Prospero, with his enemies in his grasp, chooses to be guided by his 'nobler reason'. Alcibiades is thus faithful to the maxim he had urged in his dispute with the Senate, that justice should be tempered with equity and mercy.

England's evolution had gone far enough, this play shows, for political judgments of considerable maturity to be made. More clearly than ever Shakespeare is recognizing the decay of an old social order, without welcoming the new one taking its place. Each has its better attributes, which he would like to see combined in one whole. His Alcibiades is among the earliest sketches of a populist dictator, with army backing, coming to purge society and promote justice and progress, as in Cromwellian England only forty years later, and as in so many outdated fantasies of our modern world. The senators offering surrender address Alcibiades as 'Noble and young' (V.iv.13); it is fitting that those in Shakespeare who undertake this vanguard role should be young men like him – Fortinbras, Edgar, Malcolm, Octavius. Their youth augurs a new springtime of rejuvenation for their people. Athens is opening its gates to the future.

7

Antony and Cleopatra (1606–08)

In the sixteenth and seventeenth centuries Antony and Cleopatra were often reunited on the stages of Europe. In the preface to his own version of their story, *All For Love* (1678), Dryden accounted for their vogue by 'the excellency of the moral', the lesson that we must learn to keep our passions under control. We could have learned it in fewer words from Iago; and Dryden could have found a better key in the fitness of the story to the mood of a changing Europe, stumbling out of one epoch into another, half-lamenting what had to be left behind, half-resentful of what had to be adopted. Danby thought of Shakespeare's play as a discontinuity, a monument standing by itself in his tragic series (*Fool's Hill* 128.) It is indeed a unique trophy of his 'infinite variety'; none the less, its underlying meanings mark it as belonging to the tragic continuum.

Our escape here from the sombre bleakness of the previous dramas, and *Timon of Athens* in particular, is one of Shakespeare's most astonishing transformations. Somehow the elements have rearranged themselves as if in a kaleidoscope. The basic antithesis is more sharply defined than ever. Problems of poverty have disappeared, though only to return with a vengeance in the next play; with them have vanished most of the more sordid aspects of both old and new, so much in the foreground in *Timon*. Instead we are given the brilliant aspects of both, in a blaze of poetry that made Quiller-Couch call it 'in some ways the most wonderful' of Shakespeare's masterpieces (186). Yet the two chief personages are a middle-aged pair, each with a very chequered past. We may fancy the poet, himself middle-aged now, turning his imagination loose to revel in autumn colours.

More deeply, he was recovering, by some kind of self-purgation, from the lowest point of the tragic descent, the rejection of life by Macbeth and Timon; he was discovering vitality in what was passing away but deserved to be perpetuated in memory, and new values to be added. In *Timon* nearly all human ties were broken, and the hero's fate was a solitary death; now the tragic destiny can be accepted joyfully, because, as in *Julius Caesar*, there are two to share it. Shakespeare has given himself strength by returning from shadowy legend to a firm bedrock of history, and to a Rome – not now the city, but the empire or civilization that goes by its name (Miola 117) – which by itself confers a sense of permanence. Few of the scenes are laid in the capital; yet some of the institutions cradled there remain to foster effective organization of power, and endowments unknown to barbarian peoples or decadent kingdoms round the frontiers. With this inner strength of Roman tradition to sustain him, and knowledge of many glories still to be added to the Roman name, Shakespeare can find exhilaration instead of gloom in the spectacle of change. Individual fortunes are, as Traversi says, linked throughout with 'the fortunes of a universal empire' (79). These may at times seem no more than prey for adventurers to fight over like wolves; but the ideal Rome remains, fitfully intermixed with the strife.

Fault has often been found with the play's construction, as too loose and sprawling. With more insight Granville-Barker called it 'the most finely spacious piece of play-making he ever did' ('Henry V to Hamlet' 72); and Stauffer thinks it equalled in grandeur only by King Lear – 'For the last time Shakespeare exercises simultaneously all of his magnificent powers' (232). One complaint of the objecters is that it is too much overcrowded with miscellaneous incident, and jumbles up love and politics (e.g. Boas, Shakspere 473–4). But this combining and blending is a vital part of its achievement; and a lavish lay-out was needed to contain an era of European history. Most of the other tragedies are played out on much narrower stages. Even in Julius Caesar we only see the empire's capital and a corner of one of its provinces; now we are awed by its real extent, and unending expansion. Two words that haunt the pages are 'great' and 'world'. Caroline Spurgeon found prominent in the imagery the ideas of globe, sky, ocean, vastness; and 'world' occurring forty-two times (Imagery 350–52). Bethell followed her in stressing the 'Brobdingnagian imagery', indulged in not by one or two speakers but by all, and linked to the dual themes of empire and love (117, 119). Charney contrasts the profusion of imagery of all kinds with the spare diction of Julius Caesar (28). We may see this as reflecting a Roman state grown hollow but still apparently firm in the earlier play, and the fluid situation of the later, where a flood-tide of events sweeps Rome towards an unknown future.

Much of what can seem puzzling in the play must be due to its author having to follow history, which he could not always explain, and which he often readjusted but seldom knowingly falsified. Underlying this is the fact that his tragic world lies between an old social and moral order and a newer one; bewilderments over right and wrong, uncertainties of duty, are inescapable. Old and New are clothed in the guise of East and West; as always, Shakespeare is both appreciative and critical of each. Antony's

155

desertion of Rome for Egypt tells against him, but also, obliquely, against Rome and what it prizes. With the lovers, we can 'call great Caesar ass' (V.ii.306). Discordant ideas lie behind verbal likenesses. Octavius looks forward to winning 'the last of many battles' (IV.i.11); Antony wants to live long enough to give Cleopatra 'Of many thousand kisses the poor last' (IV.xv.20). He alone has a foot in both worlds. So has Shakespeare, and a subject splendidly fitted to bring together many of his clashing thoughts, and allow him to bathe dramatic contradictions in the most brilliant colours.

In one scene (III.iv) Antony is living in Athens; but there are other things to make him and Timon of Athens less incongruous than they appear at first sight. Both men after dazzling careers have dropped out of active life, where we would have expected to see Timon still playing a part instead of holding banquets, as Antony does at Alexandria. Both their plays open with scenes of magnificence, but with an undercurrent of censure, ominous for the future when Timon will be abandoned by his partners, and Antony will see the flatterers he has enriched turn away to 'melt their sweets on blossoming Caesar' (IV.xii.22–3). He is brought before us in the very first words as a great man fatally in decline.

But he is not really, as censorious followers like Enobarbus think him, a rugged fighting-man seduced into sloth by a vampire. He has always had a double nature, characteristic of times like his. He 'revels long o' nights', Caesar said of him tolerantly (*JC* II.ii.116); Brutus underrated him, as no more than a devotee of 'sports' and 'wildness' (II.i.189), and spared his life; Cassius at Philippi called him 'a masker and a reveller'. He is more divided in personality, or attitude to life, than any of the other heroes. This means that he is tugged in opposite directions, more persistently than even Hamlet. He succumbs to the charms of an exotic mode of living, more fascinating than ever in its twilight hour, and thereby condemns himself to share its fate. He is left stranded in an Alexandrian Eastcheap, repudiated by Rome as Falstaff was by Henry V and his court.

He has been cold-bloodedly ready to kill, in his time, when it was expedient in the struggle for power. Having won this, he wants to keep it; but there is nothing very much that he wants to do with it. He can afford to give way to a haphazard good nature: 'men did ransom lives of me for jests' (III.xiii.180–81). No one would ever win a pardon from Octavius by cracking a joke. In Egypt, politically null, there is no opposition to contend with. He is not accused of playing tyrant there. Nor is Cleopatra. Between them they reveal another facet of that disillusion with what authority can perform, or simple weariness of its demands, that has been filtering into Shakespeare's thinking.

Antony wants to enjoy the easy-going life earned by long years of warfare when he bore its rigours, by Octavius's testimony, 'with patience more than savages could suffer' (II.iv.61). But Octavius understood by instinct, and

Antony did not, the grand lesson that Andrew Marvell was to draw from his country's coming broils –

> The same arts that did gain
> A throne, must it maintain.

In an alien land, shut up in an oriental palace filled by Cleopatra with a magical luminosity, Antony is gradually losing the realism, the willingness to face facts, that he still likes to plume himself on (I.ii.99–100). His grumbling lieutenant Enobarbus sees this only too clearly. 'Men's judgments are parcel of their fortunes' (II.xii.29; cf. 195 ff.). Lear too, with a better excuse from his age, wanted to be free of all business, and yet keep the trappings of royalty.

Yet while Antony is in one sense slipping back into the dissipations of his early life, in another way he has grown, or mellowed, along the only line his nature permits. He has turned his back not on a well-ordered Roman republic, but on a Rome of factions, a political life, as Wimsatt calls it, of 'treacheries and back-stabbing' (cited by Lerner 242). Withdrawal from that brutal arena to tranquil Egypt is as near to repentance as he can come. When a 'Roman thought' strikes him (I.ii.84), it is not of any duty owed to his country, but recollection that every man of position must take care to keep his footing in a competition sharpened by the recent civil wars. It would be as perilous to drop out of the game too long as for a London merchant to stop adding to his hoard. In *Julius Caesar* Antony was proposing to Octavius that they should join to oust their stupid fellow-triumvir Lepidus; only by painful steps does he come to understand that the fate intended for Lepidus is now to be his own.

His 'Roman thought' calls him away from lotus-eating in Egypt to politics in Italy. All those in Shakespeare's theatre who knew their Virgil must have remembered Aeneas quitting Dido, another eastern queen, for an Italian bride. Antony's new match is Octavius's sister, and he can assume a proper demeanour when he talks to her of the duties of his 'great office' (II.iii.1). When leaving Egypt he had told himself that he must break away from his 'enchanting queen', or risk 'ten thousand harms' (I.ii.129–30); yet he had promised Cleopatra new kingdoms, the sovereignty of the East (I.v.45–7), which ought to be Rome's. The inevitable feud breaks out; Octavia goes to Rome to attempt mediation; he leaves Athens and hurries back to Egypt.

Octavius is quick to make patriotic propaganda out of his backsliding. His unconcealed liaison with Cleopatra is proof of his 'contemning Rome' (III.vi.1). Governments at loggerheads in Shakespeare's time directed a great deal of printed indignation against one another. Prudence as well as masculine prejudice makes Antony's own lieutenants consider Cleopatra no better than a 'whore' or 'trull' (III.vi.67, 94). Antony suffers from a sense of inferiority when he is with Octavius (II.iii.34 ff.), because, we may guess, his rival is a Roman to the backbone, while he himself has turned renegade. Macbeth recalled this precedent when he felt abashed in Banquo's presence (III.i.53–6). Antony feels a pang of regret, when in ill humour with Cleopatra, at having thrown away his chance to beget 'a lawful race, and by a gem of women' (III.xiii.106–8) – Octavia, unexciting but dutiful, the model of a Roman matron of better days.

Antony has no 'party' to lead, but he is the head of a loyal faction of officers, clients, dependants; by abandoning Octavia he provokes another civil war, in which they all stood to lose. Hence their dislike of his conduct. Timon was left in the lurch by his friends, Antony is doing the opposite. In Egypt he is sinking back into the easy luxury of an old court, of the moribund sort that the British lion's paw was to strike down so many of in years to come. Faced with ruin, he looks back on days when he 'with half the bulk o' th' world' played as he pleased (III.xi.64): a revealing gamester's phrase. Timon would have liked to 'deal kingdoms' to his friends (I.ii.214) – irrespective of how their inhabitants might like it; Antony has done so, crowns and coronets have dropped from his pockets (V.ii.90–92), but this was no serious training for politics. Irresponsible power degenerates into petty tyranny when he orders Octavius's messenger to be whipped, and invites his master to take revenge on a freedman of his own (III.xiii.147 ff.).

Love and friendship save Antony from being no more than a grand egotist, but in him Renaissance magnificence soars to its highest, forgetful of the earth it stands on. 'Kingdoms are clay', he declares; 'the nobleness of life' consists in the embraces of a pair as splendid as him and his queen (I.i.35 ff.). 'Nobility' has taken on a strange new meaning. 'Honour' too has changed from what it was to Brutus and his associates. It is not now recognition of a duty to the public weal, but a demand for respect. At best his honour is 'sacred' when sworn obligations to allies are in question; it may even compel him to offer them a limited apology (II.ii.85, 97). As defeat approaches he feels that his 'dying honour' can only be revived by fresh bloodshed, though his own blood too may have to flow (IV.ii.6–7). By withdrawing from the naval battle and following Cleopatra in flight he proves the strength of his love, which has grown by stages (cf. Adelman 161); but he has also played the coward, and humiliated himself. 'I have offended reputation' (III.xi.49), that treasure so precious to soldiers in these plays. He begins to see how men's blindness leads them to their ruin (III.xiii.111 ff.).

It is the desertion of Enobarbus, his closest comrade in arms, that first penetrates his consciousness and forces him to realize how hopelessly he has gone astray. Staring at a cloud, he feels as if he too is losing shape, dissolving (IV.xiv.2 ff.). To some readers he has seemed to be sinking into a maudlin sentimentality, as he exchanges greetings all round with friends, followers, servants (Sanders and Jacobson 116). Rather it should be said that a better side of himself is reviving; he reminds us now of the Macbeth who heard men's curses and pined for their respect and good will. This solace at least Antony has not altogether lost. Some lessons he has been learning from harsh experience, as a tragic hero must, and we can feel that he has expiated some part of his wrong-doing. In death he is acquiring a philosophy of life, a stoical willingness to 'bid that welcome which comes to punish us' (IV.xiv.135 ff.). In his last words before calling on Eros to kill him, and in his last speech of all, it is his manly nature that prevails; but he can die both a true Roman and a true lover.

After his death he has a kind of apotheosis in Cleopatra's imagination, such as he himself once bestowed on the dead Caesar (III.ii.79 ff.). She thinks of him as a superman bestriding the world; a man so great must be beyond the invention of dreams; in him Nature for once outdid human fancy. Real or unreal, a man who can be or seem like this must be self-destructive, through his own excess of strength. A 'royal' mien seems to invest Antony. He could be given a semi-divine ancestor in Hercules – 'the god Hercules, whom Antony loved' (IV.iii.18). His mode of speech befits his role; his tongue has lost none of its eloquence since the funeral speech, though it is no longer addressed to a citizenry. It is full of striking images, some forty in Act IV alone.

The tale of a European succumbing to the languorous spell of the East was to be repeated many times in later history. But the purple passages of many commentators on an Antony sunk in oriental degeneracy are too much in the vein of Horace's partisan ode on the death of Cleopatra (e.g. Boas, *Shakspere* 475). Life at her court may not be edifying, but it is not a round of nameless orgies. Antony has to admit to Octavius that when he answered the latter's envoy too brusquely he had been feasting three monarchs, and was not himself; some 'poisoned hours' had kept him from attending to Octavius's claims (II.ii.75 ff.). More damaging is the report (though we only hear it from Octavius) of the two paramours enthroned in the public square, Cleopatra robed as the goddess Isis, with their bastard offspring, to whom sundry eastern provinces of the empire were being assigned (III.vi.1 ff.). Historically Antony can be seen as a presage of the future orientalizing of the empire, a centuries-long trend towards adoption of Hellenistic culture and local deities like Isis. In Shakespeare's time there was once again a growing European interest in Asian life, as described by merchants and diplomats, and particularly in the life of the harem, which was taken to be the essence of eastern existence. Cleopatra's curiosity about the sensations of a eunuch (I.v.12 ff.) was meant to titillate such inquisitiveness.

Nearly all the Egyptians who appear are eunuchs or women, in contrast with the sternly masculine temper of the Romans. Octavius has a disdain for women (III.xii.29–31) unaffected by his real regard for his sister. Enobarbus is more bluntly contemptuous of them. Antony's attitude to women has been 'courteous' (II.ii.222), but Octavius considers him to have become no more 'manlike' than his mistress (I.iv.5–6). A lingering shadow from *Timon* falls across the sunlit scene when his catalogue of Antony's frivolities includes a hint at a risk of venereal disease (I.iv.16 ff.). New and Old, West and East, mean also male and female, as often in the imperialism of later times.

It is easy to see why Cleopatra's claim to a valid place in the tragic world has been queried (Barroll 131). Her nature is a complex one, as Stewart sees (69–70). All her life she has been thrown into complicated situations, and forced to improvise, manoeuvre, to keep her footing in a decrepit kingdom on the edge of the Roman empire. Like Antony for other reasons, she gives us few glimpses of her inner self (Adelman 19). It is needful for our impression of a mysterious Oriental queen that we should not be allowed to see her too distinctly. Court business at Alexandria is little more than a chase after amusements. Cleopatra has never acquired, what Antony has been losing, a serious interest in government; power means to her only royal trappings. Iras and Charmian, her attendants and confidantes, are as eager as Macbeth to have their fortunes told (I.ii.1 ff.), but their questions could not be more empty-headed. Only death is to ennoble these women, as it does their lady. When Antony goes away Cleopatra is left to boredom, and can only turn for relief to billiards, music or fishing – harmless diversions enough. Her prank of hopping forty paces through a street suggests a regime grown light-headed, playing the mountebank. There is all the same something endearing in the thought of an unconventional queen strolling about her city, close to her people in this manner at least. Our modern personages, royal and other, have learned to go on public 'walk-abouts'; hop-abouts might prove still more popular.

Cleopatra must have reminded many of Mary Queen of Scots, a more than half-foreign woman, fond of billiards and of wandering the streets, and England's enemy as Cleopatra was Rome's. Cleopatra and Octavia on the other hand are among Shakespeare's most sharply contrasting pairs of women, the one emancipated from all restraints, the other demurely virtuous. Shakespeare does his best to admire Octavia too. There is another pair of opposites in Cleopatra and the Fulvia whom we do not see, that 'great spirit', as her estranged husband Antony calls her when she dies (I.ii.123), a Roman lady who plunges boldly into politics and war. When Cleopatra tries to emulate her for once, and insists on joining her fleet, as 'president' of her kingdom (III.vii.16–18), all that follows is that she runs away and ruins everything. As with Portia and Lady Macbeth, a woman embroiling herself in the brutal affairs of men may have heroic intentions, but her nerves are likely to give way.

Cleopatra incarnates an *ancien régime*, with all its seductive and repulsive qualities, the essence of an aristocratic life grown archaic and artificial. She is witty, provocative, capricious, and yet capable of a grand passion. She is also capable of striking a messenger who brings unwelcome news, and threatening him with worse (II.v.61 ff.). There is a sinister suggestiveness in her casually mentioned pursuit of 'conclusions infinite of easy ways to die' (V.ii.354–5). They may have been animal experiments, but it is a likelier guess that she has been testing poisons on human beings. As with Duncan's unlucky grooms, we see the complete insignificance of the plebeian by comparison with the lady or gentleman.

Believing that she has played him false, Antony can call his queen a 'foul Egyptian', and 'a right gypsy' (IV.xii.10, 28). This was a term derived from 'Egyptian' and bestowed on a tribe of wandering entertainers from India, some of whom reached Europe by way of Egypt, and by the sixteenth century were percolating into England and Scotland; they were viewed as thieves and nuisances. Antony is calling Cleopatra a 'native', not a decent 'white' woman like Octavia. He and Othello are opposite cases, but each has stepped too heedlessly out of his own sphere, and when trouble comes the question of blood or race will come up with it. Antony lives to be reconciled, but he, like Othello, has had thoughts of killing his partner, as a traitress whom it is his duty to save other men from. 'One death might have prevented many' (IV.xii.41–2).

The Cleopatra of the final scene can never have thought of handing over her lover to his enemies, as some allege. She may have thought of running away again, as she did from the sea-fight, and going into hiding for a while. Even this would disqualify the play as a tragedy. She must not be over-romanticized, it is true. She can be as Machiavellian as Octavius (Nandy 179), but only so far as petty arts and wiles are concerned. She may be 'cunning past man's thought' (I.ii.146), but only in the short-sighted wisdom of her own courtesan lore. She looks back with pride on her conquests of great men. Otherwise she is a child of nature, who wants her Antony great and glorious – 'The demi-Atlas of this earth' (I.v.22–4) – but keeps him loafing and lotus-eating at her side. He sees too late how his giving in to her has demoralized men like his faithful Enobarbus (IV.v.16–17). Something of the truth may have dawned on Cleopatra after his death, when she recollects him, as though in a vision, restored to his prime as world-hero.

This Egyptian woman can admire the Roman character, without any desire to emulate it; but when it reasserts itself in Antony she knows that it must part him from her. She herself, however, will end with Roman thoughts, and be worthier of her lover than ever before, when she resolves to die rather than be taken captive to Rome, a showpiece in Octavius's triumph. Brutus and Macbeth made the same choice of death instead of public degradation. She was proving that she could feel this sense of honour equally with a man; for this at least Horace would find praise. She could call the dead Antony now her 'husband' (V.ii.186–7).

She has to struggle with Egyptian thoughts, of an escape with a shipload of gold. Other heroines may have to pass through ordeals in order to win love, hers come in her last days. Honour calls on her to 'be noble to herself', by rejecting her enemies' blandishments (V.ii.190–91). Her death is truly tragic, as Bradley felt (*Tragedy* 299); poetically, the most inspired death-scene that Shakespeare ever wrote. She has been weighing up the hollowness of worldly grandeur, and there is a sardonic note in her pretended submission to the omnipotent Octavius. All power is unmeaning: it is the great who deserve pity (V.ii.133–5, 175 ff.). Resolved to die in 'the high Roman fashion' (IV.xv.86 ff.), she can face conquering Rome as an equal.

Royalty and common humanity are merging. If Shakespeare's finest men have been coming to see that there is nothing higher they can aspire to than to be true *men*, Cleopatra is making a similar discovery on behalf of women. When Antony dies she feels the same emotion that a servant-girl might (IV.xv.73–5). The clowning interlude of the yokel bringing the poisonous asps adds to this sense of a world shared by human beings of every rank and station. He, it is true, has the same conviction as any Roman of women's inferiority. A woman may be 'a dish for the gods', but half the dishes are spoiled by devils (V.ii.272 ff.). Cleopatra is about to vindicate woman against man, as well as East against West. Before the end she remembers her royal ancestry, puts on her robes of state, and feels 'marble-constant', emptied of all feminine weakness – as Lady Macbeth had wished to be. Not only a queen but an ancient and famous realm is reaching its end, and as always Shakespeare is ready to pay tribute to all true greatness for which the past with all its sins has provided a scaffolding. Dying, she feels like a nursing mother sucked asleep by her infant. Humanity is restored to its one-ness: queen and commoner, high and low, capable of the same sublimity, the 'immortal longings' (V.ii.280) higher than any earthly ambition, of which robe and crown are now only symbols.

Cleopatra is left with no loyal friends except her two women, and her farewell to them is as moving as any Roman leave-takings. Her better self comes to the front, and these two court butterflies, hitherto so frivolous, are learning the same lesson as their mistress. They are the best testimony of her nature having goodness enough in it to deserve such fidelity. She is strengthened by their sharing her resolve; Charmian and Iras are worthy companions for her journey, 'kind' and 'noble' (V.ii.229, 91), and ready to meet death first, as Antony's freedman Eros, 'thrice-nobler' than himself, had done (IV.xiv.95.). In them too women are showing themselves equal to men, even Romans, the masters of the world.

Royal station and untrammelled freedom have made Cleopatra her lover's equal – except in battle –, as Desdemona and Othello could never have been. Like Lady Macbeth she ruins the man she loves, and herself with him. Cleopatra, however, does not lure Antony into crime, only into weakness. Lady Macbeth wants to thrust power on her partner, Cleopatra to make him careless of it. In both cases the hero finds himself increasingly isolated, Macbeth because of what his wife has made him do, Antony because of what his mistress has kept him from doing. This most superb of all Shakespeare's women is an alien, an outlaw, not amenable to any conventional judgments; he can take her as she is, or as he makes her, a spirit moving beyond good and evil.

She brings love back into what was in danger of becoming a loveless world; one that it can only enter by doors of its own, not by any legitimate contract known to lawyers. It is love between a man and woman from two very different cultures, traditions, epochs, separated by barriers far higher than the trivial family feud which stood between Romeo and Juliet. They are lovers weary of the lives they have led before meeting, for whom reality has grown so dull or distasteful that they are losing consciousness of its meaning and its pitfalls, above which their charmed palace is reared. It is only a love of this extraordinary kind that Shakespeare can bring himself to believe in now, and he has to take pains not to slide into credulous sentimentality. Our faith in it is kept balanced against scepticism.

Antony and Cleopatra are both long past romantic youth. Their connection is dogged by the running criticism of friends and enemies alike, as Timon's friendships were by Apemantus and his caustic dissent. We hear in the first words that to Roman thinking Antony is doing no more than pander to 'a gypsy's lust'; Cleopatra's entry, and first words, in her most bewitching language, are a denial of this. It is an adulterous love, the only one that Shakespeare ever lent his sanction to, but its physical aspects are carefully draped. Whatever its traducers make of it, there is an absence of grossness or sensuality that has impressed many. As Granville-Barker said, there are no voluptuous love scenes: hero and heroine are never alone together on the stage ('Shakespeare's Dramatic Art' 55). They are in a way spiritualized by intensity of feeling, bathed in an aura that can transfigure poor human bodies into 'a race of heaven' (I.iii.36–7). What is sensuous is not common passion but a poetical idealizing of the senses. Dollimore's 'sexual infatuation' is a poor definition of it (217).

Each lover is carried out of the captivity of a too cramping environment by the fascination of strangeness. Shakespeare himself must have fallen under Cleopatra's spell; his imagination was in search of something not to be found in humdrum England. It was not taking leave of reality, however, as Antony's was. Such a relationship cannot be stable and unruffled, though this has nothing to do with commonplace temptations. Antony is unfaithful only reluctantly, under political pressures; Cleopatra in his absence has no thought of consoling herself with other men. But there must be times when the liberation she has brought to Antony becomes in turn a bondage, and he feels that his 'strong Egyptian fetters' must be broken (I.ii.117). He sets off to Italy in the third scene vowing loyalty, but he and she are not together again until half-way through the play, and we do not witness their reunion. In the fourth Act he dies. Out of forty-two scenes in all he appears in twenty-two, Cleopatra in sixteen, but they are together only in ten, and in five of these there are quarrels. Yet meanwhile Antony has learned something of how to live, and has taught Cleopatra in turn how to die, when the time comes; and they each die more in love than ever.

Antony cannot drive away for long the knowledge that his enchantment is enervating, and that hedonism unmixed is a deceptive siren. Man's nature demands activity, weeds grow in stagnant minds. 'Would I had never seen her', he is exclaiming very soon (I.ii.110–11, 153), much like Othello with his 'Why did I marry!' In another way Cleopatra is conscious of danger: her thoughts of him are 'most delicious poison' (I.v.27), but she is more brilliantly reckless, or else irresponsible. The frank openness typical of Shakespeare's heroines cannot be hers, and her arts and subtleties cannot bring about a marriage of true minds, or not until they have only their love left to comfort them on their way to the shades.

Cleopatra has been Antony's 'conqueror', and held him enslaved (III.xi.60 ff.); all the recriminations come from his side, except the first, when he suddenly decides to leave her. Her flight from the naval battle transforms his fantasy of love as the elixir of life into a feeling that it can only have been an illusion conjured up by a witch (IV.xii.16 ff.). This oscillation of feeling goes on until their final embrace, when reconciliation sheds its light back over the play, and helps to account for the fact that although a tragedy it has often so buoyant a tone. It is a reunion not of two lovers only, but of two ages of mankind. Neither partner, it is true, is more than half representative of the civilizations they grew up in; their magnetism for each other lies in this. Antony is a man of a newer age who feels a powerful attraction towards an older one; Cleopatra is not an 'oriental' simply, but has always been in close contact with the 'West', and is well able to admire what is impressive in it. Through the two of them we are left with a sense of finer qualities of distant birthplaces coming together, and a twilight of the gods bringing new daybreaks in sight.

These lovers have had to bring love back to life in a world hostile to it, and to any aspiration of women to choose their own path. Womanly virtue is infirm even in prosperity, Octavius is convinced, and need will corrupt a vestal virgin (III.xii.29–31). To remain what she should be, or protect her reputation, a woman in these later tragedies must turn herself into something very unlike the active, free-spirited Comedy heroines; she must hide in a corner and confine herself to conventional occupations. Octavia promises Antony to pray for him while they are apart (II.iii.3–4); this is scarcely what he is accustomed to ask women for, and Enobarbus foresees that with her 'holy, cold, and still' disposition she is likely to have no helpful influence on his relations with her brother (II.vi.119 ff.). Her lament over the opposite tugs of husband and brother is extorted by one of the various conflicting allegiances that pervade this drama. It was a common fate of highborn women, treated as counters in the great game played by men. Blanche in *King John* was another of them.

In a group of contenders for power who have floated up out of the wreckage of the republic, Octavius is the one most single-mindedly bent on supremacy. This future Augustus, grand-nephew and adopted son of Julius Caesar, is a political man to his fingertips. Shakespeare makes no attempt to paint him in rosy colours; yet we come to think of him as the man of destiny, the leader whom Rome needs to inaugurate a new era. After his long series of English Histories, Shakespeare could scarcely fail to see a likeness between England's rescue from the Wars of the Roses by Henry VII and the Roman empire's from its civil wars by Octavius. Before the concluding battle the winner hails 'The time of universal peace', when all the world 'Shall bear the olive freely' (IV.vi.5–7). This is his mission; the current of history is on his side. Various allusions are heard to the steady success of the 'full-fortuned Caesar' (IV.xv.24). Antony may well be jealous of a man who has supplanted him as champion of the Rome to which he himself has become half a stranger, and who is, moreover, a younger man still full of youthful energy. This disparity of age helps to mark Octavius as the representative of the future. To Antony he is 'the boy Caesar', 'the young Roman boy'; to him the Antony who challenges him to a duel is 'the old ruffian' (III.xiii.7; IV.xii.48; IV.i.4).

Octavius is not a bloodless, passionless instrument of destiny: he has all the emotions that a politician can have, and expresses them at times eloquently. But Shakespeare cannot make him a man interesting to us in the way that Antony is. He is habitually reserved, impersonal. In his presence heroics are out of date. In him we see reason, intellectual ability, baffled in *Hamlet*, and in *Othello* and *King Lear* ranged on the wrong side, restored now to its rightful position, on the side of what must be called, if only as the lesser evil, progress. Octavius has a single warm attachment, to his sister (e.g. III.ii.39 ff.); he has no other kin, and the brother–sister relationship was in Shakespeare's eyes precious. This does not hinder him from making use of Octavia as a pawn, by marrying her to Antony. Dynastic marriages were a stock in trade of diplomacy in Shakespeare's Europe, and for centuries longer.

In the brother and sister Shakespeare draws a pair of puritans. He is as genuinely disgusted by the tipsy revels of Alexandria as any sober London citizen could be (I.iv.16 ff.); he detests having to take part in a drinking-bout (II.vii.98–9). He is ruled by a habit of mind, a discipline prescribed by the need of unremitting vigilance. His like could be found in England among either the bureaucrats of the Tudor monarchy or the City business-men, two species with converging interests and outlooks. He is capable besides of drawing round him competent lieutenants, bound to him by no such chivalrous attachment as Antony can kindle, but not torn like Enobarbus between loyalty and common sense. In his circle something like a party, a movement, is taking shape.

These men understand, as governments in Shakespeare's time increasingly did, the importance of propaganda, and hold up Roman virtues against the contagion of oriental vice. 'Let Rome be thus informed', says Maecenas when his leader has been dilating on Antony's reprehensible conduct at Alexandria. Agrippa assents: Rome is already 'queasy with his insolence' (III.vi.19 ff.). Enobarbus by comparison is no more than a rough soldier, whose blunt tongue calls for rebuke in the conference of the triumvirs; he wants to hear his master 'speak as loud as Mars' (II.ii.104 ff., 3 ff.). His wrestlings with himself are a microcosm of the play as a whole, with its two poles; his inner division, which brings him at last to desertion, remorse and death, makes him a tragic figure. His going over to the enemy, who he soon finds will not trust him, moves Antony to his most magnanimous act.

Altogether this is a highly political, as well as romantic, drama, a many-sided picture of imperial Rome refracted through the mind of a keen observer of politics in his own day. The meeting of the triumvirs to settle their differences and feast together is one of Shakespeare's great scenes of public life. All the idealism of *Julius Caesar* is gone. There at its close Antony could pay tribute to the defeated Brutus as the noblest of Romans; now he can only talk of him as 'the mad Brutus' (III.xi.38) – mad because a believer in ideals of freedom, a futile martyr. To Antony kingdoms are little more than toys for the great to play with, or get tired of. 'Let Rome in Tiber melt', he breaks out impatiently. 'Melt Egypt into Nile', Cleopatra says on another occasion (I.i.33; II.v.78).

The Roman people has disappeared from sight, though there are frequent mentions of it as a volatile force, to be manipulated as well as may be. Octavius cultivates public opinion, but puts little reliance on it. Taxes have to be collected, and to gather money is to lose hearts (II.i.13–14). It is an axiom with him that a man will only be looked up to before he comes to power, or after he has lost it (I.iv.41 ff.); which Shakespeare may have thought true enough, considering how little people owe to their rulers, and how their minds always run on better things once upon a time, or some day to come. Public favour ebbs and flows quite irrationally, Octavius concludes; and away at Alexandria Antony is saying something very similar about the 'slippery people', who he fears are transferring their goodwill to Pompey (I.ii.186 ff.).

Brutus and Cassius were both with Pompey's father when Caesar defeated him and the republic at Pharsalia. There is no hope left of the old constitution being restored, except the flicker kept alive by Pompey the younger, last of the republican old guard. Shakespeare shows a certain nostalgic liking for him and what he stands for, though his object is in part revenge for his father. When the tribunes are banqueting on his ship, his piratical ally Menas proposes to put out to sea, and kill them. Pompey rejects the plan as dishonourable, though he cannot help wishing that Menas had carried it out without asking for his approval. Menas resolves to follow his 'pall'd fortunes' no longer; a chance thrown away is lost for ever (II.vii.84 ff.).

Meanwhile the triumvirs, whom Pompey has paid a bitter compliment as 'chief factors of the gods' (II.vi.10), are feasting and tippling, until Lepidus has to be carried out, and the others join in a tipsy dance, their legs reeling under them. The high and mighty are being shown in their human littleness (cf. Leggatt 172). Even the servants discuss 'these great fellows', as Menas dubs them, with shrewd disrespect, especially the drunken Lepidus (II.vii.1 ff.). Octavius keeps the best hold on himself, as befits the man born for success. We are being given a brilliant illustration of how farce can be blended with tragedy, as it always has been in history. Pompey's reward for his forbearance is to be attacked before long by Octavius and Lepidus, and murdered by an officer of Antony. Octavius goes on to attack the muddle-headed Lepidus and throw him into prison. Now the empire is left, Enobarbus comments, with only one 'pair of chaps' (III.v.1 ff.), to fight it out like pugilists.

Man and superman are further contrasted in the scene in Syria (III.i), where Antony's general Ventidius, victorious over the Parthians, rejects advice to pursue the beaten foe into Media. By accomplishing too much he would arouse Antony's jealousy: it will be better instead to flatter him by attributing all the credit for what has been won to the prestige of Antony's name. Both he and Octavius have always owed most of their successes to their officers, Ventidius remarks. In other words, these two paladins owe their stature chiefly to self-advertisement and myth. Critics have often cavilled at this scene (Leggatt and Traversi are exceptions) as adding nothing to the story; but it tells us much about Shakespeare's political philosophy, which he clearly wants us to comprehend. All power and greatness are an artificial pageant.

While Antony's gaudy clients desert him, loyalty survives among his humbler dependants, and he, unlike Timon, has enough generosity of spirit to appreciate this, and to feel again his kinship with men of common clay. Among his soldiers he can always be a man among men; he addresses them now, colloquially, as 'lads' (IV.iv.25). His old servitors are his 'good fellows' (IV.ii.20), and even the surly Enobarbus is moved by the spectacle of Antony's thanks to them. They are in tears, and their master's words

– 'Grace grow where those drops fall' – carry us back to the funeral speech and the weeping crowd, and 'these are gracious drops'. Then it was only demagogy; now it is genuine feeling.

Here is one side of Shakespeare's picture of common humanity; another, which haunts the tragic scene, is of plebeians collectively, crowds gathered for a Roman holiday to hoot at captives following behind a conqueror's chariot. For Cleopatra to be exposed to the 'shouting varletry', burlesqued by 'quick comedians', 'enclouded' in the 'thick breaths' of 'mechanic slaves', is the worst horror she can conjure up (V.ii.207 ff.). Antony feels the same dread, like Brutus before him (IV.xiv.72 ff.). Shakespeare can hardly have failed to see links between Roman imperialism and the degradation of the Roman masses, the shameful scenes for which the ruling classes were most to blame.

Noise of battle is seldom far away, but there is no fighting on the stage. Antony sets off to the field, and returns from it, exhilarated by his sword-work – 'the royal occupation', 'business that we love' (IV.iv.17, 20). He sums up all the martial virtues that Shakespeare has, if always with a tinge of reluctance, admired. But war itself is losing its bright plumage, and by the cold light of day Antony is only a brawny bully, past his best. Egypt is no breeding-ground of warriors. Raw landlubbers are hastily conscripted, as they were so often in England, to man Cleopatra's fleet (III.vii.2 ff.). Octavia's finest words are of peace: conflict between the two world-sharers will be like the earth splitting, and the chasm having to be filled up with corpses (III.iv.30–32). Her brother, victorious at last, professes to have done his utmost to avoid a breach (V.i.73 ff.). Yet Shakespeare, as at the close of *Timon*, has still not laid to rest his – and his contemporaries' – old enigma: peace through its inner contradictions must turn back into war; 'quietness, grown sick of rest', will welcome any 'desperate change' as a purge (I.iii.53–4). It was a riddle built into the fabric of late feudal or early modern society.

Egypt has its superstitions, but among the leading figures on both sides there is a rationalizing outlook; the gods are as a rule further off from earth than in ancient Britain. Cleopatra may impersonate Isis, but does not pray to her: the charade in the market-place could only be designed to dupe the masses. She thinks of 'the injurious gods' only to abuse them (IV.xv.76). It is her lips and eyes, and her lover's, that are endowed with eternity (I.iii.35). If she has any conviction, it is that Fortune, or chance personified, rules all things. Contemplating suicide, she speaks of entering 'the secret house of death' (IV.xv.81).

On the Roman side men have glimpses at times, however dim, of a guiding Providence at work. A scene in Sicily opens with an exchange of thoughts about 'the great gods' between Pompey and Menas. Pompey considers that they ought to aid the deserving, and not let delay render their aid useless. Menas is for patience: we often beg them for things that would harm us, so by turning a deaf ear they may do us a kindness (II.i.1 ff.). This is giving them all the benefit of the doubt; Pompey breaks off with an expression of trust in his own resources. For his part Antony, when things are running against him, is driven to think of 'the wise gods' blinding us to our own follies, or 'viciousness', and laughing to see us 'strut to our confusion' (III.xiii.lll ff.) – a conception not unlike that of the gods as 'wanton boys' in *King Lear*. It is appropriate that the man with fewest doubts about them should be the winner. Octavius has a firm consciousness of being an instrument in the hands of 'the high gods'. They will make him and his friends their 'ministers', he assures his injured sister, and do her justice: she must not repine (III.vi.82 ff.). She prays 'the Jove of power' to help her weakness.

A firm Roman realism can underline belief in either the providential or the accidental; it is an acceptance of painful facts, as summoners to action. Roman history is undergoing a grand transformation; we are not concerned with hero and villain, but with the shift from republic to principate which Shakespeare began studying in *Julius Caesar*, and for which Egypt is the catalyst hastening its completion. The inevitability of the conflict is emphasized by recurrent allusions to 'destiny' and 'necessity'. Life's hard laws must be faced with equal hardness. 'The strong necessity of time' commands Antony away from Cleopatra for a while, he tries vainly to make her comprehend (I.iii.42). Octavius bids his sister not to be perturbed by the 'strong necessities' of the time (III.vi.82–3). A will to power is one of Shakespeare's chief themes, and more and more he sees how it is instilled into men of ambition by the air they breathe. In the English Histories it is a thing of course; in the tragedies it is questionable, often felt as morbid, lamented sometimes by those it drives on to success. They are left to regret their own triumphs, Agrippa says after Antony's death, their 'most persisted deeds' against their opponents (V.i.28–30). Octavius himself talks feelingly of having been compelled to defeat, or be defeated by, a man for so long his comrade, his 'mate in empire', 'friend and companion' in war (V.i.36 ff.).

Bradley could find nothing 'decisively tragic' in the first three Acts (*Poetry*). But these are required to make the last ones tragic, by showing what vicissitudes the love of Antony and Cleopatra has had to pass through, before it could become so vital, and fatal, to them. To each of them it has brought something like a redemption, or rising above self; and this is in one way the essence of the drama. He thinks of her and her fate as he lies dying; his death emboldens her to follow him. They will share the same tomb, like Romeo and Juliet. Those two by dying reunited Verona, though that was not their purpose. Now Shakespeare is weaving romantic and public themes together again, though on a far vaster loom; in something like the same way, Antony and Cleopatra have to 'sacrifice' themselves, by their too-daring love, in order that the empire may be reunited and pacified.

Antony is doomed when Cleopatra takes flight, and he follows – a repetition in brief of his abandonment of Rome – and then furiously reproaches her. It is tragic, as in other tragedies, to see two beings who have meant so much to each other whirled apart. No doubt we are compelled to ask why we should feel so strongly for such a pair, who so often seem no more than supreme egotists. We can only feel so because their example proves how closely human beings *can* be joined, when we know the price they will have to pay; and because this fate, as it draws near, humanizes them, renders them conscious of belonging to the human community they have soared so high above. Both die; fate never allows Shakespeare's lovers to die together.

We are made to feel from the first lines that hero and heroine are gambling with life. As the end nears we listen to words of unanswerable finality, as of a light being extinguished. 'Unarm, Eros, the long day's task is done', says Antony, hearing the false report of Cleopatra's death. 'Finish, good lady, the bright day is done', Iras says to her mistress, after Antony's death (IV.xiv.35; V.ii.192). As Antony lies dying Cleopatra calls on the sun to burn its sphere, the earth to sink into night (IV.xv.9–10). Antony has, indeed, burned the great sphere he moved in; an age is passing away. This finality is clearest of all in Cleopatra's death, and with it the coming to an end of an archaic style of monarchy, to make room for the new one that will be inaugurated by Octavius – one so modernizing that its law code was being adopted in early modern Europe by one country after another. There is a sense in which everything in history dies when it chooses to live no longer. Metrical convenience cannot explain why Antony addresses Cleopatra near the end by her royal style: 'I am dying, Egypt, dying'; she has always been for him a queen as well as a fascinating woman, He himself is encircled now by images of royalty; he has been 'the greatest prince o' the world', 'the crown o' the earth' (IV.xv.54, 63). Cleopatra's death is worthy of a descendant of 'so many royal kings': the past, though not the future, will belong to her. Calling for her royal insignia, she tells Charmian that after this last service she will be free 'to play till doomsday' (V.ii.231), much as Prospero calls at the end for his court dress and promises Ariel his freedom. Charmian's last act, surely symbolic, is to try to straighten her dead mistress's crown, which has fallen awry, just as the Romans break in.

Antony is adrift between two eras, and affords Shakespeare the opportunity for his most realistic, many-sided picture of a 'great man' – a phenomenon that always intrigued him –, but a great man cashiered by history. Antony has dazzled the empire with remarkable qualities as a soldier and leader of men, if with little idea of where he was leading them; in the shipwreck of the republic, and a time of chaotic competition, he has found no worthy task to harness his energies to. He is in great part a creation of men's illusions, as Cassius called Caesar, but still a superlative creation. With his passing 'There is nothing left remarkable' (IV.xv.67). Imagery reinforces this impression of mankind impoverished: Antony is a jewel stolen from the earth by the envious gods (76–8). His legacy is no tangible achievement such as Octavius will leave, but a revelation of human energy, courage and the power to love, even though he has destroyed himself by not knowing how to use these gifts.

In the comedies Shakespeare had tried, often with sparkling success, to combine and thus preserve the assets of an old order and a new; in the tragedies they collide too violently. Only on the poetic plane can they be brought together, for the admiration and emulation of later days; a more precious legacy than the money or gardens bequeathed by Julius to his people. The lovers scale a height from which they can see that the victor is only 'Fortune's knave', not a free agent (V.ii.1 ff.; cf. 284–6). Greatness in the worldly sense may prove a mirage, but the greatness of soul it has sometimes helped to incubate is free now to break its shell. Humanity has had to learn its own capacity for greatness by the elevation, at first, of a few on whom have been imposed exorbitant privileges and inordinate compulsions. Antony and Cleopatra share in a very special degree a super-abundant vitality, a vibrant energy lacking to ordinary mortals, along with a spontaneous naturalness and *joie de vivre* very rare in tragedy; they can love each other because they love life.

Like Hamlet and Othello, and like Enobarbus (III.xiii.46), as the end draws near Antony can still think of how his name will stand in the record, and wants to feel that he has earned his 'chronicle', or title to fame (III.xiii.175). His last words of all are not about love, but about his career of glory, and its not inglorious finish: he is 'a Roman by a Roman valiantly vanquished' (IV.xv.51 ff.). He is making his own epitaph, as at Philippi he made that of Brutus, a kind of reconciliation under the sanction of Roman national spirit. It is left to Octavius to preside over a healing of the wounds of civil war; whoever has won or lost, Rome will go on. He, like Antony, is sometimes called 'royal', and in some ways is so, though less sponta-neously; a statesman in the making, but at present busy climbing 'young ambition's ladder' like Julius before him. It is characteristic of him to break off a nobly sincere tribute to his dead rival, and turn to scheming to capture Cleopatra by guile and false promises, which he does not hide from his entourage (V.i.56 ff.). He can be magnanimous when there is nothing to be gained by being otherwise. He praises Cleopatra for her 'royal' death, and will bury her and Antony honourably together (V.ii.333 ff.).

He can be called now the empire's 'universal landlord' (III.xiii.72) – a phrase redolent of the English countryside and its busy accumulators of land. It is the victory of new over old, not good over evil; but Octavius can be believed to have learned some lessons, and to be chastened by success won at such cost in broken friendships as well as in labour and peril. He has no 'immortal longings', but he closes the drama impressively with a speech faithful to the tragic nature of all historical advance. 'High events as these strike those that make them': men both act, and feel for the consequences of their actions to others; what brings glory to the winner stirs at the same time pity for the loser (V.ii.359–61). Both are strands of what is being woven on the loom of history; and we too are elevated by a consciousness of being ourselves part of the weaving. The world is not being left empty and desolate.

8

Coriolanus (1608)

From the lurid sunset of *Antony and Cleopatra*, Shakespeare carries us backward in time to the grey overcast morning of Rome. *Coriolanus* may have been written early in 1608. His 'most exclusively political play' raises sharp questions about his political bent (Palmer 250). But 'political' now includes social and economic affairs, those basic interests that most concern common people, as well as issues of government. We do not hear of performances in Shakespeare's lifetime. There may have been fear of it stirring up trouble. Harry Levin (*Revolution* 47) tells us that he was present at a Paris production before the last war which provoked rioting, and led to a general strike and the fall of the government. One can visualize Colonel Blimp, the well-known British cartoon-Tory of those days, puffing and huffing at such an event. 'Gad, sir, Coriolanus was right!'

Caius Martius, dubbed 'Coriolanus' after his feats in the battle at Corioli, is – apart from Prospero – Shakespeare's last superman. To accentuate his character, and what becomes his fatal isolation, he is set very much apart. Plutarch's statement that his bull-headed nature was further inflamed by 'all the lustiest young gentlemen', who formed a party round him (cf. Brockbank 21), is omitted. Shakespeare is growing tired of great men, however, and one like Coriolanus must necessarily be destructive and self-destructive, because he cannot really be a *man*. He is an embodiment of aristocratic arrogance, almost a mechanical contrivance; an impression that grows stronger after he has become his country's implacable foe. Cominius, his old commander, says that the Volscians whom he has joined look up to him as if 'a thing made by some other deity than nature' (IV.vi.92 ff.). His old friend Menenius gives a similar picture of him, as he is now: 'when he walks, he moves like an engine, and the ground shrinks' (V.iv.17–18). He is in fact a 'non-person', one reader feels (Long 76).

He has an ancestry among the haughty barons of Shakespeare's Histories, impatient of any check on their will. 'Would you have me false to my nature?' he asks his mother Volumnia, when she tries to dissuade him from the folly of antagonizing the people for nothing; but in spite of Polonius's adage, by being true to himself he becomes false to his country, even to his class which means far more to him. His overweening hatred and contempt for the commons show in his very first words, an angry rebuke to the 'dissentious rogues' (I.i.158). His intransigence gets his fellow-nobles into difficulties, and he is then outraged by their unwillingness to stand by him at the cost of civil war – though Cominius has been quite ready to threaten this (III.i.202–5; cf. 196). Banished, he departs with an image of himself as a 'lonely dragon' making for its lair (IV.i.30).

Coriolanus is the champion of power, or might is right. The word 'power' occurs much oftener in this play than in any other of Shakespeare (Patterson 143). This goes with his military habits and temper. All the other heroes have some martial qualifications, but Coriolanus has very few others. 'Valour is the chiefest virtue' in Rome (II.ii.84), and he resembles the bulk of the European nobility of Shakespeare's time in being fit for nothing except fighting. Why Rome and Antium are chronically at war, we are never told. But Shakespeare comes fairly close to saying or implying that the real motive on each side is to keep a ruling class in power, and to feed it with booty; and he takes very few pains to varnish this blunt fact. Coriolanus dislikes peace, in part because it makes the commoners 'proud', or insubordinate, feeling no more need of their governors (I.i.169): a very Tudor thought. To him the best way of satisfying their hunger, when food is scarce as it has been lately (in England also), is to march them off to plunder the Volscians' stocks (247–8). In much the same way Jack Cade's malcontents in *Henry VI* were urged to join in another expedition to France, and fill their pockets with loot. The rich have no desire to share their 'superfluity' with the poor; they would rather get rid of the poor by sending the 'musty superfluity' to fight someone else (224–5).

With Coriolanus we are back in a rude age of warfare, far removed from the Renaissance ideal of soldier, courtier, scholar, all in one. His mode of fighting, as his general Titus Lartius says, is simply to hack and hew with 'thunder-like percussion' (I.iv.59). The rank and file are much less eager for the fray, and break out instead in 'mutinies and revolts', or so Coriolanus declares (III.i.125–6). One of his grudges against the plebeians is their unwillingness to join heartily in his juvenile game. As a field officer he resembles the ferocious Talbot of *Henry VI*, instead of the silver-tongued Henry V. He warns his men that he will cut down any who run away. Yet when he is compelled to resort for a moment to persuasion, and appeals to their patriotism, they follow him with spirit. Part of what inspires them is the prospect of plunder, and as soon as they are inside Corioli they ransack it for 'cushions, leaden spoons, irons of a doit', instead of being content to feed on glory (I.v.5–6). Cominius, a more sensible leader, encourages his troops after an opening reverse, instead of abusing them, and assures them that they shall have their fair share of the spoils. Altogether these battle scenes give us a composite picture of war as Shakespeare now thought of it. There is little left of what made war appear so romantic to Othello.

It is a military patriciate that rules Rome, not yet very civilized, not yet decadent. Cominius, general and ex-consul, has a Prussian sense of duty. He loves his country's good, he assures the people, with a devotion 'more holy and profound' than his love for self, wife or child (III.iii.111 ff.). But his 'country' is the Rome of his own class; privately he talks of 'the dull tribunes' and 'the fusty plebeians' with as much scorn as any of his fellow-nobles (I.ix.6–7). He and his brethren recognize no duty except to take the lead in wars which they themselves may have provoked, and which can bring few benefits to the commoners conscripted to fight. The play is a striking exposition of how aggressive nationalism and acute social division not only may, but must, go together; the former not only as a means of hoodwinking the poor, but as a way for the rulers to throw dust in their own eyes and have a good conscience to bolster them. Coriolanus idolizes Rome, but his Rome is no more than a dumb idol; the great majority of its inhabitants he only wants to trample on. Baulked by them of the consulship, which would enable him to tyrannize over them more effectively, he goes off in dudgeon and joins the enemy, as in the sixteenth and seventeenth centuries many of Europe's blue-blooded patriots were accustomed to do.

In later Roman times the hero's mother Volumnia might have taken an active hand in politics, like Antony's wife Fulvia; as it is, her vituperation of the tribunes is in the strain of the railing termagants in the Histories. When a tribune hints at her over-masculine temper, she seems quite proud of it. 'Was not a man my father?' (IV.ii.16–18). She instilled into her son, he recalls, a belief that plebeians, those 'woollen vassals', ought to be treated as an inferior species (III.ii.8 ff.). By doing so she is to prove the cause of his ruin, and almost the cause of Rome's. But we may also attribute to her influence much of the puritanical atmosphere with which family life is invested. It is not an inhuman kind of virtue; on the contrary, only within the family can some of the softer emotions find a sanctuary; and only through it can the poet open the way towards his later plays, escaping from the tainted air that has hung over all the tragedies since *Julius Caesar*, as well as the problem plays.

Recovery dictates some straining or excess of language and attitude, as it did with the Puritanism of history. There is no need to credit Coriolanus with any revulsion from food, as Robert N. Watson does (150 ff.). Puritans were hearty eaters, not only in Scott's novels, like all practical men with work to do. But love is apt to be sublimated into a metaphor for the ardour of battle. On the stricken field, covered with foemen's blood, Coriolanus feels as 'merry' as on his bridal night (I.vi.30–32). His mighty opposite Aufidius likewise, when they meet at last as friends, feels even happier than on his wedding-night (IV.v.116–19). Volumnia affirms that if her son were instead her husband, she would rather have him away fighting than at home in bed with her (I.iii.2–4). Timon denounced gold for its power to 'thaw the consecrated snow that lies on Dian's lap!' (IV.iii.375). When the ladies of Rome come out to his camp to beg him to spare the city, he compliments the family friend Valeria – somewhat irrelevantly: she may be about to perish with the rest – on being 'chaste as the icicle that . . . hangs on Dian's temple'; and he can assure his wife Virgilia that he has kissed no other woman since his exodus (V.iii.65–7, 44). She is his 'gracious silence' (II.i.174), and they have been a devoted couple. The family survives its ordeal, when all other ties are unavailing, and saves Rome; whereas in other tragedies, *King Lear* above all, disintegration of the family is at the heart of social disruption, until in *Timon* it has disappeared, except as a target for some of the hero's tirades.

Restored morality might have been expected to come in company with a deepened feeling for religion; but there is scarcely any sign of this. Even the supernatural echoes of sublunary events, such as are heard in several previous dramas, are missing here. When naked class conflict has become the theme, with all obscuring veils swept aside, there is no need of shadows on the clouds; a hard daylight prevails. Coriolanus talks irreverently of women's soft eyes 'Which can make gods forsworn' (V.iii.27–8). In a passion he 'will not spare to gird the gods' (I.i.250), as well as his fellow-men. On the battlefield he and Titus Lartius both prefer to invoke 'the fair goddess, Fortune' (I.iv.44; I.v.20). Shakespeare must be smiling at sanctimonious Puritan manners when Aufidius, in the first flush of his alliance with Coriolanus, 'turns up the white o' the eye to his discourse', as if to a holy man's (IV.v.195–7). There is a brief change of tone when Volumnia warns her son that the gods will 'plague' him if he disregards her appeal to pardon Rome. At the point of surrendering to his kneeling mother, he himself is lifted into a momentary vision. 'Behold, the heavens do ope' – though what they disclose is the gods *laughing* at this 'unnatural scene' (V.iii.166, 183–5).

Coriolanus has at least enough statesmanship to understand the proper function of religion, that of cementing the social order. His dictum, that it is the senators, 'under the gods', who must keep the populace in awe, is not much different from saying that the gods, under the senators, have a duty to keep the oligarchy in power. He fears, however, that the teaching of 'divines' is thrown away on the rabble (I.i.185–6; II.iii.59–60), and indeed the citizens show scarcely more religious feeling than their betters.

In this early Rome the ruling class is not disrupted by internal feuds, but it is confronted by discontented masses who are learning to organize. Rome is in a state of rancorous division, or, in a phrase of Menenius on another subject, 'violentest contrariety' (IV.vi.75). Each side is completely convinced of its rightness. Patricians have the same contempt for commoners as Shakespeare's noblemen in the Histories on their prancing steeds; this has goaded the masses into a class consciousness of their own. The shrewd '1st Citizen' accuses the rich of enjoying the misery of the hungry poor, because it gives more zest to their own luxurious style of living (I.i.16 ff.). This may or may not be well founded, but it is a true enough index at least of social embitterment.

There are no clownish blockheads; the commoners in Rome and Antium alike are remarkably articulate. Whereas in *Julius Caesar* the citizenry of Rome were little more than a stylized stage mob, now they are more diversified, more real, and they have spokesmen. Politically they are less frivolous; still more, they are acutely conscious that their problems centre on food and hunger, which in the earlier play scarcely find mention. There are other grievances. Shakespeare refers to usury, an evil so familiar to so many of his listeners, only briefly; but he knew from Plutarch of harsh laws, and debtors sold as slaves (4–5).

There is a dearth, and the play opens with a riotous crowd demanding food and threatening Coriolanus as the loudest objector to their claim. This is forcibly urged by the '1st Citizen', who does not, however, go unchallenged. What he is arguing is that the rich ought to part with a share of their 'superfluity' (I.i.16). Shakespeare had preached this in *King Lear*; now, more realistically, he was opening his eyes – or wanted to open his hearers' eyes – to the fact that the rich concede little except when compelled. The poor must take up their pikes, not in thirst for revenge but as the only alternative to starving. When Menenius intervenes the 1st Citizen replies in energetic prose to the aristocrat's verse, and then seems to brush aside the difference of rank by talking verse himself, and holding his own in spite of his overbearing opponent's interruptions. Shakespeare was recognizing that in such a crowd there might be individuals capable of leadership.

Their demonstration wins for the people a political concession, the right to choose tribunes to represent them, with a regular place in the constitution; also – although our author forgets to tell us this until later on – a free distribution of corn, sternly condemned by Coriolanus (I.i.209 ff.; III.i.43, 113 ff.). Things quieten down, and when he returns from campaign, with his new title and garland, the plebeians give him the same vociferous welcome as we have heard their descendants giving to Pompey and Caesar. Class animosity overrides all other feelings except this intoxicating thrill of victory, so often the most potent brew that governments have been able to regale their subjects with. The newly appointed tribunes deplore the levity of this yielding to the siren-song, but rightly feel sure that the hero will soon give the people cause to remember their old grudges (II.i.195 ff.).

The people have their failings, but this grand failing is not the one that critics – most of them, like Menenius in his own words, belonging to 'the right-hand file' (II.i.39–40) – have harped on. Clemen does not improve his study of Shakespeare's imagery by telling us that in this play it reflects 'the baseness of the "rabble"' (cf. Margolies 122), and the poet's 'intense dislike of the masses' (154). Their two tribunes, Brutus and Sicinius, have borne the brunt of anti-popular prejudice. They are 'the crafty tribunes' (Charney 175), 'clever but mean-minded' (R.B. Parker 270). They fare better in Shakespeare's hands than in those of most of his commentators, or of his authority Plutarch, who blames 'the flatterers of the people', among them 'two seditious Tribunes', for stirring up trouble (13). They are not themselves men of the people, but upper-class individuals who have under-taken a role as guardians of the people's rights. They talk with the notables on equal terms, and sometimes in similar accents. Brutus contrasts 'the kitchen malkin' and her 'reechy neck' with 'our veiled dames' (II.i.197–8). His casual words about 'half my wealth' (IV.vi.160) inform us that he is a man of property. Menenius talks to them unreservedly about the 'beastly plebeians' (II.i.94–5).

Whether they are inspired by sympathy with the poor, or by ambition, Shakespeare does not make altogether clear; he may not have made up his mind about them; their motives may well be mixed. Commentators have found fault with them as more concerned with their own office than with serving the people (e.g. Leggatt 197). But their first duty was to guard and consolidate this newly created office and its authority, which Coriolanus and his like would do their best to abolish. Palmer (whose chapter on this play is the weightiest in his book) points out that these magistrates see themselves, rightly, as 'watch-dogs of the people', and intend to be 'alert and vigilant' (258–9; cf. Mehl 187–8). They indulge in no demagogy; they are not hot-headed young radicals, but men of years and experience. Sicinius is addressed as 'aged sir', and less civilly, by Coriolanus, as 'old goat!' (III.i.175–6). They show no desire to feather their own nests. Certainly Shakespeare does not mean us to take for gospel Menenius's abuse of them as 'a brace of unmeriting, proud, violent, testy magistrates, – alias fools' (II.i.21).

But they are not inflaming the populace, only teaching it political lessons already familiar to the higher class, of which they are members. They may have acted from prudence, or a sense of obligation to the poor, or from both motives, and an understanding of how recklessly Coriolanus was behaving. Yet Harry Levin (*Revolution* 140) taxes them with 'unequivocal cynicism', and demagogy; this, he argues, not democracy, is what Shakespeare is attack-ing. A charge of demagogy can, however, be levelled far more justly against their enemies, the senatorial party. The play is in many ways, along with the mature English Histories and *Julius Caesar*, a study of aristocratic flattery and cajolery of the people, for the purpose of duping them. A correct instinct guided Shakespeare to this subject, destined to immense importance in modern Europe. Thanks to its social and political evolution England was more advanced in the art than any other country, and was to retain the lead for very long.

Menenius knows that there are times when his class must sacrifice dignity to security. He is a jolly old toper, with no worse sins to his account that we know of, and a warm admirer of Coriolanus, 'always factionary', as he says, on the hero's side (V.ii.29). An easy-going affability towards his poorer neighbours has won him a cheap reputation as 'one that hath always loved the people' (I.i.46–7). In the food crisis he treats them with a mixture of soft soap and threats. The patricians, he assures them, have 'most charitable care' for them; if they are hungry, it is the gods who are responsible for the dearth. But 'Rome and her rats', he winds up by dropping his mask and warning them, are at the point of battle, and they will be the losers (I.i.60–1, 155).

To Coriolanus this conclusion comes as something natural and obvious. He looks down on the people as animals, 'curs', that 'would feed on one another' if not prevented (I.i.162–3). Yet with the lack of logic common among such fire-eaters, he fears that the granting of tribunes must 'make bold power look pale': having felt their strength the plebeians will advance in 'insurrection', until the governing class is overthrown (I.i.209 ff.). To distribute corn will be a fatal admission of weakness. In the campaign he hurls at his soldiers 'All the contagion of the south', 'boils and plagues' (I.iv.30). This is the language of Timon, close to madness, or even of Caliban. Coriolanus affects the plainness of a man of few words, like Henry V, but is really a man of a great many words, and as truculent in argument as in battle.

The conservative party wants to turn its champion's fresh laurels to account, and win a 'khaki election', by running him for the consulship. For this it will be necessary to gain public assent, by appearing in the market-place and asking for votes. All his prudent friends want him to submit with a good grace to what is little more than a formality. Even his mother urges him to play the modest candidate; she can even recommend him to kneel with mock-humility to the crowd. If 'policy', or trickery, is necessary in war, why should it not be made good use of in civil life too (III.ii.46 ff.)? Under pressure he consents – as he sulkily tells the voters – to 'practise the insinuating nod', to 'counterfeit the bewitchment of some popular man' (II.iii.90–92), just as candidates do today. To such deception he has no objection of principle, but he chafes at it as beneath the dignity of a man, a garlanded hero, like himself. To have to play a part, like an actor, revolts his 'noble heart' (III.ii.100). Moreover he is one of those reactionaries who by temperament are always scenting revolution, and are impatient to nip it in the bud. Neither the citizens nor their shepherds are revolutionaries; but in such situations there is always an extreme right wing, ready to argue that to give way an inch must open the floodgates of rebellion.

Coriolanus is quite prepared to thank his peers, the senators, for choosing him as consul – 'I do owe them still/My life and services' (II.ii.137–8) – but he refuses to be beholden to any commoners. His Rome is very much the patrimony of the 'four hundred families'. Any need for votes ought to be done away with, in his opinion. When he is induced to beg them, the battles he has been in, the number of scars he bears (like a Prussian officer in the duelling era), are his sole title to the supreme office; they carry the day, but before his inauguration can take place the tribunes, seeing the menace to the popular cause and their own office, reproach the people for their heedlessness and persuade them, without much difficulty, to change their mind. Coriolanus is enraged at finding himself baulked, and declares that it is part of a plot to overturn the power of the nobility (III.i.38–41). His friends and his mother manage to calm him, and get him to try again. But the citizens stand firmly with their tribunes; they have been learning from the controversy. When a senator warns them that civil war will lay the city flat, Sicinius rejoins 'What is the city but the people?' – and they echo him: 'True, the people are the city' (III.i.198–200). Their enemy's ungovernable temper does the rest. 'The fires i' the lowest hell fold-in the people!' he is soon shouting (III.iii.68).

He is banished. What exasperates him is not his rejection by the lower orders, whom he despises, but his being left in the lurch, as he sees it, by his fellow-aristocrats. He is trying to save them from the consequences of cowardice, retreat, self-betrayal. Shaking Rome's dust off his feet, he vows that he will still 'exceed the common', and distinguish himself (IV.i.32); so in truth he does, but only by turning against everything he has hitherto revered. Misfortune teaches him no positive lessons, as it does to Lear. He may be forced to sleep 'under the canopy' (IV.v.37), in the open, exposed to privations like those of the poor – which he must often have shared on campaign; but this brings no change of heart. The sole change is that he now hates all Romans, instead of only the poor.

Cut adrift from fatherland and family, he becomes a rampant egotist, bent on destroying Rome as some émigrés from the Revolution wanted to destroy Paris. He himself can scarcely understand what has happened to him; he can only talk, in a rare moment of soliloquizing, of the world's 'slippery turns', and friends estranged, enemies united (IV.iv.12 ff.), as if feeling himself to be in the grip of an unmeaning but irresistible destiny. His words show at least a sense of the value of friendship, though also of its fragility, which a nature like his makes inevitable. He resembles Timon, so eager to see his Athens put to the sword, in a total incapacity for self-criticism.

Coriolanus and Aufidius of Antium, the Volscian war-chief, have long felt a chivalrous admiration for each other, and the former at length seeks out his old sparring-partner and complains to him of the 'dastard nobles' of

Rome who have thrown him to the wolves (IV.v.76). Aufidius welcomes him magnanimously. He has a likeness, with the splinters of his spear scarring the moon (IV.v.109–10), to Hotspur, and knightly honour over-leaps national boundaries: aristocracies are born to fight one another, but they have no ill will except against their own commonalty. He is delighted at the thought of wiping out 'ungrateful Rome': we may see in his attitude an upper-class instinct of solidarity against mutinous plebeians everywhere, the same feeling that was to inspire the coalitions against the French or the Russian revolutions. Here is one of many points in the story where we should have liked Shakespeare to be more explicit, though a need for discretion is understandable. Aufidius at any rate finds no fault with his new ally as a renegade and traitor.

In Rome, Sicinius mocks the conservatives for being disappointed by the public tranquillity after Coriolanus's expulsion: they would rather have had disorder than heard 'Our tradesmen singing in their shops' (IV.vi.4 ff.). None of the patricians, or the banished man's family, have been molested. But a Roman in the Volscian secret service tells a Volscian colleague and old acquaintance that the patricians 'are in a right aptness to take all power from the people' (IV.iii.23–5). They are planning a counter-revolution, and can be expected to welcome foreign aid (*selon les règles* of political history); they will deserve no sympathy when it turns out that the foreign sword is to fall on them as well as on the plebeians. One of Aufidius's servants shrewdly predicts that the Roman nobles will emerge from their burrows like rabbits after rain, to join Coriolanus when he draws near, 'and revel all with him' (IV.v.209–11).

When it proves that he is not coming to put himself at their head, but to pay them out for their reluctance to stand by him, no united resistance by them and the people is conceivable. For all their loud patriotism, not one of the patricians except Volumnia blames him for returning with a foreign army; he has a right to his revenge. He will take Rome 'by sovereignty of nature', Aufidius says, like a bird of prey (IV.vii.34–5). This unhappily is what the plebeians too are paralysed by feeling, despite the military training and service many of them have had. They each suddenly remember that they were against the banishment (IV.vi. 140 ff.). Their tribunes, formerly so intrepid, can give them no lead, so it is not very surprising to hear that a mob has seized one of them and is threatening to 'give him death by inches' (V.iv.35 ff.). A Volscian soldier derides their 'violent popular ignorance' in driving out their strongest defender (V.ii.37). A people must submit to its masters, or be overrun by foreign marauders.

Coriolanus camps at the gates; some incoherence in the narrative ensues. He offers terms, and renews the offer as a favour to Menenius; apparently they are rejected, though Rome still has no thought of fighting. In the end he imposes a treaty, sufficiently shameful to Rome, he says (V.vi.71 ff.), and

181

withdraws; Aufidius, present throughout, raises no objection. What stands out is the great scene of Volumnia's appeal to her son, all the more powerful because her language is simple and homely. She rises at last above her rigid class attitude, and pleads for the Rome of all Romans; she can even hold up forgiveness as an ideal —

> Thinkst thou it honourable for a noble man
> Still to remember wrongs?

He is tearing out his country's bowels, and this country is 'our dear nurse'. If he persists,

> we will home to Rome,
> And die among our neighbours.

She can even urge her plea as beneficial to Romans and Volscians alike; all will share the blessings of peace and reconciliation (V.iii. 132 ff.). All this is strange doctrine from the Volumnia we have known until now. But the spectacle of an idolized son transformed into arch-traitor might well be enough to work such an upheaval in her thinking; and we can guess too at some contrition for her teaching of him in early life. It is easy to conjecture at the same time that Shakespeare is making use of her to preach something of his own, a higher, unaggressive public spirit, an ideal that he has been working his way towards. It is in any case striking that he has chosen a *woman* to deliver this pronouncement, one of his most momentous, for him.

Coriolanus warns his mother that his withdrawal from Rome may imperil his life; but he is not seeking death, and has no thought of suicide. Extraordinary as it must seem, he is nursing ambitions for a new career, in Antium, and thus sharpening the jealousy and dislike that Aufidius has not been slow to feel. The Volscian leader's list of his rival's failings sums them up well: pride, 'defect of judgment', military brusqueness of manner (IV.vii.35 ff.). Freed from former ties and respect for older men, Coriolanus has let his dictatorial propensities take control of him. Brutus earlier on taxed him with talking of the people as if he were 'a god to punish' (III.i.80–81), and the faithful Menenius, after meeting him outside Rome, shakes his head: 'He wants nothing of a god but eternity, and a heaven to throne in' (V.iv.24–5).

Both rivals are deteriorating (Traversi 226). Envious thoughts of treachery beset Aufidius; his nature is growing envenomed. He accuses Coriolanus of luring his supporters away from him 'with dews of flattery' (V.vi.23–4): another strange turn, the hero practising arts he has until now spurned. Aufidius's friends remind him that his return to Antium has been ignored, while the townsfolk, those 'patient fools', have been splitting their 'base throats' with applause for the man who killed so many of their kin (V.vi.50

ff.). Ordinary Volscians it seems are as easily carried away by the excitement of a public spectacle as Romans; and their rulers are as contemptuous of them as Roman patricians of their plebs. Aufidius is advised by these friends to kill Coriolanus before the interloper has a chance to address and sway the crowd. Coriolanus enters, escorted by a throng – Aufidius stings him into a wild fury – the people remember the deaths of their kinsfolk, and shout for him to be torn to pieces – the conspirators stab him. Aufidius comes to himself, and pronounces a last tribute to the great warrior, like Antony's to Brutus, Octavius's to Antony; and though so long a foe of Antium the Roman shall be given a noble memorial.

The manner and cause of his death add to the difficulty of seeing it in a truly tragic light. What might have been made so was his breach with the class he had idealized and served unsparingly; or the moment when he renounced his revenge and turned away from Rome a second time, to go back to Antium and meet his fate. All Act V is something of an anticlimax. But he has given way at Rome to family feeling alone, with no opening of his eyes to the barbarity of what he had intended. Like Timon he has failed to reach any comprehension of how his world has been altering round him. Such stragglers from an older time must be disoriented when compelled to breathe a new air.

There may be, nevertheless, a different way of looking at the final events, and seeing the hero's death in a more positive light. Shakespeare's text shows things as they appear to Aufidius, who is eager to discredit him. This does not exclude the possibility of Coriolanus being a changed man, at least on the issue of war and peace, as his mother when they were last together was a changed woman. He might well be deeply affected by her example, and the collapse of his creed of aristocracy, and by his paradoxical situation in a strange environment. He has come back to Antium bringing a treaty of peace, which he believes Aufidius to have endorsed, and which he must persuade Antium to accept. He has risen by war, but now he wants this war to end; after what has happened he cannot look forward to a life of continual fighting against his native land, even supposing him able to supplant Aufidius as head of the army. He may even be in a mood to renounce the sword for good. If he tries to cajole some Volscians who, as Aufidius's supporters, must be adherents of a war party, it may be with the aim of winning them over to peace, rather than of gaining their favour for ambitions of his own.

We may then give the populace that applauds him credit for good sense; they want peace, and Coriolanus is bringing them peace with honour. Aufidius has accused him to 'the Lords', or governing body, of throwing away the fruits of victory (V.vi.65 ff.); but when Coriolanus appears, and hands his treaty to them, Aufidius has to intervene, to keep them from reading it, and provokes him into the rage which turns the public against him and excuses the assassination. However Coriolanus's ideas may have been altering, his nature cannot; his explosive temper gets the better of him now when he is trying to serve the people, just as it did in Rome when he was trying to deceive them. Tragic irony could scarcely go further; the apostle of war is killed preaching peace; more than any other hero he dies a martyr, a sacrificial offering.

At Antium the war party has regained power. In Rome there has not been even an approach to the kind of radical shift that a lasting peace would have represented. There is relief, jubilation, at the lifting of the death-sentence on the city, a fraternizing of rich and poor which we can only feel to be a transient mood. No moral is drawn as to better relations in the future. There has been no social purgation, and we are left with no hint, such as all the previous tragedies give, of its possibility. Shakespeare takes leave of a republic deadlocked, with no way out except perpetual war and conquest. From now on he was turning away from any direct grapple with his 'great argument', the destiny of human society. The Romances which followed were his admission of problems insoluble in his epoch, or as far in the future as any eye could reach.

There is much in the play of the time-honoured parallel of human society and human body, but it is taken over woodenly, as Spurgeon says, from Shakespeare's source (342). He cannot be supposed to take it seriously now (if he ever did), when the fact of class division and hostility stands out so patently. Scarcely any non-partisan views are expressed, the social chasm seems unbridgeable. A mythic harmony of classes under impartial paternal government is fading. Both aristocracy and people cringe before the assailant, as the Senate of Athens did before Alcibiades. What the play leaves us with is a 'bleak and uncompromising pessimism' (Rabkin, *Meaning* 111). Its underlying causes are economic. It has always been clear that, in the opening scenes especially, Shakespeare must have had in mind some of the hardships of the English poor, brought to light in 1607 by food shortages and unrest in the Midlands.

His Roman commoners, however, are not countryfolk; they must be modelled chiefly on those of London, or one large section of them, shop-keepers and artisans, cobblers and ironworkers and the like. Coriolanus turns up his nose at 'all the trades in Rome'; his mother wants the 'red pestilence' to strike them, 'and occupations perish!' (III.ii.134; IV.i.13). A generation later the Levellers referred to their supporters by terms such as 'leather aprons', which seem to point to the same social grades. In England the franchise was beginning to broaden, for such impersonal reasons as property qualifications being reduced by inflation (Patterson 2). In Rome as in the later English Histories ordinary folk are acquiring a lively curiosity about affairs of State; to Coriolanus's indignation, they love to gather round the fire and gossip about politicians and factions and marriage-alliances, about 'who thrives and who declines' (I.i.185 ff.) – 'Who's in, who's out', as Lear put it. Already it pays a man with aspirations to be 'supple and courteous to the people' (II.ii.26–7).

Questions of war or peace came often into English politics. An opposition movement in the making, Puritans and parliamentarians, merchants and colony-hunters, often favoured war; they had an eye to its profits, and also it must be supposed to the need to allay social friction, in a London where the lower orders were suspected of dangerous thoughts. At the time of this play England had just been conquering Ireland, as Rome has been annexing neighbouring territories. Roman sway is evidently not liked there, unsurprisingly in view of what we see of government in Rome itself. Coriolanus is a product of nascent Roman imperialism, as well as of class conflict. While he is marching on Rome we hear that 'all the regions do smilingly revolt' (IV.vi.103–4), just as Ireland was always ready to do when French or Spanish forces landed on its coasts.

A sidelight on war and the people is the light-hearted chatter in the servants' hall at Aufidius's mansion, where there is the same fondness for politics as at Rome, and the same relish for new words as among servants in the Comedies. 'Directitude' is one that puzzles a hearer. Servants in a great household, especially that of an army man, would of course not be typical plebeians; they would take their cue from the high table, and they might be sheltered from conscription. Shakespeare may be poking fun at a feather-brained lower class, or giving us a parody of upper-class thinking. 'We shall have a stirring world again', says one, a fresh campaign being in prospect. 'This peace is nothing, except to rust iron.' 'Let me have war, say I', another chimes in: '. . . it's spritely, waking, audible, and full of vent', whereas peace is 'deaf, sleepy, insensible'. These kitchen-philosophers look deeper, however. Peace 'makes men hate one another'. – 'Reason: because they then less need one another' (IV.v.225 ff.). Unexpectedly, in this odd corner, we are faced again with one of Shakespeare's besetting problems, the social disharmony which can only be smothered by foreign war.

Another revealing conversation among onlookers, in this drama of ideas, is between a pair of attendants at the Capitol, before the consular election (II.ii.1 ff.). They comment cynically on the class relations that have been evolving. 'Faith', says one, 'there have been many great men that have flatter'd the people, who ne'er loved them', and many whom the people have loved without knowing why. In these words Shakespeare was epitomizing a good part of England's political future. Among the great men is Menenius, whom we see sneering at the petty utilitarian concerns the tribunes busy themselves with. They have laboured 'To make coals cheap – a noble memory!' (V.i.17). Shakespeare knew that such things might mean more to the poor than any battle, however brilliantly bloody.

Rome's Senate cannot be equated with Parliament; it is the stronghold of the oligarchy, the government of Rome, whereas Parliament had as yet only an intermittent existence. The House of Commons was drawn chiefly from the landed gentry; it might at times be against the government, seldom against the rich. The tribunes harp on the people's 'ancient strength', or rights, forgetting that Rome has only just become a republic; Parliamentary lawyers and historians did the same, stubbornly insisting on precedent and prescription. James I referred more than once, with distaste, to leaders of the Commons as 'tribunes of the people' (Patterson 123). He and they were drifting apart from very early in his reign. Coriolanus might be denouncing talkative politicians in general when he argues that if old custom is always to be followed, 'The dust on antique times would lie unswept' and hard facts be buried out of sight. He inveighs likewise against the mischief of divided responsibility: authority must be one and indivisible, or muddle and ineffectiveness must result (II.iii.17 ff.; III.i.107 ff.). Stuart apologists maintained that this was what would happen if Parliament were allowed to encroach on the royal prerogative.

Coriolanus's disdain of applause, his condemnation of 'false-faced soothing' and flattery (I.ix.42 ff.), made him in some ways eligible for Shakespeare's approval. Shakespeare had lost faith in monarchy, but he had lately been thinking of a substitute in the form of enlightened dictatorship, headed by an Alcibiades or an Octavius. In Coriolanus he tried, and rejected, a third variation. England had made some progress, and might hope to make more. So had Rome; a Coriolanus would strip the public of all constitutional rights, its 'liberties' and 'charters'. It was, besides, only too clear that he would always be on the side of the rich minority against the poor majority. Those who might object, he proposed to massacre (I.i.196 ff.).

A good many earlier writers had made use of the Coriolanus story in anti-popular diatribes; far more have done so since. The baneful influence of imperialism shows in the readiness of some of them to admire Coriolanus as the Strong Man, a replica of the kind of governor who was sent out to govern troublesome colonies. Rossiter falls below his usual level when, allowing that Coriolanus has faults, he insists that 'his convictions about the State are good and right' (243). Saintsbury, having condemned Cassius's 'pseudo-patriotic hatred of Caesar', goes on to rebuke the 'sordid spite' of the tribunes in *Coriolanus*, and contrast the 'malignity', 'meanness', 'ingratitude', of the plebs with the lofty grandeur of the hero (197–8). This was written in 1943, when Britain professed to be at war in defence of democracy.

An American writing a year or two earlier must have had his own Democrats and their New Deal in mind when he hailed the play as an illustration of the 'dire consequences' of disregard of natural law, and of attempts at 'democratic redress of popular grievances' (Phillips 149, 169). Since then two of his countrymen have confessed to 'a tremendous surge and lift of exultation' when the hero shakes off 'the dirty encumbrances of political jobbery' (Sanders and Jacobson 159): when, that is, he determines to submit no longer to his country's quarter-democratic constitution. It is stranger to read, in a work offered as 'a Marxist analysis', of cowardly patricians allowing their champion's 'unjust banishment' at the behest of 'power-seeking tribunes' (Siegel 107). A refreshing exception to the roll-call is Annabel Patterson, one of whose objects has been to controvert a dogma, long in the ascendant, of Shakespeare's scorn for the common man (1).

PART IV

Tragic Themes

1

The Hero

Tolstoy wrote in his diary in 1853 that his forerunner in Russian fiction, Pushkin, now seemed out of date, because his characters were drawn too much from outside, with too little revelation of their essential selves (63). Something like this may be typical of any cycle of literature, and certainly helps to distinguish Shakespeare from his predecessors. To say that his heroes' inner consciousness matters much more than their relatively scanty doings (Bayley 6) may suggest neglect of the outward business of life, action and its motives and consequences, which in Shakespeare always form an equipoise with inner feeling. It can at any rate be said that the tragedies form part of a human groping towards better self-understanding and mutual understanding, in both of which faculties mankind has been lamentably deficient.

Shakespearian tragedy does not show character evolving along what may be called the line natural to it, as comedy may do; like revolution, it involves violent displacement into a new orbit. There is the same individual still, but with an extreme disproportion between the man or woman we have known or learned of, and their behaviour under new and unexpected stresses. An unfamiliar situation has to be confronted, an unknown future such as mankind is perpetually moving towards. Tillyard considered Hamlet not fully tragic, because he underwent 'no great revelation or reversal of direction or regeneration' (17); but this jumbles up different things. Few heroes could claim either revelation – Othello thought he had received one, from Iago –, or regeneration; but a stormy change of direction, in a world suddenly strange, is what they all undergo.

Tragic emotion cannot be aroused if there is too little admiration or sympathy for the protagonist (H. Hawkins 76). Great though he may be, by station and by endowment, he must not be too far separated from common human feeling. We have a special liking for the earlier heroes, Brutus and Hamlet, in whom we can see humanity's better impulses at work, even if baffled, and through whom we can feel ourselves in close contact with their creator. From Othello on, heroes are less companionable beings, whom we can scarcely regard as intimates, and whom Shakespeare himself may seem to find more baffling, as denizens of a world he is finding more incomprehensible. However eloquent their words, their selves are in a measure closed to us, in a way that Hamlet's is not. From *Timon* onward Shakespeare was never fully able, Empsom thought, to 'identify' with his heroes; even in *Antony and Cleopatra* he stands 'somehow above his characters' (138). He is furthest removed from his last hero, Coriolanus – of whom Poole asks whether there is any real 'self' inside him (52).

How much of Shakespeare's own self, a secret self perhaps, went into their making can only be speculation. They all came into the world within a few years, but only Hamlet wears a youthful look; the rest are nearing or past their prime, like Shakespeare himself, and one is very old, as Shakespeare may have shrunk from the prospect of being one day. His diverse offspring are remarkably independent from him, and we may always have to suppose a complex, even half-inimical relationship between him and them.

A hero or any other prominent character must hold our interest by force of his own personality, not simply as a type, or, as English lawyers called their sovereign, a 'corporation sole'. His 'representative' self, both meaningful and mysterious, should be like his shadow, everywhere with him but not obtrusively. The social ambience, the temper of the times, are never lost sight of in these dramas; some minor persons have the duty of giving voice to them. A hero may seem to be in the grip of a power outside himself, or within him but not under his conscious will; the stronger this impression, the more distinctly we can see him as embodying human destinies, or currents that sweep us all onward, or that we must struggle to resist. He is a 'great man', and one who is or has sometimes been greatly good, or whom we can believe capable of such greatness; the highest art must be concerned with mankind's highest aspirations, and the causes of their frustration. His grandeur marks him as a scion of our collective self, subject to the human condition which we all share. In this light, tragedy is something that draws us together by making us conscious of how much we are indeed one whole. Whoever the hero, the drama is a tragedy of mankind; in Wordsworth's language, of 'poor humanity's afflicted will/ Struggling in vain'.

It is not only the protagonists who may be felt at times to be speaking for us, as well as for themselves. Many others can speak on occasion the magical language of Shakespeare's theatre, unparalleled in the world's literature. They break out in its accents in excited or exalted moods, when their thoughts go far beyond their customary bounds. At such moments the words seem to spring not from habitual selves but out of unplumbed depths of feeling hidden in all human beings; they resemble the 'bardic' or 'prophetic' utterances of early times. But these speakers must have a footing, however modest, in the heroic world. They cannot be menials, or money-grubbers. A London alderman gulping his turtle soup might be a deserving enough person in his own way, but he could not be made to look poetical, or taught to speak naturally in blank verse. And after all, Shakespeare's instincts were first and foremost those of a poet. His tragic heroes and heroines are beings whom we can believe to possess in a unique degree the faculty of revealing in a few words or sentences whole panoramas of human experience, as though from a hilltop.

It was natural to choose for their roles men and women occupying some towering position in the world. As Schopenhauer said, royalties were useful, though not indispensable: 'the misfortune in which we should recognize the fate of human life must have sufficient magnitude', in order to impress us (2.347). A nobody, an Apemantus, can serve as a sharp-tongued cynic; a Danish prince can be listened to as a serious critic of the way we live. Shakespeare could count on the mystique of monarchy, or other high descent, to capture public imagination. Nature herself might feel a similar bond. When Oedipus unknowingly sinned, plague struck his kingdom. 'The heavens themselves blaze forth the deaths of princes' (*JC* II.ii.30–31), or of men like Julius Caesar, while beggars die unnoticed.

Moretti thinks of the hero as a supreme, one-sided individualist (61); but this is only true of a hero in an early, adolescent stage, like Hotspur, or Chapman's Bussy d'Ambois. These men are anarchical forces, driven either to defy the centralizing State, or, like Richard III, to seize power over it. Doubtless many ordinary men could feel in some degree such impatience of control by others, or such desire to control others. Shakespeare's more mature heroes set out with no ruling ambition, but are forced into action, and then broken apart by painfully conflicting impulses. They are thereby enlarged, even universalized. It is by being thus turned into contradictions that they are qualified, more deeply than by externals of rank, to speak for us. As Bradley said, Shakespeare is not concerned now with the situation of 'an undivided soul' facing a hostile environment (*Tragedy* 18). His heroes are always at odds, first and foremost, with themselves, like the communities they belong to. Brutus felt the likeness between a man wrestling with himself before carrying out a terrible deed, and 'a little kingdom' in 'insurrection' (II.i.67–9). Our environment is not outside us only, but is part of us as well. Garaudy found fault with modern writers who have ascribed to a changeless human being 'the contradictions they find in themselves, which are those of a class and a social system' (40).

Bradley's singling out of a 'tragic flaw', which condemns a hero to disaster, can claim some warrant from Shakespeare. Hamlet talks of a defect that can dull the lustre of all a man's good points (I.iv.23 ff.). Agrippa acknowledges the dead Antony's remarkable gifts, but adds that the gods 'will give us some faults to make us men' (V.i.32–3), and some of these have been the cause of his downfall. There is also here a recognition that all men, as well as heroes, have their faults, which may matter little until circumstances throw them into prominence. They can then bring about actions which work harm on both individual and community.

A Shakespearian hero is attached, by a strong part at least of his emotional make-up, to things of the past, a stage of history now due to be left behind. For him the past, as he has known it, stands for an ideal, however fallacious, to be safeguarded or restored; or, as with Macbeth, a temptation not to be resisted. In *Julius Caesar* the conspirators are firmly planted in a great tradition which, like the chivalric Honour of the English plays, has come close to its end, and is living on its past. Brutus's ideal of a free republic clearly seems preferable to Shakespeare, as against a dictatorship or the ruthless rule of a trio of *condottieri*. But the behaviour of the irresponsible citizenry proves that an ideal republic, if it ever existed, cannot now be revived. Brutus is a shining exemplar of an old school of patriotism, but it did too little for common folk to cement their allegiance. He and his friends saw their duty in a narrow, negative way, like latter-day liberals, as simply removal of a threat to 'freedom'.

Timon, Antony, Coriolanus, all persist obstinately in old habits, convictions, allegiances, when wiser heads are coming to terms with a new life, a new dispensation. Hence Timon finds himself deserted by his associates – Antony by many old comrades in arms –, Coriolanus by his class. Hamlet's more creative spirit was thwarted by the obligation imposed on him from beyond the grave, again simply destructive, and tied to the past and the coercive memory of an admired father. Othello is very ready to defy convention by his marriage, but he succumbs to primitive patriarchal notions of a husband's right against a disloyal wife. Most obviously Lear carries the past with him; he is a living anachronism, and what we learn or guess of the condition of Britain under his rule is not attractive. Coriolanus is an equally evident case of refusal to accept change, or dilution of the power of a ruling class. In all these cases there is no straightforward antithesis of good and bad; the old order contained good, the new contains evil. Tragedy lies in the impossibility, betokened by the hero's fate, of harmonizing the better elements of the two.

In his essay on Hegel's theory of tragedy Bradley points out that its external conflict between good and ill nearly always has an extension in conflict within the hero (*Poetry* 88). It is in essence, we can add, a struggle between the principles of an older and a newer order. For us the inner divisions, which reach our minds more intimately or nakedly, may mirror an age of social turmoil more faithfully than any external conflicts can do. Awkwardly stranded between two anchorages, to both of which he half belongs, the hero has a recurrent sensation of being out of place, a fish out of water. Brutus was born too late, Othello in the wrong latitude. Loyal to the past when he contrasts his father with Claudius, as an intellectual Hamlet is ahead of his time rather than lagging behind it.

Tragedy disrupts a heroic personality before bringing about its death, most patently in the cases of Othello, Macbeth, Coriolanus. In Brutus the goodness of the hero and the badness of much in his society, which he overlooks, remain as a rule apart and separate; in Cassius they mingle somewhat. In Hamlet we see the process beginning that makes the hero feel society's venoms circulating in his own veins too; this helps to unnerve and demoralize him, and he is not altogether pretending when he charges himself with so many sins. He is realizing that the world is what Polonius, that old curmudgeon, thinks it; and he himself is a part of it, and cannot be free of its taints. 'Better my mother had not borne me' (III.i.121).

A hero is constrained by collective pressure of tradition or conviction – of duty to revenge a father, for instance –, which he cannot reject without ceasing to be himself. The society he is cooped up in is disintegrating, morally and politically, and this process has a closer and closer parallel within him. Accepting the time-honoured duty of revenge for a kinsman, Hamlet grows callous to the shedding of other blood as well. Macbeth finds that by reverting to barbaric habits of the past he has created a situation where things cannot simply continue, and that to maintain his footing in Scotland he must kill more and more fellow-Scots. Lear would like to wipe out a world too wicked to be allowed to go on. Timon is in Lear's company when he wants Athens wiped out, Coriolanus when he wants to wipe out Rome. The Roman or feudal spirit of conquest has turned against itself.

A persistent feature of this is that the hero is the man with courage and resolve to go to the limit, to act out in full what he feels drawn to do by duty or choice. Many Romans who perished in the proscriptions had wanted Caesar put an end to; Brutus and Cassius led a few men to kill him. Many men and women have indulged in dreams of romantic love, but few have tried to turn them into reality as Othello and Desdemona did. Timon laid his whole fortune on the altar of friendship. Coriolanus's aristocratic friends detested the plebeians, he was prepared to unsheath the sword against them. All these were great individuals, but at the same time embodiments of collective feeling and fantasy; what only an individual feels is not heroic but freakish. We cannot withhold some admiration, even when it is unwilling, for those who are not afraid to advance thus boldly on their goal, and are ready to pay the price. Attributes such as they possess belong to the human inheritance, even though there is a vital need of means to keep them within bounds.

In one aspect the hero may be humanity challenging fate: in another he is ambition, or self-righteousness, challenging humanity. He must always tread a path where he will be threatened with loss of his own humanity.

Macbeth is steadily more brutalized, though not so deeply in inner feeling as in outward behaviour. Lear is so for a while, until suffering humanizes him; it is the infliction of suffering on others that brutalizes. Other recurrent features can be seen, diverse though the heroes are. It is a prodigious leap from Lear's Britain to Cleopatra's Egypt, yet there is some likeness between an aged king exchanging power for leisure and an aging triumvir turning away from Rome in search of eastern bliss; or, again, a rich Athenian giving everything away and then wanting his money back.

Hamlet is the most exceptional among the heroes, as one who shrinks from action, recoils from a duty not of his own seeking. Because most of us are similarly 'infirm of purpose', this hesitation brings him closer to us, while some of the others, like Othello, grow more remote. He is a reader, one of very few in Shakespeare, and we may suppose that while away from Denmark he has been led to ponder his country's condition; and that his father's death and its repulsive sequel stir up misgivings that have been gathering in his mind. When he reflects on the ills that flesh is heir to – the man-made ones, such as the insolence of office, the proud man's contumely – we must take him as Shakespeare's spokesman for common humanity. He is learning early what Lear stumbled on in old age. Satirizing the higher classes, from a landowner in foppish youth to a councillor in his dotage, he is as clearly speaking for a censorious middle class.

His sole prescribed task is to punish his father's murderer, but this commission swells up in his brooding mind into that of a public reformer; he thinks himself called by heaven to be its 'scourge and minister' (III.iv.176). We are close here to the Puritan denunciation of human wickedness, and the thirst to purge it. But this is something manifestly impossible for any young man, single-handed, to carry out. He is popular with the people, but he never thinks of looking to them for support, as Laertes with his far simpler objective does. Moreover Claudius's death would not put an end to any of the country's plagues, for which he can scarcely be blamed; his reign has only just begun.

Amid Hamlet's self-questionings, practical business recedes into the shadows; the human condition at large, and his own responsibility in it, engross him. Inner conflict reaches a point close to a complete dislocation between his two identities, his hours of introspection and of febrile activity. He feels impelled to put on a mask of madness, because he cannot trust himself to behave normally in front of others. He is too morbidly conscious of his unrevealed secret, and the thoughts he cannot disclose – his 'mystery' (III.ii.321). Countless others, near or far, have felt entangled in some such dilemma; the play has been a crystal ball for generation after generation to peer into. Indecision has its supreme expression in the soliloquy 'To be or not to be' (III.i.56 ff.), a speech scarcely possible to find a coherent meaning in, yet overflowing with meanings or half-meanings. They seem to drift away from the private to the general, as his thoughts often do; the idea of resistance to oppression forms a bridge. It is the people, rather than any individual, who are faced with 'a sea of troubles', and who 'grunt and sweat' under the burden of life, though Hamlet can feel the weight of his own burden equally. Suicide cannot be a remedy for the multitude, though it may be for him. But here Shakespeare must stop; it may be one of many points where he felt, as in Sonnet 66, that his art was 'made tongue-tied by authority'.

In his last tragedy the commoners do rise up against injustice, at first with no guidance but their own. Throughout the series, social evils have been a lurking shadow in the background. Lear and Timon have thundered against them. Alcibiades, as Timon's substitute, has undertaken action against them; the coming to power of the austere Octavius is an unspoken pledge of reform. But as yet this worse side of the old order keeps its hold, whatever may befall its good side. The weight of the past, in Marx's famous words, presses like a nightmare on the brains of the living. From the early tragedies, where life imposes on the hero duties, real or illusory, there is a progression to a world holding out temptations, which it may be as fatal to resist as to yield to. Pompey's son rejects a triumph to be won by treachery, and is murdered by those he has spared. Coriolanus resists the temptation to gain the consulship by what he deems to be pandering to democracy. Macbeth's surrender is the steepest moral descent anywhere in the tragedies, apart from the treason of Coriolanus. The witches' unholy influence helps to give the play an unusual touch of allegory. Adam too was led astray by Satan and by his wife.

Lady Macbeth reminds her husband that he has sworn to kill Duncan (I.vii.68–9). He is the last of those who are pushed by others into under-takings repellent to them. Brutus dismisses the proposal of an oath to bind the conspirators together, in one of his noblest speeches, as unworthy of Roman patriots (II.i.114 ff.). But the Ghost exacts a vow from Hamlet, and he in turn from his companions, though only one of silence. It seems that tragic life is throwing up tasks impossible to face except under such compulsion. Othello kneels and takes a 'sacred vow' of 'wide revenge' on Desdemona, and Iago in a sinister parody kneels and vows to aid him (III.iii.460 ff.). Lear, Timon, Coriolanus, can rush on their fate more spontaneously, because it is folly, not crime, they are perpetrating; they feel nothing wrong in it, nothing to make them hesitate and think, like Hamlet or Macbeth.

Action may grow more unfettered, but a sense of incalculable consequences deepens, because in the tragic world everything is so precariously balanced that a small disturbance may bring it down in ruins, like a pebble starting an avalanche. Macbeth has an uneasy premonition that Duncan's 'surcease' cannot be 'the be-all and the end-all' he would like it to be

(I.vii.2 ff.). Before his deed he wavers, once committed he regrets it. As Bransom says, for Shakespeare action is set in motion by character, but once started it may escape from control (202). Yet any cloistered shrinking from life's storms is alien to the tragic spirit, which is akin to the wildest currents of human existence, often vagrant but always moving on afresh. The hero must act, as Hamlet so painfully feels, or life would stand still. He must gamble, not knowing what the outcome will be.

But Hamlet at least can only act in a sort of paroxysm, when his reflective mind is blindfolded; this begins with the killing of Polonius, which, although unintended, has dire results. Macbeth finds the speed of events around him growing vertiginously. He sets himself to win his race with time by translating thought into action the moment it is born (IV.i.142 ff.), but this only plunges him into a frenzy of violence, each crime worsening his plight. Antony, like Hamlet, goes through abrupt turns from inactivity to galvanic action, while Octavius, like Julius before him, is 'constant as the northern star' to his purpose. In an era when society is 'out of joint', without cohesion or rationality, no tragic hero could be so inflexibly consistent. All of them are doomed, because, in the end, history is against them. England when these plays were being written was such a disjointed society, drifting towards disruption.

Hence the paradox that tragedy must have great men and women, who can only be great through action of some striking kind, but whose deeds are too often self-defeating. Shakespeare was not belittling qualities that could bring them to the forefront, whether derived from older times or from those now dawning: nobility, honour, courage, on one hand; prudence, foresight, organizing capacity, on the other. Both kinds would be needed for the building of a better era. But the heroes themselves are drawn from the older order, approaching eclipse: they must be *noble*, and in an age of much ignoble strife this virtue might prove as often a weakness as a source of strength. So it proves above all for Brutus, with his aristocratic frankness and freedom from suspicion. Hamlet, Othello, Timon, and in a more truculent fashion Coriolanus, all win esteem by their openness of disposition. Othello is too credulous, and then far too ready to distrust. Hamlet has to learn to be suspicious, but he is then unable to trust Ophelia, as well as his mother.

His faith in a single person, the taciturn Horatio, remains unshaken, and saves him from the black cloud that overwhelms Timon; this is indeed Horatio's role in the play. But what Hamlet learns of his own family is the starting-point of a comprehensive disenchantment with his whole surroundings, which in their different ways all the heroes have to undergo. This is 'the collapse of the subjective world' of which McElroy speaks (238); we can equate it with that of the old order in which the hero has grown up.

Macbeth, even while dreaming of the joys of sovereignty, has looked forward to an honoured old age. Already old, Lear promises himself carefree years cherished by loving care and respect. All the heroes pass through some such traumatic awakening as theirs, from blissful illusion into harsh reality. They have all inherited or achieved grand positions, with (except for Lear) splendid possibilities stretching ahead; all these come to nothing, through malign external influences working on their failure to decipher themselves and their environment. They are condemned to a painful discovery of how things really are, by contrast with how they appeared to be. It is, as Hubler says (xxiii), 'a change from ignorance to knowledge', profounder in Shakespeare than in the Greeks. But this knowledge, this learning and unlearning, comes too late to save them from disaster. To Caesar it comes latest of all, at the moment when he is stabbed by men whom an hour ago he has invited to take wine with him and accompany him, 'like friends', to the Capitol (II.ii.126–9). Another hour, and the Rome worshipped by Brutus has shrunk, like Caesar's triumphs, to a very little measure.

Brutus, Timon and the rest are all in their own ways romantics who have wanted to believe the life around them very different from what it actually is, instead of seeing the necessity of first transforming it into what they want it to be. So far from setting out to challenge society, each has accepted it only too willingly, but has dressed it up in false or over-beguiling colours. It proves to be not what he thought. Timon's friends are not a bevy of affectionate brothers and sharers. Coriolanus's ideal commonwealth, a warrior aristocracy holding undisputed sway over a docile mass of drudges, grateful for any crumbs thrown to them, is a similar fantasy. All these Aladdin-palaces are edifices that may disappear overnight.

Lear has been deceived not only by his daughters but also by the lifelong flattery that has made him think himself a god (IV.vi.96 ff.). In such states of mind there is much of the naïve egotism of children, and he is in his second childhood. His illusions are blown away by the storm, which shows him the Britain he has inhabited, and himself with it, as a mirage. Othello thinks himself betrayed by Desdemona, and is disillusioned at the same time with the glittering Venice he has fought for – with more reason, since Venice really is a breeder of scorpions like Iago. But the hero's mis-conceptions of his community, beginning with individuals known to him, are not his alone; they are, or mingle with, those of society itself, which always spins round it and its members a web of 'false consciousness', a softened, bland self-image. To sustain this requires an ever-thickening tangle of deceptions and self-deceptions.

Meanwhile evils multiply, to which society, presided over by those who benefit from its injustice, shuts its eyes. To expose them on the stage in a naturalistic manner was only possible fragmentarily; it was a task requiring the novel, then still in its infancy. In poetic drama it could be accomplished in a surrealistic way, through sudden recognition of social ills by a hero who is shedding his own private illusions. Two parallel processes are turned into one: an individual's discovery of what has gone wrong for him, and a community's recognition of things amiss in its collective fabric. It is in this equation between personal and social consciousness that the hero's 'representative' role shows most clearly; most clearly of all in the revelations that descend on Hamlet, Lear and Timon. Shakespeare's great characters do not 'develop', as orderly wholes; rather, changing situations bring up, like earthquakes, unexplored continents from the floors of their minds. It is in like fashion that collective consciousness sometimes advances.

When the hero is made to feel that his fellow-creatures are turning into enemies, his first – and sometimes last – impulse is to accuse them of ingratitude, 'more strong than traitors' arms' (*JC* III.ii.186). Charges of ingratitude pervade the tragedies. More often than not they are launched by someone who is blaming others when he ought to be blaming himself. Lear ought to have known his daughters better; but as one of them says, even in his younger days he had little gift of sober thinking (I.i.290–93). Timon ought not to have mistaken superficial acquaintances for dear friends. Coriolanus ought not to have been so wildly resentful of the other patricians' unwillingness to follow him into civil war. All these men have been living in a fool's paradise, from which they are being banished. In several of them disillusion breeds misanthropy, disgust with mankind at large. Brutus is not one of these, because he has not lost his faithful friends. He ought to have known the Roman people better, but he does not reproach it for his failure.

Part of the hero's penalty may be the painful memory, brought back to mind by events, of sins of omission like Lear's neglect of the poor, or sins of commission like the 'good sport' that gave Gloucester a bastard son (*KL* I.i.21–2). The early heroes are forced into crime by the demands of their mission. Necessities of war compel Brutus to share in money raised by Cassius through extortion and sale of offices; he is thus besmirched by the vices of the republic he is defending. The nadir is reached by Macbeth, the only one who sins knowingly and intentionally. Great energies misapplied make a woeful spectacle; but the moral test of such a man is how far he realizes, before fate overtakes him finally, the extent of his guilt. Macbeth is tragic because he comes to share our own sombre vision of him. If he does not feel remorse, he does feel bitterly the hatred his acts have brought on him. Coriolanus leaves his worst crime unperformed, but only under emotional family pressure; he is incapable of self-reproach.

It is the common fate of the heroes to find themselves adrift, isolated from their fellows, alone with their destiny – as any human being may feel at some moments in life. This alienation is the more painful because of the frank openness of the hero's nature, untouched by distrust or concealment.

Hamlet in particular has been trusting, communicative, good-hearted, liking and being liked. If this is true in essence of all unwarped human nature, tragedy may well be believed to have a close concern with the blight that has fallen on mankind since social division turned friendly trust into hate or suspicion. An image one may guess to have haunted Shakespeare is that of the poor man in the stocks, to whom the fallen Richard II compared himself (V.v). Lear's servant the disguised earl of Kent is put in the stocks and left to himself, while round him the kingdom cracks and totters. A hero may be numbed by painful shocks, like Hamlet. Lear is soon too deeply absorbed in his own new thoughts to be conscious of what is happening. There may be a touch of the somnambulist in each hero, transformed into a stranger, an outsider, though it is only Lady Macbeth who succumbs literally.

'I am that I am', says Shakespeare defiantly in Sonnet 121, and his heroes find a similar bedrock within themselves to fall back on. But it is at least as habitual a part of his thinking – doubtless also by itself one-sided – that what we are is very much a matter of what others think us to be: we are in great measure social creations. One can see oneself only in the mirror of opinion, Brutus and Cassius agree (I.ii.51 ff.). For the hero to be cut off, thrown on his own resources, after being accustomed to praise and admiration, is part of his tragic purgatory. By entering a solitude, which must always be part of the human condition, he is enabled to represent Everyman more faithfully. Exile is a frequent outward sign of isolation, as Hunter says (*Studies* 267). Duncan's sons have to flee from Scotland, Cordelia has to find a new home in France, Coriolanus is banished from Rome, Othello has been a lifelong exile. It is of interest that a house where Shakespeare lodged was that of a Huguenot refugee; his London, and south-east England, swarmed with foreign refugees or immigrants.

Hamlet, the one who feels his aloneness most poignantly and longest, retreats more deeply into it because he cannot talk about what has befallen him to anyone except Horatio, and very little, in our presence, even to him. He talks to himself instead, as he struggles to digest his new thoughts and bring some order into the inner chaos he has been thrown into; a struggle so exhausting that it leaves little energy to spare for tasks outside himself. Macbeth has no one to take counsel with after his partner fails him, as he has failed her in his panic at Banquo's ghost. Most of the later heroes die alone, morally if not physically, the ultimate penalty they are called on to suffer. All of them have a keen sense of the value of human ties. Coriolanus strives in vain to expunge mother, wife and son from his memory. Because Shakespeare lends so much significance to all such ties, their rupture is the more searing. It is a warning memorial of how the warmest attachments can be broken, how fragile is their hold. They are at the same time parables of social disruption.

Friendship was always among Shakespeare's treasured themes, and in the tragedies it has a more prominent part to play than love. It is only conceivable between good men, or between good women, like Volumnia and Valeria. Portia, Ophelia, Lady Macbeth, Cordelia, lack such intimates, if only because there are few women on the scene. Male friendship is seen only between heroes and others; Rosencrantz and Guildenstern hunt as a couple, but show no mutual regard. Kent and Gloucester are amicable acquaintances rather than friends. It is in the first two tragedies that friendship is firmest. Horatio is ready to die with Hamlet, and only lives on to do him better service. But Hamlet and two other friends become deadly enemies, and from then on ruptures are habitual. Othello has to dismiss his only close friend, Cassio, from his post, which must have made him more ready to think Cassio unreliable in other ways too. Macbeth and Banquo were friends before one murdered the other. Enobarbus dies of shame after deserting Antony. Coriolanus and Menenius, that ill-assorted pair, meet for the last time coldly. Coriolanus and Aufidius become bosom friends suddenly, and before long quarrel fatally. All these fatalities are fuel for the tragic funeral pyre.

The final alienation, short of death, is madness. Nervous instability may seem allied to greatness. Brutus suffers at times from hallucinations, as does Hamlet at one point: he has just killed Polonius, which must be a greater shock to him than he allows himself to realize. (If the Ghost were real on this occasion, as earlier, he would surely take note with some regret of his old counsellor's corpse, or commend his son for having at least made an attempt.) His mother thinks him mad. Macbeth has a similar delusion just after his murder of Banquo, and while carrying on his reign of terror he suffers from 'terrible dreams'. Caesar has an epileptic fit while being offered the crown, Othello while listening to Iago's tale (IV.i). Ophelia and Lear, a young woman and an old man both wrecked by the shock of abandonment, go out of their minds. Hamlet and Edgar simulate madness.

Timon's conduct would have entitled any family to have him shut up. The buffoonery of his last 'banquet' is, as Nuttall says, more comic than tragic, and in the wilderness a 'half-infantile, Caliban-like second self' peeps out (82–3, 101). We may choose to think him infected with venereal disease (Soellner 105). Sex and disease obsess his mind from the moment of his ruin, and this would be a plausible explanation of his crazy wastefulness. It would not be very surprising if Shakespeare were sometimes beset with gloomy misgivings about his own condition.

Macbeth expresses for us the bitterness of all who find their successes turning to dust because they have thrown away for them what made life worth living. He dies knowing that he has earned more infamy than power, and ruined a loved wife by giving way to her. Othello is not alone in seeing, too late, that he has thrown away his most cherished possession. Hamlet has the same feeling at the sight of Ophelia's grave. Lear drives his dearest daughter away from him. It is always, after Brutus, the hero's sharpest pang that he has been unwittingly his own arch-enemy, thanks to the cross-grained times that divide individuals into jarring double selves, as well as societies into classes.

For the tragic hero, and often for those close to him as well, death is in a very special way what Caesar calls it, 'a necessary end' (II.ii.36). He is compelled by his nature and the demands on him to live his life intensely, dangerously; to live it to the full he must be prepared to risk the loss of it. Mackail was only half right in saying that Romeo's death is not fully tragic, and 'moves pity, but not fear', because it is brought about too much by accidents, instead of being inevitable (45–6). Romeo has pawned his life by a secret marriage with a Capulet, and by his duel with Tybalt, and further perils must certainly await him. All life is incalculable, for those who venture to embark on it. Death is the forfeit to be paid for aiming at anything too high. There may be a happy ending for humanity, but not for the hero, the destined victim. But *fear* of death, rare at all times in Shakespeare, scarcely enters the tragic world. Rome, with its strenuous attitude to life, and acceptance of death as part of it, gives the tone.

Roman example, and Latin literature familiar to all educated men, could be looked to as liberators from vain fears of things beyond death too. In the tragedies, as in the English Histories, death is annihilation. Only in *Hamlet*, to make room for the Ghost an after-life has to be admitted, by the hero without much conviction. In the end, as Bolt writes (72, 75), 'felicity' means to him peace, Nirvana, and Horatio's 'flights of angels' are no more than a literary flight of fancy. Shakespeare himself must have been feeling at times, as he entered the later years of an over-active life, that he had out-lived his best days. An array of passages seem to show him beginning, like Macbeth, 'to be aweary of the sun' (V.v.49), and envying Duncan who now 'sleeps well'. 'You do me wrong to take me out of the grave' are Lear's first words when brought back to consciousness (IV.vii.45). For Cleopatra death becomes the place of refuge. We can hardly think of Hamlet wanting to go on living, if the poisoned rapier had missed him, even as king; or of Macbeth defeating his assailants at Dunsinane and continuing to reign over the country he has blighted. The hero and his world have been thrust so far apart that no accommodation between them is conceivable. Only in death can he find a sort of reconciliation.

Readiness to die may take, under the sanction of Roman honour, the extreme form of suicide. It is not something to be turned to lightly. Life is in spite of everything the supreme value. A man must endure all pains and perils as long as he can hold out; self-inflicted death is the last recourse, when the only remaining alternative is ignominy. It is then not mere denial, refusal to live, but a vindication of life's worth. 'Cassius from bondage will deliver Cassius' (I.iii.90). Brutus would rather choose, if free to do so, 'patience' in defeat, submission to 'some high powers that govern us' (V.i.100 ff.). It is a philosophy heard not seldom in later tragedies, and debated by Hamlet, again in language partly religious. Brutus seems at once to contradict himself, when the prospect of being a captive at Rome, hooted by the mob – the republic, in his person, disgraced as well as defeated –, comes into his mind. Suicide is then his unhesitating decision.

Othello too kills himself to avoid public shame, but also as an act of repentance and of leave-taking from Desdemona. When the blinded Gloucester wants to put an end to his life, Edgar takes elaborate pains, in the grotesque scene on the cliff, to reclaim him, and leave him time to prepare himself for death instead of rushing on to it. 'Ripeness is all' (V.ii.12). Timon has no one to restrain him, and his farewell to himself has no tinge of resignation. Lady Macbeth is reported to have taken her own life (V.viii.69–71), like Portia before her. Cleopatra and her attendants are women who choose death more deliberately, and more ceremonially, than any of the men. Here too women are claiming equality.

Experiences like those of the tragic heroes and heroines, if on a pettier scale, have come the way of countless men and women, most frequently in societies like Shakespeare's, unstable, competitive, full of clashing purposes. Minor art of many kinds has found its soil in particular social groups; the highest art must have roots in an entire community, whose components are being forced into unwonted interaction by a period of critical change. To be worthy of such an art, heroes must be truly great, endowed with brilliant human gifts and abilities. Yet something turns these endowments against them, like the malign influence that turned the swords of republicans against them at Philippi. It is no unapt warning to the erratically brilliant human race of what its fate may be if its self-violating genius cannot be tamed.

In each case a man of splendid name and fame is compelled by his own nature and that of his environment to lose everything. Whether or not their deaths are to be self-inflicted, they seem to be steering straight towards the reef on which they will be wrecked. Much of the blame for the isolation that befalls them must rest on themselves. Lear, Timon, Antony, complain of being deserted by men and women whom they ought never to have trusted, and whose fidelity they have tried to win by wrong means. Devotion to duty in the early tragedies gives way to self-serving ambition, but in either case the hero is impelled to undertake things beyond his strength, or the limits of what history will allow. Superb energy and vitality come to nothing, either because their world demands too much of them, as it did from Brutus and Hamlet, or because they demand too much from their world, as Macbeth does when he steals the crown, or Othello when he steals a daughter of the Venetian aristocracy. All these men must disappear and make way for another order of things, a future perhaps better, at all events new.

In this microcosm of mankind's destinies, glowing in the magic light of poetry, we catch sight of vaster meanings. Whatever future is in store for man, hitherto his record has been of astounding talents and creations, coupled with abysmal follies and crimes. In good and bad alike each human being has had a part, direct or vicarious. The hero who 'represents' us becomes in the end our expiatory sacrifice, whom we must feel with as well as condemn. Even Coriolanus, whose death is most visibly a punishment visited on the sins of his class, has been applauded by all Romans, high or low, for his brutal violence against neighbouring peoples. All this carries with it associations with the scapegoat sacrificed to rid the body politic of a taint. Hamlet has to die because Denmark is 'rotten', and with him the whole royal family under whose auspices things have become what they are. In an age so fiercely theological as Shakespeare's, neither he nor his audience could be forgetful of the doctrine of atonement; little as he was moved by religious dogmas, this one was too deeply rooted in social consciousness to have no meaning for him as a writer of tragedies.

Christ was sacrificed 'To appease an angry god', as Malcolm feared he might be by a treacherous Macduff wanting to appease Macbeth (IV.ii.17). Obscure associations make us somehow think of the hero as the sacrifice offered by a human race thirsting for change, for a new life, a new name. As such he belongs in part to the realm of myth, however distinct his individual features. In him are concentrated the energies and the conflicting impulses that are to shift the world into a new orbit. He breathes life into visions still only latent in the crowd. His extraordinariness may take either a good or an evil direction. His ambitions are very diverse, but all in some sense dangerous – as Caesar boasts of being – to the settled order of things. Macbeth wrecks the social brotherhood that he hopes to dominate; Timon tries to restore it, but in a fanciful, unmeaning way, sure to do more harm than good. But while to others the hero may appear an incarnation of anarchic will, to himself he seems more and more inextricably in the grip of fate, of a destiny which is his image of overpowering historical forces. His struggles and his ruin owe their aspect of inevitability to their being governed by a collective necessity that overrides all private freedom of the will.

2

Villains and Revengers

Heights and depths in the tragic realm cannot be neatly compressed into an antithesis of Hero and Villain. There are no accredited 'villains' in the Roman plays, though there is no shortage of bad men. How bad we consider any characters depends very much on the greater or less emphasis put on their worse deeds by the author. Nothing in all the tragedies or English Histories can equal in atrocity the proscripion, or mass murder, so coolly agreed on by the triumvirs in *Julius Caesar*. Shakespeare might have left it out, but did not; on the other hand he offers no comment, and Brutus and his friends, learning of the outcome, are not provoked into outbursts of indignation. Shakespeare may already have had in mind a sequel, and hence did not want to compromise its star characters too damagingly in advance.

It was not his way to view life as a clear-cut contest between good and evil. Claudius has no malice against Hamlet until his nephew's hatred of him comes out into the open. It is only in *Hamlet* and *Macbeth* that the drama is set in motion by a villain, or rather by a villainous act, and in both cases its perpetrator is sufficiently self-critical, or old-fashioned, to be conscious of his guilt. Hamlet's play does, as he hopes, 'catch the conscience of the king' (II.ii.617), though it does not make a good man of him. In general we are made to think of good and evil forces or impulses as confusedly mingled, and of conflict often raging within the hero more than between him and his opponents. Heroes have some bad propensities, worsening in all those after Brutus, even though Macbeth alone (Claudius might be added) grows into an inveterate malefactor. He and his wife are horror-struck by their crime even while they are committing it; nothing could impress us more than this with its enormity, and the impossibility of their ever putting it behind them.

A potential for wrong-doing is most patent in Hamlet, because in him the contrasting good qualities shine most captivatingly. His acute consciousness of the duality of human nature (II.ii.286 ff.) – a painful discovery of Lear's too (IV.vi.124 ff.) – must relate to himself as well as to the rest of mankind. It relates also to Shakespeare's conception of tragedy as the touchstone that shows men and women able to soar high, or sink into abysses. Hamlet descends to a cruel rejection of Ophelia, and unfeeling mockery of her father as an old man – unless this is palliated by a belief of Polonius being his uncle's creature. His self-denunciation (III.i.119 ff.) must be forced on him by hidden promptings, things of darkness besetting his shaken mind, more than by actual misdeeds.

In the Histories political ambition was as ubiquitous as the force of gravity. In the tragedies it remains the strongest motive for action that most men, and some women, can feel. Shakespeare's interest in it is now of a different kind, however, less in the prize sought and the pursuit of it, more in its consequences for the power-seeker and those within his reach. Claudius and Macbeth cannot revel in wrong-doing as Richard III did. Iago can, but he breathes and schemes on a lower than political level. Claudius has committed a horrible deed, but apart from it he seems a commonplace fellow enough. He·and Macbeth are both drawn on from one unforeseen misdeed to another; it is part of the nature of evil in these dramas to be self-perpetuating, and to rob the guilty of their freedom like an enslaving drug. Most engrossing to Shakespeare are the circumstances, the seductions, that warp the natures of men and women. Like Montaigne he can contemplate Julius Caesar as a great man corroded by megalomania.

Thirst for revenge is another powerful force, and one whose many variant forms, higher and lower, can often serve as tests of character and feeling. From a more professional point of view, revenge was a motive that could be relied on to set going dramas full of action and excitement; while it could at the same time appeal to an audience's wider social consciousness. Before *Hamlet* the most celebrated revenge play was Kyd's *Spanish Tragedy* (*c.* 1585). This must have owed much of its impressiveness, for many spectators, to its recurrent lament that justice has fled from an earth polluted with sin and oppression of the weak by the strong. Tragedy in this mood could be a vehicle for social comment and protest, parallel to the satirical style but far more weightily emotional. Shakespeare took it up and made the most of it. Demands for satisfaction for injury haunt his tragedies, like the Ghost haunting Elsinore or 'Caesar's spirit ranging for revenge'; though only in *Hamlet* does it dominate an entire play.

Revenge had been a prominent motive in Shakespeare's two early tragedies, *Titus Andronicus* and *Romeo and Juliet*; and an early villain of his, Don John in *Much Ado* – a bastard like Edmund – sought revenge for reasons not unlike Iago's, and by the same method of dishonouring a woman. In the mature tragedies this motive gathers strength. Life is full of blatant wrongs, and of things regarded by individuals as wrongs done to them, from which public law affords no protection, and for which it gives no redress; they can be punished only by private retaliation. Victims may be driven by their sense of injustice into alienation from mankind and indiscriminate pursuit of revenge, like Macbeth's murderers, reckless what they do to spite the world (III.i.107 ff.). Edmund is a more calculatingly ruthless man of this type. It swells into huge proportions in Lear and Timon with their fantasies of genocide.

A revenge-seeker may be a hero, like Hamlet, whose aim is punishment of injury to another, not – or not mainly – to himself. He may be a villain, like Iago, or anything between. We are in a borderland, once more confronted with irreconcilable dictates of an older era and of a newer one still crudely immature. For Shakespeare the impulse to retaliate is interwoven with the affairs of communal life; and the general criterion we are given, or encouraged to give ourselves, is whether or not it can be felt as also fulfilling a duty neglected by public authority. Private revenge, Mangan reminds us, far from being approved by public opinion, was 'vociferously and unanimously condemned' (69) – by the learned, that is: doubtless by the man in the street, or theatre, much less. Sisson quotes Bacon's severe verdict on it as 'wild justice', and recalls that it was basic to Tudor centralizing policies to suppress private reprisals, and substitute public justice (44 ff.). This was plainly what the march of progress required. But the same is true of the ban on duelling, a practice of which James I was a determined opponent, if more consistently in principle than in practice. Revenge was often its motive. In spite of the weight of moral and legal disapproval, often shared by duellists themselves, the compulsion on a gentleman to fight when challenged or insulted, under pain of being branded a coward, lasted for centuries. In his soliloquy at the end of Act II Hamlet thinks of himself as a man grossly insulted – called a liar, having his nose pulled – and tamely submitting to the disgrace.

Discrepancies between official and personal or class ethics have been many; and the duel could be defended as at least an advance in refinement on the brawls and blood-feuds of older days. Throughout the tragedies feelings at work are at various stages of evolution, in this field from wrath ready to erupt to justice seeking vindication. Brutus and his friends can have no public warrant for killing Caesar, but they expect, and immediately after the deed ask for and receive, public endorsement. At Philippi Octavius vows not to sheath his sword until Caesar's death 'be well avenged' (V.i.54–5); but he and Antony profess to regard the republican cause as a rebellion, and its leaders as 'traitors', to be subjected to the penalties of law. Laertes, with the same grievance as Hamlet, first appeals to public opinion; it is only when he is assured by Claudius that Hamlet cannot be prosecuted for Polonius's death, because too high in popular favour, that the young man is induced to stoop to disguised assassination. He is succumbing to the creed of the old order from which he has sprung, and his action proves as disastrous as Hamlet's inaction.

Othello tries to exalt his anger against Desdemona to the level of a public 'cause' or issue, with himself judge as well as executioner. Her alleged seducer must die too, but Othello feels no wish to be the killer. Iago by contrast wants no more than to pay him and Cassio out for the wrongs he believes they have done him. Lear indulges in daydreams of fearful revenges; his resentment turns against the whole human species, until thoughts of the lifelong injustice and misery endured by others break in at intervals on his mind, and calm his self-pity. When Cordelia comes to his aid she speaks only of restoring him to his throne, but victory for her foreign army would have unloosed the spirit of revenge among Lear's adherents. Edgar would have ample justification if he hankered for reprisals against his half-brother; but when he comes forward against him it is as prosecutor of a criminal. He has found and given to Albany a letter from Goneril to Edmund inviting him to kill her husband and take his place; and it is as Albany's champion in a trial by battle that Edgar enters the lists (IV.vi.259 ff.: V.i.40 ff.). Malcolm urges Macduff to drown grief in anger against the tyrant who has butchered his family, and Macduff goes into the fray thinking of them; but he has already taken the patriotic road to rebellion and Scotland's liberation. For himself Malcolm, like Cordelia, seems too saintly to have any thoughts of revenge, either for his murdered father or for his own exile; to rescue his country is his sole aim.

Timon seeks no retribution against individuals. He resents his friends' collective desertion of him, and the ungrateful Senate's attitude; and as with Lear, this mounts into a frenzy against all mankind; this, however, is not allayed by any pity for innocent sufferers, and all that is left for him is to put an end to his life. Lear saw that many men and women behave badly; Timon is convinced that *all* men and women *are* bad, and ineradicably so. It falls to Alcibiades, as – like Edgar and Malcolm – a sort of deputy-hero, to take action. At first he is only out for vengeance on behalf of a friend unjustly, in his eyes, condemned by the government, though his protest is also against ungenerous treatment of the whole army. He is soon taking a much broader view, and threatening chastisement of the governing body for all its wrong-doing.

Antony and Cleopatra is the sole play virtually free of revengeful passion, except Pompey's as son of another murdered hero. Antony and Octavius are simply fellow-adventurers who have fallen out. They could no more hate each other as both hated the republicans, than they could love each other as Brutus and Cassius did. Octavius has an ill-used sister to warrant action against his brother-in-law, besides his own self-aggrandizement; but he founds his publicity campaign on Antony's behaviour in Egypt, as prejudicial to the Roman name and damaging to Roman sovereignty in the East. Coriolanus plans for Rome the same wholesale slaughter that Timon would have liked to see inflicted on Athens – 'wild justice' indeed. At least it can be said for him that he intends no worse punishment for the obnoxious tribunes in particular: they are beneath his contempt, and it is his own recreant class that his fury burns hottest against.

To seek private revenge, for personal satisfaction alone, is to join the ranks of the villains. Shylock was partly saved from this by his purpose of asserting not only his own but his community's right to equal treatment. But he, like Laertes, descended to an attempt at revenge by what was to all intents murder, when he might well have been satisfied with his public humiliation of the bankrupt Antonio, and done far more thereby for his community's credit and standing. In the tragedies the two professed villains – both young, and ravenous for a place in the world – feel that unfair treatment has been their lot. Iago's grievance, if valid, of military service ill rewarded, was shared by a great many others; so was Edmund's, unquestionably valid, as a despised bastard son and younger brother, doubly disinherited. Both complaints were widely acknowledged by public opinion. But neither man cares a straw about any fellow-victims; they are obsessed by their own wrongs, and bent on righting them by unscrupulous self-help.

When *Hamlet* was written, *Othello* was on the horizon. Iago might be called a coarse-grained, cankered imitation of what is morbid in Hamlet. These two both love to soliloquize and theorize; both are estranged from their fellows, disillusioned with women, the one by learning things about human nature that the other has always known, or believed. They are even close in age, Hamlet thirty, Iago (I.iii.306–7) twenty-eight. Iago is repulsively impressive as a study of how a gifted individual may be alienated from society as he knows it, and dehumanized. But he never towers over the scene as Shylock some-times does, because his discontent is simply egotistic, and indiscriminate: he thinks himself entitled to work it off against anyone better favoured by fortune than himself. Hence with all his cleverness Iago remains no more than a second-rate criminal, whose dupes, Roderigo and Othello, are pathetically easy to fool. He never rises above the mentality of the assassin, and it is in his nature to put the blame for the wounding of Cassio on the wretched Bianca. He speaks much, but only for himself; he speaks openly only *to* himself.

He is a small Machiavelli, a cynic philosopher, full of carking envy and grudges; so much wedded to his unhallowed principles as to risk his all to maintain them, and end by losing all. He is a true if diseased intellectual, one of very few in the hostile climate of the tragedies. Othello admires in him 'a learned spirit of human dealings', or insight into conduct (III.iii.261–2), a tribute curiously similar to Caesar's praise of Cassius (I.ii.199 ff.). On his weaker side he suffers from a sense of others being his superiors, especially in attractiveness for women. Sisson is right in thinking him genuinely hag-ridden by the marital jealousies he talks of, and dragged along by schemes of revenge that he loses control of (43). They destroy him as well as Othello; passion and delusion have got the better of his boasted intellect, too perverted to be a safe guide.

Some of Shakespeare's creations seem to have been born wicked, others have wickedness thrust upon them. On Edmund it is thrust by his base birth, and an irresponsible father. He has been brought up as a gentleman, but with no means to support his claims. His breeding has given him at least a more buoyant, less morose temperament than Iago, an attractive vitality that helps to make his fortune. He feels little personal animosity against his father and brother; they are merely obstacles to be got out of his way. He is no less unbounded an egotist than Iago, and relies on trickery as mean. Only at the end, when he has won the place he deems his due, and can feel ennobled by success in love and war, does he rise to better things, and show what a different man he might have been. He risks his life in single combat in order to prove to himself and the world that he is worthy of the rank he is now invested with. Dying, he can 'exchange charity' with his brother, as Laertes does with Hamlet, and make a final attempt at reparation. Nobility cannot be entirely extinguished; Iago is irredeemable.

Among Shakespeare's tragedy villains these two best fit Kernan's description of the type as 'rationalists, skeptics, and new-style men of practical affairs' (*Playwright* 90). *Othello* and *Lear*, plays side by side in the series (*Timon* might be added), are the pair where two philosophies, old and new, confront each other most obtrusively. Edmund can feel a nostalgia for the values of the old order, or its feudal crust. These were masculine values, which could have only limited or second-hand meaning for women. Good women here, like Cordelia, are so by nature more than by instruction, it would seem; emancipated women can discard old rules completely. It is to this newer race that Goneril and Regan belong, one that has not yet had time to become aware of any duty except to self. In them we are shown the new individualism in its most misshapen form. Moral isolation makes them dangerous, and they turn by rapid degrees into monsters.

Goneril's steward Oswald is one of the more interesting among a set of assistant-villains, confined to the non-classical plays, who help to darken the scene. In him we see the old type of loyal servitor deteriorating in the blighting atmosphere of the new age. He has a modest place on the feudal ladder, and a rapacious desire to climb higher. He is mercenarily faithful to a wicked employer, and quite prepared to seize on an old blind man in order to win a reward for his capture. Roderigo is an independent agent, only half-guessing that he is being made Iago's pawn. Rosencrantz and Guildenstern are simply a couple of young men, good talkers, with their way to make in the world, who pay dearly for letting themselves slip into the service of a villainous monarch.

A right or duty of revenge is accepted by a good many characters without demur. In the first excitement of the Ghost's disclosure, Hamlet is unhesitatingly ready to 'sweep to his revenge' (I.v.29–31). Only in more sober moods does he come to realize what it is that he, in many ways so modern-minded a man, is committed to. It is not to punish, but to revenge, his father's murder that the Ghost has summoned him. He grows anxious, Sisson holds (73), for report to be able to say of him after his death that he was not pursuing mere private satisfaction. This is plausible; but we have the same difficulty as so often during this play: why does Hamlet never tell us so himself, in plain words? We can be sure as time goes on that killing his uncle is not an act he is eager on his own account to perform. He never debates, as thousands of duellists did, the ethics of resort to bloodshed by an individual. But there is no public authority for him to appeal to, and no evidence that he can lay before public opinion.

Possibly to Shakespeare's audience this dilemma would be patent enough. But Hamlet also does not confess aloud, what we must surely suppose to have been entering his mind, a gnawing doubt, not of the Ghost's veracity, but of whether even a loved and murdered father has the right to demand a revenge which can only be the killing of another man – and his killing, since he is now king, by some kind of secret stratagem; there can be no question of a fair fight. Is this why he hesitates to confide in Horatio, and so, he must fear, implicate his one close friend in the crime he has vowed to commit? Shakespeare may have trusted his actors to convey a good many things he did not put on paper, especially in a play like this, already over-long.

Locked into a painful clash of emotions, while days go by with nothing accomplished, Hamlet may well have a sensation of paralysis; and self-distrust makes it easy for him to find an explanation in misgivings about his courage. They take possession of him and torment him. He practises fencing (to guess once more) as a relief from them. We cannot really suspect him of cowardice. Failure of physical courage is a very rare weakness in Shakespeare, and never found in his heroes – or his villains, for that matter. Only his distraught condition makes Hamlet accuse himself of this sin of sins, as it must be for any man of birth. His mother is puzzled by his strange alternations of mood between febrile restlessness and apathy (V.i.251 ff.). They must correspond to two equally sombre conclusions that he can draw from what he sees of the world about him. One is that, if the law can put no curb on wickedness, individuals must devise their own remedy. The second is that in an age so far decayed, so deeply sunk in unrighteousness, no effort that a single arm can make will be worth making, even if it loads the stage with as many corpses as crowd it at the close of *The Spanish Tragedy*.

We are left with a general impression that for Shakespeare individual acts of retaliation are to be condemned. The offences that interest him are of a more or less public nature, and constitute crimes, which deserve to be punished. Private injuries are better forgiven, as Lear's treatment of her is forgiven by Cordelia; this, not any fulfilment of his thirst for revenge, is what brings him peace. Alcibiades abandons the thought of indiscriminate reprisals against the whole Senate of Athens, though the miscreants responsible for its abuses of power must be made to smart. Coriolanus outside Rome, ready to give the city up to sack and massacre, tells his mother not to think of reasoning him out of his 'rages and revenges' (V.iii.84–6). In her long appeal, compared with which Portia's speech on mercy is only a schoolroom exercise, she touches a sensitive chord with her question

> Think'st thou it honourable for a noble man
> Still to remember wrongs?
>
> (154–5)

From Volumnia these are astonishing words; an actor should show their effect on her son. To be a Roman nobleman has been his whole pride; to be a *noble man* may be something different, and better.

Writers of revenge-plays were kept busy for another fifteen years or so after *Hamlet*, turning them out sometimes, it may be guessed, to satisfy popular appetite more than their own taste. None of them showed a nicety of moral discrimination like Shakespeare's, but there was a certain tendency in a similar direction. *The Revenger's Tragedy* (c. 1607), and *The Atheist's Tragedy* (1611), are ascribed to Cyril Tourneur. In the first it may seem that 'revenge is a binding duty' still, but perhaps an atavistic one (Vaughan 179). The wicked atheist D'Amville, accidentally wounded, dies repentant, if very unconvincingly. An irresistible temptation was for authors – like today's – to pile on more and more sensational thrills in their search for novelty. These two works are 'almost parodies' of the revenge-play, with their 'unspeakable cruelties and calculated horrors' (Ruoff 425).

Chapman's *Revenge of Bussy d'Ambois* (c. 1610–11) has been called by his editor a studied contrast with *Hamlet*: Chapman with his Stoic philosophy could hardly feel much sympathy for a waverer like the Prince of Denmark (Parrott 573). Revenge has only a limited share of the play, which is really a study of French history, or fragments of it stuck together, and of political philosophy; it has much to say about the sacredness of kings, against whom only passive resistance is permissible. King James must have relished this. Early in the second decade of the century Webster brought up the rearguard of the great tragic drama; revenge is still stirring, but does little to give his two masterpieces their thrilling life. With audiences the taste wore out very slowly, and revenge-plays, some of them in the old blood-and-thunder vein, were still being put together by playwrights like Shirley on the eve of the Civil Wars, when England was preparing to bring its own rulers to book.

3

Man and Superman

Rousseau blamed Tragedy for fostering an unwarrantable faith in Great Men. Supermen had been invented by Machiavelli and the Renaissance, as embodiments of dynamic new forces then stirring. Napoleon liked to think of himself as one of them; appropriately, he loved tragic drama, and, like Frederick the Great, was fond of declaiming scenes from it. Its heroes, he held, ought to be presented by playwrights in full perfection, marble statues unwrinkled by any marks of weakness. He would have made a poor patron for Shakespeare, who must be exempted from Rousseau's stricture. There is no Tamburlaine in his works, though some of his heroes may cherish world-consuming fantasies; and it is important to count up what a writer does not give us, as well as what he gives. His heroes have among them many frailties, and all end in failure. They represent mankind with its good side and much of its worse side; with all its vulnerability also, which in a way strengthens mankind by making men more conscious of their mutual need, as Brutus and Cassius are at the end of their quarrel – a scene that Napoleon would have vetoed. Shakespeare goes out of his way to humanize these towering figures, by revealing the tensions underlying the stately eloquence.

Shakespeare's great men have had to climb 'young ambition's ladder' (*JC* II.i.22) by laborious effort. When we meet with them at the top the impression made on us is of any inordinate grandeur in individuals being unnatural. Caesar offers an ideal target as a superman inviting ridicule, as Glendower in *Henry IV Part 1* did with his supernatural pretensions. Caesar is bombastic and posturing, credulous and superstitious. An afterthought about him, 'turned to clay' and serving menial uses, comes from Hamlet (V.i.180–83). Yet some greatness survives both in the living Caesar and in memory. Shakespeare may be an iconoclast, but he is a level-headed one.

Caesar is never so impressive as after his death, in Antony's funeral speech; Antony towers highest after defeat and death by his own hand, in Cleopatra's apotheosis of him. All an old world's illusions of rank, power, glory, and the supermen who incarnate, historically, the domination of a class over the rest, have their sunset glow in *Antony and Cleopatra*. Coriolanus comes last, and is drawn from the start with grotesque exaggeration. His right arm turns the scales of battle, he forces his way into an enemy town single-handed. His mode of insulting and browbeating plebeians and common soldiers is surely meant to demean him more than them. In him the arrogance of a whole ruling class is visibly concentrated. Ordinary mortals are hypnotized. 'He is the rock', says a watching soldier when he is encamped outside Rome, 'the oak not to be wind-shaken' (V.ii.101–2). Yet he is, more praiseworthily, about to be shaken by a woman's breath.

On 26 July 1665, Pepys noted in his diary that, having sat listening in the royal barge with all loyal respect to Charles II conversing with his brother, he could not help feeling how little difference there was 'between them and other men'. Shakespeare had anticipated him by a good many years. In his tragedies there are no doubt some very meritorious rulers, but we see nothing of them, or very little. They are not realistic portraits, but are brought in to afford dramatic contrasts; Cordelia's husband, for instance, with her father, or Duncan with Macbeth, who acknowledges his high claim to respect (I.vii.16 ff.). Edward of England is, a dreamlike picture of a saint, still more sharply counterposed to the nightmarish visage of Macbeth, and with a 'heavenly gift of prophecy' (IV.iii.157) to contrast with the hellish gift of Macbeth's witches. But apart from these pre-eminent virtues, none of the kings, or other heads of State except Caesar, is a superman by nature; any aura of greatness they owe to their office.

In the tragedies, more broadly than in the Histories, Shakespeare was gathering together his thoughts on men's collective behaviour. In this complex monarchy had always been important, but by the time the Histories were finished it counted for less with him, by itself, than the State growing up behind the royal façade. It is noticeable at once that five of these eight tragedies, if we exclude the Egyptian scenes of *Antony and Cleopatra*, have republican settings. In two of the Roman plays, it is true, republicanism is fading, a new monarchical system looming up; and that in the third, and in Athens, the republic is working badly. Government altogether, not monarchy alone, has become questionable. Venice has a competent Doge, but Athens, and the Rome of *Coriolanus*, seem to have no heads of State at all. No kings, or their equivalents, meant no courts, and this could be construed as a gain. Now as earlier, Shakespeare shared with all his contemporaries, except successful courtiers, an assumption that any royal court was likely to be a sink of iniquity. The court of Elsinore may not be this, but it is unimpressive, and is virtually the only one we see. Of Lear's we have his own unflattering memories. Macbeth is too isolated, Cleopatra too frivolous, to preside over any regular court life.

Divine kingship in antiquity, and lingering on in remote Asia and Africa, may be supposed to have signified a conviction of the sanctity of the community, the familial bond uniting all its members. In late medieval and early modern Europe the doctrine of Divine Right, though partly designed as a shield against foreign meddling, also revealed a drifting apart of monarchy and people, the king claiming mystical authority against his subjects instead of as their representative. But society by now was growing too complex and sophisticated to agree on thinking of any human being as commissioned by heaven to rule it. This would be foreign meddling indeed.

In England as well as abroad, however, monarchy was increasingly in need of a religious costume, to ward off criticism or opposition. Its sanctity is invoked at times in the tragedies, most eloquently when a king suffers or is threatened with molestation. Macduff is shocked by the discovery of Duncan's death into exclaiming that 'sacrilegious murder' has broken into an 'anointed temple' (II.iii.67–8). Regicide when it came in England in 1649 sent a similar shock through the nation, irrespective of what people had thought of Charles I. Charged with treason, Gloucester cries out to his tormentors that he could not bear to think of Lear's 'anointed flesh' being violated (III.vii.57). Shakespeare is forgetting that his Britons are not Christians.

Claudius, and Gertrude too, are at their best when defying Laertes and his rioters; but the main effect of the outbreak is to show how physically weak authority is in Denmark – or in England. Claudius's Swiss guard is not to be seen, and he is reduced to calling on the 'divinity' that hedges him. He does so with dignity and seeming conviction; but no such high protection had shielded his brother, and we must take Shakespeare's intention as ironical. Likewise the conventional speeches in Act III Scene iii on the monarch as the hub round which all national life revolves are given to a pair of self-interested sycophants; they are quite undramatic, unless their purpose is to convince Claudius that he can safely entrust any villainy to them. Laertes has no share of their 'most holy and religious fear' of any harm befalling their sovereign. Nor does Hamlet, in spite of his often pious language, ever think of his father's death, or his own desire to kill Claudius, as sacrilege. It is a long way from Richard II's belief that all the seas could not wash off his magic ointment, to Macbeth's realization that all the seas cannot wash Duncan's blood off his hands or his conscience, and his sleep-walking wife's that the perfumes of Arabia will never cleanse her hands (II.ii.60–63; V.i.49–50).

Hamlet's father is not painted in ideal colours, as Duncan is. Horatio does not take him to be a saint, and at sight of the Ghost is ready to ascribe his restless visitings to heinous offences he may have committed; one is the hoarding of 'extorted treasure' (I.i.137). It is confessedly for 'foul crimes' that he is in purgatory (I.v.12). He seems to deny any conjugal misbehaviour, and his son can think of him by contrast with his murderer as an exemplary man and king. All the same we should not forget that during his reign Denmark's taint of 'rottenness' was growing, or at any rate was not set right. Claudius's 'oafishness', 'ignorance', 'crassness', may not be as patent to all readers as to Michael Long, for whom 'Elsinorean philistinism' seems the worst failing Denmark is afflicted with (130–31, 138). But Claudius, like Macbeth, is a murdering usurper. Lear may be for his loyal Kent 'the old kind King' (III.i.28), but he has been a careless shepherd of his people.

All the three ruling families shown to us are plagued by internal treasons or dissensions. Royalty is in decline, morally or, like England's Queen Elizabeth, in vitality. King Fortinbras of Norway is 'impotent and bed-rid', deaf to what is happening (I.ii.29). Lear is turned eighty, Duncan is old; Macbeth lives to feel that he is sinking into the same 'sere and yellow leaf' (V.iii.24). 'The brontosauruses are doomed', Maynard Mack comments irreverently (80). A further weakness is their shortage of offspring to carry on a succession. Greedy for a crown, Caesar is also absurdly anxious in his old age for a son to leave it to. Claudius marries a woman too old to give him an heir. Macbeth is obsessed with the idea of handing on the sceptre to his descendants; but he has none, the sceptre soon comes to appear useless, the hope fades from his mind. Antony has no such thoughts, only an occasional regret. Octavius may have many, but he never voices them. Lear has no son, no grandchildren, and two of his daughters would be a disgrace to any throne. They and their consorts assume royal power, but not titles of royalty.

There is no monarchy based on strict heredity (the rules in Egypt, if there are any, we know nothing of). In old Denmark and Scotland the crown was, as Shakespeare treats it, semi-elective, though usually within one family. Hamlet seems at times resentful of the throne having eluded him, and we may suppose him to be thinking that with it he would be better able to bring his uncle to book and set about reforms. But this is one of the many doors that we are led past without being allowed to open. In Shakespeare's ancient Britain the country is the king's patrimony, and he disposes of it as he chooses, even by cutting it up. Here is another source of insecurity. Duncan's time on the throne, disturbed by 'malice domestic, foreign levy', was a 'fitful fever' compared with the tranquillity of the grave (III.ii.22 ff.). Some such notion of the heavy weight of a crown was no doubt an accepted commonplace. In *The Spanish Tragedy* (c. 1585) the viceroy feelingly laments its drawbacks, perpetual anxiety and hollow flattery and so on (III.i). But Shakespeare raises them all to a far higher pitch. Monarchy has left its healthier days behind, and is going downhill. All the crowned heads, and the dictator so eager to join them, come to a bad end.

This spectacle could be contemplated by Shakespeare, and his more understanding auditors, as a representation of processes of decay, and, less definably, of rebirth. 'Authority melts from me', Antony in defeat exclaims (III.xiii.90). All Lear's story is of authority melting from him, and leaving him to discover that it was no blessing either to him or to those subjected to it. Morally it had long been wilting. The play begins with him renouncing power, and ends with his son-in-law Albany declining to accept it. Egypt has sunk into a condition where no native successor could keep it going: Cleopatra has no lack of offspring, but they are ciphers. Only a Roman governor can be the next ruler. Nothing is left of the monarchy except the memory of Cleopatra's descent from 'so many royal kings' (V.ii.325–6), which nerves her to her finest deed, suicide. Her ancient crown becomes in its last hour a symbol of human greatness. Antony is not weary of power, but he is tired of having to keep fighting for it and toiling to keep it; in far-off Egypt he feels comfortably free of any challenge, like a London merchant retiring to a country estate. Here the theme of Old order and New is very directly presented in the contrast between a decrepit oriental kingdom and a dynamic European absolutism.

About the new wielders of power Shakespeare had many doubts. They centre on Julius Caesar, whose shadow falls across sundry of the plays. There is a wavering between respect for superb achievements and an impatient suspicion that his grandeur has turned into a deception. We see only through unfriendly eyes his ambition of promoting himself to a throne. It is by adroit flattery, that bane of crowned heads which Caesar professes to despise (II.i.202 ff.), that he is lured to the Capitol on the Ides of March. There can be better hopes of the young Octavius. Overcoming all rivals, restoring the unity of the empire, he has the air of a sixteenth-century European king quelling feudal broils and establishing law and order. He has the warrant of history, as inaugurator of a new polity; and the more persuasive recommendation of the great Augustan poets.

Only Lear comes to have a glimmering of something further required from those in power, a sense of duty to protect and care for the poor, in Shakespeare's day the great majority of the population everywhere. Ordinary 'good', that is, strong, government has no remedy for their wants. A hapless plaything of the storm, he cries out to the 'Poor naked wretches' of his land, who cannot hear him any more than formerly he could hear them. This is the first time that any of Shakespeare's rulers has addressed his people, except in the way of self-interest and demagogy; and the speaker now is close to madness. Margot Heinemann points out that we have no record of *King Lear* being revived after its first production ('Political Drama' 193–4). It may not be too rash to guess that its reception in conservative quarters was unfavourable; and that Shakespeare's next play, Scottish and well stocked with roundabout compliments to James, and sketches of ideal rulers, was a peace-offering. But clearly he had been finding monarchy much flawed, and kingship itself dehumanizing (Traversi 16). He could not of course propose that it should be replaced with republicanism, and this was proving an equal failure in his Rome and Athens, as before long it was to prove in England.

Tragedy may exalt the individual, even though it may also in due time put down the mighty from their seat; but in another light it can be a leveller. Like Antaeus in the myth, the hero must draw his strength from the common soil of life; and it seems part of his experience to be compelled in one way or another to learn that he is after all only a human being like the rest. This does not reduce him, but on the contrary expands his moral being, and this in turn enlarges our sympathy with him. In one sense he is likely to find himself cut off, bereft of the props an artificial society has given him – all mere 'lendings', like the clothes that Lear throws off (III.iv.108). In another, more vital way he is being brought closer to his fellow-men. A hint of this in an earlier play, *As You Like It*, is the lesson learned by the banished Duke in the forest, where Nature's rudeness teaches him that he is no more than an ordinary mortal. Macbeth comes to understand, more painfully, that he is only one more fool on his way to 'dusty death' (V.v.23). 'Life's but a walking shadow'. Some of the same thoughts and words come into Hamlet's mind. 'Our monarchs and outstretched heroes' are no more than 'beggars' shadows' (II.ii.250–51). A tragic poet is pondering over his own creations, and coming to suspect at times that human existence is merely collective illusion – as India has judged it.

This is the negative side, a levelling down of all humankind to the same nullity. Its converse is a levelling upward, towards an equally high place for all the deserving. Dr Johnson, no leveller, could declare that 'Shakespeare has no heroes', only *men*, behaving as we feel *we* might (14). Human dualism implies that the grand divide is not between high and low rank, but between the good and bad within all men. All men at their best, or their potentially highest, come little short of the angels; all in their lower or weaker selves are what Hamlet in dejection calls himself, a pitiful fellow 'crawling between earth and heaven' (III.i.124–5). The highest any of us can aspire to is to prove ourselves in the fullest sense *men*. It is the ideal of unadorned humanity, of worthiness to be counted among true human beings, all petty titles and blazons laid aside. It was very prominent in *Macbeth*, but it shows itself over and over again elsewhere. Brutus dead on the battlefield is extolled as above all one who 'was a man' (V.v.75). Kent disguised as a servitor answers Lear's question by calling himself simply 'a man' (I.iv.11). As Robert Burns was to say, 'a man's a man', and men ought to be brothers.

Amid the frenzy of evil in *King Lear*, humble folk keep, as Mehl says, their faith in 'basic human values', forgotten by so many of those above them (97); and some of these superiors attain to a higher moral pitch through being dragged down to a lower social grade. Danby reminds us of the late-medieval versions of equality, which Shakespeare must have known something of, the heresies of the Anabaptist sects (*Nature* 187–9): they were still not extinct in his time. It is no surprise to find in him, after his years of study of power and glory, a measure of the republican spirit, combined with an egalitarian spirit lacking in Rome. Compelled at last to come to terms with the triumvirs, Pompey recalls in memorable words, and with a touch of self-disgust, the unyielding dead – 'the all-honoured, honest Roman, Brutus', and his friends, 'courtiers of beauteous freedom', whose creed was to 'have one man but one man' (*AC* II.vi.21–3) –, while the three masters of the world drink themselves stupid. Not many decades after this was written there would be a party of Levellers in the field in England, an earth-shaking challenge to the hierarchical doctrines preached through the ages by Church and State, and sometimes by the theatre.

If death is a leveller, another is humour, and laughter is not without a place of its own in tragedy as written by Shakespeare. His plays, as Dr Johnson said, were strictly speaking neither tragedies nor comedies, 'but compositions of a distinct kind' (15). Underlying those we reckon as tragic are a society's crumbling foundations, whose creaks and groans will torment men's ears, but have also their more bizarre qualities. There are few wits in these plays; farce has an easier entry than polished verbal skirmishings. Hamlet is the only hero with a sense of humour, it has been noticed, certainly the only one capable of a joke. Othello's 'Clown' is a jocular servant whose witticisms are for outsiders, not his employer, and are of the indecent sort that constitutes another, inferior, species of levelling. To keep a Fool is one of Lear's old-fashioned habits, not inherited by his daughters. He is the least witty of Shakespeare's jesters, and in the play his broad earthy sallies are not meant to amuse.

Hamlet's wit has struck some readers as too sardonic, but he makes good use of it to bemuse the affected young fop Osric, whereas Iago tries to degrade all humanity to one low level. His reception of the actors brings back a readiness of his previous life for light-hearted gaiety, and for amicable relations with acquaintances of any rank. It is not untypical of him that his very first words are a wry pun, and among his last is a grimmer one as he forces the poisoned goblet on his uncle. Punning was an authentic part of the popular tradition Shakespeare was so much at home with (Ferguson 293–4; Adams 331); it was outlawed by eighteenth-century snobbery, and has never recovered its deserved place. *Julius Caesar* opens with a crowd-scene full of knockabout humour and word-play. In *Coriolanus* citizens are leaner and hungrier, and frivolity is left to the well-fed servants in Aufidius's mansion.

Light humour is less common after the earlier plays; the best of it comes, unexpectedly, with practical jokes played on her lover by the Egyptian queen. There is carefree banter too at her court, but in the later plays wit, now barbed and derisive, has gone over, like intellect in general, to the camp of the malignants, with Iago and Edmund, leaving behind that sour native of no-man's-land Apemantus. An undercurrent of cynicism accompanies tragedy throughout, opposites though the two moods are. Men like Edmund must convince themselves that everyone else is as bad as themselves, or only not bad because stupid. But their running commentary on the human scene contains much valid satire, and delineates sharply much of what in Shakespeare's eyes is wrong with the times.

Higher and lower ranks both contribute to those astonishing strokes of art where humour of an unconsciously macabre sort comes, like a sudden lull in the storm, before or after tragic events. Of this kind are the grave-diggers' scene in *Hamlet*, the porter's soliloquy in *Macbeth*, the prattle of Lady Macduff's little son just before her castle is attacked. Most unpredictable of all is the rambling chat of the countryman who brings Cleopatra her means of death, and whom she listens to, or hears, without impatience. After the many great and famous men she has known, this peasant is the last man she will ever see. Tragic vision is magnified by being framed within the reality of daily life. But the effect goes beyond this, to a revelation that there is only one world, and one air breathed by prince and gravedigger, lord and gatekeeper, queen and clodhopper. Tragedy would be meaningless if it concerned only a few.

4

War

War is the poet's grandest theme, said Dryden: 'all other greatness in subjects is only counterfeit', by comparison with a hero's readiness to face danger for his country (191). In Shakespearian tragedy war still keeps the sovereign place that it held in the Histories, as the touchstone of courage; without its looming presence tragedy could not, it seems, be its authentic self. Also, of course, drums and trumpets were among the easiest stage effects, and the most exhilarating, for the theatre to make use of (Jorgesen 3). This association with war helps to give the tragedies their 'public' or monumental character, overarching the fates of individuals. In all the Roman plays there are battles; also in *King Lear* and *Macbeth*, and wars and armies in the background of the other three plays. Feverish preparations for war give *Hamlet* and *Othello* their start, though no hostilities follow. *Julius Caesar* opens with the dictator celebrating a triumph for his victory in the civil war, *Macbeth* with thrilling tidings of battles just fought and won. These are reported in inflated language, to make up for the absence of real cutting and thrusting. Of nearly all the encounters we hear much more than we see. Shakespeare may have concluded that there was little to be gained by trying to put battles on the stage. In *Coriolanus* he returns to fighting in full strength, perhaps with more desire now to show it as chaotic folly than as glorious heroism.

But all the heroes except apparently Hamlet, the youngest, are or have been warriors. Brutus and Cassius are both old soldiers, priding themselves on their experience. Macbeth is Scotland's greatest fighter. Even the aged Lear, who while out of his mind imagines himself drilling raw recruits, at the end recalls his old days with the sword, and has strength enough to kill Cordelia's hangman (IV.vi.86 ff., V.iii.274 ff.). But with him, as with Timon, the heroic days lie in the past. Hamlet feels the baleful fascination of war all the more because he has no first-hand knowledge of it; his doubts and heart-searchings are coloured by thoughts of it and of the warlike virtues which he seems to himself to lack shamefully. His sea-fight must be supposed to have dispelled the gnawing doubt, and sent him back to Denmark more composed, if still with no plan of action. He dies fighting, and earns a soldier's funeral honours, a distinction won also by Antony and Coriolanus.

Edgar's single fight with Edmund appears to one critic 'strangely pointless', like much else in *King Lear* (Boorman 200). But it is a sequel to his fight with Oswald, a further proof of the courage he must possess if he is to be worthy of the power soon conferred on him. History as known to Shakespeare is forged on the anvil of battle. This 'duel', moreover, makes up for the incoherence of the battle just fought, by embodying Right and Wrong in two armed champions. In a man to man contest we can enjoy seeing the better man win, as we know he will.

Shakespeare has been thought, from his frequent allusions, to have been an admirer of Hercules, of whom Antony has a cult, or of the unflagging prowess he stands for (Boas, *Elizabeth* 79 ff.). But Shakespeare's feelings about war had always been ambivalent, and were now more heavily divided between admiration for its ideal qualities and disgust with its horrid realities. Othello is romantically in love with his vocation of arms, but we are meant to see him, it may be, in part as a barbarian dazzled by the pomp and circumstance that Europe was learning to invest its armies with. Courage can best be displayed in hand to hand fighting, but this is increasingly outdated, and for a commander to be no more than a brawny swordsman, like Antony or Coriolanus, can begin to savour of the ridiculous. Coriolanus especially makes a battlefield look like a shambles. Rome is always bent on conquest, but elsewhere it is some alleviation of the clash of arms that war, or preparations for it, are now as a rule defensive, not blatantly aggressive as in *Henry V*. Venice is under attack from the Turks: this continues to be part of the play's atmosphere, but as to any detail of events M.C. Bradbrook may well point to 'a marked indifference' (146). Denmark is threatened by Norway, Scotland is invaded by Norway. Antony is attacked by Octavius, whatever provocation he may have given.

Revulsion from war could draw some reinforcement from the new king's very unwarlike disposition. James was only too familiar with violence in his unruly Scotland, no more than half-civilized and especially so in the Celtic north where the scene of *Macbeth* is chiefly laid. Shakespeare does not conceal war's horrors, but rather compels us to see them vividly. They are paraded in Antony's blood-curdling threats of reprisals for Caesar's murder, as they were in *Henry V* by the invader at Harfleur. A common stock of images of this kind, for writers to draw on, was accumulating. They acquired a 'formulaic character', Barbara Donagan has found (73–4), with their 'infants spitted on pikes' for instance, and were used again in propaganda by both sides in the English Civil Wars.

All the same, Shakespeare was not obliged to insert such a speech as Antony's, which has no connection with the sequel. His sources do not account for its 'apocalyptic tone and frightening power' (Miola 103).

Shakespeare's purpose seems to be to alarm us. The narrative passage chosen by Hamlet for the actor to declaim is another gory piece of rhetoric. Listening to it he can be supposed to think of the strife that his mission may before long bring on his Denmark. In what may be termed the official view, such slaughters were deplorable at home, legitimate abroad. We may hope that the poet had never fully shared it, and was now less and less ready to do so. He may reasonably have felt that on balance he was contributing something to the humanizing of war, the most that could be looked for since there was no chance of its abolition, whether he judged this desirable or not. He had made his Henry V forbid all misconduct by his soldiers, all pilfering, or contemptuous treatment of the French; 'lenity' is a quicker way to win a kingdom than 'cruelty' (III.vi.104 ff.). Would Shakespeare like to have heard of similar conduct being prescribed in Ireland?

Hamlet's father was a warrior steeped in the ideas of a bygone day, who won the fiefs of a Norwegian prince by accepting a challenge to single combat and staking Danish territory on it: very cavalier treatment of his own country, we may say, even though his son does not. Young Fortinbras, son of the defeated prince, debarred by his uncle the king of Norway from attacking Denmark to win back the fiefs, goes off to win renown by a senseless campaign against Poland. But time is moving on, and warlike fame, meaningless adventure, are losing their bloom. Antony's challenge to single combat is a futile attempt to turn the clock back, which Octavius derides. What is out of date, however once brilliant, becomes ridiculous. There is little room now for the chivalrous respect of noble enemies; it is one of the adornments of war that Shakespeare can prize, but the end of *Coriolanus* shows how it may turn out. What is being lost of the old spirit is not being made up for by a growth of modern patriotism. Hamlet takes no interest in the prospective war with Norway, but neither does the fiery Laertes, who is going off, with paternal and royal approval, to amuse himself in Paris. It is time for fighting to be left to professional forces.

Only in *Coriolanus* does the martial ardour of *Henry V* revive, and then only among the patricians, who will be its chief beneficiaries. Plebeians are everywhere no more than accessories, collected by pay or compulsion. Fortinbras's levies are 'lawless resolutes', or desperadoes, from the Norwegian borderlands (I.i.97–8); the rebel Macdonwald has gathered similar recruits from the Gaelic fringes of Scotland (I.ii.9 ff.). Shakespeare does not repeat his fairytale experiment at Agincourt of bringing leader and soldiery together for a heart to heart colloquy. Brutus does not think of haranguing his troops before the battle. Coriolanus hurls dire threats at his men for giving way to panic; it was always a prime duty of officers in the new European armies to prevent their men from running away. Desertions and mutinies were common in English forces of Shakespeare's day, Jorgesen reminds us (145, 153); soldiers scattering to plunder are heard of both at Corioli and at Philippi.

In *Troilus and Cressida* there is a dawning recognition of the importance of planning and strategy. What we observe in the tragedies is rather an increased interest in organization, and in weaponry. Before Caesar's death ominous cloud-shapes of soldiers are seen over Rome, 'In ranks and squadrons and right form of war' (II.ii.20). Roman order and discipline offered a model for European armies in course of formation. Marcellus's account of the war-preparations in Denmark (I.i.70 ff.) sounds very up to date, with its casting of guns, impressment of shipwrights, buying of foreign munitions, things all familiar to Londoners. Othello talks grandly of cannon as imitators of 'Jove's dread clamours' (III.iii.356–7), and of the perils of storming a breach; we see him going out to inspect the building of a new fort (III.ii.5). New-style fortifications and artillery both had need of mathematics, and Iago is behind the times when he criticizes Cassio as too much a mere 'arithmetician' (I.i.19). Hamlet thinks of warfare in terms not of crude hacking and slashing, but of sappers digging mines and countermines (III.iv.207 ff.). It is not often that we are reminded by him of Marlowe's Tamburlaine. Yet both men have a mission to 'scourge' a wicked world, and gunpowder, that grand new arbiter of human destinies, could very well stand as emblem of an explosive, revolutionary purgation. Tamburlaine longed to 'make whole cities caper in the air' with its omnipotent help (*2 Tamb*. III.ii). Hamlet exults in the thought of how he will blow his enemies at the moon.

With all this, it does not seem that Shakespeare was growing more interested in military matters on their own account. One advantage of his sojourns in Rome was to allow him to dodge modern technicalities – though a cannon charged with 'sulphur' finds its way into *Coriolanus* (V.iii.151–2). He may not, it seems, have been very well informed about army ranks and titles (Jorgesen 63, 100 ff.). Generalship still plays little part. Brutus loses his war by insisting on fighting the wrong battle, in the wrong place. Cassius, it is true, knew better. Their enemy Antony, when it comes his turn to be the loser, fights a sea engagement, to gratify Cleopatra, instead of staying on land. A sophisticated touch is Aufidius's respect for the well-organized intelligence service that Rome, like his own government, maintains abroad (I.ii.1 ff.; IV.iii). Living as he did under the shadows of witch-hunting, heresy or treason trials, espionage at home and abroad, Shakespeare seems to have taken a special interest in this department of State-building. 'I have eyes upon him', Octavius tells his sister of her husband (III.vi.62–3).

War is often civil war, as it was in the Histories, though with less sense of the poignancy of fratricidal strife because it is not now Englishmen who are fighting one another. But even foreign wars were coming under increasing criticism in Europe; two high-water marks shortly after Shakespeare's death were Robert Burton's *Anatomy*, in 1621, and a few years later the treatise on international law by the Dutch scholar Groot, or Grotius. It must have struck the poet not seldom that some of the conflicts he wrote about were as nonsensical as the 'ancient grudge' of the Montagues and Capulets. While war as a technology grew rapidly more modern-minded, in its psychology it could remain childishly atavistic.

In its early Roman setting war is endemic, and businesslike enough. Territory is at stake; plunder is another prize, with attractions for both commanders and rank and file. It is an opportunity for a man like Coriolanus to win applause and political advancement. Similarly in Shakespeare's Europe war was above all a buttress of the nobility, headed by the new-style monarchies. It is not giving him too much credit for political acumen to suppose that this truth did not escape him. An advantage which could be claimed was that nobles enrolled as officers in regular armies were under firmer royal control, and their aspirations confined to legitimate channels. Othello talks of 'the big wars that make ambition virtue' (III.iii.349–50), instead of a menace to order. This would reduce the danger of civil war, which a senator in *Coriolanus* warns his countrymen against as 'too bloody, and the end of it/Unknown to the beginning' (III.i.325–6). Yet a successful commander might be a political menace of another kind, if he were tempted to use his position and prestige to usurp power, like Caesar or Alcibiades.

Fortinbras will not be seizing power in Denmark, but his sole qualification for the throne is his fighting spirit, and the fact that as a soldier he can be thought to stand outside the paltriness and rottenness of civil life: a claim often to be made for the military in Europe in years to come. Kernan surprisingly talks of his army 'achieving the honor it seeks' (*Playwright* 90). No one but its commander has been seeking glory, or notoriety, by the sacrifice of lives of men forced into service by hunger. As often, Shakespeare leaves us to draw the moral: the egotism of power and ambition, the qualities that can win a throne. Fortinbras can be expected to embroil Denmark in much unnecessary warfare, but that may be the price of peace and order at home. So Elizabethan statecraft held, and Shakespeare often said, if with diminishing conviction, and the idea was to prove very long-lived in European thinking. It was at bottom a bungling attempt to rationalize the outlook and interests of a military ruling class jealous of the growing wealth and weight of a bourgeoisie, and wanting to appear indispensable. A cycle of causes and effects was postulated, from which mankind could hope for no escape. In one neat form it was charted in the satirical play *Histriomastix*, an anonymous work refurbished in 1599; it runs from Peace, through Plenty, Pride, Envy, War, to Poverty.

When Shakespeare is talking, or leaving his characters to talk, on conventionally slipshod lines, peace is often in this way assumed to breed softness, enervation, feebleness, along with material prosperity, a degenerate condition for which war is the only antidote. Too much 'wealth and peace' can cause an internal 'imposthume', which must end fatally, Hamlet reflects as he watches Fortinbras's men on the march, unless war brings timely relief

226

(IV.iv.27–9). In pre-scientific days it was not poets alone who thought chiefly in images, and an association of ideas must be suspected between this reasoning and the medical practice of bleeding patients for all kinds of ailments, which ran alongside it for a very long time. Hamlet's image is a contorted one; what he is really brooding on is the antithesis between his own lassitude and another man's energy. But behind the hackneyed phrases lies a vista of competition for wealth, piling up social rivalries and discontents that will destroy society if not drained off: the morbid condition of Timon's Athens.

Recent conflicts with Poland, Norway, England, have not preserved Hamlet's native land from the rottenness supposedly brought by peace. And no one could pretend that the labouring poor in Shakespeare's England were suffering from a plethora of ease and plenty. It may be regretted that Shakespeare, who read his Plutarch so carefully, neglected in *Coriolanus* some openings his author held out to him: the plebs complaining of being harassed with constant army service 'for defence of the rich men's goods'; or the dearth being caused by warfare which kept the fields from being sown (xxxi, xxxvii). Still, among the many contradictions in his society which Shakespeare was sensitive to, war, ennobling and brutalizing, may have seemed to him the sharpest of all. It may do much to explain what impelled him towards tragedy-writing.

We cannot turn him into a pacifist, even if on the critics' rack he can be got to confess almost anything. It can all the same be felt that he was coming to make less of physical courage, and more of moral courage, something far more rare in history. War comes to seem in his poetry less a brute reality, more an ideal wrestling, akin to Blake's 'mental fight' and 'arrows of desire'. Cordelia braves her father's wrath. The tribunes in *Coriolanus* break away from their class to champion the people. Macbeth, on the contrary, a paladin fresh from the battlefield, lacks resolve to say no to his wife. These are tests less primitive, more complex, than those of war, and call out a deeper-laid strength of character. We are seeing one kind of manifestation of old 'noble' values refined and renewed by intermingling with those of a newer social order.

But it would be very long before more civilized ideas could find entry into the sphere of international relations, and challenge the naïve mentality we find in an early Elizabethan tragedy attributed to Thomas Preston: *Cambises, King of Persia.* When Cambises announces his intention of attacking Egypt, a worthy councillor applauds: a ruler should avoid stay-at-home temptations, and find all his satisfaction in 'martial feats and kingly sport'. A king is a wild beast, it seems, never so harmless as when turned loose to devour foreigners. This time things go wrong; Cambises comes home from Egypt a blood-thirsty tyrant.

5

Political Shadows

*If we look at writers through the ages we see that they have always been political
. . . To deny politics to a writer is to deny him part of his humanity . . .
Writers flourish in a state of political flux, on the eve of the crisis . . .*
Cyril Connolly, *Enemies of Promise* (1938;
Harmondsworth 1961, pp. 108–9)

All the tragedies bear the names of their 'heroes', one of them coupled with
a heroine, but they are always concerned with affairs of State as well, and the
two planes form a counterpoint with each other. This greatly strengthens
the spectator's readiness to feel that the fortunes of an individual or the State
are his as well; without it he might ask himself 'What's Hecuba to me?'
Shakespeare was always 'passionately interested in politics', and its meaning
for him was expanding as he wrote the tragedies (R.B. Parker 263–5). Each
drama is also a political study, though the conclusions it points to may at
times appear equivocal. Conservative readers have thought it natural and
proper for Shakespeare to hold strong political convictions, identical with
those of government and ruling class; when this has sounded too unconvincing they have fallen back on the view that he had no political opinions
at all. Grierson, for instance, found in him a lack of interest in any grand ideas
or principles like republicanism, or in anything but story and characters. But
without such ideas there would be no story or characters worth our notice.
It is not much better to say, with M.C. Bradbrook ('Shakespeare' 14), that
whereas Ben Jonson was drawn to political and social matters, Shakespeare's
interest was in mankind. Deprived of political and social dimensions
mankind is a mere abstraction.

Some expressions in Sidney's *Apologie for Poetrie* 'suggest a vision of
tragedy which is both radical and political'. Pointing to this, Mangan (64)
remarks on how English tragedy absorbed into itself much of the spirit of
social satire. This had been in vogue shortly before with both playwrights
and poets, and on the stage it persisted, most remarkably in Jonsonian
comedy and in Shakespearian tragedy. Oscar. J. Campbell can speak of

Hamlet as, in one light, 'a malcontent satirist', akin to the Jaques of *As You Like It* (149). Hamlet is realizing by painful degrees how deeply things have gone wrong in Denmark, between the vices and follies of the rich and the wretchedness of the poor. He sees people currying favour by buying pictures of Claudius (II.ii.333 ff.); he pours scorn on drunkenness, as Shakespeare does elsewhere as well. (It must have been a nuisance in the theatre, for one thing.)

Plebeian resentment finds a clumsy outlet in the gravedigger's objection to Ophelia, a suicide, being buried in holy ground by royal order (V.i.20 ff.). Some barbed comments on established society are left to croaking voices like that of Apemantus. But in *King Lear* the bitterest of them all come from a king, dethroned vagrant though he may now be. All the heroes after Brutus are themselves dogged by derisive criticism, whether they hear it or not: Hamlet from himself, Othello from Iago and Emilia, Lear from his jester, Macbeth from the witches, Antony from Enobarbus, Timon from Apemantus, Coriolanus from some of the shrewder citizens.

It is scarcely possible not to link Shakespeare's tragic feeling with what he was seeing of social injustice and cruelty. In a kind of surrealistic way, and under the weight of his own wrongs, this awareness dawns on Lear, abruptly conscious while out of his mind, or habitual mind, of social realities hitherto ignored. Life has gone awry because wealth and poverty exist side by side, and one is very largely the cause of the other. In a far-off corner of the Roman empire we have heard Brutus expressing his repugnance at the need to 'wring from the hands of peasants their vile trash', to pay his soldiers (IV.iii.72 ff.) – something that English landowners were daily doing, to pay for their own pleasures. Thomas More had called the State a conspiracy of the rich against the poor. A world where the stronger feed on the weaker like beasts of prey cannot be anything but a nightmare.

Hamlet is tethered to the old order, and cannot escape a sense of sharing in its guilt. His self-reproaches to Ophelia, his painful distress over the vices of his nature, cannot be all pretence, or hysteria: he feels a real horror, in the distraught state of mind he has been thrown into, not so much at how he himself has lived, but at how the social levels he belongs to behave habitually. He has got away from them for a while, and now would like to get away from them again, to the refuge of a quiet scholastic life. Malcolm too, in the indictment he invents against himself, must be taken as uttering a general confession on behalf of an old ruling class. He himself may be all virtue, but he knows feudal aristocracy to be deeply stained. More than Hamlet he concentrates its sins into a charge of sexual depravity, something that for Shakespeare is becoming a summation of all social morbidity. Lear and Timon seem to denounce the entire human race, in the violence of their recoil from it; but most of their accusations are only, or mainly, applicable to the rich and the powerful.

The tragedies mirror societies in disarray, and liable to frightening confusion, within men's minds as well as all round them. Their under- lying problem is that of finding an equilibrium between institutions and individuals, something that no stereotyped homilies, calls for acceptance of ready-made doctrines, could achieve. Shakespeare's picture of the feudal spirit found room for a lavish magnificence, a careless indifference to cramping prudence. Many heads had to be chopped off in Europe before this could be curbed. Warlike qualities bred by it were needed now for new purposes, but they had to be brought under control and tempered by civil law. Even a soldier as admirable as Othello ought not to kill his wife and set one of his officers to murder another.

With its former cohesion the old order was losing what moral authority it might have claimed. Its deeper disintegration is revealed in the tragedies in men's distrust of one another – and of women –, or in trust misplaced, and ability to outwit a neighbour as the skill most highly to be prized. Self- seekers are free to reject old social platitudes as mere humbug. Iago expresses the belief of a competitive age that the devil will take the hindmost, and only fools waste tears on those he catches. *Macbeth* can be said to contain a some- times prophetic parallel of capitalist aggression (Ryan 65). Such egotistic individualism flourishes when one norm of conduct is breaking down and another has not yet established itself.

In many ways this situation appears to Shakespeare warping and crippling. Nevertheless it can bring an exhilarating sensation of freedom, of life discovering new capabilities. Individual consciousness of this more benign kind could accentuate the wish to find associates sharing similar ideals. How 'honour' could take on a higher meaning we see when Macbeth promises added honour to Banquo in return for his support, and Banquo agrees on condition that he will not have to sacrifice any honour (II.i.25 ff.).

Brutus and his companions kept their honour, and their fellowship, intact to the end; but they lost their struggle, and in the other plays any such banding together of like-minded men in a common cause is scarcely to be found, except near the close of *Macbeth*. In *Hamlet* the player-king's long speech about the mutability of human attachments is, in the context of the sub-play, undramatic; it sounds like a summing up of Shakespeare's observations of high life, where great men flourish or fall, and their clients' loyalty flows or ebbs. Commercializing trends, rusting of old links, can be found in Shakespeare's writings from the outset; but their effects are now intensified.

Now as before, he does not set out to portray the mercantile classes which were in the van of 'progress' in his England. We see not them, but their dark shadow advancing in front of them, bringing men's surrender to the dominion of money. In this shape the unseen presence is felt clearly enough. Legal and financial phraseology abounds in *Hamlet* (Mack 96).

Athenian writers and artists have to be as strenuous in flattery as any courtiers (Nuttall 14–15). Money peeps out of unexpected quarters; to Cleopatra music is the food 'of us that trade in love' (II.v.1–2). It does *not* show in a quarter where it might be looked for in some other playwrights. Both Polonius and Laertes are emphatically free from that vice of depraved courts that made men willing to sacrifice a daughter's or sister's reputation to royal favour.

Goneril and Regan have a kind of sanctimonious heartlessness, before their mask comes off; their condemnation of Lear's extravagance, in the accents of puritan parsimony, contrasts with his protest that even 'basest beggars' will cherish some small unneeded possession (II.iv.260–61). Timon uncovers the underlying cause of what now moves and threatens to wreck human life, greed for gold, the blighting of an old generosity of spirit by the fever of avid accumulation. A poet must have deep roots in the past, from which he sucks most of his nourishment, and it is natural for him to look back emotionally as often as intellectually he looks forward. In his tragic world Shakespeare shows us more of the worse than the better sides of the new way of living. This may be true to history: in any new social outlook the bad elements are likely to reveal themselves more precociously than the good, which need more time to ripen. In these dramas the forces of evil are defeated, but less by any superior strength of virtue than by their own voracious appetites and jealousies.

Out of the turmoil of change is emerging a stronger public consciousness, a desire to know how affairs are being managed, a feeling of what things ought to be altered. Public opinion in this half-formed sense was already gaining ground in the Histories, and we continue to hear of its workings and their importance for the seekers of power. After Polonius's death Claudius admits gloomily to Gertrude that scandal-mongers will not hesitate to traduce the king himself (IV.v.93). In *Antony and Cleopatra* there are, as Hunter notices, sundry allusions to fickle public favour (*Studies* 268). Othello must be sent to take charge in Cyprus, the Doge declares, although there is a trustworthy man there already, because 'opinion, a sovereign mistress of effects', has more reliance on Othello (I.iii.222 ff.).

Shakespeare was not prophesying, or recommending, any single way out of the maze. Political speculation evidently attracted him, and at a time when no organized parties and programme were yet in the field he could allow his thoughts to rove. A variety of possible futures were floating in his mind. What seems to have been his firmest conclusion was that monarchy, as Englishmen had known it, could have no future. Poetically all the tragic heroes – none of them with any resemblance to King James – can be thought of as masks worn by monarchy: they are all 'royal' figures, in the way that Antonio of Venice was a 'royal merchant', a man of something like superhuman stature. But supermen are no longer what the times require, and thrones do not radiate happiness. In Denmark and in Scotland the temptation of a crown brings a usurper to power, in Britain an aged monarch confesses himself a failure. Aristocracy, an inevitable accompaniment of monarchy, is represented by the aging Polonius and his family, and the brainless Osric, and by Scottish nobles unable to offer the least resistance, unaided, to a tyrant. Macbeth is preceded and followed by a good ruler, but both are strangers to us, who can weigh little in the balance.

The bankruptcy of monarchy has a place in *Antony and Cleopatra* too, with a frivolous queen who plays on her people's superstition by impersonating the goddess Isis (III.vi.16–18), and an adventurer who speaks of himself as a great 'prince' – unlike his rival Octavius, who cultivates a Roman gravity and restraint, consults sage advisers and studies public opinion. Friends of Order, so strongly represented among Shakespeare's expounders, look up to monarchy as its firmest bulwark. Others, however, have realized that many of the disruptions we witness have been caused by criminal or irresponsible conduct of kings, or men wanting to be kings (e.g. Moretti 46). Oligarchies can be guilty of similar misconduct; and wherever resistance breaks out against those in power, it is the rebels who are entitled to our sympathy.

Moretti draws his formula too closely when he argues that the 'function' of tragedy is to put an end to the mystique of monarchy (42 ff.); the more so because he insists that all tragic monarchy must be *absolute* monarchy, of which England had less than most other kingdoms. A mystique had indeed been relied on more by the Tudors than by other rulers, to make up for lack of armed force and for the weakness of the national Church after its enforced jumps from Protestantism to Catholicism and back again. But by this time, with Elizabeth gone and an unimpressive foreigner on the throne, it was already fading, and scarcely needed a phenomenal outpouring of dramatic poetry to give it the last rites. For Shakespeare monarchy was only a part of an old order which in many ways he cherished; his besetting anxiety was for the English people and its destinies, not the throne. He saw the inadequacies of the monarchy as it was, but he also saw much that was problematical about any alternatives in sight.

Absolute monarchy has never existed as a literal fact; there were always many things, good or bad, that kings could not do or get done. Still, royal authority had varying degrees. It had been greatly intensified in Spain, where the Cortes was a small and, by comparison with England's Parliament, insignificant body. Further east royal authority was being built up by the other Habsburg dynasty, at Vienna; and, more spasmodically, in France, whose States-General or parliament met in 1613 for the last time before 1789. In all these three cases it had the ardent support of the Catholic Church. That the same might happen in England was the fear of a good many Englishmen, whose numbers grew in the next reign; they were suspicious of what they took to be Catholicizing tendencies in the Church of England, encouraged by a French queen. It was a fear that did much to turn a parliamentary party against the crown in the early 1640s. Shakespeare along with most Englishmen who thought about things liked to think of his government ruling by consent, within a framework of legality unheld by Parliament and law-courts. In *Henry IV Part II* the Prince of Wales is put under arrest by the Chief Justice, and when on the throne thanks the judge for doing his duty, instead of revenging himself.

Shakespeare must be supposed capable of imagining most of the political types that the coming years were likely to give birth to, and their outlook. Poole (58–9) finds evidence in Coriolanus's tirades of a 'vision of an ideal state'. If so, it will be one run for the benefit of an aristocracy, as all European kingdoms really were (or as England today is run for the benefit of a plutocracy). His soul aches, the hero declares, to know which side will win, if rival parties are to be allowed to compete (III.i.108 ff.). In England crown and Parliament would soon become two such competitors. Not many years after Shakespeare's death the party or faction headed by Strafford and Archbishop Laud were bent on answering the question; they wanted a more autocratic, centralizing monarchy. Ranged against them were the dauntless Hampdens of the Puritan-parliamentary opposition, landowners cherishing their independence, men with a strong family likeness to Brutus and Cassius. As governor of Ireland Strafford could try out the policy of 'Thorough' that he and his allies hoped to impose on England. He was executed in 1641 on a charge, among many others, of planning to make use of an Irish Catholic army to trample on English liberties, somewhat like Coriolanus coming to punish rebellious Rome at the head of an army of Volscians. King Charles, a reader of Shakespeare, may have preferred blander analogies, Cordelia's French army, Malcolm's English army, coming to rescue him and his country from parliamentary usurpation.

For reasons embedded in England's economic and social structure, this country was moving not towards the Continental model of rule by royal bureaucracy for the benefit chiefly of a court aristocracy, but instead towards direct rule by a landowning nobility. Parliamentary opposition to the Stuarts was preparing the ground. It represented a side of England not without an affinity to the republican regimes in these plays, although they are more urban-based. They are as unattractive in their diverse ways as his monarchies. All their governments are oligarchies, those of Venice and Athens of a highly money-conscious sort. Venetian society, we can take it from Roderigo and Iago, is corrupt, even if the government is not. Rome is full of murderous feuding; in Athens usurer-capital is in the saddle, and Timon, the grand aristocrat, has only a marginal place, and only until his money is gone.

Dictatorship is on the scene from the outset, in the ambivalent personality of Caesar, winner in a civil war for which no motives are hinted at except ambition. Our sympathies can only be on the side of his republican enemies, but republicanism in Rome is as worn out as monarchy elsewhere. Athens is under a regime which has made itself unbearable, but which is overthrown not by the people, but by the army, whose leader becomes dictator. He has mixed motives for his action, some of them higher than any that Shakespeare credits Caesar with; and the army is the only organized force ready to act. Still, we may suppose an unspoken thought in the background that it would be unwise to call the people to arms, because it might not be so willing to lay down its arms when told to.

Our twentieth century has abounded in autocrats and dictators and their admirers. In 1940 Phillips (174) claimed general agreement with the dictum of MacCallum, writing in 1925, eight years before Hitler took office, that 'the rule of the single master-mind' is the lesson of *Julius Caesar* and *Antony and Cleopatra*, as sole solution for Rome's problems in that age. It would be less incautious to think that by the time Shakespeare got to the end of the second play, and was left with no alternative to Octavius, he was willing, with the warrant of history, to hope for the best, without raising any fine expectations. Octavius is an embodiment of *raison d'état*. We are not surprised either at his threatening to kill Cleopatra's children (V.ii.130 ff.), or at his not carrying out the threat when it can serve no useful purpose. At Athens Shakespeare had seemed more sanguine, climbing out of the depths of pessimism by hailing Alcibiades and his military coup as a short cut to social reform. Now he is more realistic; and finally, in *Coriolanus*, another army leader and would-be dictator is eager to quell not a disorderly patriciate, but the common people trying to claim their rights.

Turning back from this point, and venturing to read between some of Shakespeare's lines, we can feel lurking in the background a recurrent upper-class fear of revolts of the people. A prime service of the mystique of royalty, in the long interregnum between feudal and modern, was to hoodwink or hypnotize the masses into seeing in each king a 'new Messiah', as the historian Michelet was to call him; into fancying that in him they had a true friend and protector against their petty tyrants, a 'little father' as Russian serfs learned to call their grand tyrant the tsar.

Respectable opinion in Shakespeare's time would not endorse a rebellion of the masses, on their own initiative, against the worst of governments. Even under reputable leadership a summons to the people would be looked at askance; political excitement might too easily ignite social discontents. The 'Glorious Revolution' of 1688 owed its glory to the great care taken by the Whig magnates who stage-managed it to avoid any need for common people to have any share in it. Lear's partisans plot against his daughters, and find some support, but the serious threat to Goneril and Regan comes from the French army. It comes not to liberate the people of Britain, but to restore Lear; as a consequence, Shakespeare perhaps implies, it is defeated.

In *Macbeth*, where he had to be particularly circumspect, a similar situation arises. A rising of the Scottish nobility, at the head of the nation, would not commend itself to James. (There was to be one in 1638, against his son.) Foreign intervention is again the solution, this time with happier results. It comes from England, and metaphorically from heaven, as if at the call of the 'holy angel' whom Lennox rhetorically implores to fly to England and seek deliverance there for poor Scotland (III.vi.45 ff.). Malcolm has a valid claim to the throne, and a clear mandate to free his country from a usurper. He gains the support of the Scottish lords; the common people are left in the background. At the end the nobles can troop happily off to Scone for the coronation and their rewards; no benefits are mooted for the people.

Sudden riots, disorderly demonstrations, were endemic in London. Popular feeling was lively but volatile, at a time in history when an old world and its modes of thinking were running down faster than any replacement could emerge, especially for the less literate classes, for whom time always moves more slowly. It cannot have been beyond Shakespeare's comprehension that if commoners sometimes appeared feckless, even demoralized, the conditions they lived under were to blame. Smirnov was right in saying that he did not view them with contempt, but was aware of their immaturity (83). There is an archetypal case in *Julius Caesar*, after the coup carried out by an aristocratic group which feels no need to ask anything from the people except applause. In return Brutus has nothing to offer the poor except the word 'Liberty'. Antony offers them sentimental rant, and a bribe, and they swallow both. Their human feelings are generous enough, but they have no political ballast. Government by 'the Senate and Roman people' has been no more than official fiction. The two funeral speeches show the potency of words in swaying the incautious one way or the other. As a professional speech-writer Shakespeare must have grown highly conscious of this, and his Roman crowd is in one light a caution to his English public.

At the opening of *Julius Caesar* a republican tribune is exasperated by a shoemaker's light-hearted playing on words. There is a kind of echo of this when Hamlet in the graveyard complains of the 'peasant' nowadays wanting to be as fine-spoken as the courtier (V.i.142–3) – though the same Hamlet has reproached himself with being a spiritless creature, 'a rogue and peasant slave' (II.ii.560). With all his good nature he still belongs by habit of mind to a pre-democratic society, with its incomprehension of the common man, its readiness to despise the poor if they fear to resist their betters, but to turn against them if they want a better place. Europe had haunting memories of peasant upheavals and other mass risings across the Continent.

Hamlet has more feeling than Brutus for the hard lot of the poor, but he can have little inkling of how to improve it. For him as for Brutus it is impossible to resort to violence without a legitimate public mission. He makes no attempt to gather a following against the government. Laertes does so, with easy success. But his aim is simply to revenge a private injury; and the whole affair as Shakespeare leaves it has an enigmatic air. A tumultuous crowd follows Laertes into the castle, shouting for him to be made king; a display of very scanty respect for monarchy or government. It is not easily 'quelled and cowed', as Sisson will have it (63), but withdraws at Laertes' courteous request, and is seen no more. This behaviour looks odd, because the messenger who brought warning of its approach made it sound like an earthquake, a doomsday eruption of anarchy. There is no need of this, so far as the play and its plot are concerned. We must take it as another of Shakespeare's touches of surrealism, a momentary clairvoyant prediction of some monstrous revolution to come – a distant peal of thunder, a proclamation that all oppression the people suffer under will one day be set right, by the people, by force.

Shakespeare must have been visited by more hopeful moods, and glimpses of something like a true democracy, stable but progressive, some day to be born, a Utopia of the future instead of the past. Most of his plebeians have had a close tie only, if at all, with someone above them, a relationship of the old master-and-man kind; in *Coriolanus* this comes to an end. Aufidius's servants, chatting among themselves, show no undue reverence for their master (if Coriolanus has any, we do not see them). The Roman citizenry are an independent class, finding self-respect and seriousness in combination with their fellows. Since *Julius Caesar* they have evolved; Shakespeare, in other words, has been thinking and learning in the course of his tragic journey.

It is in *King Lear* that the curse of poverty has been brought up most forcibly, but the poor are not yet on the stage. They have a mad old king, and a young nobleman simulating madness, to serve as overwhelming images of mankind fallen from its high estate, and of the way human beings treat one another. In the final tragedy the poor are ready to speak up for themselves. They are rebelling because they need food to keep themselves and their families alive. No revolt could well appear more justifiable. What two remorseful old men in Britain have told us, that the means of life ought to be portioned out more equitably, instead of some feasting while others starve, is repeated now by the hungry, and backed by a threat of action. This, not moralizing, compels the reluctant government to consent to a distribution of food.

Moreover they now have some organization, and accredited spokesmen with an official standing, again won for them by their show of strength. Their tribunes have been called unscrupulous; but as Kenneth Muir wrote, they are 'much less unscrupulous than their opponents' ('Shakespeare and Politics' 76). For once Shakespeare gives us individuals from an upper class who are genuinely leading instead of misleading the people. Class is arrayed against class, the underlying reality of all modern history revealed. A compromise is reached, only disturbed by the intransigence of Coriolanus, his expulsion, and then his return at the head of a foreign army. Demos is still under-age, and easily thrown into a panic. In the end Rome is saved, but the democratic experiment is cut short.

Shakespeare's tragic dilemma is something far deeper than the waning of monarchy, or even the passing away with it of a whole era and its way of life. What is tragic is the spectacle of men struggling for power and profit, and for too long the most ruthless winning, the idealists going to the wall; the inability of human beings to build a civilized social organization within which to combine freedom with orderly justice. The forms of government known to him shared the same fundamental vice of being based on human division and inequality; the ability of a minority, through one political machinery or another, to enslave and exploit the majority. Behind the sheltering façade of legality the rich are comfortably protected from justice by their wealth – as Claudius and Lear, two very dissimilar heads of state, both understood.

In the later Histories Shakespeare had expatiated, sometimes perhaps tongue in cheek, on the unbearable responsibilities and burdens of high office (though he never showed us his weary Henry IV or Henry V doing anything useful, beyond suppressing feudal plots and revolts). Now he seems compelled to regard power as twice-cursed, equally burdensome to those who wield it and those who have to submit to it. There would appear to be a steady drift in his thinking, away from faith in any models of government known to him; a drift towards despair, not of mankind, but of all authority, all power of man over man, perhaps too of man over woman. Lepidus had to be got rid of because he was 'too cruel', his 'high authority' was abused (III.vi.32–3). So we are told by Octavius, who never forgets to speak edifyingly of public duty as well as of his own aims. But power over others was certain to be abused, Shakespeare may have been more and more convinced. It was something that no being, mortal or immortal, could fitly be trusted with, from the malign gods of ancient Britain killing human beings for sport down to the beadle with his petty parish office and his whip. Such a conviction had inspired the Utopian anarchism of some of Europe's Anabaptists, and was to inspire Karl Marx's faith, as an ultimate goal, in the withering away of the State.

In these tragedies monarchy is worse than unimpressive; republicanism is stable only in Venice, and is nowhere in the least democratic, any more than in Shakespeare's Europe apart from corners like the Alpine cantons of Switzerland. What was growing, under one constitutional form or another, was the coercive power of the State, though Shakespeare's vaulting imagination may have endowed this with a strength it did not yet fully possess. Menenius is trying to frighten an angry crowd when he talks of the State towering above common humanity, a juggernaut as irresistible as

237

the heavens, 'whose course will on' in spite of any puny efforts they make to arrest it (I.i.61 ff.). Volumnia demands submission to her son, whose worth the rabble can as little judge as she can 'those mysteries which heaven will not have earth to know' (IV.ii.35–6).

The resources of the State were being built up for the purposes of war abroad, and to cope with mounting tensions and discontents at home. 'Let Rome in Tiber melt', and its empire lie in ruins, the poet must at times have felt, – and London in Thames. Reading him, the conservative Dr Johnson, who wanted to see British monarchy strengthened and American defiance of it put down, felt obliged to lament that 'all human advantages confer more power of doing evil than good' (xxx). Hamlet might have echoed him, and have thought 'the cease of majesty', so alarming to the loyal Rosencrantz, a consummation devoutly to be wished.

6

Women and Men

There is great diversity among Shakespeare's tragedy women, as there is among his men. Cleopatra is the most complex of them; the others are as a rule more single-minded and consistent. Conventional moralizers were hard on her (Charney 113, citing F.M. Dickey). She, a foreigner, is the only 'bad' woman in the Roman plays, where women seem as naturally chaste as men are brave. She and Antony's new wife Octavia make the most opposite pair imaginable, one as completely emancipated and self-willed as the other is virtuously domestic. Other contrasting pairs are Gertrude and Ophelia, Desdemona and Emilia, the clamorous Volumnia and the tongue-tied Virgilia.

In a time when new things and ideas were pouring into men's minds, their curiosity about women – still very much an unknown quantity –, and women's about themselves, were sharpened. Opinion was in a state of flux. From Aufidius we hear a truly masculine or military dismissal when he accuses Coriolanus of selling the fruits of victory for a few womanly tears, 'which are as cheap as lies' (V.vi.46–7). Among the puritan middle classes horror of sin, and suspicion of women, or Eve, as its root cause, were active; but so was the countervailing belief that proper upbringing could greatly improve them. Here lay an essential contribution to the flowering of a new social culture. Shakespeare's hope lay in the same blending of higher class assets that he seems all along to have wished for, an infusion of middle-class seriousness into aristocratic fineness. Any such ideal combination might be more easily embodied in feminine shapes, less fixed and more malleable.

If Shakespeare's good men were moving towards a common standard of manliness, with degrees reckoned only by merit, his women could think both of a similar standard among themselves, and of achieving equality with men wherever an equal test might be possible. In dignified self-respect they do not fall behind even the noblest Romans. Ophelia tells Hamlet that a 'noble mind' compels her to return his gifts (III.i.100–101), and the same feeling forbids Cordelia to stoop to her sisters' hypocrisy. Egyptian women can die as bravely as Roman men; and Cleopatra's waiting-women can die as untremblingly as their mistress, just as Antony's freedman can show him the way to death.

In the Comedies women had often taken the lead; in the tragedies some of them are ready for self-assertion of a more serious kind, a claim to a share in the great world's doings. Not many are free to act as independently as the Comedy heroines. Cleopatra, and Antony's unseen wife Fulvia, are exceptions, and Regan when widowed. When an old order and its man-made rules are breaking down, however, there is more room for women of rank – always in Europe accustomed to authority at least in the domestic sphere – to emerge, though this is likely to require willingness to live dangerously. Dowden may have been right in thinking of Shakespeare's 'new women' as beings of simpler composition than his men, less prone to hesitation (110). They may have underrated the risks because unfamiliar with the world of action. Certainly it is hard to imagine a feminine Hamlet among Shakespeare's characters, except possibly Ophelia.

Portia, the first of them, has no wish beyond being taken into her husband's confidence, allowed to share his secret. She stands her ground when rebuffed, and wins her right by a self-inflicted wound, in emulation of a soldier going into battle. But to be able to display this spirit is one thing, to be able to grapple with the consequences is another. Portia and Lady Macbeth both give way under the strain, and Portia's breakdown shows signs of beginning the very next day, as she waits tremulously for news from the Capitol. Lady Macbeth pays an oblique tribute to womanhood when she feels, as a woman, incapable of a brutal crime, and has to invoke the spirits of evil to 'unsex' her (I.v.39 ff.). Davenant may not have departed too wildly from Shakespeare's intention when he inserted in his Restoration arrangement of *Macbeth* a scene where Lady Macbeth reproaches her husband, who as a man ought to have overruled her, for giving way to her instead. She urges him vainly to surrender the crown; she is haunted by Duncan's ghost, and is going mad (Spencer 131–3).

There is love between man and woman in all the tragedies except *Timon of Athens*: it may be amorous or married love, or the love of mother and son, father and daughter. Whichever it is, nearly all these women, good or bad, have an ambivalent part to play in contributing to the ruin of their men, and with it their own. Claudius seems really attached to Gertrude (Mack 111, as against Mangan 123), and if desire for her as well as for the crown has lured him into crime, she must bear some blame for accepting his gifts too willingly, as the Ghost accuses her of doing (I.v.42 ff.). Far more deliberately Lady Macbeth makes a murderer of her husband. Edmund comes to grief through overreaching himself when Goneril and Regan raise his ambition too high by offering him their love.

Even when no guilt is in question, women are capable of much undesigned mischief. Desdemona tries tactlessly and meddlesomely to persuade Othello to reinstate her suspected lover Cassio. Volumnia is shrewdly opportunist in recommending her son to learn how to throw dust in the people's eyes, but she has made this impossible by instilling into him from boyhood an unbridled aristocratic arrogance. Even without any such clog, good advice is apt to be unavailing. Calphurnia cannot dissuade Caesar from going to the Capitol on the fatal day. Octavia goes to Rome and tries to avert a breach between her husband and brother. She does this as a family duty, not from any inclination to take a hand in politics, but she too fails.

Cleopatra is the chief temptress of one kind, as Lady Macbeth is of an opposite one. Her joke of dressing up a drunken Antony in her clothes, while she wears his sword (II.v.21–2), may be called an epitome of how she lures the hero into idleness. Yet it is his supremacy as warrior and conqueror that has captivated her. Contradictions reach their climax when she insists on a naval battle, and then runs away from it with her ships, leaving Antony exposed to defeat and his love to extinction. For a time she wavers, half-prepared some have (unconvincingly) suggested to go over to the enemy (e.g. Summers 125). More likely she is disoriented, prostrated by finding her great man in despair and turning against her – but reviving as soon as he recovers himself. 'I have nothing of woman in me now', she exclaims, steeling herself at last for death (V.ii.237–8) – a death that might be called, though she does not feel it so, an atonement for her whole life.

In the Comedies love was as a rule laughable, to all but the lovers, and had a running accompaniment of mockery, sometimes self-mockery; in the tragedies there is a continuing vein of condemnation. In *Twelfth Night*, nearly contemporary with *Hamlet*, women are said to have 'waxen minds', shallow and impressionable; this may be jocular, but the phrase had appeared earlier, in the tragical story of *Lucrece*, in pointed contrast with the 'marble minds' of men, and with the inference that women should not be blamed for their comparative inconstancy (lines 1240 ff.). We must take the player-king's sententious talk, and his queen who 'doth protest too much' (III.ii.136 ff.), as a comment on Hamlet's own family. (This couple have been married for thirty years – Hamlet's own age, so the parallel with his parents is close.)

As a highly independent and emancipated woman, Cleopatra can still see the ridiculous side of life, which men are becoming too serious and self-important for. She is not a wit, but enjoys practical jokes, just as she can enjoy hopping through the streets. Hamlet and Iago may be witty in a sardonic vein, but Cleopatra is the only tragic character who keeps alive the light bantering humour of the Comedy heroines. Jane Adelman finds the play's whole vision 'subjected to the comic perspective'; she instances Charmian teasing her mistress about her youthful affair with Julius Caesar (52). Remembering, we may guess, his own juvenile idyll at Stratford, Shakespeare had always seen love as from one point of view absurd – even in *Romeo and Juliet* when the hero suddenly exchanges one passion for another. At any rate love is a leap in the dark, which onlookers can see to be imprudent.

Polonius shakes his sage head over amorous excitements, much like Friar Laurence, as fuel for 'desperate undertakings' (II.i.102–6). He is borne out by all Shakespeare's tragedies of love. Ancestral sins have corrupted the world, and made it impossible for love to flower healthily; this is part of the tragic fatality. Comedy love had a separate existence of its own, whatever its tribulations; now it is in danger of being choked by the alien life crowding round it. Shakespeare was too much a realist, Dr Johnson observed, to treat romantic love as 'the universal agent' that other playwrights made it, instead of as one passion among many – in the Doctor's view if not in the poet's, with 'no great influence upon the sum of life' (13). In earlier plays, moreover, falling in love was simply something that happened, like catching a cold, or a lamp being lit; now each relationship has its own peculiar origin, and runs its own course.

All loves now are, at least from a rationalistic point of view, foolish, or reprehensible. A contradiction comes in sight here: a self-isolating individual, like Timon as he becomes, relapses into barbarism, but if he ventures too far out of his shell, in pursuit of 'such fair question as soul to soul affordeth' (I.iii.133–4), he will fall into a trap. Hamlet is a man who breaks out of a trap he thinks he has got into; instead of thereby eluding his problems he becomes responsible for Ophelia's madness, and later in part for her brother's death and his own. He breaks with her because his mother's conduct has disillusioned him with all women. Disillusion may have been creeping on him even before this final blow. He is not a very young man, and has had time to discover that ladies of the sort he meets are very much a compound of paint, powder, costume, artificial manners – that there is more *couture* about them than culture (cf. III.i.13 ff.). Perhaps he went off to live and study abroad in order to get away from them. We ought not to forget, even if not reminded by Shakespeare, that for a royal prince to live abroad as a student, consorting with nobodies, is a very extraordinary thing indeed.

At any rate much of his paralysis of will must be traceable to this source. If not, then the story of Ophelia has no significant connection with his own tragedy, and is no more than a romantic embellishment. Ophelia has been taxed with not coming to her lover's aid by giving way more ardently to love, throwing herself into Hamlet's arms (e.g. Adams 204, 206). She is 'pathetic and irresponsible', in one stern critic's words, merely 'playing with love' (M.D.H. Parker 96). But her mad song about the false lover and the girl who gave in to him shows at least a doubt in her mind as to what would have been in store for her if she had given in to Hamlet. It is after all the sober conviction of her Denmark that a young man's fancy, as her father and brother warn her, is no more than 'a fashion and a toy in blood'

(I.iii.5 ff.). She is the only heroine with a brother, and to Shakespeare the brother–sister relationship is important. Hamlet has after all drifted into love-making heedlessly; he has not offered marriage; he could not in fact do so without the royal consent. One of the many unauthorized conjectures we may indulge in is that he was on the point of seeking this consent when things were cut short by his father's death. Another is that the badness of his verses to Ophelia betrays an uneasy conscience.

He breaks with her under cover of a pretended madness which deceives her, and must in a way console her. Their failure in love is thus the fault of neither, but an act of God. He may have concluded, like Othello in the end, that he had loved 'not wisely, but too well' (V.ii.340), if by these words Othello meant that he had been wrong to let friendship with Desdemona turn into love. She, unlike Ophelia, threw herself into a lover's arms, with terrible consequences. Othello knew himself to be a man better fitted for a 'free condition' (I.ii.26) than for marriage: he gave way, as Desdemona did, to a swift infatuation, which left them no time to think of prudence or propriety. He was hoping for happiness at the cost of a family which had befriended him. We must admit some likelihood in Iago's assurance to Roderigo that the 'violent commencement' of this love must have a stormy sequel (I.iii.334–5). Or in Johnson's more prosaic language, deceits must always prove 'obstacles to happiness' (198).

In a distrustful or hostile world, love's ordeals bear witness to the fragility of all vital human relations, an inescapable element of the tragic. Only in a poem like Sonnet 124 can love be 'builded far from accident': the life men and women live is too closely hemmed in by the accidental. Once Antony's suspicions are aroused, Cleopatra becomes for him a 'whore' (IV.xii.13). Desdemona suddenly turns into 'the cunning whore of Venice' (IV.ii.88), without it occurring to Othello to wonder why a great heiress should have wanted to disinherit herself by eloping with him. There is a more ghoulish note in the gravedigger's song about a dead man's remembrance of his youthful love (V.i.62 ff.).

In the Comedies young ladies could be innocent without being ignorant, and so they are still in the earlier tragedies, where youth still has a place. Doubtless they picked up a stock of information from gossipy attendants like Emilia. Ophelia has a shrewd notion of what sort of life young gentlemen like her brother, away from home, are likely to lead. When her mind gives way her well-taught manners and refined diction crumple up, and her snatches of old songs have occasioned some embarrassment (e.g. Adams 302–3). Desdemona has shrinkingly concealed herself from the fashionable Venice surrounding her, but she knows what sort of witticisms 'make fools laugh in the alehouse' (II.i.136–7).

Ophelia submits to Laertes' admonition to keep 'out of the shot and danger of desire' (I.iii.35), but discretion does not save her. Hamlet is only exaggerating the same advice when he tells her to go into a nunnery. He shares an acute consciousness of mankind's polarity of nature with Lear, who feels it with Manichaean rawness:

> But to the girdle do the gods inherit,
> Beneath is all the fiend's.
>
> (IV.vi.126–7)

Sex itself has been falling under a dark spell, or the 'eclipses in the sun and moon' that so alarm Gloucester (I.ii.106). Much of what Shakespeare wrote in these years aligns him with Puritan thinking (what kind of life he led may be a different matter), either in its moderate and balanced or its more hysterical mode. A pervasive odour of sexual corruption seems to hang in the air he breathes. His attempt in *Othello* to revive the romantic spirit, withdrawing for the purpose half-way into the seclusion of private life, requires love to be purged of grosser attributes, carefully screened or veiled. Desdemona's love or affection has something of schoolgirlish dazzlement with a celebrity. Her marriage is a flight from Venice and its 'wealthy curled darlings' (I.ii.68); but Venetian libertinism pursues her to Cyprus, and destroys her. Othello wanted a woman combining the refined charm of an old culture with simple virtue like his own. He is in middle age, and waning physical ardour helps to make him quickly suspicious of any physical feeling in a woman.

Even a woman 'as chaste as ice', Hamlet assures Ophelia, will not escape calumny (III.i.137–8). Still, an ice-cold temperament like Valeria's must be some safeguard. The implication is that women can only be reliable if they are free from any sexual feeling, as Victorian legislators liked to suppose them. Octavia is too 'holy, cold, and still' to be a congenial companion for Antony, as Enobarbus foresees (II.vi.121–2). None the less she has strong enough feelings; one of the most moving denunciations of war in Shakespeare comes from her, when she declares that war between Octavius and Antony will be like the earth splitting open, and the chasm having to be filled up by the dead (III.iv.30–32). Cordelia has no such objection to war, but she is another virginal figure, who takes no interest in what husband is to be chosen for her, and lets us forget her marriage to a nobly unreal king of France. All her devotion is to her father, despite her denial of this at the outset (I.i.99 ff.). Shakespeare was a father, now middle-aged, with daughters but no surviving son; there may be some undertone of craving, in all paternal feeling, for a filial devotion like hers.

With all this chorus of praise for chastity, Shakespeare as well as Antony might well feel the need of a vacation in Egyptian sunlight. Even there the voice of surly respectability dogs them. The play opens with Philo's morose speech about Antony being good for nothing better now than to cool 'a gypsy's lust'. Cleopatra's entry, and her talk of love, sweep away the impression like sunshine banishing a shadow, though not from utilitarian Roman minds. Here as with Othello, mature years are some shield against suspicion of excesses of passion. Both partners have unlimited access to more youthful attractions, but neither cares about them. Love is, so to speak, smuggled back onto Shakespeare's scene, as the young Cleopatra once smuggled herself into Caesar's presence wrapped up in a carpet.

It is hard to think of Shakespeare's couples being able to discuss difficulties between them rationally. There are two married pairs, with a foundation of mutual knowledge and trust, who are capable of debate; but what has to be thrashed out between Portia and Brutus, Lady Macbeth and Macbeth, does not concern their personal relations, and it is the criminal pair who are readiest to unveil their thoughts to each other. If lovers must in some ways remain strangers to each other, the gap between them will be widened when they come from different peoples and cultures. This is pre-eminently the case in two plays, *Othello* and *Antony and Cleopatra*, with the alien first a man, then a woman. In each case the man wrongly suspects at some point that his enchantress has cheated him – in the second case, politically. In each case love ends fatally for both. Shakespeare may not have lost all belief – all interest, at any rate – in romantic love, but he abandons it now to situations where it can only end tragically; almost as if designing an allegory of vast distances between man and woman, a gulf of separation only to be bridged in dreams.

Shakespeare's families belong to the unitary or 'nuclear' type already prevalent in his England and western Europe, not the extended clan. Within its narrow charmed circle intense relationships are forged, and it is with these that Shakespeare is concerned. Lear has no other relatives than his daughters and their husbands; Macbeth no close kin but his wife; Othello none until his marriage; Timon none, Octavius only a sister. An erosion of the family even in its closer limits shows in Antony's light-hearted sacrifice of his nephew in the proscription-list, and later, less drastically, in his separation from his wife Fulvia. Heroes grow morally more isolated as time goes on, but they may have been cut off from family ties from the beginning; they mirror the deepening isolation of modern man, in the epoch that England was now entering.

We are likely to think better of a hero who has won the love of a good woman. This can be said mildly of Caesar and Calphurnia, much more confidently of Brutus, whose scene with Portia does much to establish him early on in our respect. Macbeth has a wife he loves, who in her misguided way is devoted to him; hence in part the sympathy we are able to go on feeling for both. Like Portia's, her attachment is strengthened by shared political aspirations, and neither woman shrinks from the thought of the act of bloodshed that these demand. Round Timon there is a vacuum; we are uneasily conscious that this man of many false friends has not earned a loyal partner. It is a redeeming achievement of the fire-eating Coriolanus to have a wife who manages to love him. She has learned, maybe, to placate him by keeping quiet, the more successfully because he is usually away on campaign, gathering scars.

No marriages take place or are arranged in the course of any play, except those of Cordelia and Octavia, which are not love-marriages. No woman is forced into a repulsive marriage. In the Comedies Shakespeare was shepherding his young people towards the altar; now his interest is increasingly in couples who are already married and have been, except for Claudius and Gertrude, Othello and Desdemona, for some considerable time. Termination or breakdown of their relations takes place in every case, near the end or earlier. Breakdown of the family has an essential bearing on tragedy, because it offers a microcosm of a disintegrating society. Within it rival claims, sometimes of two generations, collide, much like conflicting classes. Family questions are entwined with all the tragic stories, except in *Timon of Athens* where the hero stands alone: one reason why this drama does not impress us as tragic in the largest sense. At the outset, in *Julius Caesar*, there are no parents with sons or daughters; this may deepen our sense of a new age opening, continuity with the past interrupted. In two plays, *Hamlet* and *King Lear*, relations between parents and children play a leading part. It is only in the final play that we come to a small but united family, man and wife, child and grandmother.

Hamlet is a tragedy of family as well as nation: both a reigning dynasty and the family of its chief minister are extinguished. Confronting Gertrude, as 'queen' as well as 'mother', Hamlet tells her that her conduct has corrupted all faith, religion, virtue, until doomsday seems at hand (III.4.40 ff.). Those who preside over society, he may be implying, are likely by their example to spread more evil than good. One of Laertes' grievances is that his father's hasty burial, with no 'formal ostentation', was an insult to his family (IV.v.211 ff.). To work the young man up to a prompt revenge, Claudius dwells lengthily on how love, in this case filial love (which might be Hamlet's as much as Laertes'), is doomed to cool with lapse of time (IV.vii.110 ff.). There seems real feeling in his words, and they recall Brutus's sadness at the thought of 'a hot friend cooling' (IV.ii.18 ff.). Claudius's married life, however begun, appears to be growing into a cordial, trustful partnership. But Gertrude is to die by poison mixed by him for her son.

In *Othello* we see first Brabantio's family disrupted, then the hero's. Brabantio is suffering the same shock of disillusion that every hero undergoes, when he warns all fathers not to think they can know their daughters' minds from their outward bearing (I.i.171–2). In *King Lear* Albany warns his wife Goneril that a woman ready to 'sliver and disbranch' herself from her parental stem, as she has done by her treatment of Lear, must come to grief (IV.ii.34–6). But this is exactly what Desdemona has done. In light comedy it is all very well to say, like Rosalind in *As You Like It*, 'What talk we of fathers', when we have lovers to think about? In serious drama things have to be judged differently. Brabantio dies, and Desdemona pays the penalty foretold by Albany. Her story came from an Italian collection, where its moral was the folly of headstrong young women who go off with strangers. 'Shakespeare's heroines were an alarming novelty' in England, Gurr remarks, and after 1600 plays were being written to discourage such conduct (149).

Othello can take a dismissively modern view of paternal claims, but as a husband, and one in high position, he is patriarchal enough. A sense of lordship and ownership shows as soon as he is ruffled. Old ideas and new are at odds again in Desdemona's death. Shakespeare must mean us to see that Othello is wrong not only in condemning his wife so hastily, but in claiming a right to punish her with death. Male jealousy is so besetting a topic with Shakespeare, and, as Dover Wilson said, so much enveloped in his most repulsive imagery (*Shakespeare* 118–19), that it is hard not to connect it with some personal experience. But Othello is the only tragic hero who suffers from groundless jealousy; Iago's suspicions of his wife form a muffled echo, fomented by his feeling of having been treated as an inferior, as Othello's are by consciousness of his age and colour. Albany is one of extremely few Shakespearian husbands who really have an unfaithful wife. Rivalries in love, the bread and butter of most fictionists, are with Shakespeare a very minor or humorous theme. They are an aberration of women, as jealousy is of men. Goneril quarrels murderously with her sister over Edmund, but we hear of this only in passing. Cleopatra and Octavia are competitors, but they have a sea to keep them apart.

Even in the murder scenes Lady Macbeth can still be a tragic figure, as Goneril could never be, by virtue of her original nature; we see in her as well as in her husband the corruption of a splendid birthright. This cannot halt the widening gulf between the two partners in crime, as each in turn fails the other under the tormenting burden of what they have done. The Macduffs have been a happy family, but Lady Macduff perishes resentful of what she feels as abandonment by her fugitive husband. In *King Lear* the question of the family is magnified into near-identity with the whole problem of society. Lear can scarcely have been a careful father and teacher; and the experience of falling foul of each of his three daughters in turn must help to open his eyes to the duty he has neglected of being a true father of his people. Feminists have not found it hard to accuse him of being an obstinate clinger to patriarchal authority, and to regard Cordelia's forgiveness of him as demeaning. Still, by then he is a changed and very contrite man. A pendulum swing is sometimes observable between play and play: if Cordelia's filial devotion is excessive, it may be a compensation for Desdemona's cavalier treatment of her father.

In all these relationships, not only is each character unique, but so is the quality or key of their attachment to each other, and it is never the same on the two sides. Desdemona's love for Othello began, he tells the Doge, as pity for his years of danger and hardship, and he loved her because she pitied him (I.iii.167–8). Later on she sympathizes too warmly with the disgraced Cassio. Love may be precious as a harbinger of a brighter future for mankind; in the here and now it is likely to spell disaster. For one lover or both, death may be the only perfect resolution of the discords and impossibilities of their lives. Antony and Cleopatra are united by their resolve to die, each in honour of the other. And whereas Cordelia and Desdemona at the end are hapless, helpless victims, Cleopatra dies royally, the grand figure of the closing scenes, the splendidest of all tragedy women. She dies remembering that she is an Egyptian queen, but following the 'high Roman fashion' she has learned from Antony's example (IV.xv.88). Here is one fusion of traditions and values, such as Shakespeare so often seems to be straining his gaze towards.

A feminist of advanced views believes (forgetting Queen Elizabeth) that in Shakespeare's eyes it was an 'abomination' for any power to be given to any woman; that in fact 'Sex itself was an abomination throughout his career', and made him a misogynist (French 325; cf. Mangan 188). He had often, it is true, from an earlier time than that of the tragedies, been preoccupied by the incongruity between love and lust. It was the text on which his Adonis lectured the goddess of love with such boyish gravity. Some other characters of his see far less difference between the two passions. Iago has a quite puritanical conviction that all desire is a vice to be firmly bridled (I.iii.319 ff.). Laertes speaks of his sister's 'unpolluted flesh' (V.i.241), meaning that she has died a virgin, unmarried – he never suspects her of having been seduced. Gloucester's punishment is a savage one, made more horrific by being carried out in our full view: for Shakespeare his real sin, we must think, was not the political offence he is charged with by Cornwall, but a sexual one.

A cloud of sexual malaise hangs over the tragedies, which we must feel as part of a wider morbidity of social life as a whole. The most heated denunciations of sex are heard from Lear, whose fury has been aroused by his daughters, and for whom any amorous experiences must belong to a far past; and from Timon, who has never to our knowledge had anything to blame women for. In these cases sexual disgust can only be an overflow from something else. Timon is ready to hail venereal disease as an auxiliary in the extermination of the human race that he hopes for. In Athens and ancient Britain the social and political order is collapsing, and sex at the same time sinking into the soulless and bestial. In Lear revulsion carries him towards the same anarchic conclusion as his growing disbelief in all authority. 'Die for adultery? No!' (IV.vi.III). It is not worth thinking about what men and women do together; animals do the same.

Sexual promiscuity, abhorrent to Shakespeare on its own account, makes a natural symbol of social and moral chaos. Lear as well as other tragic heroes sounds at times, Robson admits, 'obscenely gross'. But perhaps, the same scholar adds, the twentieth century has not been amiss in finding its archetypal tragic figure in this confused, cursing old man, rather than in the glamorous Hamlet so dear to the nineteenth-century heart (Prologue 68–9). Our era has been history's great age of revolt against social oppression. Lear discovered the injustices of class, Timon those of capitalism. With the way opened for recognition of what is fundamentally wrong in the social order, the mephitic cloud can begin to lift. As if in sign of this, Shakespeare goes back to a Rome strikingly free from the infections he has been inveighing against. In *Antony and Cleopatra* romantic love revives, in *Coriolanus* marital fidelity, and with it the family.

It is the family spirit that saves Rome, after being subjected to a heavy ordeal, and ransoms our faith in humanity, which in every other sphere has been withering. It may be that Rome's future for long years will be one of social conflict; but this is at least something rational, open to the light of common day, promising an eventual emancipation. With this, Tragedy reaches its end.

In heroic drama, as in the world of action, men necessarily had to occupy a larger space than women. None the less, women have a significant part in every Shakespearian tragedy but one, the least finished or authentic; and their place, limited and mainly passive in the first two, is very important indeed in the last two. If we then ask ourselves what these plays have told us about women, or rather about how they appeared to a certain early seventeenth-century playwright, the answer must be that they tell us very much, if not so much as about men, whom he lived among and worked with and must have known better. It is equally natural that most of his concern is with how women feel and behave in relations with men. Westlund can fairly say that 'Shakespeare portrays the tragic potential of sexuality' more strongly than any wholesomer quality in it (186). Desdemona, Emilia, Regan, Lady Macduff and (undesignedly) Gertrude end by being murdered; Goneril, Cleopatra and her ladies, and probably Portia, Ophelia, Lady Macbeth, commit suicide. Those with will and opportunity to act on their own, or take the lead, and those who hold back, alike fare ill.

Cleopatra reveals to us less of her inner feelings, except when the end is near and Antony dead, than he does of his. His involvements are of course more complex and shifting; but Linda Bamber points out that the tragedy women in general seldom soliloquize, as the men often do (7–8). They have learned to keep their secrets, perhaps like some women known to or guessed at by Shakespeare. The same writer feels a morbid estrangement between man and woman, out of which he created some nightmarish females (2). These, however, are only to be found in two middle plays, where they partake of men's worst capabilities. A conventional counting up of 'good' and 'bad' women seems to leave a reassuring balance.

Lady Macbeth strikes another critic as unique in the Shakespearian gallery in taking part in crime yet remaining 'unaware of the moral reality of evil' (Boorman 222). Goneril, however, displays far more of what is repugnant in the 'new' or emancipated woman free to choose, with a streak of self-righteousness to cover it over, and a perverted kind of feminism which allows her to feel entitled to get rid of an uncongenial husband (who may not have been her choice) by having him murdered, and to poison her sister and rival in love. In a less malignant way Cleopatra is just as indifferent to textbook morality, which after all has been drawn up by men, largely in their own interests. Jacobean moralists were much given to warning husbands against being led astray by their wives (Watson 88). Macbeth is the prime example here, but Coriolanus, more pardonably, has been led astray since infancy by his mother. It is on the whole the case that women, excepting Portia in the first play, have either a bad influence on men or, like Calphurnia, Ophelia, Emilia, Octavia and Virgilia, none at all. Nor have women much influence on one another, it may be added; there are not many within reach, to be sure, until the last two dramas, in each of which one woman holds sway within a harmonious trio.

One aspect of the history of the family has been the effect on it of old age, that disfiguring change in wait for all its members. Lear found that age makes us 'unnecessary' to others. Shakespeare apparently considered old women unnecessary to tragedy, or a blemish on it. He brings in ladies of a certain age – Calphurnia, Gertrude, Cleopatra, Volumnia –, but none who show any worse mark of the years than Cleopatra's wrinkles. A historian of old age (Minois 286) has found that it was pictured in sixteenth-century European literature in an 'entirely negative', or unfavourable, way; though he notes that the bourgeois climate might be less harsh than the feudal. An aging man with money might stand his ground better than one dependent on ability to wield the sword or drive the plough. Shakespeare knew this, and was very careful of his savings. The best that writers could find to do for old age, Simone de Beauvoir comments, was to smother its realities under a conventional heap of phrases: the author of *King Lear* was a salient exception, and Lear is the only great tragic hero since Oedipus who is an old man (183–5). He bears witness to the sufferings of the poor, and is a living example of those of the aged and forsaken. Invoking the protection of the heavens, and crying out to them 'You yourselves are old' (II.iv.185–7), he pleads for all who share his misfortune.

In the early tragedies we have portraits of two successful public figures who have reached an age when they ought to be retiring, instead of hanging on. Their decrepitude, physical and mental, is depicted in cruel detail, Caesar's by Cassius and Polonius's by Hamlet. Shakespeare may have been growing conscious of his own years taking their toll. Caesar bolsters himself with magniloquent self-praise; Polonius likes to take prolix credit for his talents as a statesman. In all but the final drama a generation gap between older and younger is made significant use of. The youthful Antony running a race in the Roman games lives to be a grizzled veteran, outfought by 'the young Roman boy' Octavius (IV.xii.49). In *Timon* there is the breach between miserly old senators and ill-paid soldiers; this time it is not the old we are called on to feel for. Edmund voices the bitterness of a younger generation at being kept from its inheritance by 'the oppression of aged tyranny' (I.ii.51–2). In him and Lear we have perfect cases of the character, both individual and representative, of Shakespeare's creations: an old king brought low, an old order in decay, a young one impatient to supplant it.

7

Religion and Philosophy

Tragedy and religion have shared common roots, and common interests in life and death. In Shakespeare's lifetime religion meant chiefly the conflict of Reformation and Counter-Reformation, forces generated by trans-formations and disruptions of European life. New social formations, with their turmoil of hopes and fears, were taking shape, old ones ferociously defending themselves. Because England alone emerged as Protestant among the four countries taking the lead in drama – the others being France, Spain, Italy – Walter Cohen concludes that the theatre owed more to Renaissance than to Reformation (144). This may be true enough, except in the very special sphere of tragedy, where the English theatre had its greatest and unique strength. Smollett on his travels long afterwards had the insight to recognize the kinship of tragedy with the Calvinist spirit, comedy with the Catholic. None of the other countries was going through economic and political changes as profound as England's. Knappen's exploration of the Puritan tension, the endless self-inquisition (393), shows it running side by side with tragedy's wrestlings of conscience and ambition.

Many have looked for religious, and distinctively Christian, elements in Shakespearian tragedy. G.R. Elliott does not go too far in saying that while the poet is often critical of Christians he is never dismissive of Christianity (he could scarcely afford to be), though he looked at dogmatics with 'marked detachment' (viii). Speaight ventures further when he writes of Shakespeare, by small religious touches here and there, 're-establishing the harmony of his universe' (65). Siegel finds 'Christ figures' like Cordelia through whom he can be heard 'expressing a Christian outlook on life', even if this does not warrant a 'Christian interpretation' of the plays as a whole (34–5; cf. Dollimore 189–90). Another reader cites Macbeth's words about the loss of his 'eternal jewel', or soul, as proof of something surviving in him from his earlier self (Mack 169). Cavell catches 'Christian stirrings and murmurings under the surface' even of Coriolanus ('Coriolanus' 246). Othello vows to tell the Doge how his marriage came about, 'as truly as to heaven' he confesses his sins (I.iii.122–3).

Harry Levin (*Revolution* 91 ff.) rejects G. Wilson Knight's 'mystagogical' teachings, and agrees with Bradley and R.M. Frye in thinking Shakespeare's outlook essentially secular. All the same he finds in the tragedies an 'unremitting quest for justice . . . a higher morality, a tragic ethos' (41–2). Morality by itself, Marilyn French says, does not make literature, but moral grandeur, recognition of the ability of individuals to rise above narrow egotism, are an important element, and are to be found nowhere more richly than in *King Lear* (335). Creech discusses interestingly three religious plays from the fifteenth century, two of them concerned with temptation, as having remarkable likenesses to passages in *Othello*, *King Lear*, *Macbeth*; a 'Shakespearian atavism' not to be found in any other writer of his time (7–9).

Shakespeare was drawn, affectionately or not, to everything steeped in the colours and odours of the past, old words, proverbs, songs; they as well as newer things of his lifetime were part of what went into his magic cauldron. Religion was as old as anything else. 'I do in part believe it', he might have said, as his cautious Horatio says of one popular tenet; but only in the most general way. In his practical approach to life he was fundamentally a secularist; or he might be called a Deist, born before his time. Unlike most of his Europe, and its governments, he felt no need of religion as a bond to hold men together – or had no faith in its ability to do so, in default of harmonious social relationships. We may regard this as one expression of his realism, his instinct for veracity and the stripping away of all disguises and pretences.

His interest was in ethics, not in theology, and Christian ethics had an undoubted attraction for him, even if he felt morality to be at bottom an outgrowth of men's mutual needs, rather than something brought to them from outside. What Knights calls 'fundamentally Christian values', at odds with mindless 'Nature' (90–91), might be better called simply human values, social virtues. It must be added that in his mind, as well as in official religion, Christian ethics were often intertwined with an opposite creed of feudal chivalry and war. But from the fanaticism so rampant in Europe he must have been as far removed as any man could be. This may be supposed to have coloured his feeling about the rival priestly corporations responsible for stirring up intolerance. There is no place in these tragedies for the amiable 'Friars' of earlier plays. Only one divine appears, the 'churlish priest' who angers Laertes by refusing religious rites over his sister's grave (V.i.205 ff.); we can see him either as an embodiment of bigotry, or as a man faithfully performing a stern duty. Brutus alludes to priests in the same breath with cowards and deceivers (II.i.129), and Caesar sends orders to his 'priests' for a heathenish sacrifice (II.ii.5). English clergymen of Tudor times had been too easily ready to swear allegiance to whatever government and creed were in the ascendant.

Loyalties were hardening now, and James began his reign by ejecting a number of Puritan pastors who were too uncompromising. Shakespeare must have respected these men, and have had a high regard for those with a social as well as a theological conscience. There were preachers bold enough to declare, as Lear does (IV.vi.164–6), that poor men were trapped by the law while great men could snap their fingers at it (Knappen 345; cf. 223, 256–7, 389). Burton says the same (II.230–31). Equally Shakespeare must have detested hypocritical pretences of goodness, as he did painted cheeks. 'Thou perjured, and thou simular of virtue', Lear exclaims (III.ii.54). Polonius blushes at his trick of setting Ophelia to pretend to be reading a book of devotions; and the listening Claudius winces at his words (III.i.46 ff.). When religion is compulsory, there will be much bogus religion. In Shakespeare's day this was not all Puritan, but Puritanism was the most sanctimonious kind of piety; and demure Puritans, if they listened to some of his speeches, might well wince like Hamlet's uncle.

Religion, philosophy, superstition, run into and out of one another in the works of this period, their boundaries seldom distinct. A shadow of the uncanny hangs over several plays. Brabantio complains that his daughter has been stolen from him by 'spells and medicines', or black magic (I.iii.60 ff.). The Doge seems to take this quite seriously until he learns that Othello, Venice's indispensable general, is the man accused; he then dismisses such charges as 'thin habits and poor likelihoods of modern seeming' (I.iii.108–9). We may welcome a chance to count Shakespeare among the disbelievers in the witchcraft supposedly plaguing England and Europe, and its Satanic connections. His Scottish play could not do without its witches, just as his Danish play needed its ghost; but it is permissible to guess that he wanted and expected his more intelligent auditors to recognize the dead Caesar, visible to no one on the stage except Brutus, like the dead Banquo seen only by Macbeth, as a hallucination of a troubled mind.

Far more prominent are the signs and portents accompanying great events, or appearing to be connected with them. As a poet Shakespeare was attracted to the residue of ancient thinking for which earth and sky, men and animals, were all parts of one cosmic whole, so that events in the human sphere might be echoed on other planes. Intellectually he may have been undecided; it can be seen from Burton's *Anatomy* that intelligent men could have an open mind on the subject. Commonly it was the death of a ruler that was thus trumpeted to the world; Cassius is an innovator in seizing on the storm and its accompaniments in Rome as good omens instead for his revolutionary cause (I.iii.59 ff.). They have all the same a rather artificial, over-elaborate air – a whole catalogue of marvels, phantom squadrons manoeuvring in the sky –, as if Shakespeare was trying to make his audience take them more seriously than he did himself.

Caesar speaks in a recognizably religious vein when he declares that events so heralded are always (like his own triumphant career, doubtless) 'purpos'd by the mighty gods' (II.ii.25–6). Casca's mind too turns to 'the most mighty gods', and an angered heaven ready to destroy a corrupt earth (I.iii.11 ff.). Caesar's hope of getting a child by means of a piece of mumbo-jumbo at the Lupercalia festival, on the other hand, is no more than superstition (I.ii.6 ff.). So is Gloucester's easy faith in Edmund's tale about his brother 'mumbling of wicked charms' (II.i.39), or Cassius's pessimistic interpretation of the fall of a pair of eagles (V.i.79–81). And Cassius was formerly sceptical of omens, and jibed at Caesar for having 'superstitious grown of late' (II.i.195).

In the opening scene of *Hamlet* Horatio recalls the portents attending Caesar's death, and says that Denmark, since the Ghost's first appearance, is suffering from similar visitations. Except for 'dews of blood', they are of a more naturalistic sort, like comets and eclipses. This shift is continued; storms become an integral part of the drama. Early in *Othello* a storm at sea wrecks the Turkish fleet; the tempest buffeting Lear's body, the madness invading his mind, seem to belong to one and the same sphere. In *Macbeth* there is a somewhat perfunctory return to the freakish, with horses devouring one another, in addition to storm and eclipse. More impressive are the strange 'lamentings' in the air, and 'prophesying' of calamities (II.iii.56–9), which go better with the inner turmoil of men's minds, Macbeth's especially after the murder.

An Act of 1606 prohibited mention on the stage of God and other sacred matters. Pagan deities had to provide a poetic substitute, and scattered through the plays are a multitude of invocations, not all of them trivially conventional, of gods, heaven, Providence, fate. They express, as Bradshaw says, very heterogeneous notions (88). Everyday religion in England was in a jumbled state. It is most often in tones of bewilderment, despair of human ability to understand divine intentions, that Shakespeare's characters now lift their voices to the gods, very different from the ringing confidence of Henry V bespeaking the services of God and St George. Many of the gods appealed to seem to have little tangible existence, and least of all in *King Lear*: they are figures of speech, ancestral outcries of suffering extorted by the way human beings treat one another. Heaven is evolving into a poetic fiction, an addition to the remnants of archaic thought which, as Engels saw, have formed the primary material of poetry.

Amid these kaleidoscopic images two overarching kinds stand out. One is of pagan deities no less irresponsible than man himself; the other, more intermittent, is a higher ethical conception clothed in the form of an emergent Providence. Taken all together, the chorus is incoherent, and heaven a shadowy abode. In English tragedy at large, as Clifford Leech writes (291), gods if any were assumed to be remote from mankind; it seems hardly plausible to say, with J. Stampfer (153), that in *King Lear* the question of God's ways to men becomes 'a key issue'. None the less, in some fundamental way all tragedy may be thought of as mankind's complaint against heaven, or the universe man finds himself in. It reveals, at least, an absence from this universe of any will, or any sufficient power and wisdom, to regulate human affairs satisfactorily. A 'grand remonstrance' like this could only be muffled and oblique when governments and Churches would regard it as tantamount to a complaint against *them*. No authentic tragedy grew up in the Spain of the Inquisition.

Hamlet feels that he is being prompted to his revenge by heaven and hell (II.ii.537). Heaven must want Claudius punished, hell must be impatient to begin his punishment. Between the two of them, this play has far more of a religious atmosphere than any of the others. It is emphasized by the awkward though useful presence of a ghost on leave from a Catholic purgatory, with his terrifying half-words about the life to come. Hamlet seems unable to contemplate death, though willing to face it, with a Roman's unmoved indifference: one of the attractions that Roman settings had for Shakespeare may have been this attitude to death. Even casual touches can add to the religious presence, like the phrase 'devoutly to be wished', where other adverbs would do as well.

Yet essentially the drama stands outside religion, as tragic drama must. This paradox involves Shakespeare in palpable inconsistencies and confusions, which Bradshaw points to as flaws (121–3). They are, however, part of what has made this play part of the European mind. It is a monument left by an age full of conflicting ideas, fragments of a crumbling world jostling with beginnings of a new one. Hamlet's fear, not of death but of what may come after, cannot be merely an excuse he is offering himself, like his reluctance to kill Claudius at his prayers. He *knows*, if he knows anything, that there is an after-life; but Shakespeare's habitual scepticism makes him stumble over the fact.

Hamlet professes respect for God's ban on suicide, but takes no account of any ban on retributive killing: for the man of honour revenge is a duty. It seems at times as if Shakespeare is deliberately laying bare the contradictions within accepted morality. Laertes' prompt action argues for the legitimacy of revenge; his being applauded and egged on by the murderer Claudius casts doubt on it, and so still more does the ease with which an honourable young man is diverted into a plot repulsive from either a Christian or a gentlemanly point of view.

Again, Hamlet shows some sporadic faith in a Providence whose inscrutable purposes can rescue human affairs from being entirely haphazard; but he cannot rest content to leave his uncle's prosecution to it. He finds its guiding hand in his success in sending Guildenstern and Rosencrantz to their deaths, chiefly perhaps because this allows him to shake off his own responsibility. But he ought, then, to see this hand in the death of Polonius too: instead, as his mother assures us, he 'weeps for what is done' (IV.i.27).

However guided, Hamlet's actions have not advanced, and in some ways have hindered, the carrying out of his mission. He does not consider the possibility that Providence disapproves of it. His faith really seems to amount to little beyond lapses into fatalism which overcome him when he is feeling impotent in a bad world ruled by secret forces. When circumstances force or provoke him into a fit of readiness to act, a state of mind to him unnatural, he has an illusory sense of a power outside himself animating and employing him: he shares its superhuman energy. This has happened on his voyage, and on his return he is simply waiting for it to happen again, as it finally does.

By contrast with *Hamlet*, in *Macbeth* religion divides neatly between the wicked, who have almost completely discarded it, and the virtuous, some of them already half-way to heaven. Any prospect of being called to account in another world, Macbeth is ready to brush aside and, like Laertes, 'dare damnation' (*Mac.* I.vii.1 ff.; *Ham.* IV.v.135). His nightmares and his wife's are a revulsion from what they have done, not fear of anything to come after death. Over against them are the 'most sainted' Duncan, the memory of his prayerful queen, and the far-away English king with his miraculous gifts (IV.iii.108–11, 141 ff.). Such formalized Christian dedication is a feature of this play alone.

Of the 'pagan' tragedies *King Lear* is the most 'religious', though in an even more incoherent way than *Hamlet*. It is so mainly from an ethical stand-point, in Lear's painful realization of how dim are the lights by which he has lived his life. We hear continually of the gods, among them Jupiter and Apollo: all the native deities are anonymous. But attempts to piece together a pattern of belief have not got far: each character conceives the gods after his own fashion and mood (Snyder 57–8). It is interesting nevertheless to notice what epithets or attributes are bestowed on them: good qualities that mankind may be thought lacking in, or, more rarely, bad qualities that men are all too well stocked with. They are omnipotent: Gloucester submits to their 'great opposeless wills' (IV.vi.38). They are incorruptible: Edgar thinks of 'the clearest gods', Lear of the 'clear heavens' (IV.vi.73, IV.iii.27). Hence they are the true dispensers of justice, with stern retribution for the wicked. They are 'the revenging gods' (II.i.45); they are 'just', Edgar reminds his dying brother (V.iii.169 ff.); Albany hearing of Cornwall's death gives thanks to the gods as 'justicers' (IV.ii.78 ff.). Those in trouble like to think that heaven will pity them. Gloucester cries out to the 'ever-gentle gods', Cordelia to the 'kind gods' (IV.vi.215; IV.vii.15).

These tributes come from well-meaning, if misguided, unfortunates; hardened wrong-doers feel no need of gods, and show very little interest in them. Edmund parodies all the pathetic appeals of sufferers with his cynical: 'Now, gods, stand up for bastards!' (I.ii.22). Among believers, notions fluctuate between what man wishes heaven to be, and what he fears it is. It is also Gloucester who says that the gods 'kill us for their sport' (IV.i.36–7).

He has sinned, and heavenly kindness does not it seems extend to pardon. At times amid all this it may appear that there are some benevolent deities, and some malevolent. But though they are always addressed in the plural (if only to free the author from any imputation of making free with the Christian God), they seem always to act with a single will. The cumulative impression is of a supernal power conceived by purblind men under many different aspects, but on the whole remote, mysterious, unavailing. Humanity is looking at its own shadow, cast gigantically on the clouds. It is the warring kings of the earth who kill humble folk for their sport, as thoughtlessly as boys kill flies. Only in calm unquestioning times when people know what to expect of life, and what is expected of them, can orderly relations between earth and heaven prevail.

There is no single inspired character in *King Lear* to lead us to the play's meaning (Goldberg 43). In times of change, of social and moral disturbance, no monopoly of truth can be expected in any quarter of the compass, and certainly Shakespeare cannot be supposed to claim it. Rather, we can look for a new vision of right and wrong coming from 'the humble, the scorned, and the exiled' (Heilman, *Lear* 221). What we are accustomed to call 'character-development' can be better thought of as expansion of self-consciousness, under external pressures, bringing to light things that have lain dormant within a personality, and through them spreading to an audience a heightened awareness of life. Shakespeare's most striking manifestation of this is the awakening in Lear of human sympathies which must have existed in him but hitherto had been buried.

'I will have such revenges on you both', he had cried in fury against his daughters (II.iv.275); but this vindictiveness is challenged by his dawning comprehension of others' adversities. We can think of his contrition over his treatment of Cordelia as mingled with repentance for his neglect of what he owed to his people. Revenge comes up over and over again in the tragedies; Shakespeare must have been drawn to it as a central problem of moral and civic conduct, but he could not put his heart into a story of revenge or revengefulness for its own sake. For justification they must depend on how far they could identify themselves with any public benefit. In *King Lear* we witness the birth of this new principle, but only by the first faint rays of daybreak. There is very little in the play's happenings to warrant M.D.H. Parker's assertion that its keynote is 'justice, mercy, sacrifice and redemption' (135). There is equally little in *Othello* to suggest Kernan's sequence of 'sin, repentance and salvation' (*Playwright* 115).

Somewhere in the borderland between religion and superstition is the realm of Fate, which shows its veiled face in innumerable junctures. It invaded religion in the Calvinist guise of predestination, a doctrine generally subscribed to, as Patrick Collinson makes clear, in the Anglican Church known to Shakespeare (81 ff.,etc.). Luther too had firmly denied freedom of the will. Shakespeare's tragic writing was drawing to a close when in 1609 the great Arminian controversy broke on the Protestant world. From then on free will was gaining ground in England, though not in Scotland, but questions about it, or its absence, had already been in the air. There would have been a sprinkling of amateur theologians in theatre audiences, and predestination finds its way into unexpected corners of the tragedies. Caesar is echoing the Almighty when he proclaims that no persuasion can ever alter his 'pre-ordinance and first decree' (III.i.36 ff.). 'There be souls must be saved', Cassio stammers tipsily, 'and there be souls must not be saved' (II.iii.106–7).

Drama may be said to have a natural predisposition in favour of some degree of free will, for if we take a plot to be unfolding under mechanical compulsion, dramatic interest can only be minimal. In his own kingdom of the stage Shakespeare would appear to believe in freedom of the will, within fluctuating limits. Twice in *Julius Caesar* the thought occurs that men can bend fate, or events, to their will if they apply their energies properly. Cassius maintains that human exertion can, sometimes at least, be decisive; Brutus agrees, on condition of the right moment being seized when it offers (I.ii.139; IV.iii.217 ff.). In another mood he can sound fatalistic enough. As with Hamlet, activity generates faith in the possibility of action. It is a matter of resolve, in Lady Macbeth's words, of screwing one's courage to the sticking-place (III.i.99–100).

Responsibility for one's own doings must be reckoned part of Shakespeare's creed, as it was, Calvinism notwithstanding, of the more boldly advancing men and women of his era. When he talks of fate, Empsom remarked, there is always 'a fairly clear suggestion that it stands for an excuse' (152; cf. 243). Shakespeare's men and women make their own fates (Stauffer 165). 'The fault is not in our stars' if we submit to tyranny, Cassius urges on Brutus (I.ii.140–41). Edmund derides as 'an admirable evasion' men's habit of blaming Fortune, or the stars, when things go wrong, instead of trying to set them right (I.ii.129 ff.). Freedom of the will goes with success and confidence; moods of failure undermine it. 'Who can control his fate?' asks Othello, about to die (V.ii.265). In common-sense terms, men may choose one course or another, but the upshot will depend a good deal on circumstances. Octavius commiserates with his sister on her desertion by Antony –

> But let determined [fated] things to destiny
> Hold unbewailed their way,

and he is already framing new plans to meet a new situation (III.vi.84–5).

To a man like him words or thoughts are meaningless unless followed by action. But action once taken, whether it turns out well or ill, cannot be cancelled. No writer has surpassed Shakespeare in capturing the sensation of action – a deed directly, physically performed –, the kind of vertigo that may precede it, the overwhelming realization of its being irreversible, and its consequences unknown. It may be from nervous overstrain, or a momentary intuition of failure to come, that Brutus and Cassius have no sooner carried out their great deed than they fall into self-communings about 'the Fates' and their 'pleasures', and about killing as the conferring of a blessing (III.i. 99 ff.). They are bewildered by their own achievement, and the apocalyptic quality of their deed, felt as if in a vivid dream.

An impression of some power shaping the outcome of men's under-takings can arise from the movement of history, the growth of events out of a multiplicity of previous happenings, in a way apparently, in retrospect, logical. Shakespeare had spent much time poring over history and trying to extract its meaning. His language and imagery show him thinking of it not in mechanical terms but as a natural, organic development. Iago is in good company in talking of 'events in the womb of time', or a criminal plan reaching its 'monstrous birth' (I.iii.353–4, 386). Time has its 'seeds', Banquo questioning the witches says, and to learn what is to come one must know 'which grain will grow and which will not' (I.iii.58–9).

Mixed up with sequences of causes and effects are the accidents that plague historians, occurrences that have their own causes but no logical connection with other series of events which they may influence. Shakespeare's men and women are apt to feel their intrusive strength most heavily as the end draws near, when they can seem like fabrications of fate. Cassius's suicide leads Messalla to reflect gloomily on the harm done by errors which can make us fancy we see 'The things that are not' (V.iii.67–70). Human beings have always wanted to believe in the existence of truths exempt, unlike the rest of the universe, from decay or interruption. Cleopatra lives to discover that the sole refuge, the deed 'Which shackles accidents and bolts up change', is to die. She and Antony, almost alone among the beings of the great dramas, catch sight in the distance of another realm, of pagan myth, waiting to welcome them (IV.xiv.51–4; V.ii.282–6); but this, even for them, can be no more than a dream, a way of making their last farewells. What is left is the 'eternal night' of the Histories.

Horatio looks back over events in Denmark as a medley of 'accidental judgments' and 'purposes mistook' (V.ii.359 ff.). Mehl calls this 'a catalogue of traditional revenge tragedy clichés' (30). It cannot indeed constitute the inner essence of the tragedy, but it stands for a real part of the working out, and to this also Shakespeare was acutely sensitive. Horatio might almost be recalling the lament of the player-king about how our intentions are baffled – 'Our thoughts are ours, their ends none of our own' (III.ii.193–4). Hamlet's more high-sounding 'divinity that shapes our ends' (V.ii.10) may come to much the same thing.

In comedy chance, coincidence, random decision, have a larger part to play, as they do in daily life. But Macbeth is only enthralled by prophecies of witches he happens to meet because they fit the secret ambitions already gnawing him. Much in comedy is quite external to the men and women concerned; tragic destiny is far more a part of our selves, or is grafted on to them. It may be more comprehensible, or less. In two plays, *Hamlet* and *King Lear*, the accidental has an exceptionally powerful influence, and stamps on them the aspect of a world relapsing into chaos, of men bereft of all familiar moorings, swept away on uncharted currents; a world where mankind is unequal to the tasks imposed on it by history. England in other words was being sucked, as Shakespeare could see or feel in advance of most others, into a historical vortex. Tragedy was a flux of forces old and new in conflict, very unlike the relatively static setting of a single day neatly unrolled in the French theatre.

Religion, or any willingness to accept the unproven, is counterposed to 'philosophy', or what came to be 'natural philosophy', or science. Western Europe was setting its feet on the twisting road towards secular rationalism, and new modes of thinking were invading old ones and engendering hybrid offspring. Astrology was becoming a more elaborate pseudo-science, theology more and more highly intellectualized. Brutus and Cassius lead the way as thinkers, and readers, though men of strong feelings too. It is a tribute to intellectuals that Caesar can think Cassius so dangerous (I.ii.21 ff.), as such men have been to many governments since his time.

In *Hamlet* reason and mystery are in sharp conflict. Hamlet is another intellectual, though the apparition of his father compels him to admit that there must be 'more things in heaven and earth' than philosophy dreams of (I.v.166–7). He deplores the way a single fault, 'breaking down the forts and pales of reason', can disfigure a whole personality (I.iv.23 ff.). He denounces his mother for behaving no better than a beast, lacking 'discourse of reason' (I.ii.150). His uncle too makes good use of the word, being anxious to pass for a very reasonable man and ruler. He censures Hamlet's excessive grief as contrary to 'reason', and assures Laertes, self-importantly, that his royal ear will always be open to any request with 'reason' on its side (I.ii.44, 103). Ophelia bewails the collapse of Hamlet's 'noble mind', his loss of 'that noble and most sovereign reason' (III.i.153 ff.).

Tragedy confronts men and women, always abruptly, with many pitfalls and perils. Wrestlings between emotional attachment and dispassionate reason are likely to break out in any time of tumultuous change. Men's need of reason to hold passion in check was an Elizabethan commonplace. It implied a dichotomy, going back to Plato, between their social, civilized selves and their instinctual natures. Another truism was that passion might overwhelm good sense with startling swiftness (Beckerman 145). In Hamlet's directions to the players as to how they should behave on the stage (III.ii.1 ff.) we may be reading also Shakespeare's ideal of how men ought to behave on the stage of life: they should be ardent, animated, full of vitality, yet always keep emotion under the wardenship of good sense, instead of letting it run riot. Man's hold on reason is precarious, only a step separates him from the breakdown that Hamlet, like Lear, feels close to. And this insecurity takes on an expanded form in the illusory solidity, the actual instability, of social existence. Hamlet's dilemmas are insoluble; under their conflicting pressures he is hurrying, or being hurried, towards destruction.

A secure ruling class takes for granted that the existing arrangement of society is, if not perfect, the best possible. It is Reason made flesh; so that any tampering with it must be senseless as well as harmful. When another class is ready to compete for the hegemony, it too will claim the sanction of Reason; much confusion will ensue. No hero after Hamlet is a true intellectual, though Octavius has a fair claim to the title. Othello, Antony, Coriolanus, all have a positive aversion to being compelled to think. Macbeth and Timon share the same simplicity, of men with an immense overplus of feeling and energy. Reason cannot liberate men from their old selves, or from convictions estimable but grown irrational through their archaic associations. It must be counted part of the kernel of Shakespearian tragedy that after the first two dramas the baffled reasoning faculty is relegated from the camp of the good to that of the unworthy, men and women ready to throw away idealism and take the path of egotistic self-advancement.

Reason is mankind's glory, but it is turning against humanity. In any such era of rapid change intelligence is likely to travel on a separate line from moral progress, and often more quickly. It is the new man, the careerist carving out his way to fortune, who has most need to rely on his wits. Iago is a very clever man cast in the worst mould of warped puritanism, who extols reason as a check on the animal passions, but not on other passions like jealousy, hatred, revengefulness. There are women too whose brains only serve them to attack or gain control over others. Goneril and Regan are among them. Hawkes sees Lady Macbeth as 'the major "reasoner"' of her play, even though not of a high grade of intelligence (141). Her mind does not support her for long, and clear-sighted egotism does not keep Goneril and Regan from falling in love and quarrelling. Side by side with reason, Nature suffers some declensions. It is 'The multiplying villainies of nature' that have made a villain and traitor of Macdonwald (I.ii.11). 'Thou, Nature, art my goddess', are almost the first words we hear from Edmund (I.ii.1).

Somerset Maugham observed that, in defiance of modern 'realism' and its rules, life is fundamentally erratic or freakish: Othello is simply the most 'wildly irrational' person in his circle (291–2). Only a specious reasonableness is spread over social life by its conventions and restraints. All tragedy, it may be said – like all war –, hovers not far from the brink of madness, because of its intensity of excitement, its hurricane release of explosive feeling long pent up. Hamlet pretends to be mad, and at times may not be far removed from madness. Lear goes out of his mind. So does Lady Macbeth, having failed to heed her own warning to Macbeth that for them to think too long and agonizingly about what they have done 'will make us mad' (II.ii.33–4). 'Some say he's mad', we hear later of Macbeth (V.ii.3). Othello the African has a sort of hysteric or epileptic seizure, and we may be meant to see him, towards the end, as a man half-frantic. Antony in his decline and fall rages like a madman – and boasts of having been the slayer, or vanquisher, of 'the mad Brutus' (III.xi.37–8). Coriolanus is an unbalanced fanatic. These men and women have followed fantasies which they became unable to disentangle from reality, and which deepen our sense of a human race infected by insanity. Yet amid all this there is sometimes, perhaps always, a gleam of the 'Reason in madness' that Edgar hears in Lear's ravings (IV.vi.174). The tragic, like the mystic, vision may pierce through the false surface of daily life and its language, into the inner, more real scenery of the mind.

Passion may reveal the individual; equally it may be said to blot out too often the true or better self, as jealousy does in Othello or ambition in Macbeth. An undercurrent in these dramas carries us towards something like a philosophy of self-control, endurance, fortitude, not to be subdued by any assault of fate. These are the gifts admired by Hamlet, who lacks them, in his friend Horatio (III.ii.53 ff.), whose emotional side is revealed only at the very end when the time comes for him to act. Othello had been admired for his impregnable firmness. 'Is this the nature whom passion could not shake?' Lodovico exclaims, astonished by a revelation of the hero's hidden self (IV.i.276–7).

This philosophy of Shakespeare's is not the ascetic puritan's ideal, or Iago's, of a dictatorial will enslaving human nature, as something separate and lower. It is rather a calm acceptance, when no resistance to misfortune is possible, of the unknowable and uncontrollable. It is not a retreat into an isolated self, but unites the individual with his fellows. One of its watchwords is 'patience'. 'Be ever known to patience', Octavius advises his sister at the end of their colloquy (III.vi.98). 'Bear free and patient thoughts', Edgar bids his blind father (IV.vi.80).

8

Endings and Beginnings

Poetic genius is kindled most brightly by the flint and steel of a divided mind, microcosm of a divided society. Tragic poetry more than any other kind belongs, as Raymond Williams said, to periods between social stability and eruption (*Modern Tragedy* 54). Europe had always been changing, but about 1600 change was accelerating, in England most of all. Hopes, doubts, fears, resentments, had a rank growth, as social shifts were kept in motion by a complex of economic innovations. In many minds they could be transposed into theological refinements; in others there was an unresolved struggle with irreconcilables.

The tragic spirit never wears the same mask in two Shakespearian dramas. Their diversity is a reminder that his conceptions of tragedy must have been evolving throughout. With his deep roots in the past, his instinctive response to change was one of regret for the vanishing of whatever of the past was once precious to men. Like Macduff he 'cannot but remember such things were' (IV.iii.222). He thought of Time, as India has thought of the goddess Kali, as both destroyer and renewer; but most often and poignantly it was 'Time's fell hand' at work on all creations of the past that came into his mind, as in Sonnet 64. Yet his use of terms like 'necessity' often betoken a recognition of change as a central strand of life. He like Beethoven might have written over his work the motto 'Must it be? – It must be.'

If his ideal hope was for an auspicious blending of old and new, in a society and culture that would join the virtues of both, he must often have seen looming up the less rosy prospect of an exchange of bad features, between a gentry growing mercenary and a merchantry growing gentrified, and new generations inheriting old maladies from the past. In any profound social mutation the forces at work must be complex and irregular; and the tragic conflict could not be between two well-ordered forces. It was a contest over the fate of civilization, with good and ill at odds on both sides. Nothing less than this could be fuel enough for the tragic blaze.

Antony's death calls up the Shakespearian thought of a world cracking, its elements flying apart. A hero's overthrow is the more portentous because it is not solely defeat by forces outside him; there is civil war within. He has come to be isolated by the collapse of the world he belongs to, and he himself is one cause of its downfall, as it is of his. Individual antagonisms are surface expressions of divisions which are rending the social whole and must go on, Macbeth is driven to think, 'even till destruction sicken' (IV.i.60). In one critic's 'metaphysical world', outside the limits of the social, what counts most is the harm men do to themselves, not to their fellows (Sewell 76). But any such distinction is unreal. Macbeth ruins himself; he ruins Scotland.

We all recognize something of ourselves in the hero and his destiny; we too feel as if we were part of a realm in peril, and are lifted above ourselves in a renewal of the human community. Men are being called on by history to learn and to unlearn: the tragic hero is one who has most difficulty in facing this need, and still clings to the past, either to its higher self like Brutus, or to its worse impulses like Macbeth. He cannot survive the shock of collision with a new reality, of finding everything round him grown strange to his expectations; but he may learn much during his ordeal. Hamlet is a learner from the outset. Lear is too old, and soon half-crazed, to learn or teach in any regular fashion. Clemen notes that some of his utterances are simply images standing by themselves (134). We might call them momentary visions; but these glimpses of truth are mixed with hankerings for revenge, a vision of rushing on his enemies at the head of a band armed with 'red burning spits' (III.vi.15-16). Yet in face of the alien, hostile universe of storm and barren heath we are carried back, or forward, into remote times before human beings were divided against one another, or after their divisions have ceased. How this is to be translated from poetry into social reality we still know little better than those who thronged Shakespeare's theatre.

Tragedy must end in death, to the hero more often than not welcome, or sought by him, though to those round him cataclysmic. Vanishings of men and women of such superabundant vitality might seem unbelievable. Antony has to repeat the word 'dead' three times before Enobarbus can grasp that Fulvia is no more (I.ii.157 ff.); when Antony is given the false news of Cleopatra's death it is the messenger who has to repeat it (IV.xiv.34-7). It is above all in their final moments that hero or heroine are mankind's orators. Cleopatra's dying scene comes as close to the miraculous as anything Shakespeare ever wrote. She is lifted up high above her old self, transfigured by love and death. It is a mark of Shakespeare being ready to turn away from tragedy that Coriolanus's last speech shows him still no more than his old raging, hating self.

In tragi-comedy, coming into fashion while these dramas were being written, deserving characters could be surprisingly rescued at the end, and life could go on as before. In genuine tragedy heroes must perish, because an epoch of history, to which they belong, is coming to an end. To say that with the deaths of Lear and Cordelia 'our sense of order is for ever shattered' (Adelman 9) is a failure to recognize this. Life will go on, but only the collective, and this will be transformed. As Tillyard (14) saw, and Nietzsche earlier, the necessity of one condition of things, good in some ways, perishing to make room for another, is 'a fundamental tragic fact of all human life'.

In the tragic close there is, then, acceptance both of death and, in one sense or another, of life. It is clearest in *Julius Caesar*: the republicans have done their simple duty, and are ready for their last journey. Thoughts of Providence have brought no peace of mind to Hamlet; 'how ill all's here about my heart', he has confessed to Horatio (V.ii.186). But he dies with at least the first step of his mission, Claudius's death, accomplished, and one friend prepared to die with him, or to live and speak for him. Othello's self-command gives way when he falls into fury, talks of 'revenge', calls his wife a 'strumpet' (V.ii.75, 78): he recovers when he is made to know that she was innocent, because this means that, although he has thrown happiness away, his short life with her was not a miserable deception. And she has tried with her dying breath to shield her husband (V.ii.125–6). It is a reconciliation of the dying with the dead, mingled in his last speech with memories of the splendid Venice he has splendidly served.

Through his wife's death Macbeth understands finally that all life is mere toil and delusion (V.v.19 ff.): which we must take not in a nihilistic sense, but as meaning that all *his* life, since he gave way to temptation, has been worthless. He has not lost his feeling of how rich the rewards of an honourable life can be (V.iii.24–5). What Antony has learned is not unlike Macbeth's experience: it can be heard in his dying words that we must 'bid that welcome which comes to punish us' (IV.iv.136–7).

Reconciliation with life can only be reached, it seems, under the seal of death. Tragedy by its 'revolutionary' nature excludes compromise: the dominant antagonism, once unleashed, must go on to the bitter end. There is no room for comedy's facile making-friends. But 'life' must be represented by some human being who has been dear to the one departing – as Lady Macbeth has been to her husband, however tortured Macbeth's farewell to her. Lear has been called the first of the heroes to die unreconciled, indifferent to mankind (Stampfer 156). Really, however, his estrangement from it has ended with his forgiveness by Cordelia; his reunion with one living being is also his reception into human fellowship, even though this is fated to last only a few hours. Another kind of love ends as quickly and immortally in *Antony and Cleopatra*. In former heedless days Antony was giving his mistress only a part of himself, and the less worthy part, which was all she asked for; and he could desert her when ambition called. What had been for both of them frivolous self-indulgence is ennobled by acceptance of death, through which they give themselves to each other entirely. And life is ennobled by proof that there are men and women who will not cling to it on terms unworthy of them.

Between heroes and others too there can be a coming together, if these others share something at least of their nobility of nature. When both are dying Hamlet exchanges forgiveness with Laertes, whose pardon he has sought before the fencing-match, and whose conscience has troubled him during it (V.ii.274) and perhaps caused him to come off second best. Othello realizes how unjustly he has suspected Cassio. Edgar and his dying brother 'exchange charity' (V.iii.167), and Edmund is moved to an attempt, too late, to undo some of his mischief. Brutus's enemies can speak magnanimously of him over his dead body, and Octavius and his allies over the dead Antony. All these men have a fellow-feeling, as members of the Roman governing class; but a foreigner, Aufidius, can feel admiration again for Coriolanus after trampling on his corpse. These scenes and their poignant last words raise the dramas above any self-centred feelings, to a universal plane; they leave us inspired by a conviction that all men are, or at least were born to be, brothers. Humanity is in search of its soul.

Every hero takes leave of us with dignity, nearly always sword in hand, or the sword only just relinquished. He may have lost everything outwardly, but he is still his indestructible self, the more firmly because so much of the illusory has been shed. He perishes, mankind will go on, somehow enriched by his memory as well as awed; he dies wanting this to happen. Antony hopes that at least he and his sword 'will earn our chronicle' (III.xiii.175). Debating with himself whether or not it is time for him to abandon his leader, Enobarbus reflects that loyalty, even on the losing side, 'earns a place i' the story' (III.xiii.46); Hamlet and Othello both desire their lives to be faithfully recorded.

These are reasons for not thinking of Shakespearian tragedy as blankly pessimistic, even if Schopenhauer must be allowed to have been at least half right when he thought of it as overflowing with all earth's miseries, under the sway of chance and error 'personified as fate' (I.253). He might have quoted Apemantus's sombre words about Athens turning into a forest of wild beasts, or Albany's about the human race growing as ferocious as sea-monsters (TA IV.iii.346–7; KL IV.ii.49–50). We are left between despair of life as it is and faith in a possible better future. Tragedy would have no meaning if it ended without both these lessons. Nor can we be consoled for our own troubles, like Lucrece staring at a picture of the Trojan war (1576 ff.), by the spectacle of worse things undergone by others.

Tragedy throws emphasis on the costliness of any human advances, the sacrifices they exact, the loss often of the most richly gifted human beings. This haunted Engels as a historian; Shakespeare may well have reached the same tragic view of history and progress through his study of England's past. Now he was pondering the same harsh truth in a more concentrated form. Death was his dark lantern; it seems to be part of tragic necessity that whatever departs from the beaten path must prove itself by readiness for sacrifice, or self-sacrifice, or both. We, the survivors, can feel as much impressed by its living memory as by its dead self. Though ruins of grandeur litter the earth, Shakespeare never seems to have lost all faith in the reservoir of human qualities which may enable man to guard himself against snares and ambuscades. About the future he tells us very little; his business was to transform or amplify the lurking impulses he was conscious of round him into vivid drama. But some process of social creation, we are allowed to feel, is still at work.

Bradley blamed Hegel for not recognizing that tragedy like Shakespeare's often ends in 'exultation' mingling with pain; the hero has never appeared so noble as in his death (*Poetry* 83–4). Wilson Knight too, arguing that Shakespearian tragedy is not 'in essence pessimistic', dwells on the paradoxical fact of our 'positive joy in tragedy' (*Crown* 11; *Flower* 289). It is not a question, as in Nietzsche's conception which abstracts human consciousness from human social life, of 'life' rejoicing in the wealth and strength which allow it to immolate so much of its best without crippling loss. We are uplifted rather by knowledge of what our heroes and heroines have accomplished, what they have stood for, and how much more they might have achieved but for a fatal failure to understand themselves and their times better. We do not regret that the tragic train of events was set in motion, however many calamities it has led to. Amid the ruins, a worm-eaten fabric has been torn down, and men and women have been compelled to resume once more their long pilgrimage, set free to realize their untapped capabilities. However costly the battle with evil, and however little the benefit to those who have borne the cost, the vision of an ennobled life is our compensation. Like its heroes, mankind has achieved much, but it is under a peremptory compulsion to scale far greater heights.

Aristotle's metaphor of a 'cathartic' function of tragic drama, a 'purgation' of *pity* and *terror*, has given rise to endless debate. We can agree with Robert N. Watson that a play like *Macbeth* can be thought of as purging us of some of our 'repressed impulses' and 'rash wishes' (85), and reminding us of the human propensity to destructiveness, of which we each have a streak (141; cf. Stewart 39). The spectacle of how much harm a man who goes wrong can inflict on himself and on others ought indeed to shock us into wanting to banish dark impulses from our minds. But why 'pity'? Perhaps because we all suffer from uneasy consciences over what is due from us to less fortunate neighbours, and tragedy concentrates or clarifies dim whisperings into active sympathy, more akin to the fellow-feeling or civic spirit which the Greek city-state required for its survival. A positive strengthening as well as a negative relief is being accomplished, a purification rather than a simple 'purging' or disinfection.

Tragedy, we might then say, by dramatizing the sluggish, straggling motion of life and history, accelerates them into a swift current, and enables us to serve in fantasy as participants, active agents instead of passive endurers. A marsh is drained off into a narrow gorge, its miasmic or stagnant waters carried away. We are liberated from a clogging weight, imbued with a fresh vitality, a renewed eagerness to alter our old selves and our old world. The energies of humanity are summoned up for their conflict with fate.

For our private distempers and sterilities to be merged in collective emotion, the tragic situation must be flexible, plastic, unhindered by too much realistic detail. For this, poetic drama, with its constellations of imagery, is the ideal medium. In Hamlet's insoluble problem are overtones of demands that life has made on us too. Catharsis and confession must share some of the same tributary streams, and analogous functions; Shakespeare's theatre may be regarded as a public confessional where men and women can gather to work out smothered tensions together; where egotistic regrets and rancours can be smoothed away, and the sense of an underlying unity, a 'general will' or shared destiny, can come to the front.

The process of purgation is thus social as well as personal. England as Shakespeare had drawn it in his later Histories contained at least as much rottenness as Denmark. All feelings and gnawings of guilt must be in origin social, and we are obscurely conscious of each of us being in our own way as blameworthy as the malefactor on the stage. In *Macbeth* we come on a recurrent thought of Scotland as a sick country in need of being purged. In various plays war is thought of as the grand purgative. A less makeshift purge is the one Timon's Athens is to be subjected to, of a more modern, political kind soon to make its appearance in England with 'Pride's Purge' of the Long Parliament in December 1648.

Watching a tragedy we are taken possession of by the unpredictable adventure of human existence. By its end mankind has learned something astonishing about itself, the explosive power of good and evil within it when set free to expand by the breakdown of customary barriers. Tragedy shows its affinity with revolution – like the 'apocalyptic' one of 1789, in Hazlitt's phrase – by enabling humanity to reach heights and depths otherwise inaccessible. Tragedy 'openeth the greatest wounds', Sidney had written, 'and showeth forth the ulcers that are covered with tissue' (124). The wicked are overcome, or destroy themselves, but their very presence is a warning; still more the fact that they often seem, as they have often been in history, stronger, better prepared, more resolute than the good.

Yet it is never simply a matter of good and bad individuals pitted against one another, and the polarizing of moral opposites is not a constant measure. In the earlier tragedies the distance between good and bad can be great; but only in *Othello*, and perhaps in *Hamlet* and *King Lear*, do we find a character or characters entirely bad, and who have never been otherwise. In the last three plays the moral panorama is more blurred. Good and evil, tossing together in the swirling torrent of history, have become harder to isolate and define. What stands out more distinctly now is the emerging antithesis between what clings to the past and what is ready for change and progress.

A play ends with no easy moral being drawn, seldom with any triumphalist celebration as in *Macbeth*; more often with hushed comment or leave-taking. There is always, however, an expanded consciousness, and the keener awareness of other human beings which is a necessary condition for any human progress. We are left, as Knights says of *King Lear*, with a great enhancement of 'the activity and wholeness of the imagination' (116). Only in figurative language can such stirrings of a new consciousness be expressed, as they are in Cleopatra's strangely evocative words after the death of Antony: 'My desolation does begin to make/A better life' (V.ii.1–2). She, and the rest, have had to be broken, pulverized, remade, like the human whole they represent. Each hero or heroine by dying sounds an alarm to rouse us to the need to turn over a new page of history. Their crimes or errors have not been theirs alone; by their lives and deaths they give mankind the incentive and opportunity for a fresh start.

Hitherto overshadowed by the towering figures contending in the arena, at the end the collective life reawakens, shaken and enfeebled at first, under a grey sky out of which warmth and colour have been drained. In simpler days no more was needed to restore Verona to tranquil happiness than to put a stop to a senseless family feud: class war in Rome will not be so easily halted, and each tragedy ends amid looming problems. Successors must be found, to take the lead in coping with them, and to embody a collective will and resolve only now being released. Any change of ruler-ship could be at least a rough and ready symbol of a new era opening. Raymond Williams pointed out that we today miss the significance of this for Shakespeare's audience, in our preoccupation with the hero, who falls and dies; what his endings promise is not a return to things as they were before, but 'a new distribution of forces, physical or spiritual' (*Modern Tragedy* 55).

Tragedy shows an era departing, though leaving behind it something of its better and something of its worse self. In the English Histories a feudal ruling class was tearing itself to pieces when no other social force was yet ready to supplant it; the post-tragic situation is similar, except that at least a stronger desire for betterment has been kindled in men's minds, or in *our* minds. Those individuals who remain to contribute to the rebuilding are few, and must seem – and sometimes, no bad sign, feel – inadequate. There are only men; the women who might have helped have all fallen by the wayside.

They are left to grope and improvise. Shakespeare had passed in review the systems of government known to him; they had each been weighed in his balance, and found wanting. He did not take it on himself to draft any new constitutions. No councils are to be summoned, except in Denmark for the formality of an election. Policies are left to those who take or accept power, whether the hero and his foes have shared the same fate, as in *Hamlet*, or one side is left in possession, as in *Macbeth*. We cannot think of them as saviours capable by themselves of inaugurating a new era. Even Alcibiades and Octavius, in the short spell when Shakespeare was readiest to bring forward 'great men', only impress us as caretakers, at most as leaders in a work of transformation that must involve the whole body politic. None of them except Malcolm is a direct heir of former rulers. Others emerge from the old order, but under stress of events have learned to see what lies round them in a new light.

Julius Caesar ends with Romans coming together, but their empire divided among three men, the least unworthy of whom will be the eventual winner. Octavius is young enough to shake off some fetters of the past, and he has endured hardship and danger, and earned firm loyalties. After years of scheming and fighting, he will be the man to unite Rome and set it on a new path. We can only regret that Hamlet could think of no better substitute for himself to recommend than Fortinbras, the reckless son of a reckless father who lost his lands and left him to seek fame by what is really banditry. Denmark must be very short of talent or merit for such a foreigner to be preferred. Hamlet's divided nature shows in his admiration for a young man so opposite to himself, who can follow unflinchingly, unthinkingly, an obsolete code – and who very likely reminds him of his own father. Cassio is another young soldier entrusted with authority, to the extent of being left in command in Cyprus, chastened we may trust by his experiences there. Shakespeare could not presume to dictate reforms to King James's country, but it is a pity that Malcolm, the only successor to power with a definite measure to announce, has hit on nothing more useful to give Scotland than a peerage with foreign titles, the last thing it could possibly be in want of.

Reactions of spectators and readers to the tragic endings have been diverse, and nowhere more than with regard to the question of what happens afterwards. Some are quite indifferent to this, Leech (51) for instance. It seems strange for anyone to be content with leaving Shakespeare's unfolding of history to come to a dead end. Tragedy would have been impossible in Western culture, Uphaus writes, but for the belief in survival (2). This can only be accepted in a collective, not individual sense. As C.P. Snow said in his *Two Cultures*, the individual lives and dies alone, the community goes on. Indeed this solitariness of the human condition must itself be a taproot of tragic art, whose emotional intensity rescues us from it by fusing our consciousness with that of our fellows. If the future we collectively face is a blank wall, this becomes difficult. Or if, worse still, Stauffer (315) is right in deeming Shakespeare so much a 'traditionalist', a 'respecter of the past', that at the close of each play he is intent only on picking up 'the shattered pieces of the state', the social order he revered – then we are being led back into a past which the poet has shown as thoroughly unworthy to survive.

In *King Lear* more than in any other tragedy, there can be no return to anything like the past; the cataclysm has been too violent. There is nothing to go back to, nothing visible to go forward to. A moribund king restored by a French army would have been a grotesque anti-climax. No better future can be looked for from the party of Cordelia and Kent, whose eyes are fixed on the past. No one wants the crown. Albany invites Kent and Edgar to 'rule in this realm' (V.iii.320), as joint governors it would seem. Kent declines; Edgar says nothing of accepting a throne, and only reluctantly agrees to take on responsibility. Anyone doing so now will have to cope with bewildering social issues, of the sort Hamlet was growing conscious of in Denmark, instead of routine political manoeuvrings or wars.

Edgar is a young man of noble, not royal blood; an ordinary enough fellow when we first see him, easily overreached, but one who since then has trodden undaunted a hazardous path and found strength to face extraordinary tests. He comes from the old corrupt order, and is very conscious of paternal sin as well as fratricidal crime. We can feel more confidence in him than he does in himself, and imagine better times for Britain under his care. It will be a new age still in the making, unlike the precocious modernity of Goneril and Regan, compounded from inhumanities old and new. For inspiration there will be the memories that Edgar, sole survivor of those who saw and heard Lear out on the moorland, can hand on.

In Rome when Coriolanus gives way to his mother's entreaties and retires, there is of course relief and rejoicing, but nothing to warrant an editor's belief that the city is now 'purged, chastened, shamed, and renewed' (Brockbank 61). It will take generations to allay class conflict so unbridled and so realistically portrayed as it is in this play. There is no one to serve as moderator; Volumnia, suddenly promoted to heroine, is disqualified by her truculent past as well as her sex. It would not be like Shakespeare to leave no cranny for a ray of hope, however. We are free to hope that the plebeians will learn more firmness and solidarity when faced by the unforeseen; and that the patricians, narrowly spared from disaster, will see the light of reason and conciliate the people by further concessions. Some men of position in seventeenth-century England, historians have reminded us of late, were actually doing this, in times of dearth, and winning the good-will of the poor. *Coriolanus* is a milestone in England's gradual entry into the long bourgeois-capitalist era of its history; and this, Moretti points out (34 etc.), by contrast with its forerunner, was to be an era of class struggle, but also compromise, co-existence within an expanding economy – a fact that Marxists have been inclined to overlook.

What keeps these plays most convincingly of all from seeming to preach pessimism is the magnificence of their language, through which we share feelings so magically and so intensely. Under its spell we are buoyed up by a conviction that no race gifted with such powers of expression can be fated to fall silent. Charney has remarked on how much more organic or deep-rooted Elizabethan imagery was than any of later days (199). It could be so thanks to the feudal England remoulded by Tudor rule being invested with the hues of a collective society, part reality and part illusion, all of its parts having an importance for all the others, interacting even with earth and heaven. Its vision of things is handed on to us by the drama, its finest distillation; through it we feel our ties with mankind in our closeness to the characters, the hero most of all.

Despite all its imperfections and masqueradings, the old life was so much more close-knit than ours that its disruption was shattering. Tragedy marked the advancing breakdown, or rather the poet's awareness of it, in a series of grand stages, more clearly defined as time went on. In *Julius Caesar* political dissolution was at work; in *King Lear* the problem of poverty stood revealed; in *Timon* social maladies were traced to the necromantic sway of gold; in *Coriolanus* class struggle broke out. A hero now could only represent his own class, and that only insecurely, as the last of the heroes found. England was ceasing to be, or more strictly was ceasing to be able to imagine itself, a true community; and with this, the molten heat of the poetic crucible was cooling.

A tragic dramatist at work must be a 'demi-Atlas', as Cleopatra called Antony (I.v.23), bearing a whole world on his shoulders. Tragedy of this intensity could not go on for many years without exhausting both playwright and audience. By 1610 or so, though a few masterpieces were yet to come, it was being pronounced out of fashion, or was diluted into tragi-comedy. Theatres were changing as well as plays. Like a Greek theatre, the Globe was open to the sky, all-embracing in theme and audience, a part of civic life. It was well fitted to foster a sense among spectators of forming an entire world, contemplating the fortunes of all humanity. By comparison the private theatres coming into fashion, too small for such vast horizons, were better suited to coterie art (cf. Sturgess 6–7, 41).

Culture was dividing between the classes. A new age of social history was taking shape, and a tragic hero of the antique mould would soon be as out of place as a knight-at-arms in the drawing-room. Tragedy would find scanty soil in a public of sturdy – or surly – individualists, though not much more in an older society glued together with holy water. England was growing rationally aware of its deepening discords, when these were not muffled by religious disputations, and learning to organize rival parties or

273

factions, sparring over specific issues. Doomsday was narrowing down into competing programmes; the clash of old and new that had forged Shakespearian tragedy was becoming a matter for politicians instead of poets.

Nothing forbids us to believe that Shakespeare had some hope of better times being some day reached. But progress would be complex and difficult, as he could not fail to realize. History would have to make long detours, as it is still doing, instead of advancing in a direct line, and with it the arts, his own among them. Meanwhile, a great epoch expiring must feel pangs of regret for lessons that it ought to have bequeathed to its heirs. Some ghostly voices of heroes at their last gasp sound as if struggling to tell us these incommunicable things. 'Oh, I could prophesy', exclaims the dying Hotspur. 'Had I but time . . . ', says the dying Hamlet, 'Oh, I could tell you –'. What they would have told is beyond our guessing; it may have been beyond even Shakespeare's.

Bibliography

(This list includes only works cited in the text. Names of contributors to collections of essays, and their editors, are entered separately.)

Adams, J.Q., *Hamlet*, Boston 1929.

Adelman, J., *The Common Liar. An Essay on 'Antony and Cleopatra'*, New Haven, Conn. 1973.

Alexander, N., *Poison, Play, and Duel. A Study in 'Hamlet'*, London 1971.

Allen, N.B., 'The Two Parts of "Othello"', in Muir (ed.).

Armstrong, E.A., *Shakespeare's Imagination*, London 1946.

Aylmer, G.E., *The Struggle for the Constitution. England in the Seventeenth Century*, 4th edn, London 1975.

Bamber, L., *Comic Women, Tragic Men. A Study of Gender and Genre in Shakespeare*, Stanford, Calif. 1982.

Barroll, J.L., *Shakespearean Tragedy, Genre, Tradition and Change in 'Antony and Cleopatra'*, Washington 1984.

Bayley, J., *Shakespeare and Tragedy*, London 1981.

Beauvoir, S. de, *Old Age*, 1970; English edn, Harmondsworth 1977.

Beckerman, B., *Shakespeare at the Globe 1599–1609*, New York 1962.

Bentley, G.E., 'Shakespeare, the King's Company, and *King Lear*', in Danson (ed.).

Bethell, S.L., *Shakespeare and the Popular Dramatic Tradition*, London 1944.

Boas, F.S., *Shakspere* [sic] *and his Predecessors*, 2nd impression, London 1902.

Boas, F.S., *Queen Elizabeth in Drama and Related Studies*, London 1950.

Bolt, S., *Hamlet*, new edn, Harmondsworth 1990.

Boorman, S.C., *Human Conflict in Shakespeare*, London 1987.

Bradbrook, M.C., 'Shakespeare the Jacobean Dramatist', in Muir and Schoenbaum (eds).

Bradley, A.C., *Shakespearean Tragedy*, London 1904.

Bradley, A.C., *Oxford Lectures on Poetry*, London 1909.

Bradshaw, G., *Shakespeare's Scepticism*, Brighton 1987.

Bransom, J.S.H., *The Tragedy of King Lear*, Oxford 1934.

Brant, C. and Purkiss, D., eds, *Women, Texts and Histories 1575–1760*, London 1992.

Braunmuller, A.R. and Hattaway, M., eds, *Cambridge Companion to English Renaissance Drama*, Cambridge 1990.

British Academy Lectures, *Aspects of Shakespeare*, Oxford 1933.

Brockbank, P., ed., *Coriolanus*, Arden edn, London 1976.

Brooke, R., *John Webster and the Elizabethan Drama*, London 1916.

Brooks, C., 'The Naked Babe and the Cloak of Manliness', in Ridler (ed.).

Brown, I., *Shakespeare and the Actors*, London 1970.

Brown, J.R., ed., *Focus on Macbeth*, London 1982.

Brownlee, A., *William Shakespeare and Robert Burton*, Reading 1960.

Burton, R., *The Anatomy of Melancholy*, 1621; Bohn edn, 3 vols, London 1923.

Campbell, L.B., *Shakespeare's Tragic Heroes*, Cambridge 1930.

Campbell, O.J., *Shakespeare's Satire*, London 1943.

Cavell, S., '*Coriolanus* and the Interpretation of Politics', in Parker and Hartman (eds).

Cavell, S., *Disowning Knowledge in Six Plays of Shakespeare*, Cambridge 1987.

Charlton, H.B., *Shakespearian Tragedy*, Cambridge 1948.

Charney, M., *Shakespeare's Roman Plays. The Function of Imagery in the Drama*, Cambridge, Mass. 1961.

Clemen, W., *The Development of Shakespeare's Imagery*, 1936; 2nd English edn, London 1977.

Cohen, W., *Drama of a Nation. Public Theater in Renaissance England and Spain*, New York 1985.

Coleridge, S.T., *Essays and Lectures on Shakespeare*, Bohn edn, London 1914.

Collinson, P., *The Religion of Protestants. The Church in English Society 1559–1625*, Oxford 1982.

Corfield, P.J., *Language, History and Class*, Oxford 1991.

Council, N., *When Honour's at the Stake. Ideas of Honour in Shakespeare's Plays*, London 1973.

Creech, E., *Mankynde in Shakespeare*, Athens, Georgia 1976.

Creighton, C., *An Allegory of King Lear*, s.l. 1913.

Curtis, M.H., 'The Alienated Intellectuals of Early Stuart England', *Past and Present* no. 23, Nov. 1962.

Danby, J.F., *Shakespeare's Doctrine of Nature. A Study of 'King Lear'*, London 1949.

Danby, J.F., *Poets on Fortune's Hill*, London 1952.

Danson, L., ed., *On 'King Lear'*, Princeton 1981.

Dekker, T., *The Wonderful Year* (1603), in Hibbard (ed.).

Dekker, T., *The Belman of London* (1608) and *The Guls Hornbook* (1609), ed. O. Smeaton, London 1904.

Dixon, W.M., 'Chapman, Marston, Decker', in Waller and Ward (eds) (Vol. VI).

Dollimore, J., *Radical Tragedy*, 2nd edn, New York 1989.

Dollimore, J. and Sinfield, A., eds, *Political Shakespeare. New Essays in Cultural Criticism*, Manchester 1985.

Donagan, B., 'Codes and Conduct in the English Civil War', *Past and Present* no. 118, Feb. 1988.

Dowden, E., *Shakspere* [sic]: *His Mind and Art*, 1875; 20th edn, London n.d.

Drakakis, J., ed., *Alternative Shakespeares*, London 1985.

Dryden, J., *Dramatic Essays*, Everyman edn, London n.d.

Eckermann, J.P., *Conversations with Goethe*, 1836; English edn, London 1930.

Edwards, G., ed., *Tirso de Molina. The Trickster of Seville and the Stone Guest*, Warminster 1986.

Edwards, P. ed., *Hamlet*, New Cambridge edn, Cambridge, 1985.

Eliot, T.S., *Elizabethan Essays*, London 1934.

Elliott, G.R., *Dramatic Providence in 'Macbeth'*, Princeton, 1958.

Empsom, W.M., 'Hamlet', in Pirie (ed.).

Erasmus, *The Essential Erasmus*, ed. J.P. Dolan, New York 1964.

Erlich, A., *Hamlet's Absent Father*, Princeton 1977.

Evans, B., *Shakespeare's Tragic Practice*, Oxford 1979.

Farnham, W., *Shakespeare's Tragic Frontier*, Berkeley, Calif. 1950.

Ferguson, M.W., 'Hamlet', in Parker and Hartman (eds).

Fitzgerald, E., *The Rubaiyat of Omar Khayyam and Six Plays of Calderón*, Everyman edn, London 1928.

Flatter, R., *Hamlet's Father*, London 1949.

Ford, B., ed., *The Age of Shakespeare*, Harmondsworth 1955.

Fox, A., 'Ballads, Libels and Popular Ridicule in Jacobean England', *Past and Present* no. 145, Nov. 1994.

French, M., *Shakespeare's Division of Experience*, London 1982.

Frye, N., *A Natural Perspective. The Development of Shakespearean Comedy and Romance*, New York 1965.

Frye, N., *Fools of Time. Studies in Shakespearean Tragedy*, Toronto 1967.

Frye, N., *On Shakespeare*, ed. R. Sandler, New Haven, Conn. 1986.

Frye, R.M., *Shakespeare. The Art of the Dramatist*, London 1982.

Furness, H.H. et al., eds, *A New Variorum Edition of Shakespeare: King Lear*, Philadelphia 1880.

Garaudy, R., *Literature of the Graveyard*, New York 1934.

Gardner, H., 'The Noble Moor', in Ridler (ed.).

Gautier, T., *Wanderings in Spain*, 1840; English edn, London 1843.

Gellner, E., *Plough, Sword and Book*, London 1988.

Given, W., *A Further Study of 'The Othello'*, New York 1899.

Goethe, J.W., *Wilhelm Meister's Apprenticeship*, trans. T. Carlyle, 1795–96; Edinburgh 1839.

Goldberg, S.L., *An Essay on 'King Lear'*, Cambridge 1974.

Granville-Barker, H., 'From *Henry V* to *Hamlet*', in British Academy Lectures.

Granville-Barker, H., 'Shakespeare's Dramatic Art', in Granville-Barker and Harrison (eds).

Granville-Barker, H., and Harrison, G.B., eds, *Companion to Shakespeare Studies*, Cambridge 1934.

Gray, J.C., ed., *Mirror up to Shakespeare*, Toronto 1984.

Greenblatt, S., *Shakespearean Negotiations*, 1988; Oxford 1990.

Grierson, H.J.C., *Cross-Currents in English Literature of the XVIIth Century*, London 1927.

Gurr, A., *Playgoing in Shakespeare's London*, Cambridge 1987.

Harvie, C., *The Lights of Liberalism*, London 1976.

Hawkes, T., *Shakespeare and the Reason. A Study of the Tragedies and the Problem Plays*, London 1964.

Hawkins, H., *The Devil's Party. Critical Counter-Interpretations of Shakespearian Drama*, Oxford 1985.

Hawkins, M., 'History, Politics and *Macbeth*', in J.R. Brown (ed.).

Hazlitt, W., *Characters of Shakespear's* [sic] *Plays*, 1817–18; London 1906.

Hegel, G.W.F., *Hegel on Tragedy*, eds A. and H. Paolucci, 1962; New York 1975.

Heilman, R.B., *This Great Stage. Imagery and Structure in 'King Lear'*, Baton Rouge 1948.

Heilman, R.B., ed., *Shakespeare: The Tragedies. New Perspectives*, Englewood Cliffs 1986.

Heine, H., *The French Stage. Letters addressed to M. August Lewald*, 1837; Scott Library edn, London n.d.

Heinemann, M., *Puritanism and Theatre*, Cambridge 1980.

Heinemann, M., 'Political Drama', in Braunmuller and Hattaway (eds).

Heywood, T., *An Apology for Actors*, 1612; London 1841.

Hibbard, G.R., ed., *Three Elizabethan Pamphlets*, London 1951.

Hibbard, G.R., '*Othello* and the Pattern of Shakespearian Tragedy', in Muir (ed.).

Hill, C., 'The Norman Yoke', in Saville (ed.).

Hobsbawm, E.J., *The Age of Extremes. The Short Twentieth Century 1914–1991*, London 1994.

Hoeniger, F.D., ed., *King Lear*, College Classics, Vol. 1, Toronto 1968.

Hubler, E., ed., *Hamlet*, Signet Classics, Toronto 1963.

Huizinga, J., *The Waning of the Middle Ages*, 1924; English edn, Harmondsworth 1976.

Hunter, G.K., *Dramatic Identities and Cultural Tradition. Studies in Shakespeare and his Contemporaries*, Liverpool 1978.

Hunter, G.K., 'Shakespeare and the Tradition of Tragedy', in Wells (ed.).

Hurault, Michel, seigneur du Fay, *Second discours sur l'estat de la France*, 1591; English trans. by E. Aggas, London 1592. (I am indebted to my colleague Mr A.J. Malkiewicz for this reference.)

Isaacs, J., 'Shakespeare as Man of the Theatre', in Shakespeare Association (ed.).

Jackson, M.P., 'The Transmission of Shakespeare's Text', in Wells (ed.).

Johnson, S., *On Shakespeare*, ed. Walter Raleigh, Oxford 1908.

Jorgensen, P.A., *Shakespeare's Military World*, Berkeley, Calif. Press 1956.

Kavanagh, J.H., 'Shakespeare in Ideology', in Drakakis (ed.).

Kernan, A., *The Playwright as Magician. Shakespeare's Image of the Poet in the English Public Theater*, New Haven, Conn. 1979.

Kernan, A.B., '*King Lear* and the Shakespearean Pageant of History', in Danson (ed.).

Kettle, A., ed., *Shakespeare in a Changing World*, London 1964.

Kettle, A., 'From *Hamlet* to *Lear*', in Kettle, (ed.).

Kiernan, V., *Shakespeare: Poet and Citizen*, London 1993.

Kitto, H.D.F., '*Hamlet*', in Ridler (ed.).

Knappen, M.M., *Tudor Puritanism: A Chapter in the History of Idealism*, Chicago 1939.

Knight, G.W., *The Imperial Theme*, Oxford 1931.

Knight, G.W., *The Wheel of Fire*, Oxford 1937.

Knight, G.W., *The Crown of Life*, London 1948.

Knight, G.W., *The Sovereign Flower. Shakespeare as the Poet of Royalism*, London 1958.

Knights, L.C., *Some Shakespearean Themes*, London 1959.

Kuhns, R., *Tragedy. Contradiction and Repression*, Chicago 1991.

Lake, P.G., 'Calvinism and the English Church 1570–1635', *Past and Present* no. 114, Feb. 1987.

Lee, S., *A Life of William Shakespeare*, 4th rev. edn, London 1925.

Leech, C., 'The Implications of Tragedy', in Lerner (ed.).

Leggatt, A., *Shakespeare's Political Drama*, London 1988.

Lerner, L., ed., *Shakespeare's Tragedies. An Anthology of Modern Criticism*, Harmondsworth 1968.

Levin, H., *The Question of Hamlet*, New York 1959.

Levin, H., *Shakespeare and the Revolution of the Times*, New York 1976.

Levin, R.C., 'Shakespeare or the Ideas of his Time', in Heilman (ed.).

Long, M., *The Unnatural Scene. A Study in Shakespearean Tragedy*, London 1976.

Lucas, F.L., *Literature and Psychology*, London 1951.

Lukács, G., *The Historical Novel*, 1937; English edn, London 1962.

Lukács, G., *The Meaning of Contemporary Realism*, 1957; English edn, London 1963.

Lunacharsky, A., 'Bacon and the Characters of Shakespeare's Plays', in Samarin and Nikolyukin (eds).

McAlindon, T., *Shakespeare's Tragic Cosmos*, Cambridge 1991.

McElroy, B., *Shakespeare's Mature Tragedies*, Princeton 1973.

McFarland, T., 'The Image of the Family in *King Lear*', in Danson (ed.).

McGee, A., *The Elizabethan 'Hamlet'*, New Haven, Conn. 1987.

Mack, M., *Killing the King. Three Studies in Shakespeare's Tragic Structure*, New Haven, Conn. 1973.

Mackail, J.W., *The Approach to Shakespeare*, Oxford 1930.

McLuskie, K., 'The Patriarchal Bard: Feminist Criticism and Shakespeare: *King Lear* and *Measure for Measure*', in Dollimore and Sinfield (eds).

Mangan, M., *A Preface to Shakespeare's Tragedies*, London 1991.

Margolies, D., *Monsters of the Deep. Social Dissolution in Shakespeare's Tragedies*, Manchester 1992.

Mariestras, R., *New Perspectives on the Shakespearean World*, 1981; English edn, Cambridge 1985.

Marx, K. and Engels, F. (*sic*), *On Religion*, Moscow 1957.

Matthews, G.M., 'Othello and the Dignity of Man', in Kettle (ed.).

Maugham, W.S., *A Writer's Notebook*, Harmondsworth 1949.

Maxwell, J.C., 'Shakespeare: The Middle Plays', in Ford (ed.).

Meek, R.L., *Social Science and the Ignoble Savage*, Cambridge 1976.

Mehl, D., *Shakespeare's Tragedies: An Introduction*, 1983; English edn, Cambridge 1986.

Minois, G., *History of Old Age: From Antiquity to the Renaissance*, 1987; English edn, Chicago 1989.

Miola, R.S., *Shakespeare's Rome*, Cambridge 1983.

Moretti, F., *Signs Taken for Wonders. Essays in the Sociology of Literary Forms*, rev. English edn, London 1988.

Morris, C., *Political Thought in England: Tyndale to Hooker*, London 1953.

Morton, A.L., *The English Utopia*, London 1952.

Muir, K., 'Shakespeare and Politics', in Kettle (ed.).

Muir, K., 'Twentieth-Century Shakespeare Criticism: The Tragedies', in Wells (ed.).

Muir, K., ed., *Shakespeare Survey 21*, Cambridge 1968.

Muir, K., *Shakespeare's Tragic Sequence*, London 1972.

Muir, K., '*The Singularity of Shakespeare*' and Other Essays, Liverpool 1977.

Muir, K. and O'Loughlin, S., *The Voyage to Illyria. A New Study of Shakespeare*, London 1937.

Muir, K. and Schoenbaum, S. eds, *A New Companion to Shakespeare Studies*, Cambridge 1971.

Nandy, D., 'The Realism of *Antony and Cleopatra*', in Kettle (ed.).

Nashe, T., *Pierce Penilesse his Supplication to the Devil* (1592), in Hibbard (ed.).

Nuttall, A.D., *Timon of Athens*, New York 1989.

O'Riordan, M., *The Gaelic Mind and the Collapse of the Gaelic World*, Cork 1990.

Overton, B., *The Winter's Tale*, London 1989.

Palmer, J., *Political Characters of Shakespeare*, London 1957.

Parker, M.D.H., *The Slave of Life. A Study of Shakespeare and the Idea of Justice*, London 1955.

Parker, P. and Hartman, G., eds, *Shakespeare and the Question of Theory*, New York 1985.

Parker, R.B., '*Coriolanus* and "the Interpretation of the Time"', in Gray (ed.).

Parrott, T.M., *Shakespearean Comedy*, New York 1949.

Patterson, A., *Shakespeare and the Popular Voice*, Oxford 1989.

Phillips, J.E., *The State in Shakespeare's Greek and Roman Plays*, New York 1940.

Pirie, D.H., ed., *Essays on Shakespeare*, Cambridge 1986.

Plutarch, 'Life of Coriolanus', trans. Sir T. North, ed. R.H. Carr, Oxford 1906.

Pollard, A., 'The Foundations of Shakespeare's Text', in British Academy Lectures.

Poole, A., *Coriolanus*, Hemel Hempstead 1988.

Puttenham, G., *The Arte of English Poesie*, 1589; Cambridge 1936.

Quiller-Couch, A., *Cambridge Lectures*, London 1943.

Rabkin, N., *Shakespeare and the Problem of Meaning*, Chicago 1981.

Rabkin, N., 'On *Macbeth*', in Heilman (ed.).

Raleigh, W., *Shakespeare*, London 1907.

Rennert, H.A., *The Spanish Drama in the Time of Lope de Vega*, New York 1909.

Ridler, A., ed., *Shakespeare Criticism 1935–1960*, London 1970.

Robertson, J.M., *'Hamlet' Once More*, London 1923.

Robson, W.W., *Did the King See the Dumb-Show?*, Edinburgh 1975.

Robson, W.W., *A Prologue to English Literature*, London 1986.

Rossiter, A.P., *Angel with Horns*, London 1961.

Ruoff, J.E., *Crowell's Handbook of Elizabethan and Stuart Literature*, New York 1975.

Ryan, K., *Shakespeare*, Hemel Hempstead 1989.

Sackville, T. and Norton, T., *Gorboduc*, in Tydeman (ed.).

Saintsbury, G., 'Shakespeare: Life and Plays', in Ward and Waller (eds) (Vol. V). Cambridge.

Salingar, L., *Dramatic Form in Shakespeare and the Jacobeans*, Cambridge 1986.

Samarin, R. and Nikolyukin, A., eds, *Shakespeare in the Soviet Union*, Moscow 1966.

Sanders, N., ed., *Othello*, New Cambridge edn, Cambridge 1984.

Sanders, W. and Jacobson, H., *Shakespeare's Magnanimity. Four Tragic Heroes*, London 1978.

Saville, J., ed., *Democracy and the Labour Movement*, London 1954.

Schopenhauer, A., *The World as Will and Representation*, 1819; English edn, New York 1966.

Schücking, L.L., *Character Problems in Shakespeare's Plays*, New York 1922.

Scragg, L., *Discovering Shakespeare's Meaning*, London 1988.

Sewell, A., *Character and Society in Shakespeare*, Oxford 1951.

Shakespeare Association (ed.), *Papers on Shakespeare and the Theatre*, London 1927.

Sidney, Sir P., *Selected Writings*, ed. R. Dutton, Manchester 1987.

Siegel, P.N., *Shakespeare's English and Roman History Plays. A Marxist Analysis*, London 1982.

Sinfield, A., Introduction to Part 2 in Dollimore and Sinfield (eds).

Sisson, C.J., *Shakespeare's Tragic Justice*, London 1962.

Smeaton, O., *Shakespeare. His Life and Work*, London n.d.

Smirnov, A.A., *Shakespeare. A Marxist Interpretation*, 1934, English edn, New York 1936.

Smith, A.J., *Literary Love. The Role of Passion in English Poems and Plays of the Seventeenth Century*, London 1983.

Snyder, Susan, 'Between the Divine and the Absurd: *King Lear*', in Heilman (ed.).

Soellner, R., *'Timon of Athens'. Shakespeare's Pessimistic Tragedy*, Ohio State University Press 1979.

Southall, R., '*Troilus and Cressida* and the Spirit of Capitalism', in Kettle (ed.).

Southall, R., *Literature and the Rise of Capitalism*, London 1973.

Speaight, R., *Nature in Shakespearean Tragedy*, London 1955.

Spencer C., *Davenant's 'Macbeth' from the Yale Manuscript*, New Haven, Conn. 1961.

Spurgeon, C.F.E., 'Shakespeare's Iterative Imagery', in British Academy Lectures.

Spurgeon, C.F.E., *Shakespeare's Imagery*, Cambridge 1935.

Stampfer, J., 'The Catharsis of *King Lear*' in Lerner (ed.).

Stauffer, D.A., *Shakespeare's World of Images. The Development of His Moral Ideas*, New York 1949.

Stephen, L., *Essays on Freethinking and Plainspeaking*, London 1873.

Stevenson, L.C., *Praise and Paradox. Merchants and Craftsmen in Elizabethan Popular Literature*, Cambridge 1984.

Stewart, J.I.M., 'Shakespeare's Men and their Morals', in Ridler (ed.).

Sturgess, K., *Jacobean Private Theatre*, London 1987.

Summers, J.H., *Dreams of Love and Power. On Shakespeare's Plays*, Oxford 1984.

Swinburne, A.C., *A Study of Shakespeare*, 1874–76; London 1918.

Tawney, R.H., *Social History and Literature*, London 1949.

Thomas, K., *Religion and the Decline of Magic*, Harmondsworth 1978.

Thomas, K., 'Numeracy in Early Modern England', *Transactions of the Royal Historical Society*, 5th series, no. 87, London 1987.

Thompson, I.A.A., '*Hidalgo* and *Pechero*: The Language of "Estates" and "Classes" in Early-Modern Castile', in Corfield (ed.).

Thomson, P., 'Playhouses and Players in the Time of Shakespeare', in Wells (ed.).

Tillyard, E.M.W., *Shakespeare's Problem Plays*, London 1959.

Tolstoy, L.N., *Diaries*, London 1994.

Traversi, Derek, *Shakespeare: The Roman Plays*, London 1963.

Tydeman, W., ed., *Two Tudor Tragedies*, Harmondsworth 1992.

Uphaus, R.W., *Beyond Tragedy. Structure and Experience in Shakespeare's Romances*, Lexington, Kentucky 1981.

Van Doren, Mark, *Shakespeare*, London 1941.

Vaughan, C.E., 'Tourneur and Webster', in Ward and Waller (eds) (Vol. VI).

Ward, Sir A.W. and Waller, A.R., eds, *Cambridge History of English Literature*, Vol. V, Part I, Cambridge 1943.

Ward, Sir A.W. and Waller, A.R., eds, *Cambridge History of English Literature*, Vol. VI, Part 2, Cambridge 1932.

Warren, M.J., 'Quarto and Folio *King Lear* and the Interpretation of Albany and Edgar', in Heilman (ed.).

Watson, R.N., *Shakespeare and the Hazards of Ambition*, Cambridge, Mass. 1984.

Wells, S., ed., *The Cambridge Companion to Shakespeare Studies*, Cambridge 1986.

Westlund, J., *Shakespeare's Reparative Comedies. A Psychoanalytic View of the Middle Plays*, Chicago 1984.

Willeford, W., *The Fool and the Sceptre*, London 1969.

Williams, R., *Marxism and Literature*, Oxford 1977.

Williams, R., *Modern Tragedy*, London 1979.

Wilson, F.P., 'Shakespeare and the Diction of Common Life', in Ridley (ed.).

Wilson, J.D., *What Happens in 'Hamlet'?*, Cambridge 1935.

Wilson, J.D., *The Essential Shakespeare*, Cambridge 1942.

Winstanley, L., *'Othello' as the Tragedy of Italy*, London 1924.

Wright, L.B., *Middle Class Culture in Elizabethan England*, London 1935.

Index

actors
  in *Hamlet* 66–7
  public adoration 26
Adelman, Jane 241
The Aeneid (Virgil) 157
Aeschylus 9
alienation 207–8
All for Love (Dryden) 154
Allen, Ned B. 88
The Anatomy of Melancholy (Burton)
  22, 225, 254
Anne of Denmark 25, 63, 105
Antony and Cleopatra 154–72 *see
  also* heroes
  character of Antony 155–9, 161,
    170–72, 214
  character of Cleopatra 159–63,
    170
  character of Octavius 165–6,
    171–2
  Cleopatra compared with Lady
    Macbeth 162, 163
  Cleopatra dresses Antony in her
    clothes 241
  fate 259, 260
  free of revengeful passion 209
  kaleidoscope within the series of
    tragedies 154–5
  love and sex 163–4, 230–40,
    243, 244–5, 249
  monarchy 170, 217–18, 232
  politics 231, 234

  power is pageant only 167
  race and love 92
  role of two women 239
  spaciousness 155–6
  Timon compared with Antony
    156
  tragic close 169–72, 265, 266–7,
    270
  war 223, 224, 225
Apologie for Poetrie (Sidney) 228
Apology for Actors (Heywood) 25
Aristotle
  cathartic function of drama 268
Arminius, Jacobus 21–2, 259
Armstrong, E.A. 27, 148
art
  creative minds moulded by
    world 15
As You Like It 91, 219
The Atheist's Tragedy (Tourneur)
  213
Austen, Jane 35

Bacon, Francis 8, 208
  New Atlantis 20
Bamber, Linda 11, 249
Bayley, John 112
Beaumont, Francis
  Knight of the Burning Pestle 26
de Beauvoir, Simone 250
Believe As You List (Massinger) 140
Bethell, S.L. 155

283